The University of Michigan
Center for South and Southeast Asian Studies

MICHIGAN PAPERS ON SOUTH AND SOUTHEAST ASIA

THE BURMESE POLITY, 1752–1819

Politics, Administration, and Social Organization in the Early Kon-baung Period

William J. Koenig

Center for South and Southeast Asian Studies
The University of Michigan

Michigan Papers on South and Southeast Asia
Number 34

Library of Congress catalog card number: 88-63416

ISBN: 0-89148-056-0 (cloth)
ISBN: 0-89148-057-9 (paper)

Copyright © 1990

Center for South and Southeast Asian Studies
The University of Michigan

All rights reserved

Printed in the United States of America

TO SHERIDAN

who loves me in spite of Burmese history

CONTENTS

Illustrations x
Romanization and Dates xi
Map of Early Kon-baung Burma xii
The Taung-ngu and Kon-baung Dynasties xiii
Preface xv

CHAPTERS

1. The Early Kon-baung Polity and its Antecedents 1

   The Geographical Setting 1
   The Rise and Fall of Pagan 2
   The First Taung-ngu Empire 4
   The Restored Taung-ngu Empire 7
   The Decline and Fall of the Restored Taung-ngu State 10
   The Foundation of the Kon-baung State 12
   The Eastern Frontier, 1759–1767 14
   Sino-Burmese Relations, 1765–1819 17
   The Eastern Frontier, 1770–1824 19
   The Western Frontier and Anglo-Franco-Burmese
      Relations 22
   Internal Developments, 1760–1819 30

2. Early Kon-baung Society 37

   Burman Social Structure 38
   System of Belief 41
   Social Ideology and Social Mobility 45
   Alternative Social Statuses 51
   Agriculture and the Economy 53
   Population and Ethnicity 58

Contents

3. Kingship and Political Thought 65

    The First King Ideal and Its Political Import 65
    The *Cakkavatti* and *Bodhisatta* Ideals 71
    The State as an Agency of Salvation 79
    Legitimacy 84
    Brahmanic Aspects 89
    Royal Authority and the Dilemma of Power 92
    The Bases of Royal Power 94
    Conclusion 96

4. Administrative Structure and Process 99

    The Central Administration 100
    The Departmental Administrations 101
    Territorial Administration 103
    The Crown Service/*Athi* Dichotomy 107
    The Military System 115
    The Fiscal System 119
    The *Myo-za* System 123
    Religious Affairs and the Maha Dan Department 126
    The Privy Administration 131
    Alternate Communication Systems 132
    Administrative Dichotomies and the Fragmentation
        of Authority 134

5. The Officials 137

    Officials as a Primary Status Group 137
    Hereditary Office and the Gentry 140
    The Appointed Officials 147
    Corruption and Control 156
    Officials and Politics 162

6. The Royal Succession 165

    The Royal Women and the Succession 166
    The Royal Men 171
    The Royal Pool of Succession 174
    The Crown Prince 180
    The Passage of Power 183
    The Dilemma of the Royal Succession 185

Contents

7. The Passage of Power, 1752–1819 189
    Alaung-hpaya and His Pool of Succession 189
    Challenges to Naung-daw-gyi 192
    Hsin-hpyu-shin and Sin-gu 199
    The Coups and Attempted Coups of 1782 204
    Bo-daw-hpaya Establishes His Heir 209
    Governance and Princely Politics, 1783–1808 212
    The Future Ba-gyi-daw as Crown Prince, 1808–1819 216

Conclusion 223

APPENDICES

    1. Population Trends, 1783–1802 237
    2. Trends in Crown Service Houses by Region, 1783–1802 245
    3. Note on Sources 249

Abbreviations 253

Notes 255

Glossary of Burmese and Pali Terms 303

Bibliography 307

Index 323

ILLUSTRATIONS

FIGURES

1. Map of Early Kon-baung Burma xii
2. The Places of the Royal Court 48

TABLES

1. Summary Population Statistics in Houses, 1783–1802 59
2. Percent of Crown Service Population 110
3. Summary Trends in Crown Service Houses, 1783–1802 112
4. The Royal Women, 1752–1885 168
5. The Royal Children 176
6. Sons by Principal Queens 177
7. Comparison of Early Kon-baung Population Summaries 238
8. Trends in Houses by Region, 1783–1802 241

ROMANIZATION AND DATES

The romanization of the Burmese-language material is that designated as "standard conventional transcription" in John W. A. Okell, *A Guide to the Romanization of Burmese*. A standardization of the imprecise and unsystematic romanization that has generally been used for historical writing on Burma in English, standard conventional transcription enables those who read Burmese to reconstruct fairly accurately the original Burmese words while it remains readily recognizable to those who do not read Burmese but are acquainted with the older romanization. As a merciful act to myself and the editors, I have opted not to indicate tone with diacritics. Voicing is generally indicated except for the *th* and *sh* diphthongs, thus *min-gaung* not *min-hkaung*, but *maha si-thu* not *maha si-dhu*.

Place names such as Rangoon, Ava, Prome, Pegu, Martaban, Tavoy, and Syriam, whose form in standard conventional transcription would be of dubious recognizability to those who do not read Burmese, have been left in their familiar English form. All other place names are given in standard conventional transcription. Thus, Toungoo appears as Taung-ngu and Hanthawaddy as Han-tha-wadi. When personal honorific titles appear, the Pali words in these hybrids of Burmese and Pali are given in their Burmese rather than their Pali form, but terms such as *dhamma* and *kamma* have been retained in their standard Pali form. The Pali forms of words such as *dhamma* and *cakkavatti* have also been used throughout because there are significant differences in meaning between these and their Sanskrit equivalents *dharma* and *chakravartin*. For the reader's convenience, a glossary of Burmese and Pali words recurring in the text is included in the backmatter of this volume.

Burmese Era dates designated only by the year have been converted to Gregorian dates by adding 638, thus 1145 B.E. is 1783 A.D. Dates which include the day and month as well as the year have been converted to Gregorian equivalents by use of the tables in A. M. B. Irwin, *The Burmese and Arakanese Calendars*.

Figure 1. Map of Early Kon-baung Burma

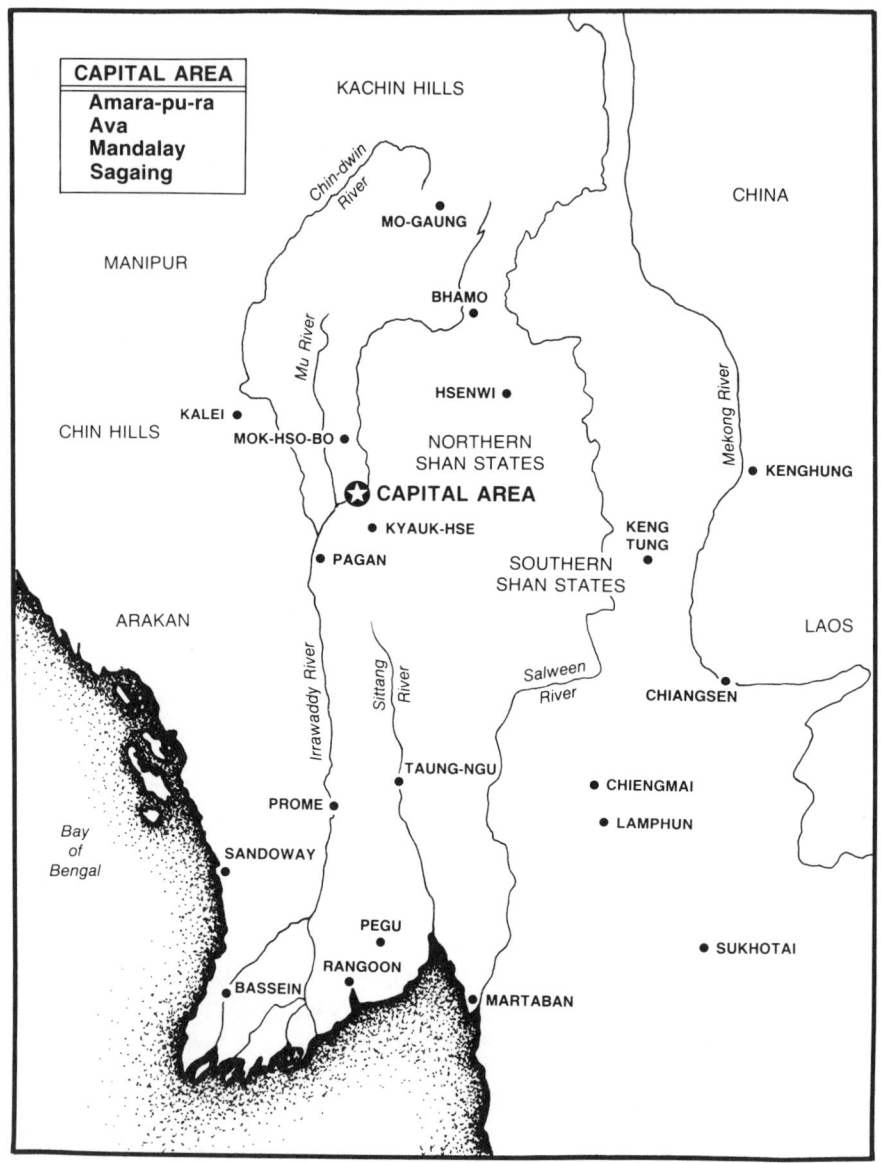

THE TAUNG-NGU AND KON-BAUNG DYNASTIES

First Taung-ngu Dynasty (1486–1599)

Min-gyi-nyo (1486–1531)
Tabin-shwei-hti (1531–1550)
Bayin-naung (1551–1581)
Nan-da Bayin (1581–1599)

Capitals:

Taung-ngu (1486–1539)
Pegu (1539–1597)

Restored Taung-ngu Dynasty (1597–1752)

Nyaung-yan (1597–1606), half brother of Nan-da Bayin
Anauk-hpet-lun (1606–1628), son of Nyaung-yan
Min-ye Deik-pa (1628), son of Anauk-hpet-lun
Tha-lun (1629–1648), son of Nyaung-yan
Pin-dale (1648–1661), son of Tha-lun
Pyei (1661–1672), son of Tha-lun
Naya-waya (1672–1673), son of Pyei
Min-ye Kyaw-din (1673–1698), cousin of Naya-waya
Sanei (1698–1714), son of Pyei
Tanin-ganwei (1714–1733), son of Sanei
Maha Dama Ya-za Di-pati (1733–1752), son of Tanin-ganwei

Capital:

Ava, 1600–1752

Kon-baung Dynasty (1752–1885)

Alaung-hpaya (1752–1760)
Naung-daw-gyi (1760–1763), first son of Alaung-hpaya
Hsin-hpyu-shin (1763–1776), second son of Alaung-hpaya

The Taung-ngu and Kon-baung Dynasties

Sin-gu (1776–1782), son of Hsin-hpyu-shin
Maung Maung (1782), son of Naung-daw-gyi
Bo-daw-hpaya (1782–1819), fourth son of Alaung-hpaya
Ba-gyi-daw (1819–1837), son of the crown prince who died in 1808
Tha-ra-wadi (1837–1846), same as Ba-gyi-daw
Pagan (1846–1853), son of Tha-ra-wadi
Min-don (1853–1878), son of Tha-ra-wadi
Thi-baw (1878–1885), son of Min-don

Capitals:

Mok-hso-bo (Shwei-bo) (1752–1760)
Mok-hso-bo and Sagaing (dual capitals) (1760–1764)
Ava (1764–1783)
Amara-pu-ra (1783–1823)
Ava (1823–1837)
Amara-pu-ra (1837–1857)
Mandalay (1857–1885)

PREFACE

The history of Burma prior to the mid-eighteenth century saw the rise and fall of three major dynastic regimes. The first of these was the Pagan dynasty, traditionally dated 1044–1287. On its demise, Burma was fragmented into several smaller kingdoms until it was reunified under the aegis of the First Taung-ngu dynasty (1486–1599), a unity reestablished by the Restored Taung-ngu regime (1597–1752). All three dynastic regimes enjoyed early periods of martial and administrative strength, subsequently went into declines characterized by the failing power of the central authority, and finally succumbed to military pressure from their enemies. The last of these dynasties, the Restored Taung-ngu, received its *coup de grace* in 1752 from an insurgent kingdom that had arisen in southern Burma over a decade earlier. After a century of progressively declining central power, upper Burma was left without a government or point of political orientation. Then occurred a remarkable renaissance of indigenous power led by the local gentry, a renaissance which soon came to be centered on the person of a local official subsequently known to history as Alaung-hpaya. In the space of five years, he and his followers militarily annihilated their southern rivals, established the Kon-baung kingdom (1752–1885), and reconstituted the central, provincial, and local levels of administration. After a period of initial vigor lasting barely forty years, the Kon-baung dynasty, too, experienced a period of declining royal power, which continued for nearly a century until its quietus at the hands of British imperialism. The course of Kon-baung history thus resembles that of the three preceding dynasties. The waxing and waning exhibited by these dynasties raises the issue of what interpretation to place on the history of the monarchical period and, more specifically, whether these recurring patterns or "dynastic cycles" share common operative causes.

The critical study of Burmese history may be said to have begun in 1883 with the publication of Sir Arthur Phayre's *History of Burma*, in

Preface

which he attempted the first overall survey from legendary times to the deposition of the Kon-baung king Ba-gyi-daw in 1837. His main source was the *Glass Palace Chronicle*, which he followed carefully and not uncritically to produce a dynastically oriented narrative. The more broadly researched survey published by G. E. Harvey in 1925 was also characterized by a pronounced dynastic emphasis. His view of the Burmese monarchy was that it was a "sanguinary despotism," which gathered everything unto the ruler and permitted no other points of power to exist. The same ground was covered by Htin Aung in 1967, with a similar monarchy-centered focus, an orientation consistently held by other writers in Burmese.[1]

Thus, the main trend in the historiography of the monarchical period in Burma has been the production of surveys of dynastic events. One common element among these surveys is an explanation of dynastic flux that depends on essentially one factor. The strength and viability of the realm in any given reign are linked directly to the personal capacities of the ruler to cope with the demands of office. Successful sovereigns are men who possess the personal strength and abilities sufficient to create a strong state, while less fortunate kings are *ipso facto* incompetent. Harvey, for example, attributed the pattern of early dynastic vigor followed by a long trend of decline to the "harem system" and marriage practices of the royal family, which, he argued, produced "effete" personalities. Other writers tend to imply chance. Little or no account is taken of internal and external circumstances, the nature of sociopolitical institutions, or changes in the structure of power and resource control.

Yet, from the time of Pagan onward, the Burmese polity was characterized by a complex social organization, well-developed political institutions and administrative systems, and a coherent body of political thought. Although the administrative records of earlier periods are meager, a substantial body of working administrative records is extant from the early Kon-baung period, making it possible to study this in some detail. In the early decades of this century, J. S. Furnivall was the first writer to attempt to understand the nature of monarchical administration and society through the study of administrative records, which he personally collected.[2] In the early 1930s, his friend and colleague, U Tin of Pagan, a former official at the court of King Thi-baw (1878–1885), prepared a monumental work entitled *Myan-ma min ok-chok-pon sa-dan* [The administration of Burmese kings].[3] The five volumes of this study are a vast treasury of chaotically organized, and for the most part uncritically presented, material on administration and society. Using some of the same sources and U Tin's research notes,

Preface

Mya Sein published the first coherent description of the structure of precolonial Burmese administration in 1938.[4]

Though valuable in themselves, these studies remained unconnected to the main trend in the historiography of the monarchical period and thus had no real effect on the interpretation of that period. A major use of administrative history to explain dynastic vicissitudes did not occur until 1976, when Victor B. Lieberman completed his thesis on the period 1580–1760.[5] His purpose was to demonstrate the roles of formal and informal changes in administration and in the control of resources, primarily labor, in the political developments of this period. Directly addressing the issue of dynastic cycles, he argued that dynastic collapse was followed by a period of reintegration and reform, which, in turn, faded into a longer period of administrative decline culminating in collapse, at which point the cycle recommenced. For the Restored Taung-ngu dynasty this cycle was the result of structural administrative weaknesses that caused a progressive decline in the ability of the crown to maintain control of its human and material resources and thus to preserve its central monopoly of power. In this conception, the relative control of resources was the basis of the division of power between the crown and its competitors.

The present study also originated as a thesis, finally seeing the light of day in 1978. It focuses on the early Kon-baung period, from the rise of Alaung-hpaya in 1752 to the death of Bo-daw-hpaya in 1819. Immediately succeeding the main period of Lieberman's study, this sixty-seven-year span encompasses the initial period of vigor and early phase of decline of the dynasty. The outlines of the dynastic history and foreign relations of the early Kon-baung period are fairly well known, but its institutions, political thought, socioeconomic organization, elite groups, and political patterns have been as yet little studied.[6] However, this is an important and fruitful period of study for several reasons. Beyond contributing to our existing knowledge of the history of Burmese society and institutions generally, this is a case study of a specific polity within the limits of a particular historical period. This period was the apogee of the precolonial polity, and a large volume of materials exists that can be exploited. In fact, the early Kon-baung polity is probably the best documented of the Southeast Asian kingdoms. Further, it is possible to study changes in the Burmese polity as a result of specifically indigenous forces, separate from the strong British pressure that was to be such an important feature of the later period.

After placing the period 1752–1819 in the context of earlier historical developments and reviewing its foreign relations and major internal trends, this study examines the society, the central political institution of the monarchy, its foundation in Burmese political thought, and the nature of the administrative apparatus through which the sovereign exercised his rule. The political roles of elite groups in society—the Buddhist monks, officials, and the extended royal lineage—are major themes. A strong case is made that monks, as an organized entity (the *sangha*) or entities (specific sects), were not major actors in the politics surrounding the throne or in the control of the resources of the society. Individually and collectively, the Burmese historically devoted substantial resources to religious ends, and did so in the early Kon-baung period. But the administrative records of the period make clear that the *sangha* was regulated and administered by the secular power, and that neither the *sangha* nor individual monks had hands-on control of lands or revenues.[7] The monks were unquestionably an elite group, but were neither politically active nor economically powerful in the early Kon-baung period. The officials and the extended royal lineage were clearly the major sources of contest for resources and the throne.

In a monarchy-centered polity, the efforts of various groups and individuals to influence, control, and even obtain the crown were the central focus of politics because the ruler was the primary arbiter of wealth and privilege in the society. Thus the two basic and interrelated areas of political conflict were the relative distribution of the resources of the society and control of the central political institution.[8] The latter area of conflict was, for the most part, focused on the royal succession. I have therefore included discussions of the nature and politics of the royal succession during the period. My argument is that, important as administrative changes and resource control were, they were not the only factors operative in the dynastic pattern. Certain features inherent in the nature of the monarchy, the royal succession, and the political ties binding the polity together must also be taken into consideration. Harvey did, indeed, have a germ of insight when he decried the influence of the harem system on Kon-baung politics. The study concludes with some observations on the nature of politics and society in the early Kon-baung period and a comment on dynastic cycles in Burmese history.

This book originated as a Ph.D. thesis at the School of Oriental and African Studies (SOAS) of the University of London. I owe large debts to Professor C. D. Cowan, my patient thesis supervisor, and Professor Hla Pe, my guide through the complexities and nuances of the Burmese sources. Perhaps they will feel repaid by finally seeing this work in print. SOAS at that time was a stimulating environment in which to work, made the more so by the interest and accessibility of such staff

Preface

members as John Okell, Anna Allott, H. L. Shorto, and R. B. Smith, to name but a few. I was further fortunate to work on my thesis alongside two fellow students—Victor B. Lieberman and M. S. Ali—who were also preparing theses in Burmese history. The intellectual interchange and friendship contributed a valuable dimension to all our work.

I wish to thank Victor B. Lieberman and Michael Adas, who both subsequently took the time to wade through the manuscript again and send me reams of valuable comments and suggestions. I have incorporated many of their suggestions, updated the text on certain points, excised here and there a little of the detail so dear to graduate students, and line edited the text. I wish also to record the contribution of two late friends—Professor Frank N. Trager and Dr. Yi Yi—with whom I enjoyed working on the Burmese *sit-tan* project and from whom I learned so much. The editorial skill and diligence of Diane Scherer have contributed much to the readability and clarity of the text. Finally, I am grateful to the Publications Committee, chaired by Professor Nicholas B. Dirks, of The University of Michigan's Center for South and Southeast Asian Studies, and Professor Victor B. Lieberman, its director, for bringing this work to publication.

Highland, Maryland
October 1989

CHAPTER 1

THE EARLY KON-BAUNG POLITY AND ITS ANTECEDENTS

The history of Burma has seen the rise and fall of three empires, the last of which was ruled by the Kon-baung dynasty. On its demise at the hand of British imperialism in 1885, Kon-baung rule had lasted only 133 years, in contrast to the over two centuries of rule by each of its predecessors, the Pagan and Taung-ngu empires. In its own time each empire established dominance over the Irrawaddy Basin and, to varying extents, was able to affect developments in such neighboring regions as Laos and Thailand. Cutting across these three chronologically defined segments of Burmese history are broader themes such as the development of political and administrative institutions, the general pattern of politics and power relationships, regionalism, and the gradual establishment of Burmese dominance over the Irrawaddy Basin. The purpose of this chapter is to examine briefly the antecedents of the early Kon-baung polity, in terms of both the course of the empires and these broader themes, to introduce the book's main subject: early Kon-baung political, administrative, and social systems.

The Geographical Setting

The geographical domain of the empires is a seven-hundred-mile-long depression not exceeding one hundred miles in width, which spans the valleys of the Chin-dwin, Irrawaddy, and Sittang rivers. Ringed by uplands, this long depression is bounded on the west by the Arakan Yoma and the Naga and Chin hills, while to the north and east a series of plateaus stretching from Tibet to Tenasserim form a natural barrier against China and Thailand (see figure 1). Only where the narrow coastal plains of Arakan and Tenasserim abut the southern tips of these rugged uplands is Burma unprotected by natural barriers. Within the central depression, the axes of the country are a series of parallel river valleys running north to south. The main river system is that of the Irrawaddy, flowing southwest from the Shan Highlands to Ava. There the river bends due west and absorbs first the Mu and then the Chin-dwin River before resuming its southern course. From its confluence with the Chin-dwin the Irrawaddy turns south until, just below Prome, it fans out into the eight main and many minor distributaries of its delta. Separated from the valley of the lower Irrawaddy by the Pegu Yoma is the valley of the Sittang River to the east, which also has a substantial delta. Still farther east the Salween River cuts across the Shan Highlands in a series of severe gorges to debouch into the Bay of Bengal at Martaban, but has no delta and virtually no lowlands over its long course.[1]

In common with the other river-valley kingdoms of Southeast Asia, the upper or northern regions of eighteenth-century Burma were distinguished from the lower or southern areas by climate, agriculture, and, to some extent, culture and ethnicity. An intermediate zone along a Prome–Taung-ngu axis separates the upper and lower regions at approximately 19 degrees north latitude. To the north of the intermediate zone lies the arid central plateau, while to the south stretches the flat plain of lower Burma.

The Rise and Fall of Pagan

The separation of Burma into two distinct climatic and agricultural areas tended to coincide with the lines dividing the country into two relatively distinct cultural and ethnic areas. Originally much of lower Burma had been settled by Mon peoples migrating from the southeast, who combined a high level of civilization with a maritime and trade orientation. One of the two main Mon city-states was Pegu, which had a mixed population of Mons and Indians. The other important Mon kingdom was Thahton, located in the more purely Mon region to the east of the Sittang River. By the end of the ninth century, Burman migrants from the northeast had established a kingdom they called Tam-ba-di-pa with its capital at Pagan. Thus, the traditional areas of Mon dominance were the deltas of the Irrawaddy and Sittang rivers, while the Burman kingdom was based in the drier hills and valleys to the north. A hardy agricultural people with a strong military tradition, in the early Pagan period the Burmans quickly absorbed many aspects of the cosmopolitan Mon culture. Over the centuries there was a certain amount of southward movement by Burmans until, by the mid-eighteenth century, a substantial portion of the northern Irrawaddy Delta was probably already Burman. While the north remained more insular and Burman in its outlook, the south, with its mixed population of Mons and Burmans, different agricultural style, and the cosmopolitan traditions of former Mon kingdoms, came to develop its own regional identity. On various occasions over the course of Burma's history the south succeeded in establishing its political autonomy as well.

In the mid-eleventh century the Mon kingdom of Pegu apparently entered into a vassal relationship of sorts with the Burman kingdom of Pagan to meet a Cambodian threat. The result of this union of Mon and Burman was the empire of Pagan. The basic institutions and social organization that were to characterize later empires are already evident in this period. The social and economic organization of the Pagan empire appears to have been complex, with a precise system of land measurement and areas of irrigated paddy culture centered in Taung-dwin-gyi, Kyauk-hse, the Mu Valley around Tabayin, and the lower Chin-dwin Valley.

The Pagan period was also a time of considerable political and cultural development. As imported to Burma from India via Ceylon, Theravada Buddhism had already lost the elite and esoteric character of early Indian Buddhism and had become in Burma a popular salvation religion, which, by the end of the period, had largely supplanted its Mahayana and Tantric rivals. The doctrines of Theravada Buddhism were well understood, the *sangha*, or monkhood, well developed, and large student populations gathered around well-known teachers in the major monasteries that were the Pagan equivalent of universities. Charity (*dana*) had become established as the most popular means of acquiring merit and was most commonly expressed in the construction and endowment of religious edifices, principally pagodas and monasteries. Pagan city itself was the leading center of scholarship and charitable endeavor.

The notion of kingship was rationalized and legitimized in Buddhist terms and was well developed both institutionally and ceremonially. Court ceremony and administration were complex, with a variety of officials serving sundry functions, but in general administration was only to a very limited extent departmentalized. There were, however, special officers assigned to oversee irrigation, land assessment, revenue collection, and crown granaries. On the local level there were district and village chiefs, while provincial administration appears to have been run as an appanage system for royal relatives and favored officials. As evidenced by the royal bestowal of personal honorific titles and use of the term *thahtei* to denote a person of officially recognized wealth, at least the rudiments of the later hierarchy of rank and status were present. A basic division of the lowland population into those in crown service (*ahmu-dan*) and those outside it (*athi*) is also strongly suggested. If not fully elaborated, in Pagan times the fundamental social and political organization of the Burmans was at least well along in its formative process.[2]

By the second half of the thirteenth century, the vicissitudes of dynastic politics, exacerbated by its unwieldy size, loose organization, and excessive alienation of lands, revenue, and labor to religious ends, had combined to bring the first Burman empire to a decrepit state. Pressure from the newly established Mongol dynasty in China coincided with a strong southward migration of Tai peoples, generally known to the Burmans as Shans, to destroy the empire before the century was out. The Mon kingdom revived in the delta and other ethnic rulers and Burman provincial chiefs gained varying degrees of independence. Even before the end of the dynasty, Shan chiefs established themselves in Kyauk-hse and, after defeating a last Mongol attempt to incorporate northern Burma as a province of the Mongol empire in 1301, they made Pin-ya the seat of their rule over much of the dry zone and uplands. A succeeding Shan ruler founded Ava in 1365. In one part or another of the upland areas, Shan chieftains fought for supremacy, while Burmanized Shan rulers at Ava controlled most of the dry zone.

The demise of the Pagan dynasty marked the initial failure of the Burmans to establish their dominance over the other peoples of Burma. But, although the political unity imposed on Burma by its Pagan rulers disintegrated, its cultural and dynastic traditions continued. Pagan itself ceased to be the political center of the Irrawaddy Valley, but its importance as the chief locus of scholarship and religion declined only gradually and did not end until well into the fifteenth century. As the former seat of a great empire, Pagan was seen by both Burmans and Shans as having a special status, and even down to the nineteenth century much of the royal religious patronage was still bestowed on that locale.[3]

The First Taung-ngu Empire

Following the sack of Pagan in 1287, Burma was split into the Mon kingdom of Pegu in the south, Burmanized Shan rulers at Ava to whom various Burman provincial authorities at Prome, Taung-ngu, Salin,

Taung-dwin-gyi, and Yame-thin were in vassalage, and other Shan chiefs in the highlands. In 1531 the Burman chief Tabin-shwei-hti began to expand from his base at Taung-ngu in a drive that was completed by his successor Bayin-naung and resulted in the establishment of the First Taung-ngu empire. The mid-sixteenth century marks the establishment under Burman rule of a kingdom virtually coterminous with modern Burma, the beginning of systematic Burman suzerainty over the uplands, and the establishment of a pattern of vassal relationships that was to endure throughout the early Kon-baung period.

In governing the largest of the sixteenth-century Southeast Asian land empires, the early Taung-ngu rulers followed the pattern of the Pagan imperial structure. This involved direct rule over a core or nuclear area around the capital, while allowing the remainder of the kingdom to be ruled as nearly autonomous appanages and vassal principalities. During the early Taung-ngu period, the core area was centered around Pegu in the delta region rather than in the dry zone. Outside the core area, the subcenters of Ava, Prome, Taung-ngu, Martaban, and Chiengmai were ruled by either younger brothers of the monarch or other princes of royal blood. These relatives of the direct royal line were termed *bayin*, or ruler, and allowed use of the five royal regalia as well as other royal prerogatives. As rulers of the major subcenters of the kingdom, they functioned as subkings, enjoying virtual autonomy in the governance of their charges. There appears to have been little use made of appointed royal officials to control the *bayins*, the subordinate provincial officials being in the main locals who were largely unaffected by the vicissitudes of royal politics. Lesser districts such as Salei, Salin, Tavoy, Myaung-mya, and Nyaung-yan were assigned as appanages to princes not of royal blood and to high officials. All were encouraged by the monarch to fortify their seats of administration and operate autonomously. Ayuthia and the highlands continued to be governed by local hereditary rulers who acknowledged the suzerainty of Pegu and rendered specified tribute.[4]

Thus, the kingdom consisted of three administratively distinct areas: the core or nuclear zone, the *bayin-* and appanage-governed districts, and the ethnic vassals on the peripheries. Together it was a vast and loosely organized federation of units which were actually encouraged to be autonomous. Ensconced in his capital in the core area, the monarch was, in effect, simply the most powerful of the *bayins*. The manifestation of royal power in the provinces was meant to be embodied in the minicourts and royal prerogatives of the *bayins* who, as men of royal blood, were all eligible for the throne. The fundamental unity of the realm rested on the consanguine ties between king and subkings and the formal extension of part of the royal charisma to the latter. The reverse effect was in fact obtained, however, because the *bayins* frequently tended to compete with the monarch, to withhold support, and at various times to contest the succession militarily. Those who held lesser districts as appanages also tended to withdraw support when the central power seemed vulnerable. The main weaknesses of the system were therefore the low degree of cohesion between the central domain and the other districts, the lack of effective institutional controls over the subcenters, and the virtual encouragement of other relatives of royal blood to become competitors of the monarch.

The short-term cause of the collapse of the First Taung-ngu dynasty was its attempt to maintain an overextended empire. Both Bayinnaung and his successor Nan-da Bayin endeavored to control a vast area ranging from Manipur to Laos and the borders of Cambodia, an area far more extensive than that needed for the stability of the Irrawaddy Valley and lowland regions. Both rulers were forced to undertake almost continuous campaigns to maintain even a semblance of control over this colossus. As the delta was the one area over which they had direct control, this task heavily drained its resources. The effect was somewhat diluted during the reign of Bayin-naung because captives from his campaigns were settled in the delta, but even so the lack of cultivators began to result in crop failures. As royal power grew weaker and began to suffer military reverses, the constituent parts of the system increasingly withheld support, causing even heavier demands to be made on the central domain. The social and economic organization of the delta disintegrated further at that time due to famine, the continuing levies of rice and men, and migration to Thailand, Arakan, upper Burma, and the Sittang Valley. Serious provincial rebellions began in 1593 at Bassein, leaving that district devastated, and in 1594 at Moulmein. Strengthened by refugees from the central delta, the *bayins* of Taung-ngu and Prome declared their independence in the late 1590s. Taung-ngu then combined with Arakan to sack Pegu in 1598.

This event marked the end of the First Taung-ngu empire, with lower Burma falling under the sway of the lords of Prome and Taung-ngu and, to a lesser extent, Ayuthia and the Portugese harbor principality at Syriam. The south had been severely ravaged and much of the population lost. The early Taung-ngu kings and the violent demise of their rule had so sapped the delta that a century and a half would pass before lower Burma would again become a major center of power.

The Restored Taung-ngu Empire

The time of troubles in lower Burma in the closing decade of the sixteenth century left the north largely untouched. As the final assault on Pegu was underway in the 1590s, a minor son of Bayin-naung was ignoring the calls for assistance from his half brother at Pegu and marshaling his own resources. Known from his appanage as the lord of Nyaung-yan, he began to expand from his base in southern Meik-hti-la and northern Yame-thin in 1597 and was crowned at Ava in 1600. Carefully consolidating his position after each success, he invested the next five years in bringing firm control over the highlands, both to protect his rear in the north and to harness Tai manpower for his next objective, the conquest of the south.

His death in 1606 left that task to his able son Anauk-hpet-lun, who by then controlled far greater resources than did any of his opponents. The march to the south commenced with campaigns against Prome in 1608, Taung-ngu in 1610, Syriam in 1613, Martaban and Yei in 1614, and finally Chiengmai in 1615. When subsequent minor campaigns came to an end in 1626, the first two rulers of the Restored Taung-ngu dynasty had established an empire reaching from Kengtung and Kenghung in the east to the Arakan border in the west, and from Mogaung and Hsenwi in the north to Tavoy in the south. To the extent that both logistics and lines of communication were not unduly extended in its defense, these boundaries formed a natural area of authority. After 1626, the Restored Taung-ngu rulers followed a pacific foreign policy aimed at defending rather than enlarging this domain.

Nyaung-yan and Anauk-hpet-lun had begun to introduce a number of important administrative changes and these were fully developed by Tha-lun. Whether by accident or design, these changes addressed the weaknesses of their early Taung-ngu predecessors. The capital was returned to Ava in 1635, and the core area of the kingdom was once again located in the Burman heartland. Upper Burma was, in fact, not only in a relatively undisturbed state in 1600, but had even been strengthened by migration from the troubled south. Well aware of the need for a strong demographic base in the core area, the monarchs followed every victory in the highlands and the southern campaigns not only with deportations to the dry zone but also reorganized previously existing crown service units. The majority of the deportees to upper Burma were settled within a seventy-mile radius of the capital, usually in the more productive irrigated areas of Madaya, Kyauk-hse, the Mu Valley, and the lower Chin-dwin Valley. In a related move, the irrigation systems were repaired and their administration overhauled. All three rulers also carried out various surveys in order to gain systematic data on the specifics of the *athi* and crown service populations, taxes, boundaries of local jurisdictions, and the claims to office of local headmen. The most extensive of these was the census or inquest carried out by Tha-lun between 1635 and 1638, which encompassed the entire Irrawaddy Valley. There were, in addition, various other measures and regulations enacted to ensure that the crown maintained administrative control over the population and received the revenues and services due it. The overall result was to alter the distribution of population in favor of the core area relative to the provinces and to concentrate the main resource of the throne—the crown service groups—in the core area generally and around the capital in particular. As Victor Lieberman has shown, this was a major administrative accomplishment and contrasts sharply with the low concentration of crown service units around Pegu in the early Taung-ngu period.[5]

Another important innovation was the change in the system of granting appanages to royalty. Whereas in the sixteenth century appanages had been distributed fairly evenly over the central lowlands, by the early seventeenth century there were few appanages south of the Min-bu area. They were now heavily concentrated in the core area, particularly in some of the less well-irrigated districts to the northwest and southeast of Ava. The uncles, brothers, and sons of the kings were required to live in the capital itself, to administer their grants through agents, and to obtain permission before visiting their districts. The male royalty continued to be involved in administration as appanage holders, leaders of military expeditions, and holders of administrative appointments, but with the demise of the *bayin* system they were no longer permitted to hold sway as provincial rulers and competitors of the king. The post of *myo wun*, or provincial governor, was first instituted on a regular basis by Anauk-hpet-lun, and in the succeeding reign of Tha-lun all provincial rulers were *myo wuns*, with one possible exception. *Myo wuns* were usually sons of concubines (and therefore had no blood claim to the throne) and occasionally of nonroyal birth. Another change was to reduce the territory of the major subcenters while enlarging that of a number of minor centers, thereby increasing the number of districts having resident, court-appointed, nonroyal governors, and, to some extent, regularizing the size of jurisdictions. In another important step, the rulers rather than the local governors began to appoint the subordinate provincial officials. A related move was to install a *nagan*, or "royal ear," in the administration of each *myo wun* specifically to report on the affairs of that jurisdiction.

In addition to curbing the power of the royalty and clamping down on provincial autonomy, the power and prerogatives of the gentry in upper Burma were also reduced. With no strong central power to regulate them, many local chiefs had amassed sizable jurisdictions and paid little attention to their revenue and service obligations. To establish control over this local elite, Tha-lun decreed a reduction of the size of jurisdictions, conducted the inquest of 1635-1638, and thereafter mandated the submission of annual reports. He also regulated succession to local office, brought the gentry into the status hierarchy, and, in various other ways, established links between local society and the court.

The structure of the capital bureaucracy appears to have changed little, but the importance of the ministers in particular was magnified by the diminution in the role of the royalty. The officials at the capital ran the government, including the establishments of the princes. Broadly speaking, the administration was divided into territorial and departmental jurisdictions. The Hlut-taw, or council of ministers, was the major administrative organ of the state and responsible for the various territorial jurisdictions. The Bye-daik, responsible mainly for palace administration, was the largest and most important of the fifty-odd departments. Official positions were not hereditary, but were usually filled by leading families, thus serving as links between court and gentry. The relationship between the center and the vassal principalities appears to have remained unchanged.

In their aggregate, these administrative changes had a profound effect on the nature of royal politics. The restriction of provincial autonomy gave the center greater control over the other areas. The curbing of the royalty and changes in the appanage system, combined with the *myo wun* system, significantly reduced the ability of the princes and subcenters to compete with the ruler. By severing the direct administrative relationship between the princes and their appanages, keeping the appanages mainly in the core area, and forcing the princes to live in the capital, the early rulers of the Restored Taung-ngu dynasty took their opposition out of the provinces and made the court the focus of politics. With the power of the central officials so augmented, the standard pattern of revolt now became the conspiracy of minister and princely aspirant leading to a palace coup. The overall result of these innovations was a reduction in the number of provincial revolts and an improvement in the orderliness of the royal succession.

Encompassing the first half of the seventeenth century, the administrative reforms of the reigns of Nyaung-yan, Anauk-hpet-lun, and Tha-lun constitute a highly important stage in Burmese political development. Although the basic pattern of Burmese political and social organization was set in the Pagan period, the final shape of the Burmese state and administration was established only during the Restored Taung-ngu dynasty. In the next century the succeeding Konbaung dynasty was to establish its rule over the same area as that of the Restored Taung-ngu state and follow Taung-ngu political organization. This administrative pattern continued, with only minor modifications, until the mid-nineteenth century.

The Decline and Fall of the Restored Taung-ngu State

Despite the centralizing reforms and martial vigor of the early rulers of the Restored Taung-ngu dynasty, as the seventeenth century progressed a declining trend becomes clearly evident. Significant as the new administrative changes were, they only altered the lines of political conflict within the Burmese polity rather than removing the basic problems. Because all sons by major queens were eligible for the throne, the main political issue remained the transfer of power. Even though the eldest son of the chief queen was the preferred candidate, there were sometimes as many as two other serious competitors for the throne. The diminished power of the princes under the new appanage system combined with the increased power of the high officials to introduce princely-ministerial factions into Burmese politics. Successful claimants gradually lost power to their ministerial supporters until, by the reign of Min-ye Kyaw-din (1673–1698), real control lay with the ministers, with the monarch reigning but not ruling. Over time, as the ministerial factions became better defined, they reached out into the countryside in what Victor Lieberman has termed "ministerial patronage networks," with gentry and provincial officials allying themselves with one faction or another in return for appointments and connivance in rapacious taxation schemes.

Ministerial patronage and usurpation of crown prerogatives to service and revenues further diminished central authority. Because the nuclear area was that portion under direct crown control and also most accessible to the capital, the rulers tended to exploit its resources most heavily. The result was a depletion of the royal sector through the mechanisms of migration out of the nuclear area, the amalgamation of both crown service groups and the *athi taings* (service and dues units) to reduce the burden of their individual members, falsification of revenue and population statistics, alienation of crown service land leading to an increase of private tenants under the gentry, and entrance into the service of royal appanage holders by both crown service and *athi* households.

The primary beneficiaries of this decrease in the material base of royal power were the princes, the ever-present competitors of the king. The increasingly intense factionalism at court, the corresponding development of ministerial patronage networks, and the eroding material power of the crown had a direct and deleterious effect on administration that combined to bring about a gradual weakening of the state. Polarized around the royal succession, the struggle between the two main ministerial factions was exceptionally intense during the reigns of Sanei (1698-1714) and Tanin-ganwei (1714-1733), when it came close to paralyzing the administration of the realm.

In imperial terms, the late seventeenth-century monarchy was characterized by stability. The core area still maintained a basic superiority over the provinces and vassals in resources and the system of administrative control still functioned adequately. But the absence of imperial activity, due in part to the pacific foreign policy pursued by the Taung-ngu rulers after 1626, meant that there were no deportations or formation of new crown service groups to offset the effect that overexploitation of the nuclear area and the intense factional politics were having on the military capability of the central authority. By the turn of the century, there were indications that the imperial structure was beginning to dissolve, as evidenced in the relinquishing of a few distant and minor vassals. This process of disintegration was further accelerated in the 1720s and 1730s as Chiengmai, the lynchpin of the eastern frontier, and the major Shan *saw-bwas* defected. Between 1723 and 1740, the northwest and the nuclear area suffered a series of major attacks by the revitalized Manipuri state under Gharib Newaz. In Ava itself, the destruction of the leading ministerial faction by its chief rival in 1735 caused the collapse not only of the main ministerial patronage network, but of the regular administration as well. This was further accompanied by severe outbreaks of banditry and disorder. Droughts, floods, Manipuri raids, and the dual administrative collapse created a condition of famine and disorder in upper Burma which, in the 1730s and 1740s, became endemic.

As upper Burma gradually slid into chaos during the first half of the eighteenth century, the concomitant rebellion of the peripheral vassals came to infect the Irrawaddy Delta. Southern politics were traditionally characterized by their polyethnic and parochial nature and common antipathy to the central authority and its local minions. In contrast to the predominantly Burman north and center, the ethnic complexion of the delta was then in transition. The historic southward movement of the Burmans was increased by the turmoil in the north and, in the closing years of the seventeenth century, the delta was likely the recipient of a substantial infiltration of Karens from the east. As a result, the south now had three distinct ethnic communities: the Mons, Karens, and Burmans. Another factor was the southern gentry, who had become increasingly alienated by the shift in the political center of gravity after 1635 and their resulting decreased access to court appointments. Lacking a central political focus or capital, the south was also traditionally and administratively fragmented into such provincial centers as Pegu, Bassein, Myaung-mya, Martaban, and Tavoy. As Victor Lieberman has shown, however, maladministration in the form of overtaxation was the major factor in the alienation not only of the vassals, but the southern provinces as well.

The issue of overtaxation led to overt rebellion in Pegu in 1740, when the populace overthrew an exploitative Burman governor on the occasion of his own attempted rebellion against Ava. A royal pretender, the alleged son of a Taung-ngu prince who had failed in the contested succession of 1714, appeared, was accepted by the Mon, Burman, and Karen communities, and crowned at Pegu. After establishing nominal control over the other southern provinces, the new regime began attacking its northern rival at Ava, which was now beset with rebellions in upper Burma as well. The north lacked the capacity to fight a two-front war and a massive invasion from Pegu swept away the remnants of the moribund Taung-ngu state in the dry season of 1751–1752. Along with his court and perhaps twenty thousand other people, the king of Ava (Maha Dama Ya-za Di-pati, 1733–1752) was taken to Pegu and became commonly known as the "king who came to Han-tha-wadi."[6]

The Foundation of the Kon-baung State

The southern victory destroyed both the formal and informal structures of power in upper Burma by physically removing the central administration and, in the process, sweeping away the remains of the ministerial patronage networks that had entwined the north. The result was a complete vacuum of power and a large reservoir of unattached manpower. Only the Mu and lower Chin-dwin valleys in the northwest, which had escaped attack since 1740, still retained military potential. A number of local and district Burman leaders in the area sought to harness this manpower and either resist or collaborate with the southern occupation to advance their own interests. One of the most firmly based and widely known of these leaders was U Aung Zei-ya of Mok-hso-bo, who is known in Burmese history as Alaung-hpaya. He systematically coopted or defeated his Burman rivals, organized the growing population under his control into service groups, and finally cleared the last of the southern forces from upper Burma in May 1754. He had already been crowned king at Mok-hso-bo the preceding year. His success was based on his innate leadership qualities, his careful formation and augmentation of his administrative and military base, and his open appeals to Burman ethnic chauvinism. The execution of the captive Ava king caused a Burman revolt in Prome in 1754, which swung the crucial intermediate zone to Alaung-hpaya and enabled him to carry the war to the delta. Pegu finally fell by storm in May 1757. With this victory Alaung-hpaya became the undisputed master of Burma and founder of the Kon-baung dynasty. The north had subdued the south for the last time and the Burmans had finally achieved a permanent dominance over the Irrawaddy Basin.

Alaung-hpaya followed the precedent set by the early rulers of the Restored Taung-ngu dynasty, as each victory or submission saw a careful organization of his new resources. Overall, the population of the nuclear zone was reorganized and expanded and a program of resettlement pursued in other regions. Apart from the nuclear zone, the eastern frontier from Kyauk-hse to the Sittang Valley was resettled as a barrier to Shan and Karen infiltration from the eastern plateau. As the lower Irrawaddy Basin came progressively under Alaung-hpaya's control, local officials and headmen were directed to gather in the people and reform their respective districts. Colonies of Burmans from the north were strategically placed at Henzada and above and below Myanaung while many Mons, made rootless by the war, were resettled in the western delta. There was even some resettlement and reorganization in the eastern Shan Highlands. The final Kon-baung victory in 1757 might well have left Alaung-hpaya ruler over a realm shattered by five years of intensive warfare preceded by the decades of disorders attendant on the demise of Taung-ngu rule. As it was, his domain emerged with an orderly administration, a relatively settled demographic base, and a strong military system.[7]

Although Kon-baung rule now embraced the entire Irrawaddy Valley, the imperial system had yet to be fully restored. Because the highlands ringing the valley remained largely outside Burmese control, the security of the valley remained in jeopardy. As successive monarchs struggled to reconstitute the imperial system, the problems presented by the western frontier, the Shan regions of the north and northeast, and the perennially troublesome eastern frontier dominated the external relations of Burma. This remained true until near the end of the reign of Bo-daw-hpaya, when relations with the English East India Company began to take center stage.

The Eastern Frontier, 1759–1767

The western frontier in 1757 presented no immediate problem, hence Alaung-hpaya turned his attention first to the Shan areas, where his initial efforts at pacification had been cut short by the Prome rising of 1754. Systematic pacification of the territory between the upper Irrawaddy and Yunnan was undertaken in 1758, concommitant with the reassertion of traditional Burmese dominance over the highlands west of the Salween. Significant forces were never sent east of that river, however, so control of the trans-Salween region continued to elude the Burmese. Also elusive was firm control over some sections of the north and northeast, where long years of autonomy made many of the Shan rulers restive at the reimposition of Burmese control. Some actively resisted and later came to involve Burma in a major conflict with her northern neighbor China. Thus, the area remained unstable after 1758 and constituted a trouble spot in the imperial system that was not rectified until the later reign of Hsin-hpyu-shin.

Control of the trans-Salween region had, throughout Burmese history, been considered essential for the security of the Irrawaddy Basin, so it was to the east that Alaung-hpaya turned his attention after the campaigns to pacify the Shans. As far back as the early Pagan period, Anaw-rahta (1044–1077) had attempted to seal the frontier against Mon and Shan infiltration with a line of forty-three military settlements. However, the eastern problem was only resolved, albeit temporarily, by the reduction of the Tai states of Chiengmai and Ayuthia to Burmese vassalage during the reign of Bayin-naung. With the end of the delta-based rule of the First Taung-ngu dynasty, the Thai for the first time began to appreciate the strategic value of the southeastern littoral, where Burmese control of the southern coast from Martaban through Yei, Tavoy, and Mergui to Tenasserim threatened the Thai capital of Ayuthia. The Mons of the southeastern littoral and Irrawaddy Delta, who had born the brunt of the exactions for the imperial exertions of Bayin-naung and Nan-da Bayin, realized at that time that Ayuthia offered an alternative to Burman rule. The first migration of Mons to Thailand occurred in the wake of the late sixteenth-century invasion of the delta by King Naresuen of Ayuthia. Thus came into being a special relationship between the Thai and the Mons of lower

Burma. The advent of the Restored Taung-ngu dynasty saw renewed Burman domination of the trans-Salween area and southeastern littoral, anchored with garrisons in the north at Chiengmai and in the south at Martaban, making these areas a buffer zone between Ayuthia and Ava.

The general pattern of the triangular relationship between Thai, Mons, and Burmans was that maladministration by local Burman officials provoked a Mon rising, more often than not centered at Martaban. This was followed by a Mon exodus to Thailand until sufficient Burman forces arrived to pacify the district and exact retribution. Such risings were encouraged by the Thai, who met the refugees at the border with supplies and gave them lands in Thailand. The Mons, in turn, provided Ayuthia with some of her best military units. The relationship with the Mons therefore tended to strengthen the flagging Thai military capability while weakening Burman control in the south.[8] Even so, this was a mixed blessing to the security of Ayuthia. Any delta-based kingdom, be it Burman or Mon, posed far more of a strategic threat to Ayuthia than did the kingdom of Ava based in the dry zone, and a delta kingdom would also have a substantial claim on the loyalties of the Mon community in Thailand. When these factors are coupled with the long-standing pacific foreign policy of the Restored Taung-ngu dynasty, it is not surprising that the court of Ayuthia reacted with considerable hostility to the appearance of the kingdom of Pegu in the 1740s, a hostility that was reinforced by Mon risings in Thailand during this period.

The Kon-baung victory over Pegu in 1757 restored the special relationship of the Mons with Ayuthia. Although there was no general Mon exodus after the bloody sack of Pegu, incidents soon occurred which brought the Mons in particular and the eastern frontier in general to the fore. While Alaung-hpaya was leading an expedition to Manipur, delta Mons seized Rangoon, Syriam, and Dala. Quickly driven out by local Burmese forces, the rebels fled to Thailand in the first Mon migration of the Kon-baung period. The rising had occurred in response to heavy taxation and was encouraged by offers of aid from Ayuthia.[9] The governor of Tavoy then seized the opportunity to rebel and offer himself as a vassal to Ayuthia. Recognizing that lower Burma and the eastern frontier would never be secure as long as the special relationship between the Thai and the Mons was allowed to continue, Alaung-hpaya determined to solve the problem by attacking the source of support and sanctuary for Mon dissidence. His plan of campaign was to march south, eradicate any remaining rebels in the delta, invade in sequence Tavoy, Tenasserim, Ayuthia, Lamphun, and Chiengmai, and then exact allegiance from the trans-Salween Shans.[10] In short, he intended the comprehensive subjugation of the Tai states east of the Salween, an imperial design reminiscent on a slightly reduced scale of the grand empire of Bayin-naung.

Launched in the dry season of 1759, the campaign quickly progressed from the reduction of Tavoy and Tenasserim to the investment of the Thai capital of Ayuthia. The Burmese forces were inadequate for the siege of that well-fortified and provisioned city and, as the siege dragged on into the spring of 1760, the besiegers were increasingly wasted by disease. With the approach of the rains near at hand, Alaung-hpaya began a retreat toward Martaban, but himself succumbed to disease on the march. Although the eastern campaign of 1759–1760 turned into a dismal failure, it was but the first of a series of operations on the eastern frontier that culminated seven years later in the achievement of Alaung-hpaya's original design.

The death of Alaung-hpaya brought to the throne his eldest son Naung-daw-gyi. Most of his reign was devoted to the suppression of two major rebellions and his untimely death in 1763 left both the throne and the eastern problem to his younger brother Hsin-hpyu-shin. Himself a seasoned campaigner, the new ruler quickly executed a classic north-south pincer operation against the Thai. One force was directed to occupy Chiengmai, Vientiane, and Luang Prabang and then strike at Ayuthia from the north, while a second force raised levies in Han-tha-wadi, Martaban, and the southeastern littoral and attacked from the south. This strategic operation was successfully completed three years later in April 1767, when Ayuthia fell by storm.

A number of factors were instrumental in the Burmese success. Hsin-hpyu-shin appointed two exceptionally able field commanders, Nei-myo Thi-ha Patei and Maha Naw-rahta, who was to die during the siege, and directed them to exploit fully the resources of Chiengmai, Vientiane, the southeastern littoral, and the Thai provinces conquered *en route* to Ayuthia. As a result, each commander arrived before the walls of that city at the head of large, if ethnically diverse, well-armed, and well-supplied armies. Of crucial significance was the fact that the campaign was sustained in the field through two rainy seasons, the troops maintaining themselves by raising their own rice. Equally crucial was the fact that events in the Irrawaddy Valley were not allowed to affect the progress of the campaign. Only once did Nei-myo Thi-ha Patei receive a directive relating to the siege, when an order of 9 January 1767 instructed him to bring his operations to an expeditious conclusion, destroy the fortifications of the city, and return to Ava with the captured Thai king and all his subjects. The reason given was that Hsin-hpyu-shin wished to lead his armies against China.[11]

Sino-Burmese Relations, 1765-1819

War had, in fact, broken out between Burma and China two years earlier over the status of the northern and northeastern Shan states, which had remained unsettled in spite of Alaung-hpaya's various attempts at pacification. These states served as a buffer between Burma and the Chinese province of Yunnan, whence caravans of merchants descended to Bhamo for an annual trade fair. As Burma lay outside China's effective range of control, the two states had only occasional diplomatic or military contact. Because the boundary between the Chinese and Burmese spheres of control overlapped, with many of the Shan rulers paying tribute to both, the regulation of the frontier tribes was a constant potential source of friction. The ostensible causes of the war were the death of a Chinese in a brawl near Kengtung and a minor dispute over the bridging of the Taping River by a Chinese merchant. The real *casus belli*, however, had arisen in 1762, when the usually Byzantine politics among the Shan *saw-bwas* had broken out into open warfare that engulfed the entire border region. Overt conflict between China and Burma was delayed three years, however, until the minor *saw-bwas* north of Kengtung sought Chinese protection to avoid the reimposition of vassalage to the Burmese. A force dispatched from Ava in December 1765 drove out a Yunnanese expedition and restored a Burmese-directed order.[12]

So began a long and hard-fought war between China and Burma. The Chinese held the Burmese responsible for the disturbances in the border area, which were, in fact, largely occasioned by the long delayed reimposition of Burmese authority in this region coupled to disruptions caused by the passage of large bodies of troops on the march to Chiengmai and Vientiane. Chinese efforts toward the pacification of the border region were, in turn, viewed by the Burmese as aggression. Many of the *saw-bwas* initially sided with the Chinese to resist the reimposition of Burmese exactions.

Three more campaigns were to follow the initial Sino-Burmese clash in 1765, as the Manchu Emperor Ch'ien Lung determined to bring the Burmese to heel. In spite of the large forces committed to the operations against Ayuthia, the Burmese generals Maha Si-thu and Maha Thi-ha Thu-ra outmaneuvered and generally outfought the three large Chinese armies that invaded Burma proper between 1766 and 1769.

In the last of these invasions, the entire Chinese army was trapped by Maha Thi-ha Thu-ra at Kaung-ton and forced to open negotiations in order to avoid annihilation. The terms of the treaty signed on 13 December 1769 allowed for the withdrawal of the Chinese and called for the return of Chinese prisoners and the decennial exchange of letters between the two monarchs.[13] The Chinese believed that the Burmese had agreed to at least a semblance of the tributary relationship so central to the Chinese imperial conception, but Maha Thi-ha Thu-ra knew full well that his lord would strongly disapprove of a negotiated settlement when the enemy was at bay. This fact was outweighed by his realization that annihilation of the enemy, well within his power, would only serve to provoke yet another Chinese invasion. Hence the Burmese general took full personal responsibility for his action at Kaung-ton and was, indeed, punished by a furious Hsin-hpyu-shin, who ignored the treaty and refused to return the Chinese prisoners from earlier campaigns. A French visitor at the court of Ava the following year recorded that a strong letter was received from the Ch'ien Lung Emperor threatening an embargo on trade and raising the possibility of another war if the treaty was not honored and the prisoners returned.[14] But the letter was ignored and a Chinese embargo was placed on both the overland and maritime trade.

No further intercourse between China and Burma occurred until a curious flurry of diplomatic missions between 1788 and 1796. The Chinese Shans of Kaingma and the *saw-bwa* of Bhamo appear to have acted in collusion with Chinese officials in Yunnan to dupe the Burmese court into sending missions to Peking, which were then interpreted to the emperor as tribute missions. The Yunnan officials were apparently anxious to have the emperor believe that Burma had finally submitted, while the Chinese Shans and Bhamo *saw-bwa* were eager to regain the revenues lost by the emperor's embargo on the overland trade. The initial result was that Bo-daw-hpaya repatriated the Chinese prisoners of war, in response to which the Chinese emperor lifted the trade embargo. The charade was exposed to Bo-daw-hpaya in 1796 and diplomatic activity ceased until 1823, but the overland trade continued to flourish.[15]

The Chinese wars of the late 1760s had several important consequences for Burma. In the contest between Chinese and Burmese power in the border area, Burmese arms had emerged supremely victorious and a Burmese controlled equilibrium was reestablished for the first time in over three decades. The border area continued to be the scene of minor squabbles among the *saw-bwas*, but these local affairs did not threaten Burmese control and, in the end, were usually adjudicated by the Burmese authorities. The fact that the early Kon-baung state could defeat three major Chinese invasions while simultaneously maintaining control of northern Thailand and besieging Ayuthia demonstrates the vitality and strength of the administrative and military system built by Alaung-hpaya. The Chinese and Thai campaigns of the 1760s also had the benefit of leadership by a cadre of able officers blooded in the internal conflicts of the 1750s. In terms of its ability to field large armies under effective leadership, Kon-baung military capability reached its peak in the 1760s.

The Chinese episode did have one deleterious outcome for Burma, however, because the very real Chinese threat to the city of Ava in early 1767 drove Hsin-hpyu-shin to send his fateful order to Nei-myo Thi-ha Patei to hasten the end of the siege of Ayuthia and return to Ava immediately. The king may have envisioned the capital itself under siege. Without this order, Nei-myo Thi-ha Patei would surely have remained in Thailand, undertaken a more thorough pacification, and left larger Burmese garrison forces. As it was, the precipitate Burmese withdrawal doomed the small Burmese detachments left behind to be quickly overwhelmed and Thailand was largely reunified under Tak Sin by 1770. Far from having solved the problem of the eastern frontier, only three years after her ultimate victory Burma was confronted with a resurgent Thailand.

The Eastern Frontier, 1770-1824

As the regeneration of Thai power provoked renewed Burmese operations in the east, the Thai-Burmese struggle resumed. As late as 1772, the Lao states of Vientiane and Luang Prabang sent tribute to Ava, but by the following year Tak Sin was raiding their borders and attacking Chiengmai.[16] In the face of the Thai challenge in Laos and the trans-Salween, Hsin-hpyu-shin attempted to repeat the successful pincer strategy of 1764-1767 by ordering Nei-myo Thi-ha Patei to proceed to Chiengmai, rally Laos, and march from the north on Tak Sin's capital of Thonburi in the Bangkok Plain. In the south the *myo wun* of Martaban was to raise levies from the southeastern littoral to mount a southern attack. The pincer strategy foundered in its second application, however, because maladministration by the Burmese governor of Chiengmai drove that key province into rebellion and vassalage to Thailand.[17] The southern expedition collapsed when the extortions of the Burmese governor of Martaban drove the conscripted Mons to revolt, followed by a large exodus to Thailand.[18]

The campaign was renewed in the dry season of 1774–1775 with more success and the troops of Nei-myo Thi-ha Patei so ravaged Chiengmai that the district was still deserted ten years later.[19] Maha Thi-ha Thu-ra was also directed to renew the assault from the south. For reasons of his own, he tarried at Martaban for a year, but then made rapid progress in the dry season of 1775–1776, smashing the Thai resistance led by Tak Sin and Chao Phya Chakri. As Maha Thi-ha Thu-ra deployed his armies for a final descent on the Bangkok Plain in June 1776, news arrived that Hsin-hpyu-shin had died and been succeeded by his son Sin-gu. The new king ordered both Maha Thi-ha Thu-ra and Nei-myo Thi-ha Patei to halt their operations and return immediately with all their forces.

The following six years of Sin-gu's rule were characterized by a marked lack of activity in either the domestic or imperial spheres. Sin-gu's sole venture was to send an inconclusive expedition against Lagun in 1777.[20] The lack of a Burmese presence in that region allowed the Thai to win the struggle for Laos the following year, when both Vientiane and Luang Prabang severed all relations with Burma and became Thai vassals.[21] With no Burmese interference for the decade between 1776 and 1785, the rejuvenation of Thailand was completed and a new dynasty established with its capital at Bangkok, with Chao Phya Chakri on the throne as Rama I.

Sin-gu was replaced on the throne of Ava in early 1782 by his uncle Bo-daw-hpaya, who was to pursue an active policy in both the imperial and domestic spheres. As had all his predecessors save Sin-gu, early on Bo-daw-hpaya turned his attention to the east. The dry season of 1785 saw a massive invasion of Thailand by four subordinate columns striking via Chiengmai, Raheng, Tavoy, and Mergui, while the main army under the king himself marched via Da-raik. While the four subordinate columns made good progress, the Thai concentrated all of their forces against the main army, which suffered from logistic problems arising from the incompetence of some officers. The Thai further harassed its lines of communications and finally forced it to retreat, making it necessary for the other four columns to withdraw as well. After fierce fighting, the Thai scored another decisive victory the following year over a large Burmese force invading from Martaban, a victory which brought further heavy losses in men and materiel to the Burmese.[22]

Following the successive Burmese defeats of 1785–1786 and 1786, the scale of the conflict was much reduced. In the wake of the Thai victories, the trans-Salween Shans were restive, but a Burmese force sent to pacify that region was driven out by Thai forces.[23] At this time

Thai imperial ambitions focused not only on Laos and the trans-Salween, but on the southern part of the Tenasserim coast, where probing attacks were made against Tavoy in the hope of provoking a Mon rising. The governor of Tavoy did rebel in 1790, followed by a Thai invasion, but the Burmese had recaptured the area by 1793. Although Thai aspirations in the southeastern littoral of Burma were blocked, the balance of power had definitely shifted in their favor in the north. After 1778 the Burmese had lost any footing they had in Laos while, ten years later, the Thai had resettled and repopulated Chiengmai. The Burmese position was further weakened as, apart from recapturing the Tavoy District, between 1790 and 1797 Bo-daw-hpaya focused all his resources on domestic projects. A further attempt to retrieve the Burmese position in the east failed in 1797. The Thai position had strengthened to such an extent that their attacks on some of Burma's minor Shan tributaries in 1801 provoked growing unrest among the Shans west of the Salween. Such a development could not be ignored, but a Burmese expedition sent to recapture Chiengmai was routed by a counterattack that also drove the Burmese out of their base at Chiangsen. In the following two years, the Thai subdued the entire trans-Salween area, but abandoned much of the territory in 1805 as too exposed to Burmese and Chinese power.[24] The main Burmese base was then west of the Salween at Mo-ne (Mongnai).

The Thai still harbored aspirations toward Tavoy and Mergui, but their large investment in Laos and the contest for the trans-Salween prevented a major effort in the Tenasserim area. Sporadic raids and probing attacks finally provoked renewed war with Burma between 1809 and 1811, but the campaigning on the Burmese side was limited to four indifferent raids on Junkceylon and on the coast of the Isthmus of Kra. Thereafter the Thai contented themselves with encouraging Mon dissidence and aiding Mon refugees until the nature of the situation in the southeast was completely altered by the British presence after 1824.

Although Thailand had undergone a remarkable renaissance, first under Tak Sin and then Rama I, it seems probable that Burma remained the stronger state until the early nineteenth century, when the two perhaps reached a rough parity. The Burmese position in the east had deteriorated after 1767 because the wars with China had allowed Thailand to reunite. The pacific reign of Sin-gu first halted what might well have been a Burmese conquest of the new Thai state at Thonburi and then forfeited without contest the crucial Burmese position in Laos. After the double failures of 1785–1786 and 1786, the Burmese no longer envisaged a total solution to their eastern problem, but were simply trying to maintain a strong position in the trans-Salween, a traditional Burmese sphere. They failed in the end because a new and less able generation of officers held field command, because the Thai evolved new strategies to cope with Burmese invasions, because internal factors came severely to affect the Burmese ability to wage war, and because the eastern frontier gained a competitor after 1784, when the western border began increasingly to claim Burmese attention and resources.

The Western Frontier and Anglo-Franco-Burmese Relations

Historically the states to the west of Burma had posed little threat to the security of the Irrawaddy Basin, where geography and climate combined to spare Burma the strategic problem faced at the opposite point of the compass. Mountainous terrain and pestilential conditions effectively sealed the western frontier against the contiguous states of Arakan and Manipur and the Himalayan states of Assam, Cachar, and Jaintia. By the time Alaung-hpaya had completed the reunification of Burma in 1757, the once mighty kingdom of Arakan was on the brink of chaos from incessant dynastic disputes and, indeed, had not threatened Burma since the end of the sixteenth century. The Ahom dynasty of Assam was also in a decline, while states such as Cachar and Jaintia were too remote to have much contact with Burma. After a brief efflorescence in the early eighteenth century, Manipur too had fallen prey to internal conflicts and presented only a sporadic threat to the lower Chin-dwin Valley. This threat was neutralized and Manipur maintained in vassal subjection by periodic raids from Burma. Alaung-hpaya in the dry season of 1757–1758 and Hsin-hpyu-shin in 1765 and 1770 raided Manipur and deported substantial numbers of people to the nuclear area of upper Burma.[25] In addition to contributing to the demographic strength of the nuclear zone, such operations also helped to stabilize the northwest by renewing control over the Tai statelets of the upper Chin-dwin area. Only in the later reign of Bo-daw-hpaya was the west to become a major scene of Burmese activity.

The first Kon-baung adventure in the west involved Arakan. That country had finally dissolved into chaos in the 1770s, prompting both migration to Burma and appeals by Arakanese chiefs for Burmese intervention, despite the fact that Arakan had not previously been a Burmese vassal. Ignored by Sin-gu, these supplications were renewed in the succeeding reign of Bo-daw-hpaya. A short campaign led by the crown prince in the dry season of 1784–1785 brought the entire country under Burmese dominion. The king, his court, and twenty thousand people were deported to Burma along with quantities of arms, horses, and elephants. With a force of ten thousand musketeers to support his administration, Min-gyi Min-gaung-gyaw was appointed *myo wun* of Arakan, with subordinate *wuns* at Ramree, Sandoway, and Cheduba.[26] The intervention of 1784 ended Arakan's existence as an independent political entity, and left it a directly ruled province of the Kon-baung state.

Arakan had posed no threat to Burma and lay outside the natural area of Burmese authority. The concrete motive behind the annexation, other than general imperial aggrandizement, was undoubtedly to strengthen the material base of Burmese power for the coming large operations on the eastern frontier. Requisitions of men and supplies came immediately after the annexation.[27] Foreign policy became subsidiary to internal projects following the major failures against Thailand and the further heavy labor requisitions that came in 1790 and 1795 were for the construction of the Min-gun Pagoda and for a huge project to expand the Meik-hti-la Lake irrigation system.[28]

Although relieved of the previous chaos, the Arakanese found Burmese rule onerous in the extreme. Numbers fled to the sparsely populated Chittagong District in the adjacent territory of the English East India Company, while others fought Burmese rule within Arakan. Although there had been previous armed resistance, the 1795 levy of two thousand men for the Meik-hti-la Lake project provoked open rebellion, assisted by armed raids by refugees from Chittagong. The rising was quickly suppressed, however, and the leaders fled to Chittagong, whence they were surrendered after a tense confrontation between English and Burmese forces inside the territory of the company. A fateful result of the Burmese annexation of Arakan was the creation of a common frontier with the domain of the East India Company in India. The border incident over the rebel Arakanese chiefs opened a new phase in Anglo-Burmese relations by showing just how sensitive this frontier had become.

There had been modest contacts of a commercial nature between the East India Company and the court of Ava starting in the seventeenth century. After the failure of an English factory established at Syriam from 1647 to 1657, a new arrangement was made for shipbuilding and repairs at Syriam and the maintenance of an agent to regulate the private English traders in that port. The company soon had a rival, when its French counterpart also opened an establishment at Syriam about 1713. The motivation in each case was not primarily commerce, but shipbuilding and repair and the procurement of Burmese teak and other naval stores. An agrarian kingdom with its capital far inland, Taung-ngu Burma did not actively encourage the growth of maritime commerce or of a colony of foreigners. The respective ventures of the English and French did continue in modest vein until the disturbances ensuing from the Pegu rebellion of 1740, which caused first the French and then the English to abandon their enterprises in 1742 and 1743.

As a result of their recurrent contests with the British, the French had come to see the strategic value of bases and influence in Burma. Hence in 1749 they reopened relations with the kingdom of Pegu, which was in desperate need of military support in general and arms in particular.[29] In the end the directors of the French East India Company decided against a major involvement in Burma, however, and only authorized the reopening of the shipyard at Syriam. French involvement with Pegu had moved the English company to counter by occupying Negrais (Haing-gyi) Island off Bassein and, desperate for munitions, Alaung-hpaya opened negotiations with them in 1755. Thus, the French and English came to be involved in the Burmese civil war, with unhappy results for both. After considerable intrigue, Alaung-hpaya captured the French contingent that had been consorting with Pegu, as well as two shiploads of arms and supplies belatedly granted to Pegu by the High Council at Pondichéry. The lack of British response to his proposals and the activities of some British ship captains in support of his enemies left Alaung-hpaya disenchanted with the English company. The company, in turn, had found its venture at Negrais of so little value that it had been mostly withdrawn when it was attacked by Burmese troops in retaliation for its alleged support of the Mon rebellion of 1758. Contact between the company and the Konbaung state ceased in 1761 after completion of negotiations for the removal of the remainder of the company's property from Negrais and did not resume until the Arakan border incident of 1794.

French interest in Burma continued, however, and the High Council at Pondichéry opened negotiations in 1770 for the release of the French nationals captured by Alaung-hpaya and the renewal of shipbuilding and commerce. One of the French prisoners, Pierre de Milard, had become extremely influential at the court of Hsin-hpyu-shin and provided a valuable entrée for the French envoy Feraud. Well received by Hsin-hpyu-shin, Feraud obtained the release of the five remaining Frenchmen, several of whom elected to remain in Burma, and permission to reopen the shipyard at Rangoon.[30] Thus, France became the only country permitted to maintain a formal establishment at Rangoon. In 1778, the entry of France into the War of American Independence left the venture at Rangoon inactive and, unable to compete with rival French designs on Cochinchina, it was abandoned for the last time in 1784.[31]

The key element in Burmese relations with both the British and French companies in the seventeenth and eighteenth centuries was a continuing need for munitions in general and artillery in particular. Artillery had been introduced to this part of Asia by the Portuguese mercenaries serving Burma and Thailand in the sixteenth century, but neither the Burmese nor Thai had ever been able to develop it into an effective military instrument by European standards. It has, in fact, been said of Indonesian and Malay rulers that by 1770 cannon were valued "rather for prestige and sacro-magical reasons than with any serious idea of using them offensively."[32] This observation had less relevance to Burma, where siege operations were often an important aspect of warfare. There was apparently no lack of cannon in Burmese arsenals, but most seem to have been of small caliber and locally cast.[33] The guns, whether European or Asian, were rarely fired and deteriorated rapidly through disuse and the ravages of climate. In common with other Asian rulers, Burmese kings usually seem to have been in desperate straits for serviceable artillery, which could only be obtained through purchase, confiscation from merchant ships, salvage from wrecked ships, or spoils of war.[34] A related problem was the lack of gunners with even a modicum of skill, one of the reasons why Milard, a French artillery officer, enjoyed high favor at court and was commander of the royal artillery.

The early Kon-baung state's main interest in maritime commerce was the procurement of arms, in return for which it was willing to allow a limited number of foreign factories and trade concessions. When Alaung-hpaya had approached the company's establishment at Negrais, he had acceded to its request for a concession precisely because he was desperate for artillery and muskets to employ in the coming sieges of Syriam and Pegu. In 1761 his successor Naung-daw-gyi had offered the company a liberal concession for trade at Negrais if the company would agree to pay for Burmese commodities with arms which, he said, were needed for use against the rebel Min-gaung Naw-rahta, then besieged in the city of Ava.[35] Feraud, too, reported that Hsin-hpyu-shin was especially interested in arms and munitions and was willing to allow the French liberal trade concessions if they were even partly paid for with these items.[36] Bo-daw-hpaya's efforts to obtain arms included negotiations with Atjeh in 1786, with the French agent at Chandernagor in 1787 and 1794, and with Ile de France (Madagascar), the latter sending two shiploads of munitions in 1802.[37]

Balanced against their desire for arms was a general lack of interest in the development of maritime trade, possibly stemming from the early Kon-baung rulers' innate distrust of foreigners and the agrarian orientation of the economy. More specifically, there was a lingering fear of foreign involvement with Mon dissidence rooted in the events of the civil war. This last point was specifically made to Feraud by Hsin-hpyu-shin in connection with the French reopening of an establishment at Rangoon.[38] In spite of these negative factors, however, the early Kon-baung rulers appear to have been willing to offer the British and French companies a limited *quid pro quo* of factories and shipyards in return for some military hardware. Each company for reasons of its own, however, declined to take real advantage of the offer. In the thirty years prior to 1794, the English East India Company had virtually no relations with Burma and the French company had officially withdrawn a decade earlier. The border incident marked the beginning of a new and different phase in Anglo-Burmese relations, as the issues of shipyards, trade, and munitions paled in comparison with the tensions produced by the growing problem in Arakan.

Having seen the potential danger raised by the Arakan situation and taking into consideration the renewed war with France in 1793, the governor general of India, Sir John Shore, feared that unless some approach was made to Burma to defuse the frontier problem, the Burmese might retaliate by allowing the French to use their ports. His concern coincided with the desires of private commercial interests in India for expanded trade with Burma, hence in 1794 Captain George Sorrel was dispatched on an informal mission to the court of Amara-pura to test the climate.[39] The results of the mission being perceived as favorable, an official mission headed by Captain Michael Symes arrived in Burma the following year to remove the cause of misunderstanding over the Arakan border and refugees, to request the closure of Burmese ports to French ships, and to negotiate a commercial treaty with provision for an English resident at Rangoon.[40] The Burmese court refused, however, to become involved with the company through the formal mechanism of a treaty or to close its ports to the French, from whom it was still trying to purchase arms. About the time that Captain Hiram Cox's tenure as resident at Rangoon was ending in failure in 1798, renewed Burmese operations on the eastern frontier caused a heavy levy of twenty thousand muskets and forty thousand men to be laid on an already oppressed Arakan.[41] There was a large migration to Chittagong, whence many raids were launched against Arakan, parts of which were heavily devastated. Burmese threats to retaliate by invading Chittagong and even Bengal intensified fears at Fort St. George, and in 1802 Symes was again dispatched to the court of Amara-pu-ra, both to propose a subsidiary alliance and to investigate the suspected presence of the French in Burmese ports. The first official British contemplation of actual intervention in Burmese affairs was embodied in Symes's instructions for this mission and its failure left Symes himself recommending the establishment of British influence over Burma.[42]

The continuing confrontation over the frontier and the efforts of the company to establish some sort of formal relations with Burma began at this time to enter into the matrix of court politics. The moderate clique headed by the heir apparent favored more amiable relations with British India, but other elements centered on several influential officials played on the king's deepening suspicions concerning the British inability to control the Arakanese dissidents in Chittagong and British motives toward Burma in general. Following the flare-up of 1798, however, the issue of the border hung in abeyance, as immigration slowed and the cross-border raids ceased after 1801. Captain John Canning was sent to Amara-pu-ra by the company in 1809 because it was feared that the British blockade of Ile de France would interrupt what was thought to be an extensive trade with Burma and thereby provoke Burmese reprisals. Canning discovered instead that there had been no contact with the French island for over six years.

The conflict between Burma and British India did not enter its most explosive phase until 1811, when Arakanese from Chittagong led by a rebel chief named Chin Pyan overran all of Arakan and massacred the Burmese population in the capital of Mro-haung.[43] When Chin Pyan subsequently offered to hold Arakan as a vassal of the company, Canning was again sent to Amara-pu-ra to try to persuade the enraged Bo-daw-hpaya of his employer's innocence of any connivance with Chin Pyan. Bo-daw-hpaya already strongly believed that the company was at least partly responsible for his troubles in the west and, indeed, some of the actions Chin Pyan undertook were intended to encourage the Burmese monarch in this belief. Arakan had already lost much of its population and productivity and, despite the fact that a Burmese counterattack quickly drove the motley forces of Chin Pyan back into Chittagong, the effort needed to protect Arakan from Chittagong-based incursions meant that rather than contributing to the Burmese effort against Thailand, Arakan was proving a net drain on the Burmese military capability.

Chin Pyan soon ceased to respect the British border as well, forcing the authorities at Chittagong to pursue him with the meager forces at their disposal. The inability of the company to cope with Chin Pyan on its own territory further confirmed Burmese suspicions of its culpability and earned their contempt for its seeming weakness. The issue only resolved itself with the death of the main protagonist in January 1815 and the dispersal of his followers.

The Chin Pyan episode was to have a major influence on subsequent Anglo-Burmese relations. The Burmese were left embittered at their losses in life and property, suspicious of British motives, and interpreted the manifest inability of the company to suppress Chin Pyan as clear evidence of weakness.[44] Burma and British India were profoundly ignorant of each other, hence one instruction given to Symes, Cox, and Canning on their various missions was to gather as much general information and specific intelligence as possible. Even before 1811, a similar medium was being employed by Bo-daw-hpaya to gather intelligence about the company and its enemies in India, who he saw as the natural allies of Burma. Between 1807 and 1817 at least seven missions, several headed by the former English missionary Felix Carey, were sent to India, ostensibly to purchase books and visit religious sites.[45] The reports of these missions must have offered the Burmese court at least a modicum of insight into the reality of British power in India and the nature of the company's relations with the Indian states.

The Burmese adventure in Arakan had drawn them into a triangular situation with the East India Company and the dissident Arakanese. As the eighteenth century drew to a close, similar situations began to develop in relation to Assam and Manipur, both of which were vassals of Burma. Assam in particular was disturbed by religious conflict and the rule of the imbecile Gaurinath Singh. British intervention was solicited by a royal claimant in 1792, but, though the British agreed to place him on the throne, they refused any further involvement on the grounds that the country was so troubled that only complete annexation would maintain order. Burmese intervention also appears to have been courted four years later when a princess and tribute arrived at Amara-pu-ra. Another tribute mission followed in 1799.[46] Similar dynastic squabbles in Manipur brought Burmese military intervention in 1806 and 1813, while royal fiat sufficed to resolve the issue in 1810.[47] In Assam the situation flared up again in 1816 when, after being refused British support, a claimant was placed on the throne by a Burmese army, only to be deposed in the wake of the departing troops the following year. The process was repeated in 1818–1819, except that the deposed *raja* now fled to British territory. Following Bo-daw-hpaya's death in June 1819 and the assumption of the peacock throne by his thirty-five-year-old grandson Ba-gyi-daw, the general Maha Ban-du-la permanently occupied Assam in the winter of 1821-1822. The now familiar problem of cross-border raids and British sanctuary for Assamese dissidents repeated itself and Burmese moves against Cachar and Manipur further disturbed the region. The ultimate end of Burmese policy was thought by the company to have been an invasion of Chittagong and Bengal, a belief which, coupled with the overall aggressiveness of Burmese policy in the west, brought a declaration of war from the East India Company in March 1824.[48]

Two relatively distinct periods can be discerned in the relations between Burma and the two European powers to approach it in the eighteenth and early nineteenth centuries. The first period was characterized by the primary British and French interest in the shipbuilding potential of Burma, with only a secondary interest in trade, and the Burmese desire for European munitions and arms. This period encompassed the years 1695-1761 for the British and 1713-1784 for the French. In each case the difficulties of maintaining its enterprise in the restricted and sometimes turbulent Burman situation led them to withdraw. The Kon-baung rulers offered both the British and French the opportunity to resume operations on modest but reasonable terms. The terms were accepted by the French, who ran a small but successful enterprise until 1784. The entrée to the court of Ava provided by the captured French officers, in particular Pierre de Milard, was undoubtedly a key factor in the reestablishment of the French position in Burma. Abandoned in 1784, French interest in Burma did not revive until later in the nineteenth century.

It was only in the second period, inaugurated by the Arakan border incident of 1794, that the British attempted to reestablish a modest position in Burma. Anglo-Burmese relations were dominated by the Arakan problem, however, hence what Hsin-hpyu-shin easily gave to the French envoy Feraud in 1770 was denied to successive British missions after 1794. The main reason for this denial was the growing Burmese sense of grievance and suspicion of British motives concerning Arakan, feelings which reached a climax as a result of the Chin Pyan episode. The tension arising from the Arakan problem, however, was clearly augmented by the inability of the company and its minions to overcome insecurities about status and ceremonial to the point where they could adapt to the procedures of the Burmese court concerning the conduct of foreign relations. The Chinese, Thai, and French, who all adapted to Burmese customs, encountered few of the procedural blocks to communication that were so prominent a feature of the journals of British envoys. Conversely, Burmese missions to the Chinese, Thai, French, and British conformed to the procedures of their hosts. Communication problems notwithstanding, Arakan poisoned any possibility of a viable commercial relationship between the company and the court, while the continuing Burmese flirtation with the French left the company in a state of understandable anxiety until 1809. The death of Bo-daw-hpaya in 1819 marked the end of the second period of Burma's relations with British India. Subsequent events on the western frontier provided the immediate cause of war between Burma and the company in 1824 and opened the final phase of Anglo-Burmese relations: the progressive dismemberment of the Kon-baung state.

Internal Developments, 1760–1819

Alaung-hpaya bequeathed to his successors a kingdom with a reconstituted and strengthened demographic and administrative base and a strong military system. This legacy made possible the great victories of the 1760s, the high tide of empire for the Kon-baung state. As expressed in military accomplishment, the first decades of Kon-baung rule were marked by rather consistent imperial success. The ability of successive rulers to sustain this success, however, was closely related to events and trends within the Irrawaddy Basin itself. The cumulative and interrelated effects of imperial activity and domestic affairs had important consequences for the general administrative and demographic condition of the country and ultimately influenced the nature of its politics at both the local and dynastic levels. Although most of the matters germane to these topics are explored in some detail in succeeding chapters, this survey concludes with a brief consideration of the broad trends of early Kon-baung history in terms of domestic affairs and their interrelationship with imperial matters.

Viewed from a domestic perspective, the early Kon-baung period falls roughly into two broad phases. From the rise of Alaung-hpaya in the early 1750s to the death of Hsin-hpyu-shin in 1776, the central authority paid careful attention to the organization and augmentation of its resources, a policy which left the realm in a generally healthy condition both administratively and demographically. The reign of Sin-gu from 1776 to 1782 is important as a transition period in which his inactive domestic and foreign policy set the stage for an accelerating trend of decline in the succeeding reign of Bo-daw-hpaya. Despite extremely active domestic and imperial policies, Bo-daw-hpaya's reign was marked by a near fatal combination of policies and circumstances that seriously weakened the administrative and demographic bases of the kingdom. There is no sharp line dividing the "healthy" from the "declining" phase, hence the consideration of the key themes of the former—efforts at increased administrative control, demographic strengthening of the nuclear area, and integration of the delta into the Burmese orbit—overlap to varying extents with the first half of Bo-daw-hpaya's reign.

Despite the administrative and demographic measures implemented by Alaung-hpaya, many of the old corrupt practices and abuses at the local and official levels that had sapped the base of the preceding Taung-ngu dynasty had either never been checked or had commenced anew. In effect, Alaung-hpaya had left incomplete the task of curbing the gentry and officials after their long period of autonomy under the later Taung-ngu rulers and during the civil war. The two main problems were the need to make central control of the local sphere *de facto* as well as *de jure*, and the need to strengthen royal control over crown revenues and services. In the former case, there were many abuses of local office by officials and, in the latter, the key devices for depriving the crown of control were alienation of crown land and peculation of crown revenues and services. Faced with mounting evidence of the erosion of central control over officials and resources, in the teeth of local opposition both Hsin-hpyu-shin and Bo-daw-hpaya issued reams of edicts and launched kingdom-wide cadastral, revenue, and population surveys in 1765, 1783, and 1802.

While the foregoing pertains to the control of existing resources, closely related was the augmentation of crown resources through imperial activity. One key factor in the restoration of the Taung-ngu dynasty in the early seventeenth century was the program of deportations from the uplands surrounding the Irrawaddy Valley, which increased the crown service population in the nuclear area. Although his main emphasis was the reconstitution of existing service units and the formation of new units from Burmans already resident in the nuclear area, a similar policy was pursued by Alaung-hpaya who, in particular, deported large numbers of Mons to the Kyauk-hse area. The main demographic renewal of the nuclear area came in the 1760s, when expeditions against Manipur, various Shan areas, the Lao states, and the Menam Valley poured tens of thousands of deportees into upper Burma. Had the trans-Salween and Ayuthian campaigns not been halted by Sin-gu, there might well have been another influx of deportees from the east. As it was, there are no known deportations from the second devastation of Manipur in 1770 to the annexation of Arakan in 1784–1785. Bringing twenty thousand Arakanese to upper Burma, that operation resulted in the last important known deportation in Konbaung history.[49] Bo-daw-hpaya's subsequent military expeditions therefore represent a net loss to the population base of the Irrawaddy Basin.

The close of the civil war in 1757 marked the beginning of the end of the division of Burma into two ethnic and regional entities. The delta was increasingly drawn into the Burmese orbit as the ethnic, cultural, and linguistic factors that had tended to differentiate that region from the Burmese heartland in the dry zone were reduced. In addition to the strategic settlements of Burmans planted by Alaung-hpaya after 1757, there was a steady southward migration of Burmans on an individual and family basis, so that the area along the Irrawaddy between Prome and Henzada became preponderantly Burman, as did the Bassein area. The Burmanization of the south received a new impetus when a policy was inaugurated in 1790 aimed at encouraging colonization. A number of former *myos* were resettled, grants of land were made to settlers, and taxes were remitted for the first few years of cultivation.[50]

As the former enemy, the Mons had been treated as a subject race since 1757. Though many fled to Thailand and others were assimilated, Mon resentment and grievances were expressed in sporadic risings in 1758, 1774, and 1783. The rising of 1774 was the most serious and brought the heaviest Burman retribution when, in March of the following year, Hsin-hpyu-shin arrived in Rangoon to place a new finial on the Dagon Hsan-daw-shin Pagoda and, at the same time, executed as common criminals the former king of Pegu, his brother the former heir apparent, and the latter's son.[51] The symbolic capping of the famous Mon pagoda with a Burman finial and the execution of the rulers of the defeated kingdom of Pegu was intended to demonstrate the final triumph of north over south and Burman over Mon. The aggressive eastern policy pursued by the early Kon-baung rulers, with its use of Rangoon and Martaban as staging areas and depots, restored to the delta the geopolitical importance relinquished in the early seventeenth century and brought closer administrative and political links with the central authority. Concomitant with its renewed geopolitical significance was the importance of the south as a source of rice and men for the eastern campaigns.[52] Over the course of its development as a frontier area for the dry and intermediate zones, the delta began a gradual transformation from the sparsely populated wilderness it had been before the civil war to an area of integral importance to the Kon-baung state.

The regeneration and integration of the south was a long-term trend not affected by the inactivity of Sin-gu's reign, but the lack of vigorous administration can only have encouraged the trend toward gentry autonomy and the withdrawal of resources from the crown sector. Yet

Bo-daw-hpaya appears to have begun his rule over a realm that was in a relatively healthy condition. The failures against Thailand in 1785 and 1786 were the real beginning of a long downward spiral. Around 40 percent of the men conscripted for those particular expeditions are thought to have been lost to enemy action, disease, starvation, and desertion.[53] These decisive reversals were followed by a decade of intensive construction of public works, while foreign policy lay relatively dormant. Construction of the massive Min-gun Pagoda, which became a virtual obsession with Bo-daw-hpaya, began in 1790 and was only abandoned in 1802 after twelve years of heavy labor requisitions. Repulse of the Thai invasion of Tavoy in 1791–1793 involved over forty thousand men, but what was probably the largest and most onerous requisition came in 1795, when there was virtually a general mobilization of the entire empire for a major expansion of the Meik-hti-la tank and canal system. Every district, including Arakan, was ordered to send a specified draft of men to work on the project.[54] The next round in the war with the Thai from 1797 to 1804 brought with it the necessity of raising new armies of conscripts with each dry season. Coupled to the constant drain on labor for military and corvée purposes were heavy taxation and special imposts.

The cumulative effect of the withdrawal of large numbers of men from the demographic pool between 1785 and 1804 was to disturb significantly the social and agricultural organization of the realm. Once removed from their native locale for military service or corvée labor, few men returned, be it from disease, starvation, combat, or desertion. Hence the constant withdrawal of labor from the agricultural sector had a long-term as well as short-term effect on productivity. As early as 1797, Hiram Cox noted to his superior, "husbandry as well as everything else seems to be on the decline" and "the wretched inhabitants particularly the Peguvians are daily emigrating to other countries."[55] The response of the population to this consistently high level of crown activity was initially flight and subsequently banditry. By 1800 communication on the Irrawaddy River was seriously disturbed by the level of bandit activity, provoking a major effort to clear the river in 1803. A large floating population alienated from both the land and crown service began to form.

Hardly had the crisis caused by the Thai victory of 1800–1804 in the trans-Salween eased when another factor appeared to place an additional heavy burden on the populace. Already faced with a severe drought from 1802–1803, 1805 marked the beginning of a great famine that started in the dry zone. Brought on by successive failures of the monsoon, the famine was called by the people the *maha thayaw* from the fact that corpses were left on the ground like the debris (*thayaw*) left by a flood. The problem was further aggravated by starving tigers who made it unsafe to work in the fields. The general lack of food caused growing outbreaks of banditry and disorder, as villages fought each other for what little was still available. Tens of thousands starved to death, others fell prey to the tigers or bandits, and the remainder sought refuge in the larger towns and cities. The famine was especially bad in Shwei-bo, Meik-hti-la, Myin-gyan, and Magwei districts, reaching its overall peak in the dry zone in 1810.[56]

In 1809, while still in the midst of the famine, Bo-daw-hpaya inflicted on his already suffering realm the burden of resuming the Burmese-Thai conflict. With Tavoy as its staging base, the plan of campaign called for an army of eighty thousand to be levied on the march from Amara-pu-ra, with every town and village being required to produce a certain number of men. Each house in Rangoon, for example, was ordered to provide one man or a sum of between two hundred and four hundred *kyats*, at the discretion of the local authorities. If neither was forthcoming, the penalty was confiscation of property and/or corporal punishment. In the face of these exactions, many families decamped to less accessible rural locales.[57]

The commander in charge of the campaign was the *daing wun*, whose jurisdiction already gave him control of the *daing*, or shield-bearing units, of the crown service infantry. The king further equipped him with unlimited power which superseded the regular authority in whatever jurisdiction he happened to be. Along his route to Tavoy, he seized all the people capable of bearing arms, except those who fled, and took their families as hostages. As John Canning wrote to the company, "His progress down the country was marked by fire and sword, and bore every appearance of the march of a hostile army.... When I proceeded to the capital in 1809–1810, traces of this barbarian were everywhere visible in deserted and destroyed villages and the general devastation of the country."[58] Only thirty-six thousand men were levied in the end, eight thousand of whom reportedly perished before reaching Tavoy, and many others deserted.

The original famine caused by the drought appears to have been confined to upper Burma, but the levies impressed by the *daing wun* caused the growth of a large floating population in lower Burma, so disturbing the agricultural system that lower Burma experienced a famine as well. Canning described the process thus:

> All of the Daiwun's [sic] violence was, however, ineffectual towards collecting half the number of men prescribed by

the king, as a very large proportion of those men whom he dragged from their habitations, in spite of all his vigilance, found means to desert with their families, and being no longer able with safety to return to their own homes formed themselves into large bodies of dacoits which still continue to overrun the country, and nearly put a stop to navigation of the river.[59]

In a similar vein, one of the British missionaries in Rangoon wrote that "the Burmans are bent on war with the Siamese, and, by taking so many of the people who cultivate the rice, etc., from their employment, it is well if famine be not added to war."[60]

The first refuge of the populace had been flight, followed by banditry, and subsequently other forms of inarticulate social protest. Amara-pu-ra was almost completely destroyed by arsonists' fires in 1809 and Rangoon was burned to the ground in 1810, 1812, and 1814. Such fires were usually preceded by letters hung on the local administrative hall decrying the oppressive overtaxation and levies. The line dividing banditry from rebellion in such conditions was very fine, and the growing pool of people with genuine grievances against the government provided ready recruits. A number of insurrections broke out in various parts of the realm, the most important of which had its origin in the Salei region. Led by a former merchant named Nga Kauk, the rebellion progressed quickly as the *daing wun* had carried off most of the able-bodied men in the region and no effective force could be mustered to oppose it. This particular rebellion soon overran most of lower Burma and even threatened Rangoon.

Although the last war with Thailand had disastrous internal consequences for lower Burma, it was continued in desultory fashion until the rebellion of Chin Pyan in Arakan in 1811 presented a more immediate problem. The general Min-hla Si-thu was placed in charge of the pacification of Arakan and ordered to Salin to collect men to augment his force of levies from upper Burma. Pegu at this time was only able to produce nine hundred men toward its quota of three thousand, while twelve thousand of the forty thousand inhabitants of Prome had already been sent to the eastern campaign. Canning heard that a large detachment of Burman conscripts "who had been dragged to the camp by force" had mutinied and joined Chin Pyan's Arakanese forces and that troops sent to counter the various Burmese insurrections were also mutinying.[61] The famine in upper and lower Burma was so severe, however, that resources were inadequate to sustain large bodies of people, hence none of the insurgencies was able to reach a size sufficient to seriously threaten the existence of the central authority.

The famine came to a gradual end between 1812 and 1814, the eastern offensive was dropped, and Chin Pyan driven back to Chittagong. The rate of banditry remained high, but the insurrections died out and the size of the floating population diminished as the people returned to the fields. The situation in lower Burma had improved to such an extent that Felix Carey wrote his father, "The country appears to be free from foreign dangers; its internal affairs also assume a more peaceful appearance."62 Although even the people of the capital had been reduced to eating tree leaves and wild herbs, through the height of the troubles Bo-daw-hpaya had maintained his residence at Min-gun ten miles away. Apart from ordering the construction of a new capital in late 1811, no major domestic projects were undertaken and only the minor interventions in Assam and Manipur were pursued in the imperial sphere. Then in his dotage, Bo-daw-hpaya spent his last years travelling about upper Burma to worship at pagodas and dedicate religious buildings. His death in 1819 at the age of seventy-five marked the close of an era. He was succeeded by his grandson Ba-gyi-daw, whose reign saw the beginning of continuous British influence and intervention in Burmese affairs and the eventual complete eclipse of Burmese power.

CHAPTER 2

EARLY KON-BAUNG SOCIETY

Early Kon-baung society was characterized by major divisions between the lowland and upland peoples, between members of the *athi* and crown service sectors, between the clergy and laity, between the titled and untitled, and between the mass of commoners and the small number of people belonging to the more privileged social grades. The primary ethnic division was between the Burmans and the subject Mons and Shans. There were, however, no real economic cleavages in this society because the accumulation of wealth was relatively low and diffuse. This last point is significant because it meant that there were no large concentrations of economic power in the form of landed, mercantile, or industrially based classes to compete with or oppose the crown. These same factors prevented the crystallization of the very real social divisions of ruler, official, gentry, and commoner on economic lines and, as a result, social classes in the Marxist or Weberian sense did not develop in Burma.[1] Instead, society was comprised of a relatively undifferentiated peasantry, a small group that can be termed gentry whose socioeconomic position depended on local officeholding rather than wealth or landholding, and a much smaller corpus of rulers whose position was rooted in national officeholding.

Social cohesion was provided by Theravada Buddhism. This popular salvation religion enabled the people to participate in a common culture and hold the same world view, which was transmitted both through the ethical and ritual texts memorized in monastic schools and through the *jataka*-derived entertainment popular with all elements of the population. By allowing for gradations of spiritual attainment, Theravada Buddhism provided an intelligible and acceptable rationale for society and the authority of the state, with some provision for present and future mobility. The conception of the social order that the

Burmese derived from their Buddhism was conducive to a rigidly structured and tightly regulated society. Such structure and control was deemed necessary for cosmic, social, and, by extension, dynastic stability. It was assumed that without this differentiation and control, people would not fulfill their moral and civil obligations. The ends of structure and control were served by a system of social grading that was enforced through customary law and sumptuary rules, economic regulations and restrictions, and even to some extent spatial restrictions imposed by various types of toll stations. Yet the social differentiation and controls were ameliorated to no little extent by spatial and social mobility, alternative statuses in the private sector, and even corruption, which could relieve some of the onerous requirements of the state. Life for the commoners tended to be unstable as a result of service levies, wars, bandits, floods, droughts, and famine. The society therefore had a certain fluidity to it that suited the Buddhist notion of life as flux.

Burman Social Structure

Burman society in the eighteenth century was composed primarily of a lowland population which, as a whole, formed a closed system of kinship. As distinct from the hill peoples, social structure was not characterized by clans, lineages, or unilineal descent groups, nor were kinship relations extended, as they were in the hill cultures. Loyalty attached not to a kin group, but rather to a place, service group, or patron. The basic social unit of the Burmans, as well as the Mons and Shans, was the conjugal family of father, mother, and children.

Burman society as a whole was endogamous, which is to say that marriages took place within its closed system of kinship. The Burmans rarely married women from other ethnic groups and never gave their own women away to strangers for marriage purposes.[2] There were no rules governing marriage except a vague incest taboo. Customary law as recorded in the *damathats*, or compilations of customary law, prohibited marriage with close kin, but never specified the degree of permissible kinship closeness. Close kin usually refers to an individual's father/mother, son/daughter, and brother/sister and, in the Burman case, probably included first cousins as well. Beyond this, each marriage was an individual affair between a particular man and woman and marriages were not contracted to create or perpetuate relationships between clans or lineages or to further trade, as was the case in the hill cultures. As Theravada Buddhism advised the abandonment of all desires and involvements, marriage was a secular and civil institution, with the ceremony itself basically a public avowal of the intent to have conjugal relations. Similarly, because there were no religious sanctions on the institution, divorce was easy and common.

Burman society was further characterized by polygamy, which was fully recognized by customary law. The *Manu-kye damathat* of 1756, for example, states that "a man commits no fault even if he takes ten wives," a statement echoed in other *damathats*.[3] This practice was largely confined to the gentry and official groups, and was more prevalent in central and northern Burma than elsewhere. Law and custom, however, recognized only one wife, who was termed the head wife (*mayagyi*). In the gentry and official groups, only the head wife was recognized by the royal court, where she was termed *pwe-det* or *pwe-win*. This meant that she had the privilege of attending the official functions and ceremonies (*pwe*) of the Western (women's) Court at the palace. A man might, in addition, have lesser but still legal wives (*mayange*) as well as concubines who did not have a formal contractual relationship with the husband and were not considered wives.[4]

Because the Burman social system was quite rigid about its detailed social and rank distinctions, gentry and official families usually arranged marriages to protect their social position and advance their interests. To marry a person of inferior social status was unthinkable, hence each party normally undertook a thorough investigation of the other. Even the *damathats* specified legal recourse against families that misrepresented their social position in marriage negotiations. The Western Court of the royal palace served, in fact, as the center for circulating the marriageable daughters of the court officials and more prominent gentry among suitable families. In this process, personally or politically desirable candidates were culled off for the royal harem or for those of the royal princes. In this way the royal lineage assured itself of firm affinal relationships with the officials and leading gentry families.

Such considerations were particularly to the fore in the contracting of the first marriage for, as the *Manu-kye* stated, "it is said that the first married shall be the head wife."[5] In the higher-status groups, therefore, the first marriage was usually arranged by the parents, with the bride becoming the head and legal wife. These considerations in marriage were much less important for the lower status groups, which usually had little property and no office to transmit, but were of paramount concern for the gentry and officials because the first marriage largely determined the prime inheritance rights within each family. Heredity was one of the most important organizing principles of Burman society, and family, marriage, and especially the conventions governing inheritance are important for later discussions of official and royal politics.

In this society of rigid and detailed social and rank distinctions, polygamy, divorce and remarriage, property rights for women, and adoption of children, inheritance was a complex subject that was treated in great detail in the various *damathats* of the period.[6] Burman inheritance was almost fully cognatic in that "all children who are legitimate shall have their proper share," but the particular proportion was determined by various circumstances.[7] The essence of custom was that inheritance never ascended if it could descend, the nearer relatives excluded the further, relatives of full blood were preferred to those of half blood, and children impaired physically, mentally, or morally had no share. The line of descent of the inheritance was children, grandchildren, great grandchildren, parents, and the collaterals: brothers/sisters and aunts/uncles.

All legitimate children were entitled to share in the estate, such children being the offspring of the head and lesser wives and also of concubines. Even so, the eldest son and eldest daughter enjoyed a special position both in the family and in inheritance. The former was termed the *aw-ra-tha*. Although the Pali form *orasa* means simply "legitimate child," the Burman usage referred to the legitimate son and heir. As the *aw-ra-tha*, the eldest son acquired a vested interest in the estate that superseded the rights of the surviving parent and other children. The *Manu-kye* explains succinctly:

> When the father has died, there are two laws for the partition of the inheritance between the mother and son: let the eldest son have the riding elephant, riding horse, goblet, betel utensils, sword, clothes, ornaments and, of the slaves, the water bearer and betel bearer. Let the mother have her clothes and ornaments, goblet, betel utensils and the female slaves. Let the remainder be divided into four parts and the eldest son have one and the mother and younger children have three.[8]

The importance of the first marriage is underlined by a statement in the *Manu-kye* that "the eldest son of a couple given in marriage by his parents is called the *aw-ratha*."[9] The same *damathat* deals with the problem raised by polygamy in a similar manner: "If there are several wives and each has a son, the son by the first wife shall be the *aw-ra-tha*."[10] The status of *aw-ra-tha* was not solely ascriptive, however, as it carried with it certain functions which had to be fulfilled for the welfare of the family. The duties of the *aw-ra-tha* were to assume the responsibilities of the father, discharge his debts, and continue the family. It was therefore necessary that the eldest son be competent to meet these obligations and, if he was not, he did not inherit as the *aw-ra-tha*. In such cases a younger son, even by a lesser wife, could be recognized as the *aw-ra-tha*. As the *Manu wunana damathat* states, "The son who takes upon himself the burdens and responsibilities of the parents is considered as the *aw-ra-tha* son, whether he is the eldest born or not."[11]

As indicated by their inheritance rights in customary law, women in Burman society were more than mere chattels. They had a certain legal position, but were distinctly inferior to men. The essence of the situation was summed up concisely by the *Manu-kye*: "Because the law preached by the Buddha has said: let a woman become a *yahan-da* [*ariya*] she is not comparable to a man on the day he becomes a *thamanei* [novice]. Considering this sacred teaching, a male is the most noble."[12] Women had divorce and remarriage rights, and also property rights in inheritance and divorce. There are many records of female holders of local office below the level of *myo-thu-gyi*, but above that level women were definitely excluded from office. There are also records of women as proprietresses of such lucrative local concessions as toll stations and ferries. Women whose husbands were members of a crown service group were also considered to be members and, as such, were required to make their contributions toward meeting the service and dues obligations of the group, even when widowed.

System of Belief

The belief system of eighteenth-century Burma was a syncretic blend of Theravada Buddhism, animism (*nat*, or spirit, propitiation), faith in astrology and various cabala, and belief in hyperphysical causes and manifestations. The dominant element was Buddhist, which provided the metaphysics of the cosmos, soteriological goals, and, drawing on the richness and depth of Indian civilization, the classical background of Burmese thought and culture. Lacking any soteriological elements of their own, the other elements were basically devices for coping with the fears and complications of mundane existence both for the individual and, to a lesser extent, for the state. Although Theravada Buddhism also contained such devices, its main function was salvation, which enabled it to either subsume the other elements as subordinate parts of a hierarchical structure of belief or to ignore them as immaterial. In its aggregate, this syncretism was the framework of the Burmese world view, from which stemmed the values and beliefs underlying social and political relationships and actions.

It is not known when Buddhism first came to Burma, but the Theravada persuasion had largely vanquished its Mahayana and Tantric rivals toward the end of the Pagan period. In their passage from India to Burma via Ceylon, the doctrines of Theravada Buddhism underwent significant modifications that changed them from the austere philosophy of a small group of Indian ascetics to the popular salvation religion Therevada Buddhism was and continues to be in Burma. In sum, these modifications were that *dukka* (suffering) was viewed as caused not by desire, but by the frustration of desire. Thus, *samsara* (existence) became graded from states of great suffering to states of great pleasure. The traditional negative view of *nibbana* as extinction was either reinterpreted in positive terms as a super paradise or disavowed as unattractive. *Kamma*, an inevitable result of volitional acts instigated by desire, was transformed from a negative fact of existence to be extinguished through nonattachment to a desirable fact to be enhanced. The goal became not the extinction of desire, but its satisfaction; not the cessation of rebirth, but rebirth at a higher grade of *samsara*. In short, the personal aspiration became more samsaric than nibbanic.

The outcome of these changes was that *kamma*, rather than being an obstacle to *nibbana*, came to be seen as its ultimate determinant in that merit (*kusala*) rather than wisdom became the means to salvation. The concept of *kamma* itself underwent important changes. Perceived of as always in flux, it could be changed by the addition of new merit or demerit. In this view, a ruler could execute his rivals and then neutralize that demeritorious act with the meritorious act of building a pagoda. Although merit could be acquired through charity, morality, and meditation, in Burma the notions of kammatic flux and neutralization caused charity to be seen as the primary means to that end. Corollaries to kammatic flux, neutralization, and charity-derived merit were merit-sharing with either the living or the dead and merit-making in which the merit was shared collectively with all living creatures.[13]

Ameliorating both the austerity and elitism of early Indian Buddhism, these doctrinal changes began to occur early in the history of Theravada Buddhism, and were probably already incorporated in the form in which it came to Burma. The emphases on samsaric aspiration, charity-derived merit as the means to samsaric advancement, kammatic flux and neutralization, merit-sharing, and collective merit-making were already quite noticeable in the lithic inscriptions of the Pagan period. The religion was given a genuinely popular base through the custom of making every male a formal member of the religious elite—the *sangha*—at least for a short period in his life. The means to salvation stressed charity-derived merit rather than ascetic meditation, which was left mostly to the monastic community. For the Burmese laity, charity merit required not the renunciation of material possessions, but their accretion. Wealth in a sense became a religious goal because merit and a better rebirth could literally be bought. Activities related to merit-making in various forms, but especially to charity, were central to early Kon-baung religious concerns and were manifested in considerable expenditure and effort at all levels of society: individuals, households, villages, provinces, and the state.

The central religious institution in society was the *sangha*, which served as the chief merit-making focus of the laity through the fulfillment of the mundane needs of monks. As the *sangha* is the primary object of charitable merit-making, Melford Spiro has cogently argued that the relationship between it and the laity is a perfect exchange system. The monk is enabled to pursue his individual quest for salvation by the people who, in turn, are the recipients of merit from the support of the monk and hence are serving their salvation needs as well. In this sense, the *sangha* serves as a collective savior for the Burmese.[14] This relationship also obtained between the *sangha* and the early Kon-baung state, and is nowhere better illustrated than in the *kahtein-daw-bwe* (annual monastic robe festival), when, with the *sangha* as the object, the village, province, and state turned themselves into corporate merit-making units.

The moral and transcendental values that Burmese society derived from Buddhism were idealized in the lives of the monks, who dedicated themselves to personal salvation and enlightenment through humility, continence, and austere self-denial. These values reached their highest idealization in the *arahats*, or fully perfected monks, who, though not deified, were attributed with special putative powers stemming from their spiritual quest. They fulfilled a mediating role in Burmese Buddhism similar to that of the saints in Catholicism. The idealized position of the monks was further expressed in their roles as preceptors to the king and princes and in the titles and honors lavished on successful "career monks" by rulers. European observers reported that the monastic order largely fulfilled the laity's expectations and, in return, was liberally supported.[15] Closely related is the fact that the *sangha* was the primary agent of political socialization because most young boys were sent to monasteries to learn reading, writing, and the basic tenets of their religion. Study of a basic set of ritual and ethical texts imparted a sense of the moral and physical order of the universe necessary to regulate life in general and social, political, and economic relationships in particular. On a more mundane level, learning in a variety of arts, crafts, and sciences was available, as monastic scholarship was competent over wide areas of secular learning.[16]

Never a homogeneous or structured group of monks, the *sangha* historically had only had reference to the secular authority structure. Crown regulation of the Burmese *sangha* probably had its roots in the Pagan period. This aspect of royal administration grew over the centuries, most notably in the reigns of Dama Zei-di of Pegu (1472-1492) and Tha-lun (1629-1648), and reached its climax under Bo-daw-hpaya. The relationship between ruler and monastic order was generally harmonious because the Burmese kings were usually lavish patrons of religion in material terms and intervened in *sangha* affairs mainly to control excessive sectarianism and doctrinal unorthodoxies.[17] For its part, the *sangha* required only that temporal rule be in accord with the *dhamma*, or cosmic law, preached by the Buddha and fulfill the historic stewardship role of Theravadin kings.[18] With no economic or administrative base or temporal aspirations of its own, the monastic order was completely dependent on the secular power, this being accepted as the proper state of affairs by both sides.[19] Although able to tap a vast reservoir of moral authority and respect among the populace, the monkhood used this power but sparingly to influence secular affairs and without notable political consequence. Nor did individual monks as such join in partisan politics or governmental affairs.[20]

The monkhood represented the orthodox side of the belief system, but there was an unorthodox substratum exemplified by a wide variety of men skilled in such arts as astrology, medicine, meditation, charms, alchemy, white and black magic, and related cabala. Often known as *weik-zas*, or wizards, such persons were unorthodox mediators for the people in dealing with the difficulties and uncertainties of life. Important in the lives of the state and the people alike, astrologers and soothsayers, for example, played important roles at court as counsellors to the rulers, preparing detailed "histories" of the future which were influential in the conduct of state affairs and politics.[21] Such unorthodox or semiorthodox arts were used in early Kon-baung society to determine auspicious courses of action, counter the power of enemies and malevolent spirits, and warn of and avert impending dangers or catastrophes. Given the credence placed in omens and prophecies, interpretations given at court may well have constituted the accepted channel for directing negative feedback and criticism to the ruler on proposed ventures and policies. Belief in the ability to foretell the future coupled with faith in the efficacy of magical means for neutral-

Early Kon-baung Society   45

izing or overcoming a rival, or even the superior power of the king, provided the background of many local conflicts and attempts on the throne and helps to account for the mercurial nature of both local and royal politics.

Social Ideology and Social Mobility

The structure of Burmese social thought, like that of medieval Europe, was hierarchical, with the cosmos seen as a merit-graded pyramid of beings ranging from demons to deities. The nature of being was a continuum ranging from ethereality to corporeality, no perception to perception, asexuality to sexuality, and incomprehensible longevity toward either end of the continuum to time measured in comprehensible terms at the level of humankind. The upper part of the hierarchy consisted of four levels of *brahma* deities, formless and insensate beings with no needs or wants. This was followed by the middle world with sixteen levels of *brahma* deities with form, but still with sufficient merit to be free from desire and sensation. Humankind occupied a lowly position in the cosmic hierarchy, below that of the six levels of spirits with form, desire, and sensation, but above that occupied by four levels of lesser creatures. Because position in the universal moral continuum was determined by *kamma*, beings were in effect classified according to their merit, which in turn meant that merit position in the cosmic hierarchy was quantifiable. Thus, *kamma* emerges as a kind of natural law giving order and regularity to the universe.

Used to account for the differences between individuals and between groups of individuals, the natural law of *kamma* also brought order and regularity to human society. All societies have differentials in the distribution of power, wealth, and status, but social stability depends less on these differentials themselves than on the degree to which people perceive that distribution to be equitable or inequitable. *Kamma* invested the social order with a powerful moral authority in that it rationalized status in this life while offering the possibility of improved status in a future life. The core of the kammatic message was that inequalities were not iniquitous, but the just and inexorable working of a moral law which guaranteed that everyone receives and will continue to receive their just due over the long run.[22] The foundation of early Kon-baung social ideology was this conception of the cosmic hierarchy as conditioned by the natural law of *kamma*.

The cosmic hierarchy of merit-related levels was the model for the social hierarchy of early Kon-baung society. The descriptions of the latter hierarchy, found particularly in the *damathats*, give a picture of a precisely defined and detailed system of social ranking. There were four main levels of society, comprising the rulers (*min-myo*), the officials (*amat-myo*), the wealthy (*thahtei thakywe-myo*), and the commoners (*thu-hsin-ye-myo* or *hsin-ye-tha-myo*). Clearly the Burmese adaptation of the four *varna* of Hinduism (*brahman, kshatriya, vaisya,* and *shudra*), this fourfold division of society had further gradations within each main division. The rulers were divided into an upper grade of king, chief queen, and crown prince, followed by four more specific grades of princes, other royal relatives, and high officials. Divided into three main grades of superior, middle, and inferior, the officials encompassed not only those holding formal offices ranging from minister of state to village headman, but also those holding appanages without office and those having honors from the crown. Also divided into three grades, the wealthy group was, in fact, a *thwei-thauk* to which men of material substance were appointed as an honor by the king and which involved minor ceremonial duties in connection with the Eastern Court of the palace. The commoners had three grades as well, the lowest being the *dun-zan-da*, or people in such degraded circumstances or occupations as hereditary slaves, beggars, and grave diggers.[23]

Social differentiation in early Kon-Baung society was made clear cut and visible through customary law and the operation of rigorous sumptuary rules. Using a system of fault based on rank and punishment based on *ko-bo*, or body price, the *damathats* contain extensive prescriptions for the regulation of relationships between the grades of the social hierarchy. The lower the social rank of the offender in relation to the offended, the greater the fault and the greater the punishment or compensation. The *Manu-kye* says "If a man of good family, a man who is reputed for his good works, any man who is a chief or head, be abused by a person of little repute, compensation shall be made in proportion to the rank and qualities of the good man."[24] Customary law was further used to maintain the social distance between the various grades and levels through punishments for what were considered to be antisocial actions or behavior.[25]

The sumptuary rules were not only the visible manifestation of social distinctions, but also the primary means of maintaining them. Every grade within each of the four levels had the style and opulence of its dress, personal utensils, houses, funerals, trappings of office, and related matters prescribed in detail. Such matters were the most important indicator of rank in early Kon-baung society. Regardless of individual wealth, for example, the sumptuary rules for commoners had to be observed unless and until the individual had been honored by the king with membership in the wealthy grades, in which case the sumptuary rules for those grades had to be followed.26 Composed in the late 1750s at the request of Alaung-hpaya by a former Ava courtier, the *Law-ka byu-ha kyan* [Treatise on customary terms] contains long chapters describing in detail the sumptuary requirements of the various grades of the ruler level, and many local officers in the lower grades of the official level recorded their particular sumptuary privileges in the *sit-tans* they submitted.

Status was broadly reflected at court and in society by a system of conferring nonhereditary personal honorific titles. Hence the most basic status division was between those titled and those not. In the earlier periods of Burmese history, the use of these personal honorifics was apparently restricted to royalty and other high personages but, at least by the Restored Taung-ngu period, titles were common among the middle- and lower-level officials and *myo-thu-gyis*. In the early Kon-baung period there were two groups of titles, those of the *min-nyi min-tha* (real or conferred royalty) and those of the courtiers/officials. Hybrids of Burmese and Pali, the personal honorifics expressed a quality or qualities perceived in the recipient or considered desirable for his post. The terms *pyan-chi* and *yaw-da*, for example, were often incorporated in the titles of military commanders, while *wei-lu* was deemed especially appropriate for secretaries. At the top of the hierarchy, the title word *thado*, meaning courageous, diligent, and of wise counsel, was often bestowed on important ministers. A similar word was *u-zana*, formerly given only to very high personages, but in the early Kon-baung period widely used for middle-level personnel as well.27 The male status hierarchy was paralleled by a female hierarchy headed by the chief queen.

A second organizing focus of the court status hierarchy had as its core the concept of *nei-ya*, or "place." The courtiers were divided into two groups: those who had place and those who did not. Place was only obtained by royal appointment and brought with it specified trappings, ornaments, and clothes to be worn on official occasions at the palace. If not a *nei-ya-daw-nei*, or "holder of a royal place," a courtier could only wear good, clean clothes on these occasions. Place, in fact, meant assignment to a specific physical location in the royal audience hall. The hall was divided into 47 sections, 23 on the right and 24 on the left, as befitted the higher status held by the left in Burmese thought, for a total of 567 places (see figure 2). The first place on the left was held by the crown prince, with no corresponding place on the right, followed by the three *min-tha* (prince) governors of the left and the same of the right, the nine great *min-tha* of the left, and the same of the right, and

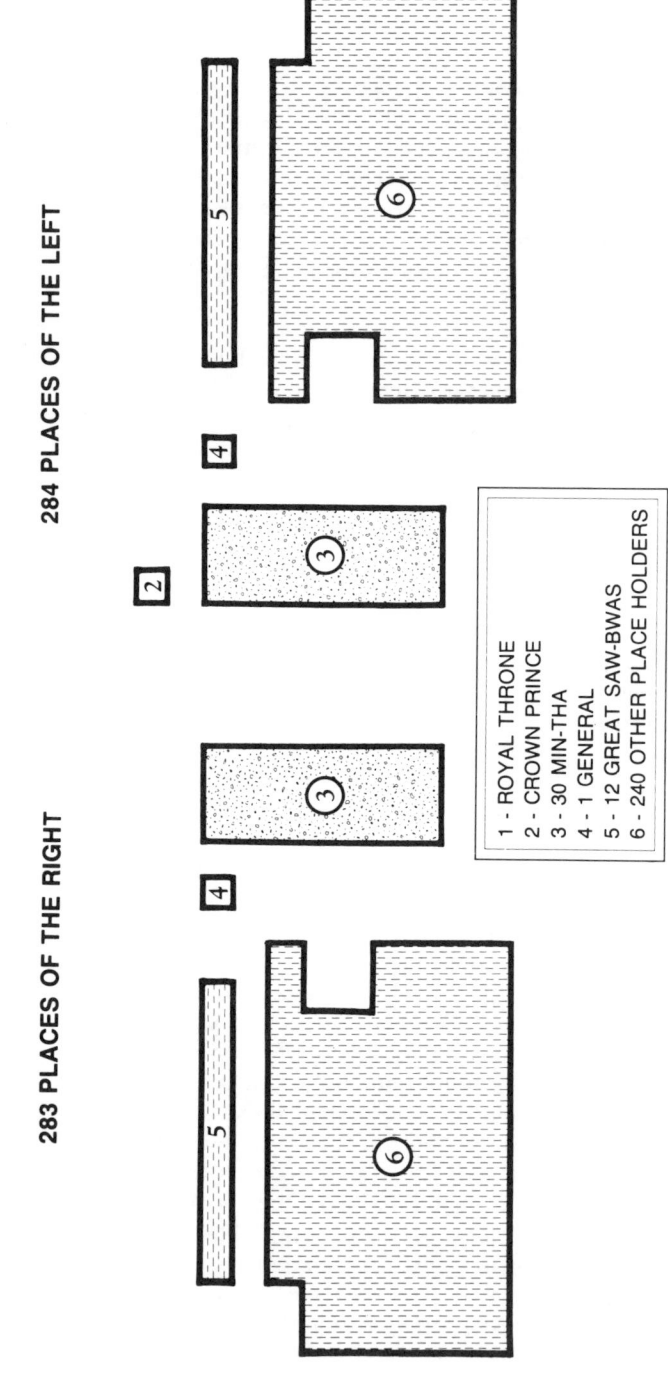

Figure 2. The Places of the Royal Court

so on.[28] A person without place generally received only a lower-class title as an indication of royal recognition. Once he began to work his way up the status hierarchy, his title advanced in class and he was ultimately assigned a place.

Rigidly observed and permeating all aspects of court and procedure, the elaborately graded status system was the formal manifestation of the hierarchical relationship between ruler, royal lineage, and officials. By assigning individuals to specific places and grades of title, it served as an important control mechanism through which the favor or disfavor of the sovereign could be immediately expressed. As such, the status hierarchy played a central role in the strict discipline to which the court was subjected. On receiving a present from the son of the crown prince in 1802, for example, the British envoy Michael Symes was informed that "the attention might be considered as coming from the king, the discipline of the court being so well regulated that not one of its members, not even the Engy Teckien [crown prince], could send a trifling present, or communicate with a foreign minister, without express permission from the king."[29]

The differentiation of rank exemplified in the sumptuary rules was based on the moral authority of the law of *kamma*. Transgression of these rules, said the *Manu-kye*, "is not in accordance with the orders of the monarch, the moral law [*dhamma*], or the opinions of this world."[30] As the duty of the state was to uphold *dhamma*, sumptuary infractions were considered lese majesty and punished by death.[31] The British envoy Symes observed in 1795:

> It has already been noticed, that almost every article of use, as well as ornament, particularly in their dress, indicates the rank of the owner; the shape of the betel-box, which is carried by an attendant after a Birman of distinction wherever he goes, his ear-rings, cap of ceremony, horse furniture, even the metal of which his spitting pot and drinking cup are made (which, if of gold, denote him to be a man of high consideration), all woe be unto him that assumes the insignia of a degree which is not his legitimate right.[32]

When officials fell from favor, the outward sign of their disgrace was the loss of some or all of their sumptuary privileges, with deprivation of the betel box in particular constituting "the greatest mark of degradation among the Burmahs."[33] Questionable practices concerning sumptuary privileges could also contribute to the downfall of officials.[34]

Although the structure of the social order was precisely defined and vigorously maintained, it still did not necessarily root people in a permanent rank. Unlike Hindu *dharma*, which militated against positional change by prescribing compliance with caste norms, sociologically Burmese Buddhism was much less conservative. Merit from past lives determined birth in a given social rank, but merit accrued and wisdom and effort employed in the present made change possible through kammatic flux. The legitimacy of such positional change is mentioned in various early Kon-baung *damathats* and other texts, while the *Manu-kye* gives a detailed illustration of precisely this point. In a previous existence, the Buddha was a *dun-zan-da* (slave) serving a rich man. He determined to have his master's daughter with such bad passion and persistence, despite severe abuse from her father, that the daughter finally begged to be given to him in order to prevent her father from killing him and thus suffering hell. In a better temper, the Buddha became a hermit and monk and obtained *janana* (wisdom), whereupon his former master made obeissance to him as a fit object for such respect. The text concludes, "Bearing this in mind, all men whatever, even of the most degraded class, are worthy to be raised to rank and station, if the habits are good."[35]

The moral of this story is that through morality and meditation, the Buddha obtained enough merit to move from the very bottom of the social order to the top, an option that is open to all men. Thus, social life was viewed as a continuous process of changing station, either upward or downward, through the working of kammatic flux. There are enough examples and evidence of positional change available to suggest that the element of mobility in early Kon-baung social ideology had at least a certain reality.

The common people appear to have held three basic goals in terms of mobility in the social order. For the socially ambitious, the greatest social distance was between the commoners and the wealthy and official divisions. Hence a common aspiration was to enter officialdom even at the lowest grade, or barring that, the less prestigious wealthy grades. The two most prevalent ways of obtaining entry to officialdom were to gain the notice of the king or crown prince with distinguished service or to marry the female heir to a local office, as evidenced by the *sit-tans* not an uncommon practice. Because there was always a strong status division in Burmese society between titled and untitled men, women, and monks, a second, closely related, social goal was to receive a personal honorific title from the crown. This usually, but not always, came about after achieving office and was a decidedly less frequent route from the common grades. A last way of acquiring social status was to be the builder of a pagoda or monastery, thereby acquiring the title of *hpaya-daga* or *kyaung-daga*, an appellation so respected that even kings took it upon themselves.

Alternative Social Statuses

In common with other Southeast Asian societies of this period, Burmese society included four social statuses which provided individuals an alternative to the administrative and status regimen of the formal social order. Slavery was an important factor in the maintenance and support of many of the religious establishments of the society. Debt bondage and patron-client relationships were two closely related statuses, the first with a primarily economic focus and the latter with distinct political implications as well. Lastly, there was always a floating population, often quite large, which provided the ultimate alternative status for the individual. On occasion, the floating population coalesced in sufficient numbers to become a political factor in its own right.

Slavery was as widespread in Burma as it was in the rest of Southeast Asia in this period. There were both hereditary and permanent slaves, the majority of whom were pagoda slaves who, along with their descendants, had been condemned to this degraded status for criminal or treasonous reasons.[36] Such pagoda slaves were quite distinct, however, from the large numbers of people who worked glebe rather than private or state land and whose produce taxes went not to the crown or an appanage holder but to the support of an ecclesiastical edifice or institution.

Far more common than outright slavery was debt bondage, an institution that tends to be well developed where labor is in short supply, as was the case in Burma. Debt bondage was a business transaction, recorded and taxed as such by the local authorities, in which individuals sold their labor or that of their families for an agreed sum of money. The arrangement came to an end when the money was repaid. Households that could not meet their tax obligations were often sold by the local authorities if the tax was more than thirty *kyats*.[37] The tax on debt bondage transactions is mentioned in almost all the *sit-tans* and its regulation is the subject of many royal edicts and detailed rules in the *damathats*.

The most common reason for entering into this transaction was relief from heavy taxation and service obligations, as was observed by the Italian missionary Vincentius Sangermano: "It often happens that a man will sell his children or his wife or even himself, to pay the taxes and imposts; though these transactions should be looked upon rather as pledges than sales, as the slavery thus entered into is never perpetual."[38] Thus, the bondsman remained a free man, but gained exemption from all taxes and service, protection, a reasonable subsistence, and sometimes even improved his social position through the association with a personage of power and rank. If mistreated, which by all accounts was rare, there was always the alternative of flight.

Also common in early Kon-baung society was the patron-client relationship. For all the same reasons that caused debt bondage to flourish, people entered the service of members of the royal family, high officials, or other powerful personages. In return for securing their livelihood and protection, the patron gained followers who owed him their sole loyalty and therefore constituted an important factor in his political position. In contrast to the pronounced decline of centers elsewhere, for example, the number of service houses in Taung-ngu increased from 1,118 in 1783 to 1,795 in 1802.[39] This increase is most probably due to the amassing of clients by the Taung-ngu prince, who was engaged in improving his position *vis-à-vis* that of his rivals for the throne. Officials also found it necessary to maintain large establishments. The *myo wun* of Han-tha-wadi was estimated to have five thousand followers to enforce his rule within his charge and to defend his position against his rivals, and his deputy and chief enemy the *yei wun* had over fifteen hundred personal followers.[40] Generalized to the full range of political conflict in the officialdom and royalty, patron-client relationships must have involved significant numbers of people.

At any given time there was also a substantial floating population of persons displaced by war or famine who were either unwilling to endure the rigors of continued service in the *athi* or crown service sectors, or simply in personal trouble. The points of organization in this population tended to be bandit chiefs, wandering troupes of entertainers, and individuals thought to have uncanny personal powers such as wizards, necromancers, and tattooers. Banditry itself was an almost respectable occupation and often enjoyed the overt support of villages. The more successful bandits survived through reciprocal relationships with local and provincial officials. In some cases banditry became an avenue to appointment to local office as well.[41] Joining the floating population in whatever capacity provided alternatives to debt bondage and patron-client relationships for the more alienated members of society and enabled them to find refuge outside of customarily accepted institutions.

Debt bondage and patron-client relationships were so similar that they were probably only variants of the same basic institution. The Burmese did not distinguish between them in terminology. Perhaps the main difference was that patron-client relationships tended to involve personages of power and status, had a distinct political undertone and, as far as can be determined, did not involve a written contract. More economic in nature, debt bondage arrangements were mostly contracted with local persons of means who probably were more concerned with economic than political gain. Even the floating population had certain important features in common with debt bondage and patron-client relationships. All three were mechanisms through which a probably substantial segment of the population escaped crown control and hence were means of depleting the material base of the central authority. In the case of patron-client relationships and banditry, the crown was further weakened politically by the transfer of loyalty to the patron or bandit chief. Conversely, these mechanisms strengthened subordinate loci of power within the society. In good times such mechanisms probably had only a marginal effect on the central authority, but in times of famine or high levels of labor conscription by the crown they became the primary means by which the common people escaped the exploitation of the state and general physical and economic insecurity for the comparatively less onerous and more secure life of the private sector. For example, during the famine of 1805–1812, patron-client relationships coupled to the prevalent desire to escape crown service played an important role in the politics of succession during the reign of Bo-daw-hpaya.

Agriculture and the Economy

Burma in the eighteenth century was largely a peasant society which, for the most part, was focused on villages. The village base of society was not necessarily stable, however, as the peasantry displayed considerable mobility, both intra- and interdistrict, in response to the poor quality of land over much of central and northern Burma, the desire to escape service and dues, and drought-induced scarcity.[42] There was somewhat less tendency toward mobility in the more densely populated alluvial and irrigated areas where the quality of the land did not require it.

Within this village-oriented society the primary unit of economic cooperation was the family, followed by the crown service unit or *athi taing*. Although the majority of these units were self-sufficient in terms of food, they were not economically independent because of their need for such items as salt, ironware, pottery, jaggery (palm sugar), and cooking oil. The food staple was rice in the south and rice and millet in the center and north.

Agriculturally, the country was divided into a northern dry zone, an intermediate zone, and the southern delta areas. The dry zone is a large lemon-shaped area centered on the confluence of the Irrawaddy and Chin-dwin rivers. Protected from the May to September monsoon by the hills of the Arakan Yoman, the dry zone receives less than forty inches of rainfall annually. Although there was some cultivation of such cash crops as indigo, cotton, tobacco, mulberry trees, and toddy palms, the agriculture of the dry zone in the early Kon-baung period was founded on five main types of food cultivation. These were wet rice or paddy, dry-season rice or *mayin*, millet and sesamum, *kaing* cultivation, and shifting, or *taung-ya*, cultivation. The three main areas of irrigated paddy cultivation in the dry zone were Kyauk-hse just to the southeast of Ava, Min-bu on the Irrawaddy midway between Ava and Prome, and the Mu Valley to the northwest of Ava near the original Kon-baung capital of Mok-hso-bo. Paddy was grown in the wet season, lasting roughly from May to September, in fields irrigated by the stored monsoon rains or on land inundated by the annual rise of the rivers. Sown in January for reaping in April, *mayin* was planted wherever sufficient water was left in low spots and hollows as the rivers receded. Combined with the low rainfall, however, the light sandy soil covering most of the area made millet the most important grain crop. *Kaing* was the term applied to the cultivation of maize, onions, peas, tobacco, and vegetables on river banks or islands receiving annual inundation. In areas not amenable to more productive forms of cultivation, *taung-ya* was practiced.

With the main exceptions of the paddy areas of Kyauk-hse, Min-bu, and the Mu Valley, in the late eighteenth century most parts of the dry zone appear to have had a mixed agriculture of paddy, *mayin*, millet, and, to a lesser extent, *kaing* and *taung-ya* cultivation. Another notable exception was the most arid part of the dry zone centering on Pagan and neighboring Taywin-daing and Ywa-tha. The Pagan land roll of 1765 records only one village as having any paddy cultivation, the records of most uniformly stating "There is no paddy or *mayin* cultivation in this tract." The majority of the villages recorded millet, pulse, and *taung-ya* cultivation, while a few reported only pulse and *taung-ya*.[43] It is little wonder that the early Mons termed Pagan the *tattadesa*, or "parched land."[44] Taywin-daing and Ywa-tha also recorded no paddy or *mayin*, but only dry and *kaing* cultivation.[45]

To the north and east of the dry zone lay the valley of the upper Irrawaddy and the neighboring Shan Highlands, both characterized by sparse populations of Tai-speaking peoples and shifting agriculture. To the south was the intermediate zone, with its foci at Prome and Taung-ngu. Located just above the upper edge of the Irrawaddy Delta, Prome was an important rice-producing area for the crown. As Francis Buchanan, who accompanied the Symes mission to Amara-pu-ra in 1795, noted in his journal, "It is said that the inland country here produces much rice, that the king has here large storehouses for collecting it. . . . We saw several of the granaries, built of wood and covered with thatch."[46] Dominating the upper end of the Sittang Valley, Taung-ngu was also a large and prosperous paddy and *kaing* area, but was left somewhat remote from the main north-south axis of the lower Irrawaddy Valley by the Pegu Yoma.

With an average of one hundred inches of rainfall annually and two hundred inches in the coastal regions, the deltas of the Irrawaddy and Sittang rivers were a different world from the frequent droughts and crop failures of the dry zone. Most of lower Burma and especially the Irrawaddy Delta were completely inundated during the monsoon season and unfit for habitation during several months of the year. As neither Burmans nor Mons had ever built more than a few embankments to control the flooding, vast tracts of fertile land in the Irrawaddy Delta, the Pegu/Sittang River Valley, and the Henzada/Tha-ra-wadi Plain still remained largely uncultivated in early Kon-baung times.[47] The alluvial soils, high temperatures, and heavy rainfall made this region ideal for the intensive cultivation of paddy. Riverine irrigation was rarely needed or used, as the natural rainfall was retained in the fields by small dams or bunds. This style of paddy culture also characterized the coastal plains of Arakan and Tenasserim at the mouths of their many rivers and streams. The Han-tha-wadi and Martaban land rolls of 1784 and 1802 record these areas as being devoted almost solely to paddy and *kaing* cultivation, with virtually no mention of other agriculture.[48] The western delta around Bassein was less developed and its small and scattered agricultural areas were devoted to paddy, *mayin*, and *taung-ya*.[49] In conjunction with the intermediate zone, however, the delta areas were important granaries for the Kon-baung kingdom based in the dry zone.

The main industries were salt boiling, the production of cooking oil, petroleum, shipbuilding, mining (silver, lead, iron, copper, and gold), pottery, and lacquerware.[50] Internal commerce was well developed through local and regional market networks in which the *myos* served as both market towns and administrative centers. On the basis of the many references to cart roads and high roads in the *sit-tans* and the accounts of European travellers, the road system appears to have been functional between the capital and the major subcenters, between the major subcenters themselves, and in the areas of overland trade, particularly the north and northeast and west over the An Pass.[51] The Irrawaddy River and its tributaries were the main artery of commerce and communication between upper and lower Burma and far surpassed the roads in significance.

International commerce was composed of both overland and maritime trade. There was a certain amount of overland intercourse with Bengal through Arakan and a large overland trade with Yunnan. The main Burmese terminal was Bhamo/Kaung-ton, where large Chinese caravans arrived for an annual trade fair.[52] The maritime commerce centered at Rangoon while Bassein, Martaban, and Tavoy were points in the coasting trade with Bengal. The main maritime imports were broadcloth, piece goods, hardware, and glassware and the main export was teak. The staples of the overland trade with Yunnan were Burmese cotton and Chinese silk. Evaluating the contemporary estimates of British visitors, Tun Wai has suggested that the annual value of the maritime trade was probably at least twice that of the overland trade.[53]

Commerce and business at all levels were carefully taxed and regulated and industry and agriculture also had their own revenue structures. The Han-tha-wadi and Bassein *sit-tans* record in detail the physical restrictions, port dues, other imposts and fees, and crown duties levied on maritime commerce. The *sit-tans* of inland jurisdictions refer to bazaar taxes; the transit dues at *te*, or land toll stations; *hseik*, or water toll stations; and the *kin* (the "chokeys" of British accounts), or crown police and customs posts. While *te* and *hseik* appear to have been simply tax stations for internal commerce, the function of *kin* was to tax and monitor intercourse between the precincts of the capital and other districts, interdistrict intercourse, and intercourse with foreign countries. *Kin* were further charged with preventing the export of rice, silver, gold, elephants, horses, cattle, and arms without a crown permit and with apprehending bandits, smugglers, and fleeing rebels.[54] All local business transactions and dues were recorded and subjected to a tax of up to 10 percent of the value of the goods or services by a special officer whose post was often hereditary and whose title varied with locality. In smaller jurisdictions where administrative duties were less differentiated, this function was often performed by the headman. Another local officer, termed *pwe-za*, or broker, in the *sit-tans* and usually a hereditary post, acted as a middleman in arranging sales transactions on which he or she took a commission. The crown itself carefully controlled the production of such precious commodities as gemstones and silver and strictly regulated the amount allowed onto the open market. Concessions in other areas of commerce and industry were often sold to groups of individuals, or "companies" as they were known, who in return for an annual fixed payment to the crown received a monopoly in a certain area of trade or industry.55

Revenue and commercial transactions were conducted in what might be termed a "raw lump currency," hence the economy was not fully monetized in the sense of having a standard coinage. Silver bullion in the form of irregular buttons and ingots was the most common standard of exchange and was negotiated in terms of the weight and purity of the metal. There were many standards of silver alloyed with copper, but the most common and the one in which crown revenues had to be paid was *ywet-ni*, or flowered silver, an 85 percent alloy. Thus, a second function of the broker in transactions was to produce the agreed weight of silver at the agreed standard of alloy. Copper was also a medium of exchange and lead was often used for purchases in the bazaars. Gold was used only for jewelry, ornamentation, and the gilding of religious and royal edifices.56

The early Kon-baung polity was therefore characterized by a small-scale economy in which food agriculture was predominant, but in which cash crops, small-scale industries, and internal and international commerce had important roles. The economy tended to grow at a very low rate under the best of circumstances and appears to have been contracting as the dynasty progressed. The low rate of expansion can be accounted for by a number of factors. The prohibition on rice exports was probably the main factor, while the lack of investment capital and labor, the poor quality of much of the land in central and upper Burma, and the pestilential nature of the Irrawaddy Delta in the south were also important. Much of the agricultural surplus was drained off by the crown through agricultural taxes, and the crown also tended to absorb surplus labor for its own uses. Although there was a domestic market in rice, it was limited by the state monopoly of the surplus and further inhibited by the fact that the market price tended to be linked to the amount of silver the crown accepted in lieu of paddy in the payment of taxes.57

In addition to the lack of market opportunities, the quantity and variety of available consumer goods was limited. Conspicuous consumption, too, was limited by the rigid sumptuary rules prescribing the style of dress, utensils, house, funerals, etc., for every element in the population. Indeed, any conspicuous display of wealth usually drew the extortionate attentions of the local officials. The requirements of large presents necessary for appointed officials to gain and hold office and to maintain followers, and the same for merchants to conduct business of any scale, prevented most from accumulating capital for investment. Only the hereditary local officers managed to avoid these requirements to some extent and they alone amassed estates, after a fashion. Such estates tended to be fractured through cognatic inheritance, however, hence even hereditary officials were limited in the capital and resources they could accumulate and transmit. Such resources and savings as were accumulated tended not to be reinvested in economic ventures, but in the pursuit of religious goals. The charity approach to merit accumulation stressed in Burmese Buddhism meant that such surplus as was not taken by the state or officials tended to be invested in a wide spectrum of merit-making activities including the erection of religious edifices, the feeding of monks, and the holding of festivals and ceremonies.[58]

The factors described above have been termed "levelling mechanisms," or ways in which many small-scale economies force the expenditure of accumulated capital or resources into channels that are not necessarily economic or productive.[59] Absolute wealth and accumulation in Burma therefore tended to remain both limited and diffuse. This did not, however, mean that the mass of the commoners was impoverished, for as the British envoy John Crawfurd observed in 1827: "In fact, the Burmese peasantry are in more comfortable and easy circumstances than the mass of the labouring poor in any of our Indian provinces; and, making allowance for climate, manners, and habits, might bear a comparison with the peasantry of most European countries."[60]

Population and Ethnicity

Comparing the extant early Kon-baung population statistics with the estimates of the various contemporary British visitors, the population of the early Kon-baung polity was probably between 2 and 2.5 million (see appendix 1). The Kon-baung statistics themselves reveal two further points. First, while the north/northwest and central areas show marked declines between 1783 and 1802, the Irrawaddy Delta, Taung-ngu, and Martaban areas remained basically static. Second, the declines are almost without exception confined to the major centers, while the smaller *myos* are in the main unchanged or show modest increases. Overall, the available figures indicate rather conclusively that the general demographic trend was downward by about 17 percent and that the historic centers of irrigated paddy cultivation and crown service population in the northern and central districts bore the brunt of that decline. These figures are given in table 1, which summarizes the data in appendix 1. The figures almost certainly reflect the drain Bodaw-hpaya's heavy military and labor demands made on both the *athi* and crown service populations after 1785. The downward trend would be even steeper if the Kon-baung records covered the great famine and social disruption which occurred between 1802 and 1812.

Table 1
Summary Population Statistics in Houses, 1783–1802

Area	1783	1802	Percent Change
Capital	20,075	22,428	+12
North/Northwest	69,058	42,543	−38
Central	57,637	47,638	−17
Prome	30,189	28,786	−5
Irrawaddy Delta	20,119	20,207	(<1)
Taung-ngu	2,332	3,163	+36
Martaban	4,707	4,707	—
Totals	**204,117**	**169,472**	**−17**

Unfortunately, the statistics throw no light on the ethnic composition of the Kon-baung state. Burmese society had been ethnically heterogeneous since the early Pagan empire and ethnicity remained an important factor in the structure and administration of the early Kon-baung state. Although ethnic cleavages tend to be well defined in contemporary Burma, in the eighteenth century the situation was considerably more fluid and the state's rationale provided a different basis for ethnic interrelationships.[61] From this perspective, early Konbaung society falls into an unequal dichotomy between the majority lowland, rice-cultivating, Buddhist peoples—Burmans, Mons, and Shans—who, although linguistically and ethnically different, shared a common culture, social structure, and history, and the animist hill peoples such as the Karens, Chins, and Kachins, who had a different type of social structure and culture.

The two most important non-Burman groups were the Mons and Shans, both of whom had been subsumed in the same political entity with the Burmans for most of the seven hundred years since the Pagan empire came into being. In its own way, each group was at the same time important to the strength of the state as a source of services and revenues, but also posed a substantial threat.

The historic habitat of the Mons was the Irrawaddy Delta and the southeastern littoral.[62] The demographic exhaustion of the delta and its subsequent devastation in the sixteenth century had resulted in the steady deterioration of their position. Following the imposition of northern rule by the early kings of the Restored Taung-ngu dynasty and the growth of the special relationship between the Mons and the Thai, Mon revolts broke out sporadically in response to misrule by Burman governors. Mon resentment and aspirations found vigorous expression in the Burman/Mon/Karen kingdom of Pegu between 1740 and 1757. The Burman repression that followed the final northern victory in 1757 left the Mon population reduced through liquidation, disease, and migration. Subsequently, the Mon population of the south was subject to heavy military levies and again suffered the maladministration of Burman governors.

Although maladministered and exploited for military service, the Mon population was viewed with suspicion by the Burmans as a serious internal threat and the Mon proclivity for the Thai was thought to make Burma more vulnerable to her eastern neighbor. Fear of the Mons was further increased by the Thai use of Mon spies and recruitment of Mon regiments.[63] There is no evidence, however, that this fear was extended to the Mon service population of upper Burma at this time.

The Mon response to Burmese misrule following 1757 was rebellion, migration, and assimilation. In direct response to maladministration by Burman governors, the Mons of Martaban and Rangoon rose in rebellion in 1758–1759 and 1774. A subsequent rebellion at Rangoon in 1783 had as its inspiration the restoration of a Mon-dominated kingdom in the south.[64] Each of these rebellions was followed by substantial migrations to Thailand, with a further large migration taking place in 1816.[65] Those Mons remaining were under heavy pressure to assimilate in terms of language and costume, the two most significant differences between Mons and Burmans. Migration and assimilation were conspicuous enough for the British visitor Francis Buchanan, a noted scientist of his day, to record in his journal: "by far the greater part of the Talain [Mon] had fled since the conquest of their country to Siam, and they continue to take every opportunity of making their escape. Those that remain have intermixed so much with the Burmas, and conceal themselves so much by adopting their language and dress, that it is difficult to distinguish them."[66] Over two decades later, the English missionary Felix Carey observed in a similar vein: "The Peguers [Mon] no more exist as a nation; they are nearly become extinct, or are incorporated with the Burman."[67] Such observations may, however, have been exaggerated because only sixty years later the Mons still made up the majority, at least in the Pegu District.[68] The accounts leave little doubt, however, that the Mon community in lower Burma had been severely depleted by the wars of the 1740s and 1750s and the subsequent military levies, rebellions, reprisals, migration, and assimilation.

The Burmans used the term Shan for the Tai-speaking population spread around the periphery of central and upper Burma from the northwest to the east and thence southward, but distinguished between them and the Thai themselves, who were called Yo-daya, and the Tai population of the Chiengmai area, who were termed Yun. Unlike the Mons, the Shans did not generally live within Burma proper, but in petty statelets at its periphery. The larger statelets were single units under hereditary chiefs called *saw-bwas*, while smaller entities were run by *myo-zas* or *myo-thu-gyis* and tended to be satellites of the larger states. Distributed over a wide expanse of upland territory, the Shans were valley-dwelling rice cultivators and, although balkanized politically, were relatively homogeneous linguistically and culturally. In addition to the Shans themselves, these principalities also included substantial numbers of hill peoples who, by this period, were in some cases the dominant internal force.[69]

The Burmans further divided the Shans into Western, Northern, and Southern. The Western Shans were situated in the Chin-dwin and upper Irrawaddy valleys, generally to the west of the latter river, in three statelets and some ten lesser entities. The Shans of this area, which contained a fair number of Burmans as well, were quite Burmanized. Administrative matters were conducted in Burmese and the appointment of Burmans as officials and chiefs was customary. By contrast, the Northern and Southern Shans had remained far less assimilated and much more on the peripheries of the Kon-baung state.[70] These peoples inhabited the territory to the northeast between Burma and Yunnan and the Shan Plateau to the east on both sides of the Salween River.

Although the Shans had dominated upper Burma from the late twelfth to the mid-sixteenth centuries, they failed to establish a unified Shan kingdom and were brought under systematic and lasting Burman control during the reign of Bayin-naung. From that time on, the Shans had remained politically fragmented and under a system of Burmese military administration that reduced their threat mainly to one of defection to China or Thailand. At the same time, levies from the Shan states constituted an important part of the military strength of the Burmese state. The campaigns of Alaung-hpaya had drawn large forces from the Western and Northern Shans, for example, and at a rough estimate Shan levies constituted 45 percent of the forces in Bo-daw-hpaya's great eastern expedition of 1785.[71] Even before the advent of Kon-baung rule, however, the military potential of the Shans was ebbing due to the gradual advance of Burmese and Chinese control, internecine conflicts, and Kachin and Karen pressure. The heavy labor demands of the early Kon-baung rulers further depleted the Shan states to a point where by the time of the first Anglo-Burmese war in 1824 the Shans may have ceased to have independent military potential.

Organizationally balkanized and situated on the edges of the realm, the Shans presented a different security problem to the Burmese state than did the Mons. While the Burman fear of the Mons focused on the internal threat of rebellion and Mon combinations with the Thai, French, and British, their concern with the Shans was the external threat of defection and assistance to Burma's enemy Thailand. Far more than the Mons, the Shans represented an important factor in the balance of military power between Burma and Thailand, a factor whose importance was demonstrated during the Thai victory in the trans-Salween between 1797 and 1804. As such, the position of its two principal minorities was vital to the strength of the early Kon-baung state, but also brought it an element of instability.

In contrast to the important role played by the Mons and Shans in the early Kon-baung state, the hill peoples, mainly the Kachins, Chins, and Karens, were marginal and generally of little concern to the Kon-baung rulers. Unlike the lowland paddy cultivators who lived in village communities, the hill peoples survived by shifting agriculture, trade, and warfare, were structured genealogically in terms of clans or lineages, lived in geographically widespread settlements, and were non-

Buddhist animists. Such peoples were able to maintain a fair degree of independence because they were not generally integrated into larger political units.

The Burmans distinguished between the Chins of the mountainous region on the western border, the Kachins (a loose term for the various groups of the northeast), and the Karens (another loose term for a congery of hill peoples) of the Salween/Sittang area and the Irrawaddy Delta. The Chins and Kachins were organized into chieftaincies, many of which were outside any semblance of Burmese control, and the remainder of which made a token acknowledgment of Burmese suzerainty through the payment of modest amounts of ivory, beeswax, raw cotton, and ginger.[72] In addition to trade and tributary relations, each group engaged in considerable raiding of Shan and Burman fringe areas. By the last part of the eighteenth century, the Northern Chins had become marginal participants as mercenaries in the local squabbles of Burman and Shan chiefs in the Kalei and Chin-dwin valleys. Farther to the east, the Kachins were in the process of eclipsing the Northern Shans militarily, with the more important Kachin chiefs among them being bestowed Burmese titles and treated as minor *sawbwas*.[73] Despite the fact that the Chins and Kachins were assuming a less marginal position, they still remained very much on the fringes of the early Kon-baung state.

Of far more significance were the Karens who, in addition to a large concentration around Kaya, were widely distributed over the Sittang Valley and Irrawaddy Delta. The Karens were divided into the Eastern Karens, who generally responded to Burmese authority only under military coercion, and the Western Karens, who tended to be absorbed in Burmese *myos* and often lived in registered houses. The Han-tha-wadi land rolls, for example, record some *myos* with substantial numbers of registered Karen houses, probably wet rice cultivators. Han-tha-wadi, Bassein, and Taung-ngu recorded large numbers of tax-paying Karens and there is also mention of Karens in the Martaban land roll. Many Karens paid a head or family tax in silver, a fixed tax on *taung-ya* cultivation, or a lump assessment in betel levied on all the Karens in the jurisdiction.[74] European observers noted the particularly onerous taxation of the Karens. Francis Buchanan, for example, recorded information obtained from the Italian missionary Vincentius Sangermano that many Karens were to be found near Rangoon and Bassein and "are most severely oppressed by the Burmas whom they mortally hate. The government has been so severe on them, that great numbers have retired to the Arakan Mountains."[75] One factor in the heavy-handed Burmese administration of the Karens, however, may have been memories of the important Karen role in the kingdom of Pegu between 1740 and 1757. In addition to being despised as animists, therefore, the Karens may also have been suffering for their participation in that unsuccessful venture.

For their part, the Karens had a traditional hostility to the Burmese monarchy. The most actively anti-Burmese Karens were those concentrated to the east and southeast of Taung-ngu around Karen-ni and Kaya, whence they raided the Burmese and actively assisted the Thai against the Burmese eastern campaigns.[76] In reprisal the Burmese sent various punitive expeditions against these Karens, with generally indifferent results. A continuing Burmese fear was that both the Eastern and Western Karens would make common cause with the Mons.[77] As a hostile segment of the population of the delta and adjacent eastern areas, the Karens, like the Mons, constituted an internal threat to the security of the early Kon-baung state and a potential, albeit minor, source of support to Thailand.

In addition to the majority lowland groups and the more marginal hill peoples, early Kon-baung society contained small and, in some cases, minute groups of other foreigners. There were, for example, small Chinese communities at the capital and several other places, an Indian-European-Armenian mercantile community in Rangoon, a handful of Catholic and Baptist missionaries, and a few other Europeans in crown service. These groups were tolerated because they performed specific and useful functions for the state, the missionaries, for example, serving as translators, physicians, and tutors for the court. These small foreign communities were of minor importance, however, as the crux of ethnicity in early Kon-baung society was the Burman relationship with the Mons and Shans.

CHAPTER 3

KINGSHIP AND POLITICAL THOUGHT

Early Kon-baung kingship rested on a broad foundation of political theory which provided a coherent statement of the purposes of government and the roles and responsibilities of kingship. In this conception, the basic purpose of the state was the regulation of human affairs that made civilized life possible. Its higher purpose was to reform the individual from degenerate to regenerate being. This regulation function was expressed in the "first king," or Maha Thamada model. Supported by selected aspects of the pragmatic expediency of the Arthashastran tradition of Brahmanic India, this model was supremely idealized in the *cakkavatti* tradition of kingship. The reformation function, expressed in the Asokan model of Buddhist kingship and a complex of state religious activities, reached its supreme idealization in the *bodhisatta* tradition of Burmese kingship. The temper of the times also provided early Kon-baung kingship with an undeniable element of messianism, which popular lore adapted from Theravada Buddhist eschatology. Comprised of both Buddhist and Brahmanic elements, kingship under the early Kon-baung rulers was shaped to no little extent by the turbulent nature of that period.

The First King Ideal and Its Political Import

Most historical and legal works of the early Kon-baung period contain an account of the origin of the world, of the human race, and of society adapted from the Pali canon. From these works can be derived the basic political ideas of the time. In the Burmese conception of time, the universe endures continuous cycles of creation and destruction called *kappa*. Ordinary cycles during which time reaches infinity are grouped into larger cycles, which, in their aggregate, are termed a "great" cycle during which a complete revolution of nature occurs. Unconcerned with primary origins, Buddhist and Burmese thought viewed this process as endless. Destroyed at the end of each cycle, the world was reconstituted by the force of nature and the first inhabitants migrated from the abode of the *brahmas*, the highest of the levels of existence. These first inhabitants were asexual and insensate beings who lived on internal joy. Over time the state of these beings began to deteriorate, as corporeality, sexuality, labor for sustenance, theft, lying, and punishment progressively developed. In response to each stage of human deterioration, the physical environment also deteriorated. Greatly concerned at their condition, the people of the world assembled and decided that the remedy was authority in the form of kingship held by a man of supreme integrity and morality. This office was given to a *bodhisatta* "just in all his proportions beyond other men, and perfect in his members; of most excellent power and sanctity, and great wisdom."[1] Because he was chosen by all the people, he was called Maha Thamada, or "acclaimed by the many."

Every cycle has its Maha Thamada, or first king, who is the originator of government and the revealer of the law. The first king ordered the demarcation of countries, towns, and villages, and appointed a crown prince, judges, military officers, and envoys. Although differing on how the law is revealed, the major Burmese accounts directly identify Maha Thamada with Manu as the first revealer of the law and law giver. The *Manu-kye* states:

> The lineal descendant of the sun, who habitually performs works of the greatest benevolence, who is the possessor of power, glory and authority, King Maha Thamada who is to men as their eyes and by his qualities enlightens all as a second sun—the rules he lays down none dare infringe. Amongst all rulers the first is called Manu. In this world of man the wonderful bodhisatta was the first.[2]

These Burmese statements of social evolution postulated an original idyllic state of nature. The gradual emergence of moral decline underscored the differences that divide people, hence social institutions developed to cope with the resulting problems. The corresponding changes in the physical environment were related to the state of immorality that developed among humanity and human corporeality was the consequence of this fall from perfection. Thus civil society originated in this moral decay, government grew out of the need for order, and kingship was seen as necessary to prevent society from lapsing into anarchy. Burmese political thought explicitly postulated a monarchical form of government, as did early Buddhist political theory.[3] Within this statement of social evolution and the Maha Thamada ideal can be found the two basic functions of the Burmese state mentioned earlier: regulation and reformation. The state must introduce and maintain order in human society, which was inherently immoral on the one hand, and bring about the moral reformation of its subjects on the other. Such tasks could only be undertaken by a person of vastly superior moral qualities who, to the Burmese, denoted a *bodhisatta*.

The appellation Maha Thamada itself was symbolic of the acknowledgment by humankind of the need for some agency to regulate human affairs in general and to rescue humanity from anarchy in particular. This latter role had a certain legitimizing tone to it and was attributed to such Burmese rulers as Nyaung-yan and Alaung-hpaya, who rose to power in times of chaos and effected a reconstitution of the polity. Indeed, there are many references in early Kon-baung texts comparing the accession of Alaung-hpaya to that of Maha Thamada. One early biography of Alaung-hpaya, for example, says that the people at the beginning of the world, lacking both refuge and support, asked Maha Thamada to rule as king, and that as Maha Thamada accepted out of his pity for the people, so also did Alaung-hpaya.[4] Another text relates that "Alaung-min-taya-gyi, full of glory and all the virtues," was approached by the forty-six chiefs of the Mok-hso-bo area who "inviting him as Maha Thamada had been invited, said, 'The time is now right; take the throne and save the people.'"[5]

Beyond his initial role as the bringer of order to a chaotic world, Maha Thamada represented the need for secular regulatory power in society. This need had both a positive and negative aspect. The former was the need for the *dhamma*, or universal moral law, to be upheld in the human sphere through the agency of kingship, and the latter was the need for coercive power in regulating human affairs. A concept central to both Buddhism and Brahmanism, *dhamma* was the law of the universe, its ethics and rationality, immanent, eternal, and uncreated. A blending of nature and justice, *dhamma* had to be upheld if there was to be cosmic harmony. *Dhamma* was intelligible to a mind with the range and depth of the Buddha, and in orthodox Buddhist thought was made known to humankind through him. Burmese sources usually ascribe the revealing of the law to Maha Thamada identified as Manu, but the point is that the universal moral law exists in and of itself and was only "revealed" to humankind. The function of the king was therefore not to be the maker of law, but the upholder of the law.

The Buddhist conception of *dhamma* connoted the supreme principle of righteousness, and was closer to western concepts of virtue than was Brahmanic *dharma*, which had a more legal tone and was tied to the maintenance of caste prerogatives. Brahmanic *dharma* had to be sufficiently flexible to allow the king to justify actions necessary for the preservation of order, even if such actions were not ethical. Although Buddhist thought also considered the safeguarding of order to be the primary purpose of the state, order was understood in more purely moral terms. Thus, *dhamma* was made the standard for all the activities of the king. This idea pervades many of the Burmese documents, the following passage from the *Manu-kye* being a good example:

> Oh King! Amongst men there are two ways of settling disputes, by *damathat* and by *pa-pathat*. By *damathat* is when the decisions are guided by the precedents recorded by kings, bodhisattas, from the beginning of time through the whole succession of worlds, in accord with the constituents of the Eightfold Path; right views, right intentions, right speech, right conduct, right livelihood, right effort, right mindfulness, and right caution. This is called *damathat*.
>
> By *pa-pathat* [Pali *papa*, or evil] is when a ruler merely from having the power habitually takes property by force, gives no consideration as to who should die and who should not, who should be mutilated and who should not, who should make restitution and who should not, who should be removed from office and who should not. This is called *pa-pathat*. *Pa-pathat* should be avoided and decisions given in accord with *damathat*.[6]

And, elsewhere: "the king who had the law for a flag, the law for a banner, and who was inclined towards the law, and who is like a slope up the side of the mountain of the law."[7] The idea that the law circumscribed and directed the actions of the king was also well established in medieval Burma.[8]

In this conception, the ruler became but the servant and agency of *dhamma* and his righteous conduct or sinful behavior infected the whole universe. If he was unjust, the realm was brought to ruin, but righteousness and adherence to *dhamma* brought fame to him and prosperity to his land. Virtue brought happiness to the people and had to be protected at all costs. The people were quick to discern and follow the example of the king: "If kings do not abide by the law, the lords will not. If they do not, the people will not and the country will go to ruin. If the king watches over the law, the lords will do the same and if they do so, so do the people of the country. The country being happy during the reign of that king is the cause of the people obtaining *nibbana*."9 Thus, morality stood between order and anarchy. Immorality led not only to the ruin of the country, but also to the dislocation of natural functions in the cosmos.

Because the ruler's role in the moral order of the universe was crucial to the welfare of both his subjects and himself, a norm of kingship known as *raja dhamma* was established. This norm pervades the texts of the Pali canon and the *jatakas*, and is common in Burmese historical and legal works both as subject and explanation. The standard Burmese formulation of this norm was expressed in the "ten royal laws": alms-giving, morality, liberality, uprightness, compassion, self-restriction, nonanger, nonoppression, forbearance, and compliance.[10] A second set of often cited principles was the "four *sangahas*" (assistances), which were to take one-tenth of the produce of the land as tax, to give grain to the troops once every six months, to lend money interest free to subjects for three years, and to speak kindly and affectionately to the people.[11] The "seven laws for the increase of prosperity" were the third important set of *raja dhamma* principles, and were to consult with ministers three times a day, to be united in all undertakings, to adhere to tradition in tax and criminal affairs, to honor old age, not to oppress the common people, to propitiate the *nats* (spirits) who guard the country, and to protect the Buddhist clergy.[12] There were yet more sets of royal duties or practices, which had as their source the *niti* literature of ancient India, and these will be mentioned in more detail below.

The Burmese adaptation of these sets of principles was very popular with both rulers and ruled. It is not surprising, therefore, that Burmese texts have Maha Thamada ruling in accord with the ten royal laws, the four *sangahas*, and the seven laws for the increase of prosperity. On those occasions when the Burmese chronicles comment on the relative uprightness of a ruler, the measure employed is always the ten royal laws and sometimes the other *raja dhamma* principles as well. Examples of the fate of kings who were not upright in this respect abound in the Burmese historical literature. For example, a text of the late 1750s says of Maha Dama Ya-za Di-pati and the end of his rule, "The king of Ava did not observe the ten royal laws. He broke the tradition of former kings. Dacoity appeared in the towns and villages and these were destroyed . . . [and the kingdom fell]."[13] Alaung-hpaya also charged his deceased former rival with failure to abide by the ten royal laws.[14] The health of both the polity and the cosmos demanded that *raja dhamma* be fulfilled. Failure in this duty was a heavy charge against any Burmese ruler.

Inherent in the need for secular authority over humanity was the use of coercion. Maha Thamada was to "revile and degrade those who should be reviled and degraded and banish those who should be banished."[15] The task of *danda* was therefore entrusted to the ruler. *Danda*, the rod of punishment, was the coercive function in government made necessary by the fall of humankind from righteousness. In Brahmanic thought, *danda* had the central role of upholding *dharma*, and was the function of the ruling *kshatriya* group. *Danda* was in a sense the negative side of *raja dhamma*, the odious but necessary use of coercive power.

Buddhist and Burmese thought tried to uphold the moral order in a more positive way by stressing *raja dhamma* and arguing for the avoidance of *danda* whenever possible. This effort was well documented in the early Kon-baung *damathats*, which were infused with a fervent spirit of Buddhist ethics. The *Manu-kye*, for example, recognizes the need for *danda*: "In all large and small villages, deceitful men who are thieves by habit and repute, all men of broken character, should be corrected according to their faults," but firmly rejects punishment not in accord with *dhamma*:[16]

> [I]t is not proper to put a man who has killed another to death in return and a king who does not put a murderer to death will be praised by all the gods and good men....
>
> It is not laid down in the *damathat* that such an offender shall be put to death or have his hands and feet cut off. These punishments are called *ya-za-that* [king's punishments].[17]

Thus, early Kon-baung thought recognized the need and fact of *danda*, but tried to tame and control its use by emphasizing *raja dhamma* and by setting Buddhist ethics as the standard for secular rule. Why, indeed, the *danda* function needed taming in the eyes of the compilers of the various *damathats* can be seen in this observation by the British envoy Michael Symes in 1795:

> The criminal jurisprudence of the Birmans is lenient in particular cases, but rigorous in others; whoever is found

guilty of an undue assumption of power, or of any crime that indicates a treasonable intent, is punished by the severest tortures. The first commission of theft does not incur the penalty of death, unless the amount be above 800 kiat or tackal ... or attended with murder or mutilation. In the former case the culprit has a round mark imprinted on each cheek by gunpower and punctuation ... for the second offense he is deprived of an arm, but the third inevitably produces capital punishment.[18]

There is one further aspect of the concept of *danda* in Burmese kingship that bears discussion here. In return for assuming the burden of "degrading, reviling, and banishing," Maha Thamada was to receive one-tenth of the people's rice. A similar concept of the right to part of the produce of the land in return for ruling was part of the consecration ceremony of the king when eight *thahteis*, wealthy men of official status, admonished the new ruler, "Oh king! After accepting the water poured by us, heed our words. Take one-tenth of the people's produce and enjoy the kingly estate, but rule in accord with the law."[19] Therein lay the right of the state to tax, but this should not be taken to mean that there was any sort of contract theory of state in which government was based on the consent of the people who had the right to take sanctions against tyranny. The ultimate source of sovereignty in Burmese political theory could never have resided in the people because the people were by definition immoral. The consecration oath of Burmese kings was actually a pledge of loyalty to *dhamma*, wherein lay the ultimate source of authority. The legitimacy of the state was rooted in its enforcement of the moral law in society.

The *Cakkavatti* and *Bodhisatta* Ideals

The first king ideal provided the basis for the regulatory function in Burmese kingship, but the reformation function was derived from Theravada Buddhist eschatology and the concepts of *cakkavatti* and *bodhisatta*. These two concepts are a part of the Buddhist theory of the superman, one who has put away "lust, speculation, and ignorance," whose mind is emancipated, and who concerns himself "with the advantage and welfare of the great masses of the people, many are the folk he has established in the Ariyan system."[20] Such a superman was recognizable by the thirty-two bodily signs, which included flat feet, long fingers and toes, forty teeth, a long tongue, blue eyes, and a bronze complexion. The exalted state was attained only on the basis of *kamma* and maintained only by righteousness. The superman had to choose between the careers of *cakkavatti* and *bodhisatta*. There can only be one of each in a world system at a time.[21]

The *cakkavatti* (Sanskrit, *chakravartin*), or universal monarch, who conquers the world is a concept found in both Hinduism and Buddhism. The idea of a state spanning the Indian subcontinent is at least as old as the tenth century B.C. A remnant of the more virile culture of the Vedic age, the Hindu conception of *chakravartin* was that of a "historical man" who in times of need emerged to save the world from whatever decay was at work in the dharmic order. An incarnation of a god, the *chakravartin* retired into legend once the cosmic order was mended. The *cakkavatti* concept entered Buddhism at the time of the rise of absolutism and the unification of India by the Mauryas in the third century B.C. The Buddhist version offered a universal king who conquered by righteousness and effected the political realization of the Buddhist *dhamma*. The *cakkavatti* concept represented the universality of the Buddhist spiritual message, the hope that interstate relations could be brought under moral controls, and the belief that adherence to *dhamma* was the most important force for the material and moral advancement of humanity.[22] The supreme temporal ideal of Buddhist kingship was embodied in the *cakkavatti*.

A king became a universal monarch only when the celestial wheel of the law revealed itself to him, an event contingent on his *kamma* and fulfillment of the duty of a wheel-turning monarch. The latter was described as "leaning on the norm, honouring, respecting, and revering it, doing homage to it . . . having the norm as thy master, shouldst provide the right watch, ward, and protection for thine own folk, and for the army, for the nobles, for vassals, for brahmins and householders, for town and country dwellers, for the religious world and for beasts and birds."[23] With the wheel rolling before him, the king then conquered the kings of the four quarters of the world and reigned with all the attributes of a universal monarch, including great retinue, great treasure, perfect health, great wisdom, popularity, and the seven treasures of the universal monarch.[24]

Monarchy deteriorated after a time, however, because kings again ruled by their own ideas and whims, in response to which society and human longevity deteriorated. When life span had decreased to ten years, the people realized the problem and returned to lives of law and piety, whereupon the process was reversed and life span increased. Then Sankha, "a wheel turning king, righteous and ruling in righteousness, lord of the four quarters, conqueror, protector of his people, possessor of the seven precious things . . . will live in supremacy over this earth to its ocean bounds, having conquered it not by the scourge, not by the sword, but by righteousness."[25] During the reign of Sankha there will appear the Buddha Metteyya, at which time Sankha will give his palace and treasure to the destitute and follow Metteyya as a wanderer to obtain *nibbana*. This is fitting because, though a *cakkavatti* rolls the wheel of the law, only a buddha rolls the supreme wheel of the law—he alone can save through his message.

Thus, the *cakkavatti* concept is part of the cycle of swings between morality and immorality, which Theravada Buddhism views as the course of human history. The original *cakkavatti* was obviously Maha Thamada, the first king to restore a declining age, whose righteousness was so great that his life reached infinity, becoming the model for all subsequent kings. Although universal monarchs appeared periodically after Maha Thamada, the world was in a state of progressive decline. At a relatively recent point, the Buddha Gotama revealed his teaching to the world, and predicted that his message would last five thousand years. Sometime after the expiration of this five thousand years—it is not said when—morality will have completely disappeared and humankind will have sunk to the lowest level of depravity. As in the Maha Thamada ideal, humanity realizes its plight and again begins the ascent to morality. At this point the last universal monarch appears to bring the world under the rule of law in preparation for the advent of the Buddha Metteyya. Maha Thamada is the beginning of the cycle; Sankha and Metteyya are the end.

As the supreme temporal ideal in Buddhist kingship, the *cakkavatti* became the same standard for Burmese kingship, which took on many of the formal attributes of cakkavattiship in its rituals and verbal formulae. Many Burmese kings tried to associate their style with that of a *cakkavatti*. At the investiture of a crown prince, for example, the assembled courtiers chanted a formula comparing him with the son of the *cakkavatti* described in the *Anguttara nikaya*.[26] Many royal ceremonies, especially the *abhiseka*, or concecration of a new king, included stock verbal formulae emphasizing his long life and good health, two of the *cakkavatti* qualities described in the *Maha sudassana suttanta*, a Pali Buddhist text.[27] Similarly, the *Glass Palace Chronicle* includes a list of the twelve duties of a *cakkavatti* in its section on *raja dhamma* and principles of good government.[28] The comparison is further implied in the standard appellation of Burmese kingship as *min-taya-gyi*, or "king of righteousness." Many other elements in Kon-baung kingship provide further evidence of the emulation of the *cakkavatti* ideal, notably the emphasis on great treasure, a large harem, white elephants, and the maintenance of Shan and other vassal rulers as subordinate but legitimate sovereigns, such that the Burmese monarch was truly a "king of kings."

Remembering the special roles of Maha Thamada and Sankha, however, it is clear that not all *cakkavattis* are of equal significance. The concept definitely contains a notion that certain times call forth a special realization of this ideal, and this was a model with which at least some Kon-baung kings sought to identify themselves. For instance, in comparing the role of Alaung-hpaya in the chaotic Burma of 1752 with that of Maha Thamada, early Kon-baung writers clearly sought to project him as a special *cakkavatti* figure. In the case of Alaung-hpaya the reason appears to have been that the *cakkavatti* concept was politically very emotive, especially in the peasant world, because of its association with the advent of Metteyya. This matter cannot be explored further, however, without first examining briefly the *bodhisatta* concept in Burmese kingship.

Historically, the term *bodhisatta* has gone through a considerable evolution in meaning. Basically denoting a being who is on the verge of becoming a buddha, it was originally applied to the Buddha Gotama between the period of his going forth and attainment of *nibbana*. Subsequently, it came to be applied to him from his conception, then to all buddhas from conception to *nibbana*, then to all earth beings who were ultimately to reach buddhahood, and finally to the gods.[29] The Theravada *bodhisatta* becomes so as a result of *kamma*, attains insight, and, after a strong plea by Brahma, undertakes the wearisome task of teaching the world out of his pity for all living beings. When his teaching is firmly established, the *bodhisatta* rejects the remainder of his allotted life and achieves *nibbana*. Although without much emphasis, Therevada Buddhism implicitly admits that as there are buddhas to come after Gotama and Metteyya, there are *bodhisattas* at work in the world performing deeds of mercy and charity, as did the Buddha Gotama during his various lives. The essence of the *bodhisatta* concept is therefore the self-renunciation of *nibbana* to assist others in their salvation. Since bodhisattahood is achieved through *kamma*, kings with their already massive merit and *cakkavatti* associations have advanced claims to this status.

The notion of the king as *bodhisatta* may be related to the strong emphasis in Burmese Buddhism on spiritual relief in the present, as opposed to the daunting lengths of time laid out in orthodox Buddhism for the next "savior" to appear. The concern with present relief is reflected in aspects such as the popularity of charity-derived merit and the redefinition of the role of the *arahats* from full realization of the monk ideal to guardians of the faith until the coming of Metteyya. The popular cults focused on the unorthodox notion of the *set-kya min*, or lower order of superman, who appears prior to Sankha to begin restoring the world to order.[30] Incorporation of the bodhisattahood of the ruler into the conception of kingship may have helped to satisfy in yet another way the popular yearning for immediate higher intervention on behalf of the public spiritual weal.

The idea of the bodhisattahood of Burmese kings was already well established in the Pagan period, when all kings styled themselves as such and many prayed for buddhahood.[31] The Shwei-gu-gyi inscription of Alaung Si-thu (1113–1165?) in 1131 is surely the most eloquent statement of the *bodhisatta* yearnings of kings of any period in Burmese history:

> By this my gift, whatever boon ensues
> Be it the best of boons, to profit all!
> By this abundant merit I desire
> Here nor hereafter no angelic pomp
> Of Brahmas, Suras, Maras; nor the state
> And splendour of a king; nay, nor the steps
> Sublime of pupils of the Conqueror.
> But I would make my body a bridge
> Athwart the river of samsara and all
> Folk would speed across thereby
> Until they reached the blessed city.
> I myself would cross and drag the drowning over.[32]

It should be noted, however, that while a *cakkavatti* cannot be a *bodhisatta*, a *bodhisatta* may be a *cakkavatti* in some of his existences, as was indeed the Buddha Gotama. Important as the *cakkavatti* ideal was as a temporal norm of kingship, it was subordinated to and incorporated into the *bodhisatta* ideal for Burmese kings. Since bodhisattahood, cakkavattihood, and even kingship itself were determined by *kamma*, the extent to which a given ruler aspired to be a *bodhisatta* in a *cakkavatti* existence, a special *cakkavatti*, or, most commonly, a king associating himself with the *cakkavatti* norm was dependent on his *kamma*. The strength of the royal *kamma* was manifested physically in the *hpon*, *let-yon*, and *a-na* of the ruler. *Hpon* was a kind of charismatic glory, *let-yon* was force of character and personal ability, and *a-na* was authority and dominion. Thus, the personal qualities of the king and the extent of his dominion were the visible measure of his *kamma*.

Rulers who on this basis had reason to believe in the strength of their *kamma* put forth higher claims.

In the most extreme case in the Pagan period, Kyan-zit-tha (1084–1113) in an inscription of 1098 bluntly claimed to be a *bodhisatta* in a *cakkavatti* existence: "the king of kings, the lord supreme, the mighty universal monarch, who makes his vehicle the white elephant, the omniscient bodhisattva, who shall verily be a buddha and save from misery all living creatures."[33] This claim was surpassed by Alaung-hpaya, however, whose style during his Syriam, Pegu, Manipur, and Thailand campaigns was to issue proclamations explaining that he was an embryo buddha and *cakkavatti* ordained by prophecy, engaged in spreading the true religion in the world.[34] In at least one instance, specific reference was made to the *Anagatavamsa*, a well-known Pali text foretelling the advent of Sankha and Metteyya. The events of his own swift and spectacular rise to power appear to have provided steady reinforcement for Alaung-hpaya's own deeply rooted conviction of his kammatic destiny, a conviction apparently shared by many, as there was a widespread popular belief that he was a *bodhisatta*.[35] In light of the reference to the *Anagatavamsa*, Alaung-hpaya probably saw himself not only in the role of a special *cakkavatti*, but specifically as the *cakkavatti* associated with the coming of Metteyya.

The progressive deterioration of Burma in the first half of the eighteenth century, culminating in the destruction of the kingdom and the sudden reversal of national fortune under Alaung-hpaya, may well have appeared to the people to herald the arrival of an important eschatological milestone. It was, of course, impossible in orthodox terms for Alaung-hpaya to present himself both as Sankha and as a *bodhisatta*, but given the undeniable physical manifestations of his *kamma* and the strong *bodhisatta* tradition in Burmese kingship, this contradiction apparently inhibited neither his aspirations nor those of the people for him. In view of the turbulence and insecurity of the times and the significance such conditions would have had to a people schooled in Buddhist eschatology, the *bodhisatta* aspect of Alaung-hpaya's kingship was probably popularly welcomed as evidence of a benevolent higher force at work in a troubled world. Alaung-hpaya's charismatic rise to power may also have enabled him to give expression to the essence of the popular messianic cults, because there is some emphasis on the assistance he received from Sakka, king of the gods, and in particular Sakka's magic lance, the basic attribute of the *set-kya min* of popular belief.[36]

Whatever the case may have been, by linking his claim to special *cakkavatti* status to an association with the advent of Metteyya,

Alaung-hpaya left his successors little room for maneuver in terms of "superman" aspirations. There is no information on the three-year reign of Naung-daw-gyi in this respect, but his successor Hsin-hpyu-shin strongly associated himself with the general attributes of a *cakkavatti*, though avoiding specific claim to that status, perhaps out of deference to his father. Both Hsin-hpyu-shin and his son Sin-gu made strong prayers for buddhahood in their espousal of the *bodhisatta* mission.[37] Possessed of a strong personality and sharing his father's deep conviction of kammatic destiny, Bo-daw-hpaya appears to have been led by several circumstances to take a step far beyond that taken by Alaung-hpaya. The fifth ruler of the Kon-baung dynasty was a man of deep and orthodox religious belief. As his reign progressed, he became increasingly disillusioned with the lax state of the *sangha*, which resisted his best efforts to reform it. The measure of this disillusionment was recorded by the British Resident Hiram Cox after a conversation with the king in 1797:

> It appears that his majesty is much dissatisfied with the present state of religion in his dominions, and meditates some great changes. He has found the priesthood in general miserably ignorant; even his arch-priest he doubts. He says they read over their canonical books when they first enter on the monastic life, as a task imposed on schoolboys; and although they have no other employment to engage their attention, they never afterwards investigate or inquire into the mystical meaning of their rites; so they are totally unfit to instruct the people. Hence the various abuses that have crept into their religion . . . all of which are cloaks for hypocrisy and unauthorized by the tenets of their faith.[38]

Given the causal relationship in Burmese thought between immorality and natural and social deterioration, Bo-daw-hpaya may well have found a connection between the natural disasters of the ensuing years, notably the great drought and famine and the attendant social disintegration and rebellions of 1805–1814, with his view of the immorality of the *sangha*. If this was indeed the case, his notion that the deterioration of the *sangha* along with the resulting ignorance and immorality of the people was responsible for the disintegration of society does much to explain the extraordinary step he took in 1812. Having already left the capital twelve years earlier for permanent residence at Min-gun, the site of a huge pagoda he had ordered constructed, Bo-daw-hpaya held a series of conferences with the leading monks of the realm to try to persuade them that the five-thousand-year duration of his teaching predicted by the Buddha Gotama had elapsed and that Bo-daw-hpaya himself was the Buddha Metteyya ready to propound a new teaching. The monks successfully demonstrated to the contrary, however, and in his wrath the king

> compelled his own head chaplain and several of the chiefs to abandon the order. As to the rest he ordered them to be conducted to the confines of the kingdom and banished forever. But as difficulties occurred in the execution of this order, it was commuted into a prohibition of supplying them with provisions or rendering them any assistance under pain of losing a hand and of calling on them to perform any act of religion under pain of death. On publication of this order numbers of Talapoins quitted the order and others fled into the villages.[39]

Despite the few known facts about this episode, taking into account the Burmese belief in the cosmic relationship between public morality and social and natural dysfunction, Bo-daw-hpaya's age (he was then sixty-seven), and his by all accounts eccentric and austere personality, it does not seem unreasonable to conjecture that his personal religious conviction and revulsion over the unorthodoxies and low standards in the *sangha* motivated his actions. Yet more than simply an attempt to purify the monkhood, as had been the tradition in Burmese kingship, Bo-daw-hpaya sought to launch a new and pure form of religion. Contributing factors were certainly a strong belief in his own *kamma* and the impetus provided by both the *cakkavatti* and *bodhisatta* traditions in Burmese kingship to repair the temporal and spiritual decay of the times. It can be further conjectured that Bo-daw-hpaya's identification of himself with Metteyya rather than some lesser but more believable expression of kammatic achievement *cum* cosmic necessity was, in his mind, the natural consequence of his father's identification, however vague, with Metteyya's harbinger Sankha.[40]

The importance of the concepts of *cakkavatti* and *bodhisatta* to the historical traditions of Burmese kingship relate directly to the dual function of the Burmese state. The *cakkavatti* concept and, in particular, the idea of the "special *cakkavatti*" as embodied in Maha Thamada and Sankha, lay at the root of the state's regulatory function, while the *bodhisatta* concept was the idealization of the reformation function. Both concepts served as reminders of the perfection and righteousness of the past and future Buddhist utopias, lost through immorality and to be regained through morality. The reformation function of the Burmese state was to turn men from political animals into moral beings so that all might gain utopia. Given the eschatological implications of the obvious contemporary moral and social degeneration in early Konbaung times, these concepts were vital and emotive to rulers and ruled alike.

The State as an Agency of Salvation

The *cakkavatti* and *bodhisatta* concepts were central and deeply rooted ideals in Burmese kingship, but they were in the end dependent on the qualities of *kamma*, *hpon*, *let-yon*, and *a-na* perceived in the individual ruler. In the sense that Burmese kingship was synonymous with the state, however, it also involved institutional aspects that were independent of kingly individuality. Although lacking the charismatic and salvational appeal of the *cakkavatti* and *bodhisatta*, these mechanisms were perhaps the most important means by which the state served to advance the salvational ends of its people.

The verbal formulae of most royal ceremonies contain a phrase which epitomizes these institutional aspects of the salvational function of the state. During the consecration ceremony of the king, for example, he is required to state: "Being free from illness and disease and having a long life, I shall be able to rule well for the welfare of the religion, my sons, my grandsons, and all the people."[41] The welfare of the people was viewed in religious terms, and meant a strict maintenance of *dhamma* and responsibility for the kammatic well-being of the populace. The most developed statement of the welfare concept is found in a panegyric composed by the royal preceptor on the occasion of Bo-daw-hpaya's second *abhiseka*, or kingly consecration. The author states that Bo-daw-hpaya showed favor to the world by forbidding demeritorious acts and encouraging meritorious works, by observing the traditional duty of kings of yore to patronize the world through the four *sangahas* and other kingly duties, and concludes: "The king strictly followed this path taken by the righteous kings of old . . . thus he showed favor to the world continuously and intermittently to a marvelous degree and in an unheard of manner."[42] A more succinct expression of the welfare idea is found in the monumental list of royal titles prefacing the royal letter of 1795 to Sir John Shore, Governor-General of India: "this great king . . . whose understanding by divine aid, is enlightened to guide his people in the right way, and preserve them in pious obedience and the road of true religion."[43]

The state concern for the spiritual welfare of its subjects basically took the form of a complex involvement in the preservation and enhancement of the *kamma* of the people. The main elements in this involvement were the enforcement of morality and the making and sharing of merit through the agency of the state. The core of Buddhist morality is observance of the five precepts of abstention from the taking of life, theft, falsehood, illicit sex, and alcohol and rulers were in the habit of urging such observance on their subjects through proclamation. At the beginning of Lent, for example, this proclamation was read aloud throughout the capital area: "Subjects, now that Lent has arrived, killing, theft, falsehood, adultery, and drinking spirit must not be done and the five precepts, the eight precepts, and the ten precepts observed. Offerings, observance of precepts, practice of meditation, attitudes of kindness and benevolence—all these should be done."[44] In like fashion, Bo-daw-hpaya had proclaimed that for five days each month throughout the country "All subjects must always observe the four important precepts," and Ba-gyi-daw on his accession ordered the people to observe the five precepts, an order he had repeated throughout the realm monthly for a year.[45]

In Burmese eyes observance of the precepts was not important in the positive sense of making merit, but was extremely important in the negative sense of avoiding *akusala*, or demerit. In this negative sense, the early Kon-baung rulers attempted to protect the level of the popular *kamma* by enforcing the precepts by the sword. Alaung-hpaya issued strong edicts prohibiting cattle butchery, hunting, gambling, use of alcohol, hemp, and opium, and the practice of animal sacrifices to village and field *nats* at harvest time.[46] Mass deviance from the precepts often occurred at *nat* festivals, hence the major *nat* festivals were subject to regulation by officers of the Hlut-taw to ensure the absence of intoxicants, drugs, and animal sacrifice.[47] Acts counter to the moral precepts were forbidden, paradoxically on pain of death, in order to protect the people from "the consequences of indulgence in these acts on their *kamma*, remembering the effect of *kamma*, which says that an evil act done habitually brings forth evil fruit even in one's own lifetime."[48]

Beyond the regulation of public morality, the king was responsible for the kammatic advancement of the people in two other respects. He was the center of a complex of state merit-making and merit-sharing activities directed at the general populace and, more importantly, he was steward of the monkhood, the chief focus of merit-making for the laity. The thrust of state merit-making and merit-sharing centered on the construction of religious edifices, mainly pagodas, the feeding of monks, and the cycle of state ceremonies and festivals.[49]

To a greater or lesser extent, all of the early Kon-baung monarchs built pagodas and other religious edifices, acts which were carefully recorded in their obituaries. Bo-daw-hpaya built seventy-five assorted pagodas, monasteries, ponds, and rest houses, but even the brief and turbulent reign of Naung-daw-gyi saw the construction of five such projects.[50] Bo-daw-hpaya's gigantic Min-gun Pagoda project and his construction of one pagoda in each of the 230 districts of the realm are excellent examples of state merit-making for the public weal.

The usual means of lay merit-making was fulfillment of the mundane needs of monks. The state was also active in this area in connection with the eight major events of the Buddhist calendrical cycle such as the New Year, the beginning and the end of Lent, and *kahtein-daw-bwe*, the annual monastic robe festival. At these times, eight monks were fed at each of sixteen specified places in the palace and surrounding fort, including the eight gates of the outer wall, the four gates of the palace compound, and the Hlut-taw.[51] The feeding of 148 monks eight times a year was a substantial act of state merit-making. That it was directed at the realm is indicated by the location of the feeding points in the palace and fort, the symbolic center of the kingdom.

A prime example of state merit-making was the *kahtein-daw-bwe*, which was a major collective merit-making occasion at all levels of Burmese society. Here again the state organized a festival centered on the palace and related festivals at the major provincial centers.[52] Crown revenues were also employed in these centers to finance the state merit-making activities in connection with the main points of the calendrical cycle.[53] There was also apparently a custom that crown funds were disbursed to at least some of the higher-status crown service units to be used for the New Year's feasting of monks.[54] There is no way to estimate the amount of crown revenue invested in such state merit-making, but it must have been substantial. The resulting network of state merit-making activities that focused on both the capital and provinces in connection with the Buddhist calendrical cycle was certainly one of the major cohesive forces in the early Kon-baung polity.

State merit-making was a minor contribution to the religious welfare of the people, however, because ultimate salvation was dependent on individual effort. The people focused their efforts on the *sangha*, which served as collective savior. The state and the people therefore had an immediate concern both for the purity and orthodoxy of the monkhood as a whole and the conduct of individual monks, whose degree of personal purity and piety determined the amount of merit accrued to their supporters. An impious, ignorant monk was of little value. The spiritual welfare of the populace did then depend to no little extent upon the standards and orthodoxy set within the *sangha*. Of even more concern was the fact that if the monks as the guardians of the Buddha's teaching became too corrupt and unorthodox, the religion would not last its allotted five thousand years. In his stewardship of the monkhood, therefore, the king was in fact ruling "for the welfare of the religion, my sons, my grandsons, and all the people."

One of the interesting aspects of Theravada Buddhism is the continuing need to purify and reform the *sangha*. This problem arose immediately on the death of the Buddha and appears to lie in the nature of Buddhism itself. There is a highly venerated set of texts that establish the authority for orthodoxy, but every monk is ultimately responsible only to himself. As such, new schools within the order constantly appear and disappear in proportion to the charismatic authority of their creators. What modern writers generally refer to as "the *sangha*" was, in fact, an agglomeration of many little *sanghas* with nothing originally linking them but doctrine and practice. Such a situation inevitably created serious problems of doctrinal deviation, especially deviation from the *Vinaya*, or canon law, of the monkhood. Deviation from the *Vinaya*, in turn, raised the issue of the ordination of new monks, which required the participation of a certain number of validly ordained monks. If the moral conduct of the ordaining monks was doubtful, so too was the ordination of new monks. At various points in the histories of Burma, Thailand, and Ceylon it was found to be impossible to assemble enough validly ordained monks to ordain new monks and royal patrons sent monks to be reordained abroad where the credentials of the *sangha* were not in question. The resolution of this problem is one of the main topics in Buddhist historical writing.

The relationship between state and *sangha* in Burma stemmed from the view of the Indian monarch Asoka developed by Theravadin historians in Ceylon. In historical terms, it is unclear if Asoka was a Buddhist or even that he had more than a superficial understanding of Buddhist doctrine and its temporal implications. He is known to have constructed but a few pagodas and confined himself to the practical side of religion. Yet Asoka came to be a figure of importance second only to the Buddha himself in Buddhist historiography.[55] Some of Asoka's appeal for later Buddhists was because he was an obvious *cakkavatti* figure who renounced martial for *dhamma* conquest. But most of his attraction stemmed from the fact that he effected the first purification of the *sangha* and thereby saved early Buddhism from its inherent schismatic tendencies.

Asoka's concern for the purity of the *sangha* derived from his philosophy of the state, which saw society as comprised of diverse social and legal status groups, each governed by its own traditional law. The duty of government was to protect the various groups of hermits and ascetics, of which the Buddhist monks were but one, from internal and external disruption, but in particular to assure preservation of their traditional law.56 Thus, Asoka saw as part of his legal duty the preservation of the *sangha* in accordance with the *Vinaya* canon. In one of the important episodes of early Buddhism, he used the authority of the state to purge the order of undisciplined and improperly ordained monks. The execution of the act was done with a minimum of interference and in accord with the principles of the *Vinaya*. Because Buddhism was brought to Ceylon during the reign and under the patronage of Asoka by his son Mahinda, his stance toward the *sangha* became the model for the Ceylonese and later the Burmese kings, who were influenced by the Buddhist commentaries and histories produced in Ceylon. In this literature, Asoka was transformed from the historical reality of a tolerant ruler attempting to apply a just law and rule in a multireligious society into a fierce sectarian of Theravada Buddhism.57

So important was the Asokan legend in Theravada Buddhism that, from the Pagan period on the model of Asoka's kingship pervaded the styles and behavior of Burmese kings. Some of Asoka's titles, such as "lord of earth and water," were taken over and became standard usage. In emulation of Asoka it was not uncommon for kings to wait three or four years before receiving the *abhiseka*. Similarly, an important source of the pagoda building tradition of Burmese kings lies in the Theravada legend, which credits Asoka with the construction of a pagoda in each of the eighty-four thousand towns of the southern island of Jambudipa. Early in his reign, for example, Bo-daw-hpaya ordered a pagoda built in each of the 230 districts of the kingdom. The *Konbaung-zet* remarks of this action: "Keen in his benevolence, the king thought, 'Like Siridhammasoka [Asoka] built pagodas for merit, I too will build pagodas for merit.'"58 The royal practice of sending missionaries to the Shan areas, Laos, and Arakan was also modeled on legendary Asokan missionary activities.

The most important aspect of the Asokan model, however, was the concept of the regulation of the *sangha* by the secular power. Over the course of Burmese history secular control was developed in its practical applications by individual monarchs in response to specific crises over ordination, doctrinal deviation, and monastic indiscipline. By the early

Kon-baung period, state control of the *sangha* was beyond question, and the *sangha* itself was administered by a secular department of religious affairs under an appointed *wun*. The Burmese *sangha* had come to be treated administratively as if it were another crown service group, which, given its central importance to the salvational function of the state, it somewhat resembled in function. Religious affairs in general and the *sangha* in particular are discussed as administrative problems in chapter 4.

Legitimacy

The legitimacy of kingship rested on the acknowledged need for some agency to perform the regulatory and reformation functions necessary to ensure both temporal and spiritual well-being. Thus, the institution was never called into question in theory or actuality, but was simply accepted as a necessary part of life. Those who came to occupy the throne, however, found it necessary to justify themselves as worthy of the office. Kingship went unquestioned, but individual kings did not. Because the rationale and models of Burmese kingship were drawn from Buddhism, it was only natural that rulers should seek their legitimacy there as well. There were basically two Buddhist-derived credentials which early Kon-baung rulers used to legitimize themselves. One drew on the doctrine of *kamma* and the other used the concept of lineage found in Buddhist historiography. Because the early Kon-baung rulers suffered problems of legitimacy not faced by their predecessors of the Restored Taung-ngu period, both of these credentials were fully employed.

The kammatic basis of kingship was part of that aspect of Burmese social ideology which used the doctrine of *kamma* to rationalize the inequalities in the social order. As the apex of the social order, the king represented a massive concentration of merit. Thus, the holding of power was not an accident of history, but the ineluctable result of the fundamental natural law that applied with equal force to all beings.

The centrality of the idea of the kammatic source of kingship is evident in early Kon-baung sources. Proclamations and edicts often began with the formula: "Inasmuch as my *kamma* has designated the kingship for me in this life." Panegyrics, court odes, and royal inscriptions also abound with such references. The usual way of announcing the death of a king was "wearied of the world of people, [he] has gone to enjoy the world of the spirits."[59] As this stock phraseology implies, kingship appears to have been the highest level of merit achievable in one's birth as a human, after which the next level of existence was expected to be that of one of the lower orders of spirits. Because the spirits were able and willing to come to the aid of humans, here may lie the explanation for the royal custom of casting and venerating portrait statues of the immediate royal ancestors.[60] Kingship was therefore a rung, albeit a high one, on the samsaric ladder. The main source of popular veneration and awe of the ruler stemmed from his so obviously superior morality, as evidenced by his kammatic achievement. As with the social order, in the case of kingship *kamma* is again seen as a measurable commodity. Because kingship was an inherently *akusala*, or demeritorious function, the king of all people was most in need of kammatic neutralization. While the nature of most of the state merit-making activity discussed above indicates that it was obviously directed at the realm, much of the pagoda and monastery building by rulers was clearly private and intended to maintain the ruler's kammatic score.[61]

Yet the sociopolitical implications of the doctrine of *kamma* are deceptive. In view of the fact that degree of merit is related to degree of morality, it becomes obvious that a ruler of low merit as manifested in his *hpon*, *let-yon*, and *a-na* could not have the moral qualities necessary to fulfill the functions of kingship. A ruler who failed to fulfill the needs of *raja dhamma* had *ipso facto* low merit because he lacked sufficient morality. *Kamma* and *raja dhamma* were therefore directly linked. In keeping with the Burmese notion of kammatic flux, the merit of a ruler could decrease during his reign to a point where it was insufficient to maintain him on the throne, or even alive. A contemporary Kon-baung comment on precisely this point is given in the *Glass Palace Chronicle* in reference to the rise and fall of King Saw Yahan of Pagan (931–964):

> Although in verity King Saw Yahan should have utterly perished, having killed a king while he was yet a farmer, he attained even to the kingship simply by strong *kamma* of his good actions done in the past. . . . [T]hough all creatures may strive hard to become wealthy and great, they shall not speed if there is not the *kamma* of their previous acts. . . . When Saw Yahan . . . stood in front of the palace and cried, "Who shall be king while I live?," the *kamma* of his past good acts was exhausted insomuch that the stone statue at the door pushed him down and he fell head foremost from the palace-front and died.[62]

In similar fashion, Alaung-hpaya and his supporters often attacked Maha Dama Ya-za Di-pati of Ava for his failure to adhere to *raja dhamma* and maintained that the *kamma* and merit of the latter had come to an end.63 Likewise, the retinue of Sin-gu attributed the revolt of Maung Maung in 1782 to the low *hpon* and *kamma* of their leader.64 Thus, kammatic flux could imbue royal politics with a certain volatility because the signs of strong *kamma* conferred legitimacy, but evidence to the contrary immediately called into question the regal worthiness of the incumbent.

Although *kamma* was the dominant factor in royal legitimacy, lineage, too, was an important royal credential because being of the royal race was one of the classic attributes of kingship. The *Anguttara nikaya*, for example, says that the first of the four qualities of a king is to be well-born, "pure in descent as far back as seven generations both of mother and father."65 Similar statements are common in the *niti* literature and were repeated in Burmese texts.66 Indeed, in the Burmese context to be of royal race meant to be part of a royal lineage reaching back to a mythic founder figure. There were, in fact, two competing origin stories of the Burmese royal lineage. In the older story, a quasi-divine hero named Pyu-saw-hti, the result of a liaison between a serpent princess and the sun spirit, founded Pagan and the royal lineage after relieving the land of preternatural oppression. The resulting race of kings was known as the solar or sun dynasty.67 This origin legend survived well into the early Kon-baung period, and was repeated in detail in the principal biography of Alaung-hpaya from that time.68 Indeed, in his earliest extant edicts Alaung-hpaya styled himself as "Alaung-min-taya-gyi of the solar lineage."69

The competing founder was, of course, Maha Thamada. Buddhist historiography gave a detailed account of the lines of kings descending from Maha Thamada to the founding of Kapilavatthu and the origin of the Sakyan line. One line of kings was traced to Okkaka of Benares, whose eldest son Okkamukha became the founder of Kapilavatthu. The origin of the Sakyan line stems from the four brothers of Okkamukha who, because no princesses of suitable blood were available, married their sisters to keep the line pure. Thus, the Sakyan or "pure" lineage came into being and descended through 82,010 kings to the grandfather of the Buddha. The first claim to a direct relationship between the Burmese royal lineage and the Sakyan lineage of Buddhist historiography appeared in court poetry in the 1770s, and entered the chronicle genre in the following decade with the compilation of the *New Pagan Chronicle*.70 This text attributes the origin of the first Burmese kingdom of Tagaung to a migration of Sakyans fleeing the destruction of Kapilavatthu. In spite of its emphasis on the Pyu-saw-hti story, the biography of Alaung-hpaya mentioned above also makes a few vague Sakyan allusions.

These claims became more elaborate over time, with later Kon-baung documents emphasizing that the royal lineage of Burma was an unbroken line of kings reaching back directly to Maha Thamada. The compilers of the *Glass Palace Chronicle* in 1829–1832 extended the unbroken lineage concept to its ultimate conclusion. By rewriting history where necessary and subjecting earlier chronicles to detailed criticism, the compilers of this chronicle completely sakyanized the early royal lineage of Burma. In the process the Pyu-saw-hti origin story was carefully demolished and Pyu-saw-hti incorporated into the line with appropriate Sakyan forebears. The chroniclers then set out to prove that the term "solar lineage" had nothing to do with the alleged original parentage of Pyu-saw-hti, but was in fact the appellation of the unbroken lineage of Maha Thamada. The purpose of this lengthy scholastic exercise, say the compilers, was "to make plain the lineage of the Burmese kings, who were descended in unbroken succession from the Sakyan race."[71] The unbroken lineage extending back to Maha Thamada became one of the stock formulae placed in the mouths of all the early Kon-baung kings by the chroniclers, and the *Glass Palace Chronicle* itself represents the culmination of a trend to reinterpret the notion of the solar lineage in terms of orthodox Buddhist historiography. Burma was made an extension of this historiography by various adjustments to early Burmese history, enabling the early Kon-baung rulers to draw on a more coherent and impressive source of legitimacy as lineal descendants of Maha Thamada, the most orthodox source of temporal political authority.

The ultimate incorporation of the original Burmese founder king by the founder king of orthodox Buddhism should not obscure the fact that the two origin stories share a common concern for the ideas of the unbroken lineage and the pure lineage. The ideal of purity represented by the Sakyan lineage was also present in the concept of the solar lineage derived from Pyu-saw-hti who was, in fact, given many of the attributes of cakkavattiship. The two lineage ideals were also expressed in the custom of having more than one major queen and the extensive sister and cousin marriage practiced within the royal family.

As the first ruler of the Kon-baung dynasty, Alaung-hpaya had to surmount formidable problems of legitimacy. Occupying the hereditary office of *kyei-gaing* of Mok-hso-bo, he came from a family that had been established as local officials in the Mu Valley area some ten generations earlier and was well intermarried with other gentry families.[72] From the fall of Ava in 1752 until October 1754, Maha Dama Ya-za Di-pati was captive in Pegu and his heir apparent, the Shwei-daung prince, remained at large in northern Burma. Thus, until he mustered sufficient strength bound to his cause, Alaung-hpaya had to present himself as an agent for the restoration of the existing royal house. Fairly early on, however, he broke with the ineffectual Shwei-daung prince, took on the attributes of a monarch, built a traditional palace, and transformed his town of Mok-hso-bo into the royal city of Yadana Thein-hka.

Lacking any immediate connection with the royal lineage, Alaung-hpaya based his claim to the throne on his undeniable *hpon*, *let-yon*, and *kamma* and the lack of these qualities in his rival Maha Dama Ya-za Di-pati. He also made good use of the omens and prophecies which circulated in profusion in Burma to identify himself as a foreordained king *cum* savior figure.[73] This effort was so successful that in the latter half of his reign he was able to present himself as a Buddhist superman. Although there are few extant primary materials for his reign, it also appears that a necessary task in his quest for legitimacy was to claim to be of the solar lineage.

Alaung-hpaya was brilliantly successful in establishing his rule on the basis of his personal qualities, but his successors needed the justification of lineage, so links between his family lineage and the royal lineage were established at two points. Alaung-hpaya's forebears were traced to the brothers Narathein-hka (1170–1173) and Narapati Si-thu (1173–1210), the son of the former marrying the daughter of the latter to launch this offshoot of the royal lineage in the later Pagan period. Kingship again returned to the line in the person of Mo-hnyin Thado of Ava (1427–1440), whose younger brother Wa-ba Naw-rahta was made an official in the northern area. The story continues that the descendants of Wa-ba Naw-rahta held posts in the various towns of this area until the birth of Alaung-hpaya in 1714.[74] Wa-ba Naw-rahta himself was probably a historical personage, but G. H. Luce and Than Tun have shown on the basis of epigraphy that despite the royal genealogies given in the eighteenth- and nineteenth-century chronicles, no such king as Narathein-hka existed in the Pagan period.[75] This strongly suggests that this connection was fabricated to strengthen the lineage basis of Alaung-hpaya's legitimacy. The interesting and at present unanswerable question is whether the royal links were developed during his reign or posthumously. Whatever the case, it was necessary for later chroniclers to continue the links to preserve the dual attributes of the unbroken and the pure lineage.

By necessity, throughout the early Kon-baung period primary stress was laid on the unbroken lineage. The corresponding claims to pure lineage had to be downplayed until the reign of Bo-daw-hpaya, when a new generation of princes and princesses were extensively intermarried, a practice that characterized the remainder of the dynasty. Although Alaung-hpaya had successfully surmounted the legitimacy problem on the basis of *kamma*, the issue of lineage remained a problem for him and, despite their efforts, for his successors. Lineage as a qualification for kingship was important enough that even such peasant rebels as Nga Hpon in 1782 and Nga Taw-nge in 1805 found it necessary to represent themselves as long lost princes of the blood. While the popular yearnings for order and grace may have been such that Alaung-hpaya and his successors were accepted on the basis of *kamma* by most of the population, there is literary evidence to suggest that some of the more sophisticated remained dissatisfied with the credentials of the Kon-baung line, at least until the reign of Bo-daw-hpaya.[76] Until the accession of that monarch in 1782, the legitimacy issue remained a factor of some importance in early Kon-baung politics.

Brahmanic Aspects

The Indian tradition had yet another powerful influence on Burmese kingship through the science of secular statecraft known as Arthashastra. This corpus of Machiavellian maxims and aphorisms on polity and politics apparently grew from the teachings of various wandering sophists and was later systematized by such writers as Kautalya and Kamandaka.[77] The influence of these works was considerable and early, a direct reference to one of them occurring in an inscription as early as 1442.[78] Such works were known both in India and Burma as *niti*, a Sanskrit-Pali word meaning "conduct" in its abstract sense, and used as a general term for any work of moral or practical guidance.

There were at least four *niti* compilations in Burma, the two most popular being the *Loka niti* and the *Raja niti*. These are thought to have been composed in the fifteenth century in Pali and later translated into Burmese. Both were popular handbooks that were much studied by the eighteenth-century Burmese, the *Loka niti* in particular being a standard text in monastic schools. An analysis of the 167 stanzas of this work indicates that 60 percent of the 90 traceable stanzas were drawn from Sanskrit-Brahmanic sources such as the *Hitopadesa*, *Mahabharata*, *Pancatantra*, and particularly the work of Kautalya.[79] The *Raja niti* were in the main derived from the Arthashastra literature. Despite the Sanskrit-Brahmanic origins of their contents, however, the *Loka niti* and *Raja niti* produced in Burma were unique in that the text was expanded and explicitly Hindu ideas were Buddhicized.

The main emphases in the *Loka niti* were the untrustworthiness of others and the need for self-protection, the value of learning and wisdom, wealth as a personal goal ("wealth in this world is a great friend"), and the absolute supremacy of royal authority and prerogatives.[80] The *Raja niti* stressed as the bases of royal power wealth, military might, fortresses, imperial aggrandizement through conquest, wise and loyal officials, and careful scrutiny and control of subjects and officials. There is a particular emphasis on the Brahmanic concept of *danda*: "The pride of low people increases by the display of too much forbearance; by the chastisement of a bad person, others should be deterred from acting like him; by chastisement he is made to desist from evil; by chastisement the king bestows happiness."[81]

The influence of the *niti* literature is also suggested by the fact that the early eighteenth-century *Great Chronicle* and the early nineteenth-century *Glass Palace Chronicle* are both prefaced with substantial extracts from the *Loka* and *Raja niti*. Some surprisingly technical passages about kingcraft extracted from the *Raja niti* appear also in some of the *damathats*:

> It is proper for a king to listen to entertainment in the first watch. In the next watch he hears about the law and customs of the past. In the third watch he sleeps. When he has awakened, standing in front of the northeast corner, saying not even a word, he cleans his teeth with a cleaner which is from a tree with sap, oil and thorn and is a hand span long.... When he has washed his face and reverenced the three gems, he dresses, smiling and with a pleasant countenance. Sitting on his throne... he gives audience first to wise ministers, then to astrologers, then to those learned in medicine, and then to Brahman reciters of *parittas*.[82]

The *Raja niti* stressed wealth as the key element in kingship because wealth enabled the king to maintain a large army to defend and extend his position. Wealth was derived from control of a large domain and the taxation of the people therein. Control was maintained through wise and able ministers. The *Raja niti* concludes: "Therefore with great zeal should a king amass wealth, by this his safety is assured."[83] The Arthashastran approach to kingship in Burma was summarized by Hsin-hpyu-shin in his Po-u-daung inscription of 1774:

> The ruler of Ava was assisted in his government by wise ministers, and was happy in the possession of trustworthy friends. He was the possessor of military weapons, soldiers, horses, elephants, and fortified towns, and received tribute from sixteen states. . . . His capital, Yadana-pu-ra, was the storehouse of all kinds of precious minerals and the repository of all wealth. He was wise, mighty, and powerful, and had reduced to subjection all the other rulers of the world.[84]

This conception of kingship was a reality to Burmese rulers, whose royal positions were based on wealth, military capability, administrative control, and the imperial system.

The Arthashastran tradition of statecraft was the most important Brahmanic element in eighteenth-century Burmese kingship, but another element is worth noting. Because Buddhism specifically eschewed ritual and mystery, Burmese kingship appropriated some aspects of Vedic ceremony and Brahmanic ritual to give itself a highly visible aura of mystery and majesty. Such ritual and ceremony, however, was always performed in a Buddhist context and given a Buddhist motivation. The most important state ceremonies of Brahmanic origin were the *rajabhiseka*, or consecration on elevation to the throne, and the *muddhabhiseka*, or rejuvenation of the royal powers.[85] Offerings were made to Hindu gods at all important state ceremonies, including the *abhiseka*, installation of a crown prince, naming a royal child, ear piercing, hairdressing, marriage, and construction of new thrones, drums, and palaces. The most popular Hindu deities were Ganesh and Bhavani, but also included Vishnu, Paramesvara, and Karttikeya or Skanda.[86]

Brahmans therefore played a prominent role in the formal procedures of the court. Most court Brahmans came from Arakan, but during the reign of Bo-daw-hpaya, who was very interested in secular knowledge and the occult, some Brahmans from India were also imported. Organized as a crown service group under a Brahman chief and a Burmese *wun* and secretary, the Brahmans were diversified in their functions, some specializing in ceremonies, some in *paritta* reciting, others in sacerdotal functions, and still others in particular aspects of astrology. Because of their technical knowledge of astrology, medicine, and science—subjects the monks were theoretically forbidden to pursue—the Brahmans were considered the scientists of the court. In that capacity they prepared almanacs, calculated eclipses, and dealt with the many and varied other astrological needs of the state.[87]

Further evidence of Brahmanic influence can be seen in the large influx of Sanskrit secular works during the early Kon-baung period. Around 60 were imported by Hsin-hpyu-shin and over 250 by Bo-daw-hpaya, all of which were translated into Burmese by the Brahmans and some learned monks. Although Buddhism did provide the king with certain idealized objects such as the wheel, the jewel, the white umbrella, the white elephant, and the flying horse, the Burmese crown derived its real paraphernalia, pomp, ritual, sense of cosmic mystery, and grandeur from the Sanskrit-Brahmanic tradition.

Royal Authority and the Dilemma of Power

The institution of kingship was imbued with absolute and overwhelming authority over all areas of human activity. As the arbiter of all political and social relationships, the ruler gave orders with the force of law and suffered restrictions from no human source. "His will is law and his voice fate" aptly observed a contemporary European visitor.[88] In their relationship to the crown, the people were the *kyei-daw-myo kyun-daw-myo*, or "royal servants," and the king the *athet-u-hsan-baing-thaw-ashin*, or "lord of the life, head, and hair of all beings." The measure of royal authority over the individual in this equation is reflected in the fact that the Burmese consider the head and hair sacred and to touch these an insult. In its application to the individual, royal authority was seen not only as total, but also as arbitrary, intolerant, violent, and often calamitous. Concerning personal property left in care of another person, for example, the *Manu-kye* states: "If the house of the receiver of the property and the property be burned, if the property be stolen, or if the king in his anger shall destroy or take possession of it, and this be proved, let the owner suffer the loss."[89] Burmese hortatory texts and proverbs often viewed kingship and government in their effects as similar to natural calamities and advised avoidance of contact whenever possible.

The omnipotence of kingship was also manifested in the mutability of edicts, offices, and status privileges. The *Manu-kye* specifically observed that a ruler had the power to void all acts and orders of his predecessors except those relating to pagodas and monasteries, and carefully listed sixteen broad categories of civil and criminal suits not prosecutable after the accession of a new king.[90] All the edicts of a ruler were considered to lapse on his death, and it was not uncommon for his successors to issue a few blanket edicts informing the populace that edicts from the previous reigns were in force until specifically modified. Indeed, the enjoyment of any political office and privilege of rank was dependent on the whim of the ruler who granted it, and came to an end with his demise. This power was derived from the Maha Thamada model of kingship in that not only was Maha Thamada to punish, but also to "exalt those who should be exalted." On this point the *Manu-kye* states: "Oh king! If any man or woman shall be exalted by the king, the lord of land and water, as superior to others, let them be considered excellent without reference to the class in which they may originally have had their birth . . . amongst men, he whom the king hath decided to be excellent, is so."[91]

Given that the king alone held the right to grant office and rank, he was the sole arbiter of the social and political order. It was customary for the entire palace establishment to resign *en masse* when the new king first entered the palace but, as with edicts, there was an immediate blanket renewal of most appointments followed by a selective up- and downgrading throughout the entire range of appointive offices. Although the same process theoretically occurred with personal honorific titles and other insignia of rank and status—the physical trappings of which were, in fact, crown property issued by and returnable to the crown treasury—there is no actual evidence that a formal blanket renewal was customary.

The absolute nature of royal authority derived from the uncanny powers or charisma associated with the person of the king. Rulers possessed mystic power as a result of their righteousness, morality, and merit in the same way that pious monks obtained the same power through the virtues accruing from their spiritual quest. This spiritual charisma was one of the attributes of kingship and reflected the moral and kammatic superiority of the monarch over the populace. These qualities made obedience to the ruler close to a religious duty and failure in this duty always brought severe punishment and often death. On this basis the authority of the king was so awesome that even the weakest kings could issue the most extreme orders and have them carried out immediately. No king was in actuality omnipotent, however, hence there are several qualifications which must be added to this point. While possessed of total authority, the real power of the king was limited by the Buddhist sanctions on kingship and his ability to control the administrative machinery of state. Hence orders affecting the capital area were generally executed because the king knew immediately if they were not, but the more general the order the less its chances of execution outside of the capital area. Finally, orders that roused substantial opposition from the people failed and had to be withdrawn, examples being Bo-daw-hpaya's attempts to introduce a coinage in 1797 and to destroy the monkhood in 1812.

Even so, the absolute nature of royal authority placed a dangerous instrument in the hands of even weak rulers and created a dilemma of power in Burmese kingship. Burmese political thought accepted the necessity of kingship to exercise power over society, but power was easily misused or abused by rulers. Thus, the dilemma lay in the association of absolute authority with an imperfect human agency. Some checks therefore had to be placed on the behavior of kings. The orthodox Buddhist interpretation of the doctrine of *kamma* offered long-range deterrence by threatening rulers with retribution in future existences, but early Kon-baung thought applied more immediate sanctions as well. There was first the ever-present deterrent provided by the notion of kammatic flux as a reflection of kingly legitimacy. A second check was the attempt to infuse the monarchy with a sense of higher moral obligation through the concepts of *raja dhamma*, *cakkavatti*, and *bodhisatta*, and the Maha Thamada and Asoka models. Finally, further deterrence came from those aspects of the Arthashastran tradition which emphasized prudence and restraint on the part of the ruler for pragmatic political reasons.[92]

The Bases of Royal Power

The dilemma of power reflected the essential dichotomy between the office and the officeholder in Burmese kingship. The authority of the institution was never called into question, but the power of the incumbent often was. It is therefore important to know what resources the king had at his disposal to enforce his authority and maintain his position. The problem is perhaps most easily approached in terms of the areas of the polity over which the rulers attempted to maintain monopolies. These areas were traditional religious values, armed force, and material and human resources.

Royal legitimacy was basically couched in traditional religious terms, as were the royal roles of *cakkavatti*, *bodhisatta*, and the Maha Thamada and Asoka models. Royal domination of the monkhood was also justified in terms of religious ideology, but further served the Arthashastran end of preventing the *sangha* from competing with the ruler for control of mundane affairs. Only in connection with the message of Buddhist eschatology did the royal monopoly of religious values fail to be complete, as the popular urge for salvational grace was not satisfied by the royal roles and charisma. The peasantry therefore continued to fasten its messianic fantasies not on the ruler (with the exception of Alaung-hpaya), but on nonroyal claimants to the status of Metteyya and his forerunners.

Under most circumstances the royal monopoly of force was also fairly complete. The palace was located inside the royal fort, or *myodaw*, which was physically the largest and strongest structure in the realm. Located within the royal fort were the royal armories, central granaries, and treasuries. It was of prime importance for rebels to seize the palace less because it was the magical center of the kingdom than because it was the main strong point and physical seat of royal power. The crown further maintained a monopoly on firearms and munitions, and brick buildings were permitted only to the crown or for religious purposes. The security connected with the royal fort and the person of the ruler was extensive, as the French envoy Feraud noted in 1770: "The king departed the fort to the sound of cannon and the gates were immediately closed. This is a precaution he takes each time he leaves. . . . One could hardly pass for the press of people in the vicinity and on the walls of the fort; 6000 men armed with muskets, lances, and bamboo staffs guarded the approaches."[93] The security was not as effective as it was impressive, however, because the rebellions of Maung Maung and Nga Hpon in 1782 both demonstrated the ease with which the fort could be penetrated.

The crown also attempted to impose a monopoly on material and human resources. In terms of wealth, most of the production of gold and silver was acquired through special units of miners responsible to the Gold and Silver Tax departments, and the mining and marketing of gemstones and other precious substances were also kept under crown control. The crown monopoly of the agricultural surplus and surplus labor has already been mentioned in chapter 2, as has the basic system of controlling the human resources of the country through the crown service groups, the *athi*, and the *kyeik-su taings*. The motivation here was not only to maximize the bond between human resources and crown service, but also to keep them free of fixed ascriptive rights or connections with other centers of power in the society. The crown monopoly of material resources was reasonably effective, but its attempted monopoly of human resources constituted one of the central administrative problems of the early Kon-baung period.

The instrument for the maintenance of these monopolies was the administrative apparatus. One goal of the monarchy was thus to provide a unified, centralized administrative framework. Such a framework was necessary to achieve the goals of the monopolies, but also required a continuous supply of resources for its own maintenance, hence the monopolies and the administration were mutually sustaining. The administrative apparatus was perhaps the most important physical base of royal power. It was the means by which the king attempted to achieve the control deemed necessary for survival in the Arthashastran tradition of rational politics, and for fulfilling the regulation and reformation functions of Burmese state ideology.

Conclusion

The concept of kingship in Burma was derived primarily from Theravada Buddhist thought and peripherally from the tradition of secular statecraft developed in Brahmanic India. The ideology of the state and the functions and roles of kingship stemmed from the former, while the pragmatic and more technical aspects of government and kingcraft were drawn from the latter. Brahmanic elements were only incorporated selectively, however, and carefully integrated into the dominant Buddhist framework. Burmese kingship was thus characterized by an unequal dualism between the idealism and utopian purpose of its Buddhist-derived ideology of state and the Brahmanic-derived craft of pragmatic politics, which aimed at coping with the problems of governance and political survival in the real world. This dualism was exemplified in the 1774 Po-u-daung inscription of Hsin-hpyu-shin, in which he presented himself with all the attributes and aspirations of an Arthashastran monarch while, at the same time, strongly espousing the Buddhist utopian mission of Burmese state ideology.

Burmese political thought contained a coherent rationale for legitimizing both institutionalized government and the holder of supreme power, and the core of the state ideology lay in the functions of regulation and reformation. Both functions were derived from Theravada Buddhism, which reluctantly accepted the necessity of force in human affairs, but gave the state the higher mission of reforming individuals from degeneracy to morality and offered an ultimate utopian goal. These functions were embodied in the temporal and spiritual ideals of kingship exemplified in the *cakkavatti* and *bodhisatta* traditions. While classical Buddhist thought restricts each to its own sphere, the ideals were merged in Burmese kingship, a merger which in theory enabled royal authority to encompass all areas of human activity.[94] The association of total authority with a human agency, however, created an irresolvable dilemma of power, a situation ameliorated to some extent by recourse to the Buddhist moral conception of kingship, the Burmese interpretation of the doctrine of kammatic flux, and Arthashastran concepts of royal restraint. In the end, the state was unable to translate its absolute authority into total power, both because of these restraints and because it lacked a sufficient level of administrative technology and cohesion, as will be discussed in the next chapter.

CHAPTER 4

ADMINISTRATIVE STRUCTURE AND PROCESS

The fall of the Taung-ngu dynasty brought with it the complete destruction of the administrative structure above the local level. The system was carefully rebuilt during the reign of Alaung-hpaya, but he and his successors made no major structural changes and faced administrative problems similar to those of their Taung-ngu predecessors.[1] The core of the administrative problem was control: of officials, of the extended royal lineage, of revenues and people, and of religious resources and personnel. As such, the administrative goal was to prevent other centers of power from developing within the polity and competing with the monarchy.

In administrative terms, the early Kon-baung polity can be aptly characterized as a "patrimonial-bureaucratic empire," as defined by Stephen Blake.[2] Royal governance was based on a personal, traditional authority, with obedience to the person rather than the office. The ruler maintained a large personal demesne, with a more attenuated rule over the remainder of the realm. Rulers typically travelled about the country often to renew personal bonds and to overcome the problem of poor communication and control stemming from geographic remoteness from the capital. The rulers also maintained extensive intelligence networks, which provided alternate communications channels separate from the formal administrative apparatus. Another form of control was to overlap the responsibilities of both territorial and functional components of the administrative structure. The early Kon-baung administrative apparatus was centralized, departmentalized, and almost minutely differentiated in its functions. *Department* here denotes administrative divisions with either functional or territorial responsibilities. This chapter explores the various aspects of the administrative struc-

The Central Administration

The administrative structure was hierarchical, with authority descending from the king through a central executive organ to a wide range of departments and territorial jurisdictions. This central executive organ was the Hlut-taw, whose ministers, usually but not always four in number, were termed *wun-gyi* and constituted an executive committee overseeing all affairs of state. The second line of management was the office of *wun-dauk*, again usually four in number. The incumbents were in each case ranked in order of importance and were commonly referred to as the first *wun-gyi*, second *wun-gyi*, first *wun-dauk*, and so forth. The two other offices considered in the same echelon with the *wun-gyis* and *wun-dauks* were the *athi wun* and the *myin-zu-gyi wun*, or chief of cavalry. Supporting them were over sixty lower officials with various responsibilities, service groups of horse and boatmen to deliver orders and messages outside of the capital area, and a service group of foot messengers to race around the capital with messages and summonses to officials.[3]

The Hlut-taw itself was a substantial structure within the royal fort with a large eastern chamber where the *wun-gyis* conducted their business, and a smaller western chamber, called the Zei-dawun Chamber, which contained a throne and was used only on those occasions when the king held audience at the Hlut-taw. Manned twenty-four hours a day, the Hlut-taw had regular rotas of night duty for its officials from the *wun-gyis* on down. No cushions, mats, or betel chewing were allowed, and proper attire stipulated that a minimum of a white turban and jacket be worn by all who entered the precincts. All of the officials of the various departments had to gather at the Hlut-taw in the early morning and again in the early afternoon to present their reports and cases for the morning and afternoon audiences of the king, which they attended *en masse* in the Bye-daik. The king rarely attended the Hlut-taw, so either the crown prince—if there was one—or other adult princes were required to preside over these meetings.[4]

The jurisdiction of the Hlut-taw was comprehensively stated in an edict of 1637 as "Let the orders of the Golden Hlut-taw be carried out in all matters."[5] In actual terms, its main concerns were revenue and fiscal matters; civil and criminal cases referred from the provinces; public works (mainly royal pagoda, monastery, and irrigation construction projects); historical and religious affairs (archives, inscriptions, chronicles, the *pitakas* and material related to the annual monastic examinations, and administration of the *sangha* and glebe revenues); and official appointments, promotions, and demotions in the royal service.[6]

The Departmental Administrations

It is difficult to estimate the number of departments under the umbrella of the Hlut-taw, but fifty would be a conservative minimum and one hundred perhaps closer to actual fact. Each department was usually headed by a *wun* (the generic title for a senior official) and a secretary, while the rank and file belonged to one or more of the crown service groups. The duty of the *wun* was to see that the functions of the department were fulfilled, to maintain discipline among his cadres, to maintain sufficient cadres, and to oversee the proper succession to the hereditary offices among them. The secretary of a *wun* usually functioned as his deputy and saw that orders were executed or transmitted to others. The actual clerical work of writing and copying was performed by young men under the direction of the secretary.

Many of the departments were of minor importance and size, but a few deserve comment. The Eastern Court administered the capital area. The Western Court was the residence of the females of the royal family and harem and fell partially under the jurisdiction of the Byedaik. The public purse and repository for revenues from glebe lands was the Kathaung-myaung Taik. Another important department was the Maha Dan, which maintained secular control over the monkhood and religious benefactions.

The Silver Tax Department had jurisdiction over the groups of silver miners spread over the upper Irrawaddy Valley, the southern Shan principalities, and Pagan and Taywin-daing districts in central Burma. Paying only a specified annual house tax in silver, these groups were exempt from all other taxes and service, including military.[7] This department had a powerful competitor in the Granary Department, which, in addition to managing the extensive crown granary system and receiving the agricultural tax from the crown demesne, had jurisdiction over the Eastern, Central, and Western Gold tracts (mainly in lower Chin-dwin, Katha, and western Mandalay districts) and some of the silver-mining groups. The Eastern Gold Tract, for example, comprised thirteen village tracts in Katha District with a total of 1,929 houses and paid an annual revenue of 295 *kyats* of gold in 1783.[8] Some indication of the relative base of the two major departments is shown in the 1783 inquest figures, when the Granary Department had a total jurisdiction of 9,045 houses as opposed to the 2,135 houses of the Silver Tax Department.[9] There was strong conflict between the two departments for control of the silver- and gold-mining groups. A small Iron Tax Department managed to maintain an independent existence, but by 1783 an earlier Gold Tax Department had already fallen prey to the Granary Department.

Another important category of department involved the administration of the crown service groups. Each type of group—artillerymen, *jingals* (musketeers), the various types of boatmen, infantry, the Yuns, elephant catchers and trainers, and so on—were under their own *wuns* and responsible only to them. The major crown service departments appear to have been the Northern and Southern Cavalry and the Daing departments. The latter was composed of units of crown service infantry whose distinguishing characteristic was the square leather shield called *daing* from which the units took their generic name. There are no figures on the size of the Daing Department, but *daing* groups appear to have formed the bulk of the crown service infantry, and the *daing wun* was an important court official.[10] The jurisdiction of the Southern Cavalry comprised 6,468 houses covering most of central Burma, while the 7,745 houses of the Northern Cavalry were concentrated in Shwei-bo and Mandalay districts.[11] Each had its own *wun* who reported to the *myin-zu-gyi wun* (chief of all cavalry groups).

The crown demesne was not part of the system of territorial administration and, in effect, functioned as several departments. For example, there were three different *wuns* in charge of various groups of crown service cultivators (*lamaing*). Their produce tax went directly to the privy purse and they were not liable for other imposts or service. These cultivators were concentrated in some of the better agricultural areas in central and northern Burma, and functioned as crown service units rather than as villages within the territorial administration. The bulk of the crown demesne apparently consisted of the major *taiks*, or "revenue departments," in that their revenues also went to the Shweidaik rather than the Kathaung-myaung Taik. Each *taik* had its own *wun* who was, in turn, responsible to the *taik wun*.[12] Little is known about the nature of the *taiks*, but there appear to have been nine—the Northern, Southern, Western, Hsin-gyei, Twin-thin, Maha Dan, Kyawzin, Ban-gyi, and Ye-hlei—with a total of 496 villages and over forty-two thousand houses, about 15 percent of the overall population in 1783.[13] Most, if not all, of the *taiks* were not geographically discrete administrative jurisdictions, but had their constituent villages spread over a number of separate districts. The Northern Taik covered almost the whole of the north above the capital area while the Southern Taik encompassed almost the whole of central Burma. Kyaw-zin and Twin-thin *taiks* had villages in Kyauk-hse as well as the lower Chin-dwin area.

The Taik Department was an important part of the central administrative apparatus, but perhaps the single most important department was the Athi Department, which encompassed all people classified as *athi* in the broad sense of the term denoting those not in crown service. The basic functions of the department were to have charge of the hereditary local officers of the territorial administration and their succession to office, to be the appellate court for legal disputes referred from the *athi* sector, and to ensure that *athi* obligations in regard to military, corvée, and revenue matters were fulfilled. The post of *athi wun* was considered so important that it was usually held in tandem with an appointment as *wun-gyi*, the incumbent being known as the *athi wun-gyi*.[14]

Territorial Administration

Some of the departments had jurisdiction over substantial portions of the population or countryside. These departmental jurisdictions coexisted with the territorial jurisdictions, which also reported to the Hluttaw. The basic unit of territorial administration was the *myo*, a term denoting a district seat of government along with its hinterland and subordinate villages, but also denoting only a town proper. Size more than any other factor determined whether a *myo* was an independent administrative entity under its own *wun* or was combined with other small *myos* into a larger jurisdiction under a single *wun*. The *myos* of northern and central Burma were mostly single wunships with a few combined wunships. In this latter category, for example, were the *myos* of Nyaung-bin, Yatha, Hnget-pyaw, Pin-tha, and Naga-zin in northern Mandalay District, which were ruled by hereditary *myo-thu-gyis* under one *wun* known as the *pyin-zala-nga-myo wun* or the "*wun* of the five *myos*." The nine *myos* of Kyauk-hse were also administered by *myo-thu-gyis* under the Kyauk-hse *wun*.

The largest wunships north of the capital were Tabayin with 214 villages, Alon (Badon prior to 1782) with 126, and Myei-du with 80. The central area to the south of the capital contained the large jurisdictions of Pagan with 96 villages, Yame-thin with 177, Salin with 105, and Talok with 58. It was southern Burma, however, that had some of the largest *myos*, such as Taung-dwin-gyi with 149 villages, Bassein and Henzada with 88 and 87, respectively, and Tha-ra-wadi with 213.[15] Because the south was smaller than the northern and central areas in overall population, the size of southern villages must on average have tended to be smaller.

In addition to these *myos*, there were four "super wunships" situated at Martaban, Taung-ngu, Prome, and Han-tha-wadi. Martaban and Taung-ngu were the southern and northern bastions of the eastern frontier and the stations of important military garrisons. Prome dominated the southern approaches to central Burma and the capital area and also guarded against Arakanese intrusions. It was also the site of important garrisons and defenses. Han-tha-wadi was easily the most important wunship in the realm because it included the port of Rangoon and its *wun* functioned in essence with the powers, though not the title, of viceroy (*bayin*). "Han-tha-wadi Myo being the outpost of the empire and the place most vulnerable to invasion" was how the 1802 *sit-tan* of the last of the super *myos* described its function of protecting the central delta and the entrance to the Irrawaddy Valley.[16] The annexation of Arakan in 1784 added a fifth super wunship called the Anauk-pyei-gyi, or "Great Western Country Wunship."[17] The importance of Prome and Taung-ngu was also accorded official recognition in 1791, when the second and third sons of Bo-daw-hpaya were given complete governance of these jurisdictions. Also given the titles of *bayin*, they became the only two viceroys appointed during the early Kon-baung period.

Apart from the single, combined, and super wunships, there were three additional wunships involved with territorial administration. The *myei-lat wun* had charge of those *myos* to the east of the upper Irrawaddy River not under the rule of Shan *saw-bwas*, thus constituting in effect one of the larger combined wunships.[18] Miscellaneous small *myos* and some villages that escaped the jurisdiction of any territorial wunship or department came under the *myo-lat wun*, while the *ywa-lat wun* had similar responsibility for miscellaneous villages that for the most part appear to have been new villages in areas of pioneer settlement.[19] Towns and villages fortified as frontier posts were also not placed under the jurisdiction of the local territorial officials, but were assigned to one or another of the central administrative officers with ongoing military responsibilities. These officers included the *wun-gyis*, *wun-dauks*, and *win-daw-hmus* (commanders of the sides of the royal fort).[20]

The essence of the administrative function of the territorial *wuns* was given by the Kyauk-hse *wun* in his 1784 *sit-tan*: "I have to attend to all the crown business and execute all the orders from the

Hlut-taw."[21] The *wuns* and their establishments were responsible for receiving the collections of taxes and fees from local officials and transmitting the crown share of the monies and the accounts to the Hlut-taw annually, adjudicating civil cases that local officers had failed to resolve, looking after crown property, assisting crown service groups in performance of their functions, dealing with criminal matters and banditry, and carrying out orders from the Hlut-taw. These orders were usually related to quotas of labor for corvée and military service and expenditure of crown revenue collected locally for state merit-making purposes.

The notable exceptions to these generalizations were the Kyauk-hse wunship and the super wunships. The Kyauk-hse *wun* administered one of the two most important areas of irrigated paddy cultivation and crown service population, the other major area being the Mu Valley. The irrigation of these regions was mainly based on crown systems, in contrast to the mostly private systems of Min-bu, the third significant area of irrigated cultivation. The wunships of the Mu area were in some cases larger than Kyauk-hse, but the irrigation system of the latter was more complex and extensive. The duties connected with the operation and maintenance of the Kyauk-hse weirs and canals, performed jointly with the Crown Weir Department, left the Kyauk-hse *wun* with far more complicated responsibilities than other *wuns*.[22] In the case of the super *wuns*, in addition to the functions of an ordinary territorial *wun*, they were also responsible for the local garrisons and the security of their frontiers, obtaining and forwarding intelligence concerning foreign neighbors, and control and taxation of international commerce.[23]

The seat of wunship administration was the *yon*, or local court, a building located in the main town of the *myo*. Here the *wun* and his establishment gathered to deal with serious civil and criminal cases referred from the villages; with revenue, corvée and military levies; and with other local business. Consultations were held with the local headmen, the chiefs of any crown service units in the jurisdiction, and the local agent of the *myo-za*, or appanage holder, if there was one. In addition to the *wun*, the *myo* administration included a secretary who passed on and oversaw the execution of orders; the *sit-ke* who, as deputy to the *wun*, assisted him in all matters, particularly police and judicial affairs; the *ahkun wun*, or revenue officer; and the *nagan*, or crown representative. The size and importance of the *myo* and the importance of the *wun* determined the size of his administrative establishment. Large *myos* often had pairs of *sit-kes* and *nagans*, as well as additional writers and other minor officials. Riparian *myos* such as Han-tha-wadi, Bassein, and Martaban had an additional officer called the *akauk wun*. Known as the *shahbandar* to Europeans, this officer was usually a European or a person of mixed blood who may or may not have been country-born and who was responsible for the port revenues. The Han-tha-wadi administration also included as deputy to the *wun* the *yei wun*, who had control of the maritime commerce and military security of the *myo*. The *sit-kes* served under the *yei wun* in this instance. The officers of the *myo* administration were important figures in the political hierarchy and, as such, were usually given honorific titles and umbrellas indicating their rank. All *wuns* had retainers, but the super *wuns* had crown service units to function as lictors, messengers, and police.[24]

The territorial *wuns* and their subordinate officers were appointed by the crown. Because these officers were appointed, promoted, transferred, or deposed in accord with their favor at court and/or with political currents, the real administrative stability in early Kon-baung Burma was rooted in local hereditary offices whose incumbents, together with their dependents and affinal and consanguine relations, constituted the gentry. The chief among the hereditary officials was the *myo-thu-gyi*, who had overall charge of the customary aspects of administration in the *myo* and to whom the village headmen reported. In contrast to the transiency of the appointed *myo* officials, most of the *myo-thu-gyi* lineages recorded in the *sit-tans* go back three or four generations, and some beyond that. The duties of the *myo-thu-gyi* were to divide equitably the quotas for corvée labor, military service, and special revenue levies he received from the *myo* court among the *athi*, *ala*, and *kat-pa* inhabitants of his charge; to maintain law and order; and to keep a detailed and current register of all the individuals in his jurisdiction with name, age, date of birth, and crown service group, if any. His authority was also to decide petty civil and criminal cases or, in a common phrase from the *sit-tans*, to make "large cases become small and small cases disappear." A last important function was the collection and transmission to the authorities of the customary fees and agricultural revenues.

Most local administrative activity was carried out by the *myo-thu-gyi* and the other hereditary officials, the most common of which were the *thu-gyi* and the *myei-daing*. The *thu-gyi* in essence performed at the village level the role played by the *myo-thu-gyi* at the *myo* level. *Myei-daings* are found at both the *myo* and village levels in the *sit-tans*. In its narrowest sense, the office of *myei-daing* was responsible for arranging, recording, and taking a commission on all sales of immovable property, mainly land. In many villages, however, the *myei-daing* functioned as the headman and submitted the *sit-tan*, while in others the *thu-gyi* in his *sit-tan* specifically stated that he performed the function of *myei-daing*. The office of *myei-daing* appears to have been clearly differentiated from that of *thu-gyi* only at the *myo* level and in some of the larger villages. Although the terms *thu-gyi* and *myei-daing* were most common, there was some variation by locality in the names applied to these two offices. Headmen of larger villages and some smaller *myos*, for example, were sometimes termed *pyei-zo* rather than *thu-gyi* or *myo-thu-gyi*, while headmen of jurisdictions in the gold and silver tracts were called *shwei-hmu* and *ngwei-hmu*. There is occasional mention in early Kon-baung documents of officers called *kyei-gaing* and *taw-ke*, who appear to have performed the duty of *myei-daing*, in its narrow sense, in localities lacking that office.

These hereditary officers carried out what was referred to above as the customary aspects of administration: the disposition of local affairs in accord with the traditional norms of each locality. Customary administration encompassed all taxes on agricultural produce, fishing, and other water-related economic activities; local tolls, ferry fees, bazaar taxes, fees on sales, brokerage, and other local hereditary concessions; the disposition of stray cattle, loose boats, and runaway slaves; the disposition of the carcasses of dead horses and elephants; and the succession to local hereditary offices and concessions. Albeit with considerable variation in detail, local customs concerning these aspects of administration were meticulously recorded in the *sit-tan* of each village and *myo*. Through its appointed *wun* the central government tended to impinge on the local administration of the *myo* only with levies for military and corvée labor and special assessments of rice and money. The state did not increase the traditional local taxes to meet specific exigencies, but preferred to make special levies through the *myo* court, which the *myo-thu-gyi* then had to apportion among his headmen. The local *wun* also made special levies of either money or rice to support a certain expense or of labor for local construction projects.[25] Thus, the customary part of local administration was generally respected and, in spite of the special levies, probably afforded the general populace some protection from the heavy taxation of the state.

The Crown Service/*Athi* Dichotomy

Administratively, Burmese society historically was divided into two unequal segments, those who served the crown directly (*ahmu-dan*) and those who did not (*athi*). The *ahmu-dan*, or crown service population, was administered by the myriad departments while the *athi* population was largely under territorial officials. Central to the Burmese conception of administration, this dichotomy was expressed by Bo-daw-hpaya in this manner: "The crown service groups [*asu*] established in the reigns of noble kings are the foundation of the state and should be distinctly established for a long time. . . . The true religion flourishes when the affairs of the country are tranquil, and these are tranquil when all the crown service groups give their allegiance and perform their duties."[26] Thus, the state viewed the crown service groups as its chief resource and devoted considerable administrative attention to their maintenance. The state also attempted to keep the nonservice or *athi* sector organized into *taings*, or service and dues units. Thus, all of the population was theoretically organized into groups for the service and support of the crown in a system that was complex but rather flexible in its actual mechanics.

The crown service sector comprised a wide spectrum of groups that performed various functions for the crown, and whose relative status varied according to the nature and degree of their service. The structure of the crown service sector was hierarchical and graded by degree and nature of service. At the top of the hierarchy were the *thwei-thauks*, followed by the cavalry, musketeers, and a large corpus of palace guards, attendants, and servants. Royal decree formed men of the same status and ethnicity into elite units called *thwei-thauks* dedicated to the close service of the monarch.[27] The rationale of the *thwei-thauk* as stated by Hsin-hpyu-shin was similar to that of Bo-daw-hpaya for the crown service groups as a whole; that is, that rulers must seek servants who are clever, strong, and can be organized as elite servants of the crown in such capacities as palace attendants, personal bodyguards of the king, servants of the princes, and in the management of state, religious, and military affairs.[28]

Divided into the interior (*atwin*) and exterior (*pyin*) sections, the *thwei-thauks* themselves constituted a hierarchy with the highest units formed from close servants, attendants, and guards of the ruler and such important middle-rank officials as *atwin-wuns*, *wun-dauks*, and *myo wuns*.[29] The elite nature of the *thwei-thauks* is further indicated by the fact that such interior units as the Lei-ze-daw and Nga-ze-daw, for example, took their names directly from certain categories in the court hierarchy of status and place, and may have included all members of those categories. Other units of the interior section were formed of courtiers and officials and yet others of their sons and younger brothers.[30] The exterior *thwei-thauks* were military units headed by less prominent personages who did not serve within the palace and had correspondingly less status because of their greater distance from the royal person. Overall, the ranks of the *thwei-thauks* were small, generally having between twenty and forty members. As creatures of the monarch, they had to be formed anew by each new king and, as a group, appear to have had no influence on administration or politics.

Ranking just below the *thwei-thauks* in status were the cavalry groups, which were considered the elite of the armed forces. The esteem in which the cavalry was held may have stemmed from the Burmese view of the horse that: "because horses and elephants are worthy of kings; they are excellent things, of power."[31] This prestige is also reflected in the court hierarchy, in which one of the most prestigious upper ranks was the *myin-hmu min-tha*, or "princely cavalry commanders." The cavalry itself was not under a single administrative department, but was split up into a number of jurisdictions under various cavalry *wuns*, the two largest in 1783 being the Northern Cavalry with 5,043 service families and the Southern Cavalry with 3,194.[32]

Palace guards, attendants, and functionaries who were not members of *thwei-thauks* but who served in close proximity to the monarch also enjoyed a high status because "they are men of good family, who attend and watch over the monarch by day and by night . . . remain in the different ranges of the palace . . . and are not masters of their own lives."[33] The palace compound had literally hundreds of different service units attached to its various parts, some units being assigned to a specific chamber or member of the royal family, others to certain stairways, and still others serving as janitors, cooks, butlers, messengers, lictors, bird shooers, musicians, jailers, and so on. The Western Court alone had fifteen identifiable units attached to it.[34] There was also a large number of military units that did rotating garrison duty at the capital and provided the manpower necessary for court festivals, processions, and other nonmilitary purposes.[35]

Overall, the main functional categories for service groups were ordinary infantry, musketeers, cavalry, elephantry, artillery, boats, *lamaing* (or crown cultivators), and a wide variety of nonmilitary units rendering special products or services to the court. These units received a certain level of basic support in return for their stipulated services, which were carefully detailed and recorded in their *sit-tans*. The nature of the duties of certain units like the elephant catchers and trainers made it impossible for them to engage in regular cultivation, hence they received direct allotments of provisions. As a general rule, however, the reward for service was allotments of cultivable land. The units appear to have been given a lump land allotment sufficient to give each member about 8 3/4 acres for cultivation and the unit chief double that.[36]

Bearing in mind their limitations, it is possible to determine the approximate percentages and identify the main concentrations of crown service people within the general population using the population summaries. These documents not only give the overall number of houses in each *myo*, but further break the figures down between *athi* and crown service. The crown service figures include the retainers of local officials and the local appanage holder, which usually amounted to a fair number of houses. A summary of these figures is given in table 2, which compares the Burney "Census" of 1783 and the "Population Summary of 1802."

Table 2
Percent of Crown Service Population

	Crown Service	Total	Percent
Burney Census of 1783[†]			
145 *myos*	83,783	228,533	37
12 *taiks*	25,077	43,508	58
6 departments	19,656	23,926	82
Totals	**128,516**	**295,967**	**43**
Population Summary of 1802			
141 *myos*	66,306	178,806	37

[†]The percentages for the "Population Summary of 1783" vary one percentage point from those given by Burney.

The figures show first that the *taiks* and departments had much higher percentages of service people than did the *myos*, which is not surprising in view of the fact that departments in particular were service oriented. The relative proportion of service people in the *myo* population remained constant, but the overall service population declined by 18 percent between 1783 and 1802, a decline in keeping with the 17 percent drop in the total number of registered houses in the same period. The overall percentage of the service sector in the population was probably between 40 and 45 percent in the early Kon-baung period.

The main geographic concentrations of the service population can be seen from the regional breakdown in appendix 2, which parallels that given for population in appendix 1. Table 3 summarizes the data from appendix 2. As the figures show clearly, the highest concentration of service population was in the immediate capital area, followed by the north/northwest and central areas. The north/northwest emerges both in absolute and percentage terms as the main center of service people, although the central area figures are distorted by the omission of Kyauk-hse. The fragmentary figures available for that district suggest that in percentage terms it was a significantly denser service area than the north/northwest, but that in absolute terms it contained at most only one-third of the population of the latter area in 1783 and may have lost up to 80 percent of its population by 1802.[37] The Taung-ngu area showed an increase of 88 percent over that same period, probably because it became the appanage of the Taung-ngu prince after 1792. The 11 percent increase in Martaban certainly reflected its role as the main depot and staging area of the campaigns against Thailand and the chief point of defense against Thai intrusions. The Martaban land roll of 1784 lists over fifty service units stationed in that town, about one-third of which appear to have been military.[38]

Unfortunately, the various population lists do not give information either on the ethnic composition of the service population or for the population as a whole. A substantial proportion of the total was non-Burman, especially in the north/northwest, capital, and central areas. The majority of these non-Burman groups were formed in the early Taung-ngu period or earlier, however, so that by the early Kon-baung period they had been linguistically assimilated.[39] On a smaller scale, the early Kon-baung rulers established settlements of Shans, Yuns, Mons, Laos, Manipuris, Arakanese, and Thai, but the impetus in this direction was spent after 1770, when Burmese military operations became increasingly ineffectual and the deportations of non-Burmans became minor and sporadic. After the end of the Chinese war in 1769

Table 3
Summary Trends in Crown Service Houses, 1783–1802

Area	1783		1802		Percent Service Houses	
	Service Houses	Total Houses	Service Houses	Total Houses	1783	1802
Capital	14,986	20,075	16,438	22,428	75	73
North/Northwest	32,655	69,058	19,974	42,543	47	47
Central	15,745	57,637	12,892	47,638	27	27
Prome	6,592	30,189	5,923	28,786	22	21
Irrawaddy Delta	4,617	20,119	4,605	20,207	23	23
Taung-ngu	1,210	2,332	2,277	3,163	52	72
Martaban	1,169	4,707	1,296	4,707	25	28
Totals	**76,974**	**204,117**	**63,405**	**169,472**	**38**	**37**

and the devastation of Manipur in 1770, there was only one large deportation from Arakan in 1784, a minor one from Chiengmai in 1797, and the resettlement of some Manipuris and Assamese between 1819 and 1822.

The number of non-Burman units named in Burmese documents and the fact that each of the ethnic groups represented in the service population was the responsibility of a specific *wun* (with the exception of the Shans and Mons) suggests that the proportion of non-Burmans in the service sector may have been as high as 35 percent overall and even higher in the capital, north/northwest, and Kyauk-hse areas. Such a large foreign population in intimate contact with the court and capital suggests a potential internal security problem, but there is, in fact, only one known incident of overt dissidence by non-Burman servicemen in the main service areas.[40] The non-Burman service population apparently remained loyal, or at least quiescent, because it was both administratively and geographically balkanized and because most of its members were culturally and ideologically similar to the Burmans and hence able to relate politically and ideologically to the Burman monarchy.

Important as the crown service sector was, some 60 percent of the population remained under the designation of *athi*. The etymology of this word is uncertain, but old Burmese inscriptions frequently use the term in reference to landowners who were not in government service.[41] From its usage in the records of the Restored Taung-ngu period, the meaning denoted by the term *athi* in early Kon-baung times appears to have been reached by the reign of Tha-lun (1629-1648). In its broadest Kon-baung meaning, *athi* referred to any household that was not registered in a crown service unit, not in the establishment of any official or royal personage, not pagoda or any other kind of slave, or not in a debt bondage or patron/client relationship. Thus, *athi* denoted households that were free of those obligations but bore a more general obligation of crown service termed *taing thu-yin* and a minor obligation called the *hse-hnahmu min-daing*. The first of these obligations involved general service and dues levied directly on the *athi* population, which was theoretically organized into *athi taings*, or service and dues units. The number of houses per *taing* varied from five to twenty-five until an edict of 1783 decreed that all *taings* were to consist of twenty-five houses.[42] Levies were made not per house but per unit of houses. The dues per *taing* were probably levied monthly and the service itself was generally done within the community and involved corvée labor, messenger duties, porterage, and similar chores. Assessments for military service were also made per *taing*. It would further appear that *taings* were found only in central and northern Burma and not in the south or border areas. The *hse-hnahmu min-daing* or "twelve crown items" were minor tokens traditionally offered by *athi* communities to the crown.[43]

Athi had a more restricted meaning, however, because in its more precise definition it referred to people with a certain legal and social position. Those with true *athi* status had to be landowners living permanently in one locale. Lands so owned were termed *athi myei*, or *athi* land, and could only be inherited by or sold to *athi* from the same community.[44] The *athi* in this narrower definition tended to be prosperous people to whom the sumptuary rules permitted a more elaborate style of housing, dress, utensils, and funerary customs than was permitted to the mass of commoners.[45] In this strict sense, then, the position of *athi* was based on permanent residence, landownership, and a special place in the status hierarchy.

People who met these requirements, however, were obviously only a fraction of the overall population broadly designated as *athi*. Genuine *athi* were probably to be found mainly in areas where the land was of good enough quality to make property rights of some relevance. Where the land was poor, the population tended to be mobile rather than sedentary. The majority of the commoners were probably not *athi* in the strict sense, but came under the rubric of *kat-pa* or *ala*. *Kat-pa* were migrants from other communities and were only allowed to work *athi* land with the permission of the local authorities. Such permission was contingent on the migrant's agreement to share the community's dues and service obligations. The *kat-pa* was then made part of the *kyeik-su athi*, or quasi-*athi*, of the community. *Kyeik-su athi* was a status recognized by the crown, which organized such people into *kyeik-su taings*, as it did the *athi* into *athi taings*.[46] In many cases the *kat-pa* probably functioned as the tenantry of the *athi* and eased the burden of dues and service through the mechanism of the *kyeik-su taing*.

Because the *athi* and *kat-pa* lived in the same communities, intermarriage was both inevitable and legally recognized. When an *athi* male married a *kat-pa* female, the offspring was termed *ala* and had inheritance rights only to *athi* land in the mother's estate. Once having inherited the maternal *athi* land, *ala* presumably ceased to be *ala* and became real *athi*. Thus, inheritance through the maternal side may have provided some mechanism for the assimilation of people to the *athi* status.

The crown service groups, *athi*, and *kyeik-su taings* were all means of harnessing the population for service and dues. Even though the crown service groups held crown land in return for service, they were also required to perform the same local corvée labor and other duties as were the *athi*. The *sit-tans* of the Kyauk-hse weirs, for example, describe how the servicemen whose land was irrigated by a given weir system were required to maintain and repair that weir.⁴⁷ A 1758 edict of Alaung-hpaya states: "If any serviceman called for the above [local] duties fails to present himself in his arrogance of service, let the authorities and elders in concerted action chastise him."⁴⁸ When not on active service, some crown service units were apparently also required to pay monetary dues in the same manner as the *athi taings*.⁴⁹ The dues and service of the *athi* and crown service sectors were exclusive of agricultural produce taxes and land rents for, in addition to their regular service obligations and the local service and dues, the crown service groups also paid agricultural taxes or land rents. A few units were exempted from agricultural taxes and/or local labor commitments by royal favor, but the majority worked alongside the *athi*.⁵⁰

It is therefore not correct to define the *athi* as taxpayers in contradistinction to the nontaxpaying crown service sector. More probably, there was a continuum running from total service without local labor commitments and land taxes at the far end of the crown service sector to mainly dues and little local labor at the far end of the *athi* sector. The cleavage between the crown service population and the *athi* was very real to the Burmese, however, and was reflected in the relative social positions of each sector and the precise administrative arrangements made to keep the two sectors distinct. Whether crown service or *athi*, however, the burden of dues and service was onerous and caused many people to seek relief in alternative statuses. Neither sector was particularly stable.

The Military System

The military system of the early Kon-baung state consisted of both a permanent professional force supported by and owing its allegiance directly to the crown and conscript levies mobilized only in times of war or emergencies. The standing force was composed of the crown service units of infantry, cavalry, artillery, war boats, and elephantry. The units of each generic branch of the infantry such as *daings*, musketeers, spearmen, and so forth were organized into departments under *wuns* who reported to the Hlut-taw. Thus, the standing military was not focused into a single concentration within the administrative apparatus, but fragmented into many smaller parts. Except for the guard units of the interior palace under the Bye-daik, during both peace and wartime the military was directly controlled by the Hlut-taw. As part of the crown service sector of society, the military units were hereditary in their membership and leadership and received allotments of state land for their support. As the soldiers of the crown, the military servicemen were expected to become proficient in their calling through training, although it is not clear to what extent this expectation became reality. In sum, the two primary characteristics of the permanent military were that it was a body of hereditary professional soldiers who held state land, and that its administration was divided into a number of autonomous departments.

It is difficult to estimate the size of the standing military because its perimeters were not clearly defined. I have already suggested that there was a gradient of service to the crown rather than a clean division between crown service and *athi* statuses. The military service units were subsumed in this gradient and can be divided into three general categories: household troops, capital garrison troops, and field levies. The function of the household and capital garrison troops was to protect the person of the ruler, the palace, and the capital area, while the field levies both provided support for the first two categories and formed the nucleus of the field forces in wartime. The important distinction is between the field levies, who were mobilized only in wartime or emergencies, and the household and garrison troops, who were assigned permanent duty at the capital. The latter two groups were on the intensive end of the service gradient, while the field troops were closer to the middle and, in at least some cases, paid taxes when not on active duty. The lack of data makes it impossible to estimate the total size of the field troops category, but the Burmese historian U Tin has provided a detailed list of the military units assigned to permanent duty at the capital that totals over twenty-six thousand. Among the force of fifty-five thousand men with which Hsin-hpyu-shin invaded Manipur in 1765 were twelve thousand men drawn specifically from the elite guard units, who manned the four walls of the royal fort. Their role was to protect the king in the field.[51] Although it is not clear whether he is referring to the early or later Kon-baung period, U Tin's list of figures for the capital garrison troops may therefore be fairly accurate for the early Kong-baung period.

The ranks of the standing military included a substantial number of non-Burmans. The household and garrison troops contained many units of Shans and Laos, which were often stationed in close proximity to the person and quarters of the king. The intimate bodyguards of the ruler were the elite *thwei-thauks* recruited from royal relatives and the families of courtiers, but just beyond these were the Shan and Lao guards. It would seem that the kings placed their first security reliance on ties of blood and self-interest, and then on alien troops dependent on the throne for support and reward. Indeed, the non-Burmans may have had a function somewhat analogous to the Swiss guards employed by the European monarchs of the seventeenth and eighteenth centuries.

From Pagan times onward, there had been a system of conscription by levying quotas of men from jurisdictions on the basis of population and jurisdictions were rated for soldiers in terms of tens, hundreds, and thousands. For example, Taung-ngu and Taung-dwin-gyi had quotas of one thousand, Pahkan-gyi four hundred, and Mok-hso-bo two hundred in the Taung-ngu period.[52] This system was replaced in the early Kon-baung period by one in which the Hlut-taw set the quotas of the provincial governors for specific campaigns or occasions on the basis of the district population registers. The governors in turn made allotments for the subordinate jurisdictions of their provinces. In 1784 the head of the Taung-bet-tan jurisdiction in Pagan described the process in these words: "When there is occasion to raise men for military or civil service, I go to the *myo* court, receive my quota, and apportion it among the 27 villages of my jurisdiction."[53] References to the traditional military quotas of towns are a routine feature of the *sit-tans* of the Taung-ngu period, but are uniformly absent for those of the early Kon-baung, the majority of which only state that the *myo-thu-gyi* was responsible for meeting the local quotas for military service. Thus, the selection of conscripts was left to the local headmen. The most common method was to group several families together as constituting one house and to require so many men from it as a unit. A shortfall in men had to be made up in money and conscripts could provide a substitute or pay a fee in lieu of service.[54] An important source of military manpower, the Shan principalities were also subject to quotas and the rosters of major campaigns recorded in the *Kon-baung-zet* usually show contingents from all the major and minor Shan rulers.

Once in the field, soldiers were organized into *tao-za* ("those who eat from one pot") of five men, *akyat* consisting of two *tao-za*, *thwei-thauk* consisting of five *akyat*, and *tat* consisting of two *thwei-thauk*. The *tat* was the unit of maneuver in the field and combinations of *tats* were commanded by field officers usually termed *bo-gyok*. Field formations were organized *ad hoc* for specific campaigns or exigencies. Officers down to the level of *tat* commander were appointed by the Hlut-taw, which also determined objectives and strategy. Large field forces normally included a contingent of crown service units to stiffen and control the less-than-reliable and often unwilling conscripts. Burmese generals in the field employed a distinctive tactical style involving temporary fortifications, ruses, feints, and ambushes. In the main battles were fought with sword and spear. Artillery and muskets were available in considerable quantities, but seldom employed effectively by western standards. Still, the central government's near monopoly on firearms gave it a significant advantage over internal competitors, and firearms have been shown to have played important roles in numerous seventeenth- and eighteenth-century battles.[55]

Conscription provided the manpower to resist invasion and project Burmese power beyond the limits of the realm, while the standing military provided security for the ruler and the capital and the ability to respond to immediate threats. Perhaps more importantly, the presence of a large body of elite troops on active duty at the capital was a constant and highly visual expression of the coercive power of the crown. The security of the monarch and dynasty rested on the strength and vitality of this force, which was the real prop of the despotic state. No force could match the standing military within Burma proper, and only on the northern and eastern peripheries did subordinate rulers, be they *saw-bwas* or Burman governors, on occasion even try.

The military system was not without its weaknesses, however. Conscripts often had to be driven into battle and the rate of desertion was always high. While state supported, even the standing military was not a true stipendiary force. Forced to grow their own food, the soldiers were tied to the land as closely as the rest of the population and were equally affected by the frequent droughts and famines. As subordinate entities within the general departmental system, the military departments tended to subject their constituents to the same kind of maladministration that characterized the nonmilitary departments. And because the military service units were both the special tools of the king and the easiest to employ, they tended to be overexploited by the rulers. Agricultural scarcities, maladministration, and onerous service demands produced the same response in members of the military units as they did in the general population. Victor Lieberman has emphasized the general flight from crown service as an important factor in the decline of the Taung-ngu dynasty, a factor that was also operative in the early Kon-baung period.[56] In both cases, however, the key element in dynastic decline was the failing overall military capability of the crown that resulted from the gradual deterioration of the standing military.

The Fiscal System

The crown's right of taxation rested on two bases. One was the classical Buddhist notion that a king was entitled to a certain portion of the produce of the land as payment for ruling and thereby making possible orderly social life. The texts of the Pali canon specify one-sixth as the crown due, but Burmese texts and documents uniformly refer to *tha-thamei-da* (Pali, *sasamedha*), which is the first of the "four *sangahas*," or ways in which righteous kings show favor to their subjects.[57] *Tha-thamei-da* required that the ruler take no more than one-tenth of the produce.[58] The other base was the conception of the king as "lord of earth and water" (Burmese, *yei-myei-shin*), a concept also derived from classical Indian thought.[59] As lord of earth and water, the ruler was entitled to his share of their produce, treasure, and minerals and could evict defaulters or claim the property of those dying heirless. It was standard, for example, for the titles of early Kon-baung kings to include the phrase "lord of all the mines of rubies, sapphires, topaz, gold, silver, amber, copper, and iron." Taxation was in this sense a return for tenancy. The proprietary rights of the king in Burmese political thought were not unlimited, however, because, as the *Manu-kye* stated, "he has a right to duty collected but he shall not take the whole."[60]

Even though the Burmese tradition of *tha-thamei-da* specified the rate of taxation as one-tenth, there were, in fact, two modes of assessment in common use. These were variable assessment (*hkun-shin*), a given percentage of the product, and fixed assessment (*hkun-thei*), a set charge regardless of the product. The practices described in the *sit-tans* reveal widespread use of each mode with respect to the various commodities and services taxed, and sometimes both modes were employed within the same village for similar categories of taxation. The rate in variable assessment was almost always one-tenth and represented the dictates of *tha-thamei-da*. Fixed assessment was often used where the land or other productive source was uneven in quality or of inferior productivity.[61] As was the case with most local administrative practice, local custom was also decisive in determining the mode or combination of modes in use in a given locality. Although the *sit-tans* at first reading show a wide variation in local tax rates on commodities and services, closer examination indicates that all taxation fell within one of the two modes and thus adhered to standard principles.

In addition to whatever fixed or variable assessments were levied, the payer was subject to other charges which were the perquisites of office of the local officials and tax collectors. In the case of agricultural produce, an extra amount was usually assessed to compensate for that part lost or stolen in transit, thus ensuring that the correct amount of tax was delivered to the authorities. Such charges added another 5 to 20 percent to the main tax (*hkun-ma*), except in the case of glebe land, whose residents often paid only the main tax. The same basic system appears to have been functioning in the early seventeenth century. The few surviving *sit-tans* from that period similarly refer to assessment of one-tenth and by the *pe* and yoke of buffalo.[62]

The primary areas of taxation were agricultural produce, nonagricultural commodities, and commerce. The tax on such agricultural products as rice, millet, pulses, alluvial crops (tobacco, maize, and vegetables), palm products, and cotton was generally paid in kind in districts where there was a crown storehouse and in specie in other districts. Nonagricultural commodities included such forest products as timber, beeswax, ivory, and betel, and such minerals as gold, silver, copper, and iron. The crown control of minerals has been discussed earlier in reference to the Gold, Silver, and Granary departments. Betel cultivation was generally taxed through a lump assessment per village or community of betel-producing Karens and upland-dwelling Burmans.[63] Commercial taxes consisted of a standard levy of 10 percent on the overland trade with China and imports through the ports of Rangoon, Bassein, Mergui, and Martaban. The crown also assessed a duty of 5 percent in silver on the value of legally exportable goods.[64]

There are no records to show the amount of crown income from these sources, but the Italian missionary Gaetano Mantegazza noted in 1784 that the port revenues of Rangoon surpassed all other sources of crown income. The British resident Hiram Cox obtained information in 1797 that the annual Rangoon revenues were 150,000 *kyats* of silver from commerce and 50,000 *kyats* from agriculture and other sources, and that Tavoy and Mergui produced 30,000 *kyats* and 40,000 *kyats*, respectively. Yet the Burmese historian U Tin gives figures from a decade earlier for the crown income from Kyauk-hse, one of the richest agricultural districts, of 92,500 *kyats* of silver and 420,000 baskets of rice in 1784 and 20,000 *kyats* of silver and 300,000 baskets of rice in 1785.[65] If these figures are accepted at face value, clearly agricultural and related revenues from the provinces alone must have been many times greater than that derived from commerce, based on the fact that 5 baskets of rice had a contemporary market value of 1 *kyat* of silver.

The crown also received income from the sale of concessions. For a set annual amount paid to the ruler, the concessionaire received the right to operate a toll station, landing stage, fishery, ferry, or to perform the functions of brokerage. Once purchased, such concessions became heritable, contingent on the continued payment of the annual fee, and could also be sold or mortgaged by the concessionaire. Closely related was the sale of commodity concessions for which the crown received a set annual sum from an individual or group exploiting a natural resource or business. For example, the Chinese silver miners of Baw-dwin were reported to have paid the king forty-eight *viss* of pure silver annually for the privilege of mining, and the ruby miners and the oil-well operators of Yei-nan-gyaung had a similar type of arrangement.[66] The sale of concessions seems almost a form of tax farming, but there is no way to estimate the undoubtably considerable crown income from this source.

Another source of crown income was what the *sit-tans* invariably classify as "fees from petty cases and the judicial fees." The officers of every *myo* and village were empowered to deal with a variety of such minor matters as adjudicating local disputes; arranging the sale of horses, cattle, debt slaves, and land; and disposing of stray livestock and the carcasses of dead horses and elephants. Indeed, almost any act taken by a local official in relation to one of his or her constituents resulted in a modest fee. Most *sit-tans* carefully specify that half of such fees had to be turned over to the crown.

The state had one other device which it employed to apparently good effect to raise revenue. Common practice was to lay a special impost on a given locality to meet a nonrecurring public expense. For instance, the British agent John Canning noted in 1810 that the cost of his trip upriver from Rangoon to Amara-pu-ra was paid for by a levy of 20 *kyats* per house in Rangoon. The Italian missionary Vincentius Sangermano observed that during the reign of Bo-daw-hpaya construction of most of the palaces and pagodas in and around the capital was financed by similar local levies. The only special levy known to have been made on a national scale occurred in 1798, when $33^{1/3}$ *kyats* of silver was allegedly collected from every household in the realm for a total revenue of 6 million *kyats*. Thus, the special levies provided the crown with a means for circumventing the limits on taxation imposed by Burmese tradition, Buddhist lore, and the customary nature of local administration. The arbitrary nature of the special levies must have been one of the most onerous aspects of early Kon-baung rule. Further, this burden on the populace tended to increase over time because it was not uncommon, as Yi Yi has observed, for officials to continue to collect such imposts as though they were recurrent.[67]

In addition to these main areas of taxation, kings also derived sporadic income from confiscation, presents, and conquests. Confiscation was apparently a fairly common punishment for displeasing the ruler or for criminal or treasonous acts. The execution of a wealthy merchant who angered Bo-daw-hpaya and confiscation of his property was described in some detail by Hiram Cox, and Vincentius Sangermano recorded that the richest merchants of the capital were required to provide any financing demanded by the crown.[68] Any holding of office or contact with the court required the submission of presents, and gifts to the king and crown prince on the ceremonial *kadaw* occasions were also traditionally part of official obligation. Military triumphs such as the sack of Ayuthia in 1767 and the plundering of Arakan in 1784–1785 brought considerable increments to the crown coffers as well. Overall, however, the sporadic nature of these sources of income probably made them of marginal importance to the financing of the state.

The available information on early Kon-baung taxation is mainly descriptive of rates and categories, leaving no way to estimate the annual income of the state. Unfortunately, the same holds true for expenditure, where the nature of the monarchy also makes it difficult to differentiate between the public and personal obligations of the ruler. Much of the revenue, especially that collected in kind, was held in the provinces in regional storehouses to meet the crown's local obligations. The local and provincial officials were supported by surcharges on taxes collected, hence the local expenditure of crown revenues tended to be mostly religious in nature.[69] Revenues that did reach the capital might be termed the "net income" of the crown and this was expended in the following broad categories: (1) public works relating to palaces, religious edifices, and major irrigation projects; (2) palace festivals and ceremonies; (3) religious offerings and related outgoings; (4) support of members of the royal family without appanages; and (5) clothes and trappings for courtiers and the traditional gifts of food, clothes, and utensils to many of the crown service groups. Public works were largely financed by special levies, but the remaining categories were supported by the net income. To the modern eye, the categories other than public works may appear trivial, but in the early Kon-baung state account needs to be taken of the enormous costs of both state merit-making and the requisite need to express national unity and aspirations in the lavish and splendid ceremonial of the court. These categories must have been heavy debits against the exchequer. Indeed, the eagerness of kings to sell concessions and extort and confiscate the assets of the wealthy suggests a chronic need for hard cash.

Although in outline the early Kon-baung state appears to have possessed a systematic pattern of appropriation and a moderately diversified revenue base, the overall ability of the fiscal system to secure revenue appears to have fallen short of the needs of the state. The combination of Burmese tradition and classical Buddhist doctrine tended to limit the amount of the national product that could be converted to state purposes. So, too, did the custom established by the Pagan and Taung-ngu kings of fixing by decree the fiscal obligations of given communities, groups, or concessions, obligations which were respected as royal tradition by the early Kon-baung monarchs. Thus, the ability of the ruler to expand income by raising the rate of taxation was limited. At the same time, many, if not most, of the fiscal obligations of the state were dictated by the ideological obligations of its reformation function and by the historic patron-client relationship between the king and his officials and crown service groups. Fundamental to the purpose and health of the state, these obligations and relationships were not really susceptible to reduction or other manipulation. Fiscal control also suffered because revenue collection was dependent on an officialdom whose livelihood and political position were too integrally related to the fiscal system for the latter to be efficient. Thus, factors outside the fiscal system tended to deny the state basic control over income and expenditures. The need for the crown to resort to arbitrary levies, extortion, and confiscation is one manifestation of the fundamental inadequacy of the fiscal system.

The *Myo-za* System

Closely related to the fiscal system was another important system of crown-allotted appanages termed *myo-za*. Literally translated the term means "to eat the *myo*," but a more correct rendering would be "to have the use of" or "enjoy the revenues of" a *myo*. Crown-allotted appanages were a feature of the Burmese administrative system as early as the Pagan period, but use of the term *myo* itself appears only after that period.[70] There were, moreover, two kinds of *myo-za*. The largest of the thirty-odd Shan principalities were governed by hereditary chiefs known as *saw-bwas*, but hereditary Shan chieftains of lesser note were usually termed *myo-zas*. Outside of the Shan areas, the term *myo-za* uniformly denoted a holder of a nonhereditary appanage. The term has often been mistranslated as "fief," which refers to land grants in return for specifically military service.[71] Burmese appanages were bestowed on members of the royalty and upper officialdom as a mark of crown favor and reward, and were neither hereditary nor necessarily dependent on specific or recurring service to the crown.[72] When the appanage was a *myo*, the holder was termed a *myo-za* and, when a village, a *ywa-za*.

The grant of an appanage did not mean that title to the land and/or people of a given district or village was relinquished by the crown, but only that the monarch temporarily alienated his traditional due to another individual. This principle is very clearly stated in most *sit-tans* in terms nearly identical to the 1784 *sit-tan* of Kyauk-maw Myo in Taung-ngu: "When there is a *myo-za*, the revenue is by tradition submitted to the *myo-za*. When there is no *myo-za*, it must be submitted to the crown storehouse in Taung-ngu."[73] The *sit-tans* further document that *myo-zas* had the power to make special levies of cash and labor for such projects as building a new house and compound or constructing a pagoda. The appanage holder received not only the traditional crown due, but also the crown's extraordinary powers of appropriation.

Nor was the system of alienating revenue rights restricted to the the simple granting of the resource and tax rights to specific villages and districts. The revenue from a specific tax obligation in a given locality itself was often allocated to individuals. The Taung-ngu land roll of 1784, for example, records that the silver tax of ten *kyats* per house in the Kyi-daung tract had been alienated to the chief queen since the reign of Hsin-hpyu-shin and the Han-tha-wadi land roll of 1802 lists other specific taxes payable to the chief queen.[74] The crown share of revenue from bazaars, landing stages, ferries, toll stations, customs posts, and even at one point small percentages of the Rangoon import revenues were also alienated to individuals. Of the twenty-one *kin* or crown customs posts on the Irrawaddy River between Rangoon and the capital, twenty were alienated to members of the royal family in 1798, including six to the king's second son and five to the chief queen.[75] Nor were glebe and service lands excluded from the *myo-za* system. The revenues paid by the latter were alienated in the same manner as the revenues from nonservice lands, as were all revenues and fees other than the main tax paid by cultivators of glebe lands.[76]

In territorial appanages the *myo-za* was not usually permitted to reside permanently in the district, and so appointed a relative or other trusted person to serve as his or her agent. Known as the *akaing*, this agent collected the revenue and the *myo-za*'s share of the local fees. One of a new *myo-za*'s first acts was to obtain from the local officials their register of houses and revenue accounts. In some cases the *akaing* served as the local judge and, in others, shared this function with the local headman, usually splitting the fees. Beyond these functions, however, *myo-zas* did not usually encroach further on the prerogatives of local officials. A few particularly favored princes received full powers of governance over their appanages and functioned as *myo wuns* as well as *myo-zas* or, in the case of Prome and Taung-ngu, as viceroys.[77]

The concentration of appanages in the core area suggested by Victor Lieberman for the Restored Taung-ngu dynasty was not repeated in the early Kon-baung period.[78] The extant *sit-tans* and other records show the country to have been blanketed with appanages, with the exception of Martaban, a lacuna which may have been due to the exposed position of that province on the southeastern frontier and its rebellious nature. The probable explanation for the difference between the Restored Taung-ngu and the early Kon-baung periods lies in the rapid increase in the size of the royal lineage and court in the latter period. This increase caused a corresponding growth in the *myo-za* system. By midpoint in the reign of Bo-daw-hpaya, for example, Vincentius Sangermano observed: "As the reigning monarch has had more than a hundred children by his numerous wives and concubines, they have swallowed up all the riches of the land; the cities, villages, and lakes have been almost all given them for their maintenance."[79] Thus, necessity dictated that no part of the country be omitted from the appanage system.

The expansion of appanages under the early Kon-baung rulers had several important effects on the political system. Because the royal lineage monopolized not only the best but the majority of appanages, its concrete control of the resources of the realm was expanded at the expense of the formal administrative system and brought a corresponding reduction in the power of the officialdom. The *myo-za* system and the formal administrative system were an administrative duality, the former the private crown-sponsored sector and the latter the public sector. The parallel between this administrative dualism in the early Kon-baung period and the dualism of the ministerial patronage networks and the formal system in the later Taung-ngu period as described by Lieberman is indeed suggestive.[80] It almost appears that the early Kon-baung rulers took to heart the lessons of the later Taung-ngu period and tried to ensure the dominance of the royal lineage through the *myo-za* system. Whatever the case, the *myo-za* system was one of the most sensitive and effective control mechanisms available to the Burmese rulers because they could bestow or withdraw this important reward at will.

However valuable in the political arena, the *myo-za* system was a distinct liability in other respects. It clearly removed a large proportion of the country's revenue base from the direct control and exploitation of the ruler, thus complementing the weakness of the fiscal system. This left the crown in chronic fiscal straits. At the same time, the preponderance of the royal lineage in appanage holding raised the incidence of overexploitation by *myo-zas* because, in the words of Sangermano: "as almost all these petty goverments have been given to the wives, concubines, or children of the Emperor, greater oppressions have been practiced by these members of the royal family than any simple Mandarin would have dared have recourse to."[81] The result can only have been to increase the flight to alternative statuses described in chapters 1 and 2. In addition to eroding the material base of royal power, the *myo-za* system enabled the more important members of the royal lineage, particularly the princes of the blood, to dominate the politics of patronage and influence, and thus to build factions able to compete in the politics of succession.

Religious Affairs and the Maha Dan Department

As discussed in chapter 3, in the state ideology the king's reformation function gave the state the stewardship of the religious well-being of the populace. This stewardship was manifested in the monarchy in the enforcement of public morality, state merit-making and merit-sharing activities, the *bodhisatta* ideal, and efforts to maintain the integrity of the monkhood. To this list must be added one further item: the preservation of glebe lands in their original endowed purpose. The integrity of the *sangha* and the endowment of land to religious purposes were related to the emphasis on charity-derived merit in Burmese religion and the monkhood itself as the Buddha's chosen vehicle for the preservation and propagation of his teaching. If the early Kon-baung state was to perform its reformation function, it had also to deal with the *sangha* and glebe land endowments as administrative problems.

The practice of endowing religious establishments with land to provide for their maintenance dates back to at least the Pagan period. Because the king, as lord of earth and water, held absolute proprietary right over the land, however, endowment of land meant not a transfer of title but alienation of the produce of the land. This took either the form of the main tax or required the cultivators to maintain the establishment in lieu of the main tax. Glebe land revenues and their related religious institutions were traditionally administered by glebe wardens, local people of influence and piety, who collected the produce, cash, or service due to their charge. The recording of glebe land and its obligations was an important function of the *sit-tans*, some of which note the absence of glebe wardens and the performance of their duties by the local officials. The major endowers of land for religious purposes were the kings, whose most extensive dedications occurred in the Pagan and Ava periods in connection with the most intense period of religious construction in Burmese history.[82] Other members of the royal family and high officials made some endowments, but people of lesser rank had to content themselves with the construction of smaller pagodas and other modest works of merit.

Although dedicating cultivators along with the land was apparently common in the Pagan period, by the eighteenth century true glebe serfs may have been few in number. They receive but a single mention in the entire body of *sit-tans*.[83] Most glebe lands were worked by ordinary cultivators who applied to the glebe wardens or local officials for permission to farm the land. Beyond rendering the tax, produce, and/or service stipulated in the original land endowment, these cultivators were in no way bound to the land or related religious institution and were free to leave at will. The only difference between working glebe land and other land was that the traditional tithe went not to the crown or *myo-za*, but to a religious establishment through the glebe wardens. It was therefore common practice to assign cultivation rights to glebe lands to crown service units who then discharged the stipulated obligations to the endowed institution.

In order to continue to receive the proper merit from the benefaction, it was necessary for the benefactor to preserve glebe lands in their original status. For the same reason it was equally important for the pagoda or monastery related to the land to remain in good repair and function. Moreover, glebe lands had a tendency to lose their original function over time, as shown in the many references to tenantless and uncultivated glebe lands in the *sit-tans*. After long cultivation by one tenant, glebe land was often treated as if it had private heritable status and was thereby mortgaged. In other instances, those working glebe lands failed to meet or denied their obligations and, in yet others, local officials taxed glebe lands as if they had no special status. Conversely, it was not uncommon for cultivators to claim that their private or service land was glebe in order to avoid payment of taxes.

Many of the most important pagodas and land endowments dated from the twelfth and thirteenth centuries. By the eighteenth century, malfeasance by the devices described above had apparently greatly reduced the amount of glebe land still serving its original purpose. After the fall of upper Burma in 1885, British settlement officers documented the extensive alienation of glebe lands in their reports. One report noted that "a large proportion of the Wuttagan [glebe] land of

Upper Burma has become the private property of mortgagees without a chance of their property ever being redeemed."[84]

Glebe lands were apparently a problem for the crown as early as the later Pagan period, when rulers first began attempts to control the land endowments and authenticate the titles of such lands.[85] During the seventeenth-century reign of Tha-lun, sporadic efforts at control were replaced by systematic administration through a crown department called the Maha Dan. Tha-lun ordered the Maha Dan *wun* to conduct a thorough accounting of the lands and people attached to religious foundations, confiscate all lands whose credentials as glebe endowments could not be verified, and thereafter maintain accurate lists of glebe lands and other ecclesiastical property.[86] Alaung-hpaya and his successors continued to be active through the Maha Dan Department in connection with the glebe land problem, which had become even more serious as a result of the upheavals accompanying the fall of the Taung-ngu dynasty and the war between north and south. Still patterned after the one of Tha-lun's time, the Maha Dan Department proved inadequate to deal with the problem of growing glebe land abuse, in response to which Naung-daw-gyi imposed a standard produce tax of one-tenth with a 10 percent commission for the headman on some of these lands. This practice was expanded under Bo-daw-hpaya, who also began the related practice of state collection of the revenues of lands attached to defunct religious foundations and major national pagodas. These revenues were paid into the Kathaung-myaung Taik as the public purse and used to finance state activities related to religion.[87]

When these measures, too, proved inadequate, the king proposed that all glebe lands that were either uncultivated or of dubious title revert to crown ownership, but the idea was dropped in the face of strong opposition from his secular and clerical advisers. He therefore issued an edict in 1793 directing that the dedicatory inscriptions of pagodas and monasteries be collected and brought to Amara-pu-ra for authentication. The project was not generally successful, however, because local people destroyed many inscriptions *in situ* while others were destroyed in transit.[88] Thus, crown control of glebe land endowments and their revenues was to some extent extended under early Kon-baung rule, but to what practical effect remains an open question.

Another aspect of this problem was the crown stewardship of the *sangha* called for by the Asokan model in Burmese kingship. The basic problems of the *sangha* were insincere monks seeking escape from personal problems or the demands of service and taxation (another variant of the idea of alternative statuses), the moral conduct of monks which raised questions of ordination validity, and the historical tendency toward sectarianism over minor points of doctrine and practice. All these problems bore directly on the mission of the monkhood as collective savior in Burmese society and custodian of the Buddha's teaching, and hence were important concerns of the state. As with glebe lands, the problems of the *sangha* and royal responses to them date from the Pagan period and were the focus of much effort both by Tha-lun and the rulers of the early Kon-baung period. The state had three basic means of policing: a judicial role in matters of doctrine and practice, control of access to and advancement in the order through an examination and reward system, and secular control and discipline through the agency of the Maha Dan Department.

Because the monastic order had no centralized structure of its own and left each monk ultimately his own agent, it lacked any internal mechanism for determining doctrinal purity and effecting discipline. The historic mission of Theravada Buddhist kingship was to maintain the integrity of the inherently atomized and undisciplined monkhood through crown imposed definitions of doctrinal orthodoxy supported by secular administrative regulation. From the time of Asoka on, doctrinal issues were debated in open council before the ruler, who then imposed a decision on the order. The early Kon-baung period, for example, witnessed the second half of a century-long and extremely bitter doctrinal dispute over the proper draping of the monastic habit. This dispute was submitted to each early Kon-baung ruler in succession for decision until Bo-daw-hpaya finally settled the matter by imposing uniformity by decree.[89] The roles of successive kings in this dispute illustrate the fact that the only structure of authority to which the monkhood had reference was the state, and that the king had the last word in all matters relating to religion.

Formal entry into the *sangha* as a "professional" monk was also a state function, dating from the time of Tha-lun, who instituted annual monastic examinations, and continuing in the early Kon-baung period. An annual royal order directed the abbots responsible for examining monks and novices in the various districts to convene at the capital to consider which candidates had demonstrated sufficient learning to be ordained. A list of the successful candidates, along with a list of the best disciples and their teachers in such areas as grammar and parts of the Buddhist scriptures such as the *suttas* and the *abhidhamma*, was presented to the Hlut-taw. Those who were to become novices were honored with such trappings as *salwes* (ceremonial sashes) and circlets, and were formally proclaimed to be members of the *tha-gi-win min-do amyo*, or the "Sakyan race of kings." If not already of a crown service unit, the parents and near relatives of the new monks and novices were entered on the rolls of one or another of the prestige cavalry units and declared free of taxation. Ordination took place several months later at the capital under state auspices and with further honors for those ordained. Promotion within the monkhood was also a crown function, as the leading monks moved up a hierarchy of status and reward similar to the upper levels of the secular status hierarchy for officials. The precisely graded ecclesiastical honorific titles, attendant trappings of rank, and status-graded funerals were reflections of the size and prestige of the monasteries to which the abbots were assigned.[90] Thus, the monkish professionals constituted a socially elite group in which membership conferred material as well as status rewards both on the individual and his family.

Obsessed with the utopian mission of Burmese kingship and discouraged by the low standards of the *sangha* professionals, Bo-daw-hpaya carried the state stewardship of the *sangha* a step further. In 1787 he appointed his preceptor, a distinguished monk named U Nyana, to be *tha-thana-baing*, or chief of religious affairs, and made him responsible for the doctrinal instruction and discipline of all monks. In addition, the Restored Taung-ngu system of district *sangha* heads, termed *gaing-oks*, was reconstituted to administer the monks of the provinces outside the home districts. The operational arm of the *sangha* administration headed by the *tha-thana-baing* was the Maha Dan Department which, in addition to its responsibilities for glebe lands, had also been historically responsible for policing the ranks of the *sangha* for lax and undisciplined monks. The department was directed to carry out the orders of the *tha-thana-baing* and provide him with routine administrative and clerical support.[91]

In sum, secular regulation of monks and glebe lands progressed sporadically from the Pagan period on and took major steps in the reigns of Tha-lun and Bo-daw-hpaya. By perhaps 1800 the process had reached its climax, with an ecclesiastical administrative structure of sorts inserted into the body of the *sangha* and supported by the Maha Dan Department. The *sangha*, in effect, had become a pseudo-member of the departmental system and was registered, administered, and exploited in much the same fashion as a crown service group. To some extent the class of land defined as glebe had also passed from local to central control and its revenues applied to the public religious weal as determined by the crown.

The Privy Administration

The Hlut-taw controlled the departments and the territorial administration, but both its officers and its jurisdiction were kept at arms' length from the king. All that related to the person of the monarch, his private affairs, his physical security, and access to him was under the control of the Bye-daik. Although in their aggregate the functions of the Bye-daik were broader than the range of business associated with the Privy Council in English history, the term *privy* is useful to indicate the very real difference in function and orientation between the Bye-daik and the Hlut-taw.

The Bye-daik was a particular part of the Inner Palace, or the living quarters of the ruler, and was divided into upper and lower levels that were known as the Upper and Lower Bye-daik. The Upper Bye-daik contained a throne and was the scene of the first two of the three daily royal audiences, the third being held whenever the king wished. As with the Hlut-taw, there were required standards of dress and a prohibition against betel chewing and spitting. Four *atwin-wuns* headed the more than fifty officers of the Bye-daik establishment with four *than-daw-zins*, or crown heralds, making up the second line of management. The Bye-daik was manned twenty-four hours a day with two *atwin-wuns* on duty at all times.

The functions of the Bye-daik fell into two broad categories. The first related to the administration of the Atwin-daw, or Inner Palace, and the privy affairs of the crown, and the second concerned communications and relations with the Hlut-taw. The entrance to the Inner Palace was through the Red Gate over which the *atwin-wuns* had absolute control, no persons or goods entering or exiting without a written order. They were also responsible for all chambers of the Inner Palace, the interior armories, the interior gardens, the carriages and palanquins, elephant and horse stables, and building maintenance and repair. With these responsibilities went control of the myriad servants and the elite guard units both of the Inner Palace and the Western Court. One very important aspect of the Bye-daik's administration of privy affairs was the Shwei-daik, or Privy Purse, which kept the revenue from the crown demesne, the personal treasure of the king and royal women, the records of the 1783 and 1802 inquests, and the annual population registers submitted by the heads of crown service groups and the territorial officers. All credits, debits, and changes in the records had to be notified in writing to the *atwin-wuns*, one of whom was assigned specific responsibility for the Shwei-daik and was known as the Shwei-daik *atwin-wun*.

In discharging their functions as chamberlains, the *atwin-wuns* also controlled written and physical access to the ruler. For example, on receipt at the Bye-daik all messages and communications were read aloud in the presence of the *atwin-wuns* on duty and important matters were taken immediately to the king. The *atwin-wuns* had a fair amount of discretionary authority and could refer individual matters back to the Hlut-taw for additional explanation or investigation before bringing them before the monarch. All royal emanations, whether formal edicts and orders or simple messages and inquiries, were formally transmitted through the Bye-daik and its corps of writers and heralds. This included the verbal orders and messages given at the morning and early afternoon audiences and the later conference with officers with specific or ongoing military responsibilities. All of these communications were channeled to the Hlut-taw as the chief executive organ for whatever action was required.

The *atwin-wuns* were further required to advise on criminal, religious, and administrative matters, a role that enabled them to serve as a check on the Hlut-taw. Because the Bye-daik received the daily reports of the *nagans*, investigative officers of the Hlut-taw, the *atwin-wuns* were kept fully informed on the problems of national and local affairs and how the Hlut-taw was dealing with these. All of the *atwin-wuns* had to agree on an order before it could be transmitted to the Hlut-taw for execution.[92] Thus, the *atwin-wuns* transcended their roles as chamberlains by also serving not as a privy council but as privy counsellors.

Alternate Communication Systems

However absolute the authority of kings in theory, its exercise depended on their ability to maintain overall control of administrative affairs. Ensconced in the palace, they were highly dependent on the Hlut-taw as the apex of the formal administrative apparatus for the flow of news, intelligence, and advice, without which it was difficult to exert that control. At the same time, the ruler needed to counterbalance the near monopoly of the Hlut-taw over administration by using alternate channels of information and counsel.

To a large extent the Bye-daik served just such purpose, as well as providing a second channel through which aggrieved officials or individuals could communicate with the throne. There was, in addition, a crown intelligence staff which blanketed the realm and kept the king apprised of developments and affairs. These intelligence officers were known as *nagans*, an innovation probably dating from the Restored Taung-ngu period, when it was adopted as part of the program to curb provincial autonomy. The Hlut-taw establishment included four crown *nagans*, whose duty was to report to the Bye-daik as well as the Hlut-taw. Charged with investigating suspicious matters, affairs contrary to custom, and boundary disputes, these officers and their subordinates transmitted to the king a daily intelligence summary prepared from the reports of the provincial officials, reports of all pending executions, appointments and depositions from office, orders from the Hlut-taw to the Bye-daik, and from the Hlut-taw to chiefs of armed units. At the provincial level, each *myo* administration included one or two *myo nagans* whose duties were to report on the affairs of that jurisdiction, including whether the local populace was oppressed, whether the local officers were upholding their oaths of loyalty or feuding among themselves, and whether correct tax and population records and revenues were submitted. This function was considered so important that an edict of 1762 directed the chief of the *nagans* to prepare a manual for the guidance of these officers in their work and to provide each with a copy.[93]

The *nagans* are somewhat reminiscent of the Chinese inspectorate or the French system of intendants and were intended to provide the monarch with an outside check on the functioning of the administrative apparatus directed by the Hlut-taw. Thus, the *nagans* and the Bye-daik were important to the ruler to balance the near complete monopoly enjoyed by the Hlut-taw over the administration of the realm. Another device employed to keep the ruler informed and to inhibit chicanery and conspiracy was the extensive use of spies and the formal monitoring of the meetings of officials and princes.[94]

The crown also had recourse to a body of independent advisers composed of learned monks, brahmans, and other wise men who held no formal offices and were therefore assumed to give nonpartisan counsel. One well-known example from the reign of Alaung-hpaya is the Atu-la Hsaya-daw, a learned monk who provided advice on a wide range of matters. His counsel was later compiled into a work entitled *Nan-zin pok-hsa* [Questions in the palace]. The author of a similar work called *Amei-daw ahpyei* [Answers to the royal questions] was the first Maung-daung Hsaya-daw who, along with the sage U Paw U, was a prominent independent adviser during the reign of Bo-daw-hpaya. The latter was purposely never given an official position by the king so as not to reduce his value as an independent counsellor.[95] A last and very important recourse of those early Kon-baung monarchs with mature sons was to use these consanguine relatives as a source of counsel and administrative support.

Administrative Dichotomies and the Fragmentation of Authority

As described above, there were at least two basic principles underlying early Kon-baung administration: the concept of administrative dichotomies and the fragmented and incomplete nature of political authority. There seems to have been an oppositional quality to administrative thought, a sense that an important center of administrative power required pairing with an inferior point of administration, with the latter keeping the former from becoming completely preponderant. The oppositional aspect of Burmese thought can be seen in the status divisions of the left and right (as will be discussed in chapter 6), the inner and outer divisions of the palace (which was seen not as a unity but a duality), and in the important division between the interior and exterior *thwei-thauks*. Because the Hlut-taw and the Bye-daik were the two most important organs of government, the dichotomy resulting from their opposition is the most important instance of bureaucratic pairing. Their subordinate organs—the Kathaung-myaung Taik of the Hlut-taw and the Shwei-daik of the Bye-daik—also reflected this pairing. On a more mundane level, the same phenomenon was expressed in the dichotomies between the departmental and territorial jurisdictions, the differentiation between the crown service and *athi* elements of the population, and between the appointed and hereditary officers of the *myos*.

An important part of the concept of bureaucratic dichotomies was the notion that the smaller side of the pair was qualitatively superior to the larger. This was apparently derived from the Burmese idea that association with the monarch was ennobling and that the closer the association, the more ennobling it became. The Inner Palace was therefore superior to the outer, the interior *thwei-thauks* to the exterior, and crown service status to that of *athi*. The *myo-za* system may also fit into this concept as the quantitatively inferior but qualitatively superior part of an administrative duality consisting of a private crown-sponsored system and the public or formal system of administration. Whether the idea of ennoblement by proximity of association to the throne applied to the Bye-daik/Hlut-taw dichotomy is not clear from the material (although I believe that it did), but definitely did apply to the departmental/territorial dichotomy. This is reflected in the respective involvement of departments with the administration of the crown service groups and that of the territorial jurisdictions with the *athi* population.

The oppositional pairing of different parts of the bureaucratic apparatus seems to have been rooted in a deeper feeling for the need to fragment all political authority except that of the king, which was deemed holistic in nature. Imbued with absolute political authority, the throne delegated authority to its officials, but permitted no official to have complete authority over his jurisdiction. The Hlut-taw may have been the central executive organ of the state, but it did not have full control of all crown service units, military forces, arms, or fiscal matters; nor did it have custody of those most important tools of administration: the population and crown service registers and the records of the royal inquests. The lacunae in its authority were filled by the Byedaik, whose authority in some areas paralleled or overlapped that of the Hlut-taw. Similarly, few of the territorial *wuns* were free of competing authorities within their jurisdictions because they had no control over crown service groups and villages under the *myo-lat* and *ywa-lat wuns* or under such departments as the Granary, Silver Tax, or Taik. The fragmentation of territorial authority is clearly stated in many of the *sit-tans*. The 1803 *sit-tan* of Mekhkaya Myo in Kyauk-hse, for example, says: "Members of the *daing* units, the crown cultivators, and palace guards live in the *myo* and its village tracts. I cannot assign crown duties to these people of the village. Only the authorities of the various crown service groups can require service of them. I only decide the petty cases and have charge of the resultant fees."[96]

Thus, part of the population and some of the villages within most territorial jurisdictions answered to other authorities. The northern and central areas had large concentrations of crown service and departmentally administered population. Hence the power of most territorial *wuns* in these areas was diluted because a large proportion of the population was not under their control. This dilution of power was less evident in the southern wunships, where the crown service population was scanty and the departments had correspondingly less jurisdiction. The southern *wuns* therefore tended to be more powerful, not only because their jurisdictions were larger and farther from the capital, but also because they had little competition from officials in other parts of the central administration. To the north of these jurisdictions, however, conflict between the territorial and departmental *wuns* was not uncommon and often had to be settled by recourse to the throne.[97]

Having concentrated political authority in the monarchy, the essence of Burmese administrative concept and practice appears to have been to fragment control of the population and countryside through the creation of various parallel jurisdictions, thereby creating administrative rivalry and conflict. Lines of specific administrative authority extended outward from the throne, mostly through the Hlut-taw but partly through the Bye-daik, to departments and territorial jurisdictions. The incomplete nature of authority within the latter and the disconnected and often small bases of the former militated against significant concentrations of power developing within the administrative apparatus. Probable points of such concentration were further balanced by an opposing, albeit inferior, point of authority. One important result of the fragmentation of authority was that within any given jurisdiction there were always alternative channels of communication to the constituent parts state power: the throne, the Hlut-taw, and the Bye-daik.

CHAPTER 5

THE OFFICIALS

The administrative apparatus was manned by hereditary and appointive officials who constituted one of the three elite groups in early Kon-baung society, the others being the monkhood and the extended royal lineage. As discussed in the preceding chapter, the monkhood was a socially elite but politically benign group composed of "professional" monks and their relatives. The extended royal lineage, on the other hand, was an important participant in the political process in several important ways to be explored in the succeeding chapter. As a group officials were more than just administrative cadres, but another key element in the political struggle of the polity, an element whose interests were often in conflict with those of the monarch and deeply involved in the struggle for the throne.

Officials as a Primary Status Group

The institution of Burmese kingship was synonymous with government *per se* and, as discussed in chapter 3, derived its legitimacy from the first king model of Maha Thamada, as articulated in Burmese political thought. This same model also legitimized the administrative apparatus and its associated personnel. Burmese sources state that Maha Thamada organized countries and appointed crown princes, envoys, generals, judges, and other officials in order to carry out the regulation functions deemed necessary for orderly social life.[1] As such, the structures and personnel of government were associated with the repressive rather than the utopian aspect of Burmese political thought. As agents or extensions of the ruler, officials were also responsible for the consequences of good or bad rule. One text of 1771 observes that

"A king who, with his good officials, is truly the refuge and support of all the people acquires fame" and links good administration by officials to the prosperity of the realm.[2] The responsibility for the social and natural dysfunctions believed to result from a ruler's failure in *raja dhamma* was, in part, attached to officials as the agents of his will. Hortatory works also laid emphasis on wise, obedient, and discreet officials as one of the important strengths of a king.[3] To preserve and advance the welfare of the realm through *raja dhamma*, a just and virtuous king required just and virtuous officials.

The ruler extended carefully measured amounts of his authority and charisma to individual officials. These measures were visible in the grade of personal honorific title, official paraphernalia, and, in the higher ranks, value of appanage. Armed with these visible signs of association with the crown and the fact of their office, officials formed a primary status group. This social position was further enhanced by the doctrine of *kamma*, which provided the rationalization for the rigid grading of the social order. Implying strong *kamma*, official position marked the incumbent as morally superior to the common people and placed him in one of the upper levels of the social pyramid. As a result of their superior moral and political positions, officials were seen as autocratic authority figures and treated with the same kind of reverence and respect reserved for kings and monks. The Italian missionary Vincentius Sangermano noted, "the Mandarins and Talapoins [monks] are by reason of their offices and sacred character . . . regarded with an excessive reverence," and a village headman instructed his son, newly appointed as a retainer to a governor, "Worship your lord as if he were a pagoda."[4] Like the ruler and monks, officials were the objects of physical obeissance and "respect language" on the part of the commoners.[5]

The elevated political and status position of officials explains the popular preoccupation with achieving some kind of crown office. This was always a possibility for the average man because the notion of kammatic flux held the promise of sudden and radical improvement in social position. Hence, as Sangermano further observed: "There is no one amongst them, however poor or mean, who does not aim at the dignity of Mandarin. For it is a frequent occurrence here for a man to be raised in a moment, by the caprice of the monarch, from the lowest state of poverty and degradation to the rank of minister or general."[6] Aspiration to the kingship was virtually unthinkable for most, but crown office was a legitimate and attainable personal goal that people went to great lengths to achieve. The popular deference to and awe of officials and corollary aspiration for office led to what might be termed a "*min* complex," a complex of attitudes defining officeholding as highly desirable and personally attainable.

From *wun-gyi* down to village headman, the relationship between ruler and official was based on the delegation of authority and concommitant rewards by the former in exchange for the total fidelity and service of the latter. The nature of this relationship was personal, as opposed to legal or contractual, and was formalized at least once a year for all officials on ceremonial occasions known as *kadaw*, an untranslatable term. These occurred at the beginning and end of the Buddhist Lent (a three-month period from the full moon of July to the full moon of October), at the New Year (falling in the first half of March), and on the occasions of coronations and audience days. All officials, chiefs of crown service groups, and Shan rulers were required to proffer their oath of fealty and specified homage gifts on at least one of these occasions. Failure to do so was considered a declaration of rebellion and punished accordingly. On the appointment of an heir apparent, he, too, became part of the reciprocal relationship between king and officials, as the *sit-tans* testify: "The traditional *kadaw* presents submitted annually (by the *myo-thu-gyi*) to the king are two pieces of cloth and a silver bowl weighing five *kyats* while the *kadaw* presents for the Lord of the Eastern House [heir apparent] are one piece of cloth and a silver bowl weighing two *kyats* two *mats*."[7]

The oath of personal fidelity was coupled to the drinking of the "water of allegiance" on the part of officials. Thus, *kadaw* represented a regular reaffirmation of loyalty not to the government or the office of kingship, but to the person of the sovereign. There were several reasons why this regular reaffirmation of loyalty was necessary. The state ideology was apparently sufficient to imbue the people with a sense of the necessity of the monarchy, but insufficient to create an active popular loyalty. Even among its officials, the goals of the monarchy—the utopian mission and defense of the royal position—were insufficient to inspire dedication. The crown therefore held out an ideal standard of service and fidelity, but at the same time bought the service and loyalty of its officials with a system of specific material incentives that included personal power, appanages and other perquisites, and social position. While the majority of the population remained passive and imposed-on by the state, a minority was recruited into active political participation through the reward system. This minority was broadly divided into hereditary and appointed functionaries.

Hereditary Office and the Gentry

Apart from the monarch and the Shan chieftains, in early Kon-baung society almost all hereditary office was at the local level. The appointive exceptions were the *akaing*, or agent of the appanage holder; the *asi-yin*, or administrative deputy primarily concerned with judicial affairs; and the *hsaw*, or local crier.[8] The highest and most important of the hereditary local offices was *myo-thu-gyi*. At the lower level, the two offices of significance were the village or local tract headmen, most commonly but not always termed *thu-gyi*, and the *myei-daings*. Among the local hereditary functionaries must also be counted the hereditary chiefs of locally stationed crown service groups. The governmental functions of these offices have been noted in the preceding chapter, and it will rather be the purpose here to examine their relationship to the structure of economic and social privilege in early Kon-baung society.

As the heads of the customary aspects of local administration, the *myo-thu-gyi* and *thu-gyi* were possessed of considerable power, that of the former expanding with the size of his jurisdiction. Thus, the *myo-thu-gyis* of Talok with 102 villages, Salin with 105, and Tabayin with 214 were far more important figures than those of Min-don with 38 villages, Shwei-gyin with 3, and Hpaung-lin and Sin-gu with 1 each.[9] The status accruing to the holders of these offices was commensurate with their power. The visible marks of this status were armed retainers, an umbrella of rank, special funeral rites and other sumptuary privileges, and a *kadaw* relationship with the monarch. Customary law allowed them to abuse social inferiors physically without fault and their families and near-relatives were exempt from taxes and labor and military service. As functionaries they were *min*, or members of the governing elite, and, as such, objects of the respect language and physical obeissance.[10]

Beyond governmental power and social status, these offices conferred important material benefits. Specific rewards were attached to certain functions of the offices of *myo-thu-gyi*, *thu-gyi* and *myei-daing*, but, regardless of position, whoever performed these functions took the rewards. Thus, the *sit-tans* record that *myo-thu-gyis* often performed the functions of *myei-daings* in their jurisdictions and/or administered vacant thu-gyiships as well. Similarly, the functions of *thu-gyi* and *myei-daing* were commonly performed by the same person. Indeed, many *sit-tans* refer to the headman as the *myei-daing thu-gyi*. One function of a *sit-tan* was to catalogue not only the duties of each local office, but also the rewards attached to each duty. Thus, the 1802 *sittan* of U-yin Village in Salei Myo states:

The traditional fee of the *myei-daing* is one basket in ten of the main tax. The *myei-daing* customarily takes one-tenth of goods measured for sale by weight. The customary fees taken by the *myei-daing* are two *mats* collected from both vendor and purchaser on the sale of a [debt] slave, two *mats* from each on the sale of a horse, one *mat* from each on the sale of a buffalo, one-quarter basket of sesamum per basket of sesamum sown, and a present of a length of cotton cloth per yoke of buffalo worked on alluvial cultivation. The *myei-daing* by custom takes the ribs when cattle die.[11]

Although with considerable local variation, the *sit-tans* agree on the general categories of income and perquisites accruing to local hereditary offices. Virtually every form of economic activity paid a commission to one or all of the local officials. There were fees from petty and judicial cases (usually 10 percent of the value of the suit) and commissions on all sales, including land. Miscellaneous perquisites were presents from all petitioners, the flesh of dead livestock, and the power to dispose of stray livestock and other ownerless property. Most local offices also had state land, usually tax-exempt, attached to them as an emolument of incumbency. The 1783 *sit-tan* of Talok Myo, for example, states "The *myo-thu-gyi* cultivates common land of the *myo* yielding 500 baskets of paddy and land allotted for his support yielding 500 baskets of paddy."[12] In a similar vein, the 1784 record of Pya Village in Salei Myo reads "Ten baskets sowing of sesamum and 60 toddy palms are by custom allotted to the *myei-daing*."[13]

The two most important economic aspects of local officeholding were the commissions on tax collections and the control of communal and vacant land. In regard to the former, although the amount received varied with locality, the 1783 *sit-tan* of Anein Village in Talok Myo gives a fairly representative picture: "Main tax of three baskets, land rent of 30 *kyats* of copper, headman's share of 30 *kyats*, wastage of fifteen *kyats*, transport fee of 90 *kyats* and *myei-daing*'s share of one basket is collected per *pe* of land with fixed assessment."[14] In a prosperous or large village or district the commissions on the various tax collections were a lucrative source of income for local officials, especially because such items as wastage and transport tended to end up in their pockets as well.

Before turning to the pivotal role of local officials in land control, it is necessary to consider briefly the nature of the land system. The king was considered to be the theoretical owner of all land and all classes of land were basically defined by the degree of his proprietary interest. *Aya-daw* lands were his absolute property and included land allotted to crown service groups, confiscated or heirless lands, land allotted to local officials as a perquisite of office, and all alluvial formations. Cultivators could have no proprietary rights to these lands and paid produce tax and/or land rent to the crown. All other land was *da-ma-u-gya, bo-ba-baing*, abandoned, or glebe. Title to *da-ma-u-gya* land was obtained by virtue of having been the first to clear and cultivate it. This land became heritable in the third generation and was thereafter termed *bo-ba-baing*, or ancestral property, which was alienable through mortgage. The tenure on land other than *bo-ba-baing* lapsed if the occupier left the jurisdiction. Mortgages to people of other districts were generally prohibited.[15]

With the exception of *bo-ba-baing* land, no land was truly private. Permission to establish a *da-ma-u-gya* tenure was granted only by the local headman. Then, if the land was abandoned before it achieved *bo-ba-baing* status, its tenure lapsed and it reverted to the control of the headman, who also controlled all other uncultivated and communal land. Indeed, the local headman's most important power was his authority to assign land to cultivators. For example, the 1784 *sit-tan* of Kyei-ni Village in Salei Myo records: "Within the four quarters of the tract, there is cultivated land measuring about 100 baskets sowing of sesamum and uncleared land measuring about 59 baskets sowing of sesamum. I the *thu-gyi* allot the land to the cultivators and get them to work it."[16] Most jurisdictions contained a certain amount of abandoned service and glebe lands as well as uncultivated *aya-daw* and other lands. Many villages also had communal land, which the headman parcelled out to residents of his jurisdiction. Local headmen also assigned uncultivated lands of whatever origin to transients or local landless people who agreed to remain in the jurisdiction and bear their share of the community's service and tax assessments. Land at the disposal of the headman was termed *thu-gyi-gya myei*.

The structure of land tenure and control in a given community was influenced by several factors. First was type of cultivation, important because proprietary rights over irrigated paddy fields were extremely important whereas the same rights in shifting cultivation were almost irrelevant. Second, a strong headman also tended to prevent the development of much *bo-ba-baing* tenure. The most important factor, however, was the periodic population shifts caused by internal disorders, regional famines, and inducements for resettlement offered by officials eager to build up their jurisdictions. The greatest restructuring of tenures in the early Kon-baung period occurred as a result of the famine of 1805–1812. This event, coupled to the widespread social disorder and rebellion that accompanied it, caused massive demographic instability and a concomitant movement toward shifting cultivation. So much abandoned land was taken over by headmen during this period that the term *daing-baw myei* came into use specifically to describe this class of land.[17]

In many cases local hereditary officials appear to have used the wealth derived from such sources as tax and sales commissions to acquire private control of substantial tracts of land through mortgage. Because land controlled by a functionary as an emolument of office often remained in the same family for generations, it tended to be treated as if it had *bo-ba-baing* status. Headmen sometimes claimed private status for other lands under their control as well, a claim made particularly to lands abandoned during the great famine. Thus, there was some tendency for headmen to use their offices to build up what might be termed "estates," which were farmed by a tenantry. Judging from the few examples available, such estates ranged from a few hundred to a few thousand acres. The estates may seem modest in absolute terms, but when it is remembered that an ordinary member of a crown service unit was only expected to be able to work five *pe* (eight to twelve acres depending on type of cultivation), they were clearly an important factor in the economic structure of communities.[18] Headmen were also able to divert tenants from vacant state and glebe lands to their private holdings. It is not clear whether the phenomenon of estates held by hereditary officials was widespread enough or the nature of their control of the land firm enough for these officials to be termed a "landed" or "landlord" group. However, it is clear that the control they held over much of the land in their jurisdictions and the existence of estates in many places made them the dominant local economic force.

Their superior social and moral status and privileged economic position therefore made the local hereditary officials an elite group in society. Because many jurisdictions contained multiple headmen and *myei-daings*, these functionaries were also more numerous as a group than might be supposed.[19] Marriage within the group was the norm and contributed to the development of a certain group identity. These factors, coupled with their socioeconomic position, make it appropriate to label these hereditary officials the gentry element in early Kon-baung society.

The foundation of the gentry was their control of local hereditary office, as confirmed by crown appointment. As Alaung-hpaya gradually brought different parts of the country under his rule during the campaigns of the 1750s, he examined local officials and confirmed in office those with a hereditary claim willing to drink the water of allegiance. When there were no hereditary claimants, he appointed loyal followers and thus started new lineages of office.[20] Successors to all of these hereditary positions subsequently were required to set forth their claims in a petition to the Hlut-taw. After investigation, the petition and recommendation of the Hlut-taw went to the king for approval. The claimant then received an official appointment order and a letter of authority from the Athi Department containing details of the appointment and an injunction to look after the welfare of the *athi*, *ala*, and *kat-pa* of the jurisdiction. These documents also had to be registered at the *myo* court. Once established in office, it was customary for the incumbent to select and register his heir on a special list at the Shweidaik as the *aya-gan*, or heir designate.

Just as the eldest son by the head wife was designated as *aw-ra-tha* and given preferential treatment in the division of the estate, so was the same principle applied to hereditary office, where primogeniture was the preferred, though not the exclusive, mode of succession. The majority of the *sit-tans*, one function of which was to record the claims to office of the hereditary officials, show succession from great-grandfather to grandfather to father to son. There are a few instances, however, where they report the succession passing from father to eldest son, then laterally through the remaining brothers, eldest to youngest, and finally to the eldest son of the youngest brother. The basic difference between usual primogeniture and this variant mode is that in the former the succession was father-son-grandson while in the latter it was father-sons-grandsons. Thus, the variant mode was still within the Burman tradition of lineal descent through relatives of full blood. The most probable explanation for the occasional deviations found in the *sittans* is that the variant mode was specified by the whim of the king first establishing those particular offices. The variant mode in itself would merit no more than a passing note were it not for the fact that conflict between strict primogeniture and the variant mode was a central factor in the politics of royal succession in the early Kon-baung period.

Heredity was necessary to establish a primary claim to office, but the claimant was also required to be minimally capable of performing the duties of the office as determined by the other local officals. The *Da-yit-za di-pani* [Treatise on inheritance] of 1811 explains:

> If the son by the head wife is blind or deaf, or otherwise deformed, and is not known to the local authorities, he is the eldest son only in name but does not obtain the status of one.

> The son who industriously performs his father's duties and is known to the local authorities is considered as the eldest son, though he may be born of the lesser wife, and he shall succeed to the hereditary office.21

The most common reasons for denial of office, as evidenced by the *sittans*, were mental incompetence and the infirmities of old age. The local authorities referred to above included all hereditary officers plus the *asi-yin* and *akaing*, who collectively decided on the succession to an office whose incumbent had died or become incompetent. Birthright was therefore contingent on competence and the consensus of the other officials, and primogeniture was qualified by the requirement of competence and the cognatic nature of Burman inheritance that gave all children some claim on the estate. Younger sons and younger brothers of the officeholder were therefore included in what might be termed a "pool of succession" to the office. In the absence of a competent lineal relative of full blood, collateral and affinal relatives could assert claims. By increasing the pool of succession through these means, a family greatly increased its chances of retaining possession of an office and thus maintaining its gentry status. Such flexibility was at times crucial, as shown in this 1806 report to the Hlut-taw, which illustrates just how such a pool of succession could be decimated:

> I, Mi E, wife of the *myo-thu-gyi* of Yame-thin, respectfully submit this report, my lords. After my husband died, Nga Ei, the son designated as heir, was reported [to the Hlut-taw] and allowed to succeed and rule. Because Nga Ei became insane and unable to administer the *myo*, the middle son Nga Min was reported and ruled with the crown seal and appointment order. The *myo-thu-gyi* Nga Min died on a military expedition. Nga Ei and Nga Min left no sons or grandsons to succeed. I respectfully report that the younger brother [that is, third son] Nga Hmon has succeeded without breaking the hereditary line, my lords.22

Hereditary succession within the family was the primary but not the only means of attaining office. For example, there were instances in which a man married a female incumbent and thereby became the officeholder himself. The descent in some such cases continued to pass through the daughters, but in others shifted to the sons, thus transforming a female into a male lineage. It was also not uncommon for an older female functionary to contract a partnership with a younger man, sometimes accompanied by marriage but more often not, to carry out the duties of her office. Male functionaries who either for personal reasons did not wish to or were unable to perform their duties made similar partnerships. Office could also be obtained through mortgage, but the heirs of the mortgager retained the right of redemption for the principal plus interest. There were, on occasion, no heirs to an office, in which case the crown made an appointment, usually on the recommendation of the local *myo-za* or *myo wun*.[23]

Taken together, such occurrences tended to create more than one line of heirs which, coupled with the question of competency, led to disputed successions. Because of their power to both appoint and depose hereditary fuctionaries, the role of local officials was central in these disputes. Bribery and the formation of factions around disputing claimants made the competition for hereditary office the essence of local politics. The central role of succession in local politics was noted by Henry Burney, the earliest student of the *sit-tans* and inquests of this period. Burney concluded: "in almost every town and village in Burmah there are two parties of conflicting interests: the local officers for the time being, and some individuals, or the heirs or descendants of some who had held office at some former period. The latter closely watch the proceedings of the former. By setting one against the other, the Burmese government generally contrives to elicit the truth."[24]

The tenure of the hereditary office itself would have been inherently secure, but the status of incumbents was often quite the opposite. The legitimacy of their titles was subject to attack by rivals who sometimes employed suborned testimony and falsified Shwei-daik records.[25] There was, in fact, so much conflict surrounding the possession of local offices that the crown attempted to assert control by regulating the succession. An edict of 1789 treated the subject in some detail: "Of estates passed from parents to children, there are those which can be divided and those which cannot. Hereditary local office is passed from the father to the son and is not divisible."[26] The edict continues that such practices as partnerships and mortgages caused the lines of succession to multiply and create continuous conflict "which even the common people of the district cannot escape." Hence, it goes on to decree, "let there be only one person ruling in each town or village by order of the king."[27] The edict concludes:

> When unable to perform the duties of office and wishing to transfer it, let it go only to the son. When the son is young and unable to perform the duties and the office is transferred to another person not connected with the hereditary

succession, let the office return to the one of the original line when he is able to perform the duties. When the office has been mortgaged, let the one of the original line redeem it with money. When the office has been transferred temporarily, let it not descend to the sons and grandsons of the one to whom it was transferred.[28]

In a further effort to address the problems, an edict of 1809 prohibited local authorities from removing hereditary officers from their posts and appointing another person without first reporting the case to the Hlut-taw and obtaining a crown order.[29] The practice apparently continued, however, as there were edicts to the same effect by Min-don and Thi-baw half a century later.

As one of the organizing principles of Burman society, heredity through qualified primogeniture was subject to both individual and political contingencies that made the struggle for local office the focal point of local-level politics in the early Kon-baung period. Because the powers and rewards of these offices were the foundation of the gentry's socioeconomic position, they engendered strong competition and the gentry resisted crown efforts to regulate access to them. In so doing, the gentry protected both its privileged position and the benefits to be derived from successful cooptation of hereditary access to office. The crown assertion of and gentry resistance to regulation of local office-holding is but one aspect of the fundamental conflict between crown and officials that is discussed in more detail below.

The Appointed Officials

Whether hereditary or appointed, all officials were designated as members of that elite group of governance termed *min*. The hereditary local officials were generically termed *kyi-yo ke-yo*, or hereditary chiefs, but appointed officials, especially of the upper levels, were usually collectively termed *hmu-mat*, or leaders and ministers. The terms *amat* (minister or courtier) and *wun*, which may or may not mean burden or responsibility, were applied only to upper-level appointed officials.[30] The *sit-tans* provide a fair amount of information about local functionaries, but there is no comparable indigenous source for the appointed officials. Because the latter came into contact with European visitors and residents, however, it is possible to exploit European sources in partial compensation.

Appointed officials manned the various parts of the bureaucratic apparatus—the Hlut-taw and the departmental, territorial, and privy administrations—described in chapter 4. Even seemingly minor functionaries such as cooks, water bowl carriers, and betel box bearers were considered *min*, and at least some of these petty posts were held by men of rank in "confidential situations."[31] Indeed, it appears that the duties of a given individual were often defined less by the constitution of his office than by the reflection of his capabilities and fidelity in the eyes of his superiors and the ruler. This point is important because the arena of official politics was made more flexible by blurring the structural lines within the administrative apparatus. All officials were expected to be capable of handling any assignment, be it civil, legal, diplomatic, or military, directed to them. And it was also sometimes the case for a second- or even third-rank official at court to exercise power and influence far disproportionate to his position in the formal administrative structure. Thus, the situation for appointed officials tended to be more demanding of personal and political skills than those required of the hereditary local functionary involved in the customary administration of the *myos* and other local tracts.

As befitted their higher position in the political hierarchy, appointed officials were permitted more elaborate houses, funerals, trappings of office, and retinues than were their local counterparts.[32] The majority of these officers was possessed of personal honorific titles and those in the highest reaches of royal favor were honored with fictive kinship with the monarch. The appointed officials and their families enjoyed the same perquisites of exemption from labor and military service as did local officials but, given the appointed and often transient nature of their official tenure, were generally in a more tenuous economic position. In contrast to local officials, with only a few exceptions appointed functionaries enjoyed no comparable benefits and apparently were often in financial straits. Many officials of all grades were granted appanages, the value of which reflected their favor and status. *Wun-gyis*, *atwin-wuns*, and other top-level officers were usually granted middle-sized *myos* such as Myei-de and Kyauk-padaung. Lesser functionaries received villages or even specified numbers of houses in a village. Such grants were held only on royal suffrance.

Members of the territorial administration had several additional means of obtaining income. In jurisdictions such as Han-tha-wadi, Martaban, and Taung-ngu they were entitled to a commission of from 10 to 20 percent on the agricultural taxes and approximately 7.5 percent on taxes on such commodities as gold, silver, iron, wood oil, and palm produce.[33] Territorial *wuns* were entitled to make levies of money and labor for special expenses, some of which found its way into the personal purse.³⁴ All officials—territorial, departmental, and privy— had the right of adjudicating civil and petty disputes among the people of their jurisdictions, for which they received a percentage of the value of the case. Another important source of income for officials was the custom of giving presents on the occasion of transacting any sort of business. As the French visitor Feraud observed in 1770: "Presents are regarded here as a legitimate debt which they know how to force you to discharge through a thousand hindrances.... You cannot approach anyone and speak of business without presents. He receives them without incurring any sort of obligation to you and even when he has been unable to serve you."³⁵

The lower officials were particularly vulnerable economically because, by and large, they did not receive appanages and were thus dependent on presents and such portions of the tax commissions and other income as their superiors cared to share with them. Against these often uncertain sources of income, all appointed officials had to maintain themselves and their families at the appropriate level of the sumptuary rules and support their subordinates and retainers. In the case of some high officials, these retainers numbered in the thousands. But perhaps the heaviest drain on an official's resources were the payments necessary to maintain his position. The *myo wun* of Mergui left this accounting of the payments he made at court in 1819: 2,353 *kyats* to the king, 1,916 *kyats* to the *wun-gyis*, 1,070 *kyats* to the *myo wun* of Han-tha-wadi (then at the peak of his political influence), and 4,479 *kyats* to "different people."³⁶ As the British agent John Canning remarked of the *myo wun* of Han-tha-wadi: "In common with other Burmahs holding high office under Government, and who without receiving any salary are obliged annually to make large presents at Court to preserve their situations, his great object is to amass wealth."³⁷

To meet the financial demands of their positions, many, if not most, officials had recourse to speculations in trade, outright banditry, extortion, and various forms of corrupt practices with respect to the tax and service rolls.³⁸ The role of official corruption is important, and will be discussed in more detail below. Although life as an official, especially in the lower echelons, was often precarious financially, competition for these situations was acute because they offered the best opportunities available for social and material advancement.³⁹

The Kon-baung corps of appointed officials had its roots in the early followers of Alaung-hpaya, who relied heavily on his hundreds of relatives by blood and marriage. The polygamous nature of gentry society meant that much of his early following was drawn from this nexus of family and marriage connections. In terms of high functionaries, this nexus produced a significant part of the leadership of the dynasty for the next half-century. The core of early Kon-baung leadership was the sixty-eight members of Alaung-hpaya's first *thwei-thauk*, which he organized in 1749, three years before the fall of Ava. Among its members, fifty-five were recipients of personal honorific titles and twenty-seven received appointive office.[40] From these sixty-eight men came all four of Alaung-hpaya's *wun-gyis*, three of whom continued to serve in the succeeding reign of Naung-daw-gyi. The fourth was executed for his support of Hsin-hpyu-shin's unsuccessful bid in the succession crisis of 1760.

The accession of Hsin-hpyu-shin in 1763 saw the retention of one of Alaung-hpaya's original *wun-gyis* from the reign of Naung-daw-gyi, the selection of a second whose background is not known, and the appointment of two others from among the members of the first sixty-eight. These were U Tha Gyi and U Hnaung. Better known by his final title of Maha Thi-ha Thu-ra and his leading role in the Chinese war of the late 1760s, U Tha Gyi served the throne from 1764 until his execution in 1782. U Hnaung, known first as the Myo-lat *wun-gyi* and subsequently as the Pahkan *wun-gyi*, served continuously from 1764 until his death in about 1800. During the reign of Sin-gu, three of the *wun-gyis* were early followers of Alaung-hpaya, but the background of the fourth cannot be traced beyond a *myo* wunship held under Hsin-hpyu-shin. Three of Bo-daw-hpaya's first *wun-gyi* appointments, including U Tha Gyi and U Hnaung, can also be traced back to service with Alaung-hpaya.

The absence of family names, the frequent changes in personal honorific titles, and the paucity of biographic material in the sources make it difficult to trace the continuity of Alaung-hpaya's followers much past the early years of the reign of Bo-daw-hpaya. Yet continuity can be seen at least at the *wun-gyi* level and in the role of the Shwei-bo area in the political upheaval of early 1782, a tale told in detail in chapter 7. Also, many of the officials attached to Alaung-hpaya and the Shwei-bo area, especially the *wun-gyis*, had consistent marriage ties with the royal lineage that lasted until the death of Bo-daw-hpaya's eldest son in 1808. Thus, the circumstances surrounding the founding of the dynasty engendered an enduring regional bias and a related pattern of continuity in its top echelon of appointed leadership that probably lasted at least until circa 1800.

However important it may have been, the bias towards the Shwei-bo area and Alaung-hpaya's relatives was diffused in its effect below the *wun-gyi* level by other factors and by the emergence of other sources of officials. One important factor was the geographic dispersal of these officials as they were posted to other parts of the realm or took up residence in the Ava/Amara-pu-ra/Sagaing area after 1760. The consequent establishment of marriage connections and patronage relationships outside the northern area and apart from Alaung-hpaya's relatives may have served to dilute somewhat the importance of the "Shwei-bo element" in the bureaucratic apparatus. Although many were originally of local gentry backgrounds, their socioeconomic base now became their appointive situations with the attendant social rank and connections. Over time, many placed daughters in the harems of the various kings and princes. Their sons became court pages and attendants of personages of consequence, later advancing to the service of officials as writers, betel box bearers, and related positions. As these sons of officials moved upward from lesser situations to more important offices, they came to constitute a second-generation of appointive functionaries.[41] Thus, there developed an upper layer of the official elite whose positions were based on appointive officeholding. Because the appointive officials had a strong tendency to intermarry, this elite was at least partially self-perpetuating through its children. Many of these functionaries appear to have maintained their local roots and used their influence and offices not only to advance themselves, but also their relatives.

In addition to the appointed officials' own sons, the primary source of appointed officials was the local gentry, whose social aspirations tended to focus on entry into the higher elite. Illustrative of this aspiration is a letter from a headman to his son serving as a secretary to a *myo wun*: "From the time of your youth, you were trained and educated to be a high official in the service of our lord the king . . . you must take special care that you do not become a failure in the end."[42] Some references to the appointment of headmen to the bureaucratic apparatus can also be found in the *sit-tans*. There appears to have been an organic connection between the lower and upper layers of the official elite, in which the former was a primary source of recruitment for the latter while the latter recognized the value of maintaining its local ties.

The gentry as a whole, however, did not have a complete monopoly on appointive office. Some officials were selected from the ranks of the professional monks, many of whom spent time at court in connection with the annual monastic examinations and as advisers to the ruler. This provided them the opportunity to demonstrate their acumen and abilities, an advantage which, coupled to the fact that their loyalties generally lay with the ruler rather than one of the political factions, made them attractive to the king. Bo-daw-hpaya, for example, appointed two eminent monks as *atwin-wuns* and a third monk advanced from tutor of the future Ba-gyi-daw to his *atwin-wun* as crown prince in 1808, and thence through several other appointments to *wun-gyi*. Acceptance of secular office meant leaving the order and, in at least some cases, marriage.[43]

It is difficult to categorize the place of professional monks in the recruitment pattern. Some did and some did not come from gentry backgrounds and the clerics overall were a numerically tiny element in the administrative corps. Moreover, it seems improbable that such a personally difficult and indirect route to possible office would be chosen by the secularly ambitious when more direct and less personally exacting paths were available.

In their efforts to find trustworthy subordinates, rulers often turned to their immediate retainers, frequently their body servants and *ein-daw-ba*, or household factotums. Such persons were often the offspring of retainers in similar positions and hence intimates of the household from childhood. Bo-daw-hpaya, in particular, was prone to reward those retainers who had endured with him his exile at Sagaing from 1778 to early 1782. These included the brothers Kyaw Hkaung and Kyaw Ywei, who were the two most outstanding figures in the group of twenty-five retainers allowed by Sin-gu. Their mother, from a village in the Shwei-bo area, had been an *ein-ba* of an official of the Western Court, hence the boys were raised alongside Bo-daw-hpaya's elder sons in the women's quarters of the palace. They were great favorites of the future king, who referred to Kyaw Ywei in particular as his "tenth son." They assured their future by their faithful service during his exile. Kyaw Hkaung subsequently progressed through a series of offices to the position of *wun-gyi*, while his younger brother served as *myo wun* of Han-tha-wadi from about 1790 until his death in 1819 and intermittently as *wun-gyi* as well.[44] Elevation as a result of such intimate association was considered to be one of the best possible bases for political loyalty. Kyaw Ywei, in particular, became an important factor in the politics of the royal succession after 1782.

As the preceding discussion shows, the recruitment mechanisms did allow for the infusion into the corps of officials of some individuals of modest origins, either as a reward for personal service or for some noteworthy feat, usually of a military nature. Thus, social ideology did have a certain reality in the early Kon-baung period because some individuals were able to advance from the bottom to the top of the sociopolitical hierarchy. The majority of the appointed officials, however, appear to have come from either the upper or lower layers of the gentry and thus to have had the advantage of socially privileged backgrounds.

Although in many instances rulers chose individuals for appointment at their whim, the general practice was that candidates for important posts were recommended to the rulers by a theoretically collegial consensus of the *wun-gyis* and *wun-dauks*. These officers were also apparently at liberty to appoint the underlings of the bureaucratic apparatus without the formal approval of the king. Yet because the latter had to be informed of and issue a formal order for the appointment of all hereditary officials, it does not seem probable that he remained uninformed of these minor appointments.[45] Lacking any formal qualifications or entrance mechanisms (such as hereditary claim or an examination system), appointment to office was obtained through personal or family influence and the judicious application of personal or family wealth.[46] Survival and advancement in office were dependent on these same factors, coupled to the development of patronage connections. With the exception of the recipients of the monarch's arbitrary generosity, wealth and influence were clearly the key factors in officeholding. How these factors were brought into play was the essence of politics among appointive officials and determined much of their political behavior. The dynamics of this behavior involved the use of office to amass the wealth necessary to buy more influence and enlarge one's body of retainers and clients; arranging advantageous connections through the marriage of offspring; connecting oneself to a major faction at court related to the royal succession; and performing the bare necessities of one's duties in order to minimize the possibility of attracting the negative attention of the king. Taken as a whole, these behaviors discouraged bureaucratic activism and made the preservation and enhancement of personal interests a fundamental necessity.

Dependent as it was on the play of politics and royal whim, the nature of appointive officeholding, especially at the middle and upper levels, was intrinsically unstable. Few officials were able to escape incurring the displeasure of the monarch at least once during their careers. Such occasions meant the loss of position and wealth at the least, and banishment and sometimes execution at the worst.[47] Officials were also subject to attack by rivals coveting their positions and/or wishing to weaken the faction with which they were associated. The most common mode of attack was accusations of treason, which invariably provoked a decisive response from the throne. The victim was then forced to expend his material resources and political influence in an effort to exonerate himself and retain his position. There were variations on this mode of attack, but it will be more illustrative to present a case in point which reflects to a greater or lesser extent the various components of the political behavior noted above.

A man whose personal name and background are not known was able to rise to the position of chief secretary of Han-tha-wadi by becoming a protegé of Jansey, the Portuguese *shahbandar* of Rangoon, who was associated with a court faction hostile to that of the Han-tha-wadi *myo wun* Kyaw Ywei. Jansey obtained an introduction for the secretary's wife to the chief queen, who subsequently arranged for their daughter to be admitted to the royal harem. Through this valuable connection the secretary rapidly advanced to the office of *yei wun*, thus becoming Han-tha-wadi's second-ranking officer. The *myo wun* was a prominent figure in the court faction headed by the crown prince, who was commonly known for his moderate views concerning relations with the East India Company. This fact enabled the *yei wun* to use his court connections to represent the *myo wun* as dangerously pro-English and open to conspiracy with the company. Despite Kyaw Ywei's intimate associations and record of fidelity to Bo-daw-hpaya, the royal paranoia was such that the *myo wun* was bound by royal order to the capital, leaving the *yei wun* in full control at Rangoon. There the *yei wun* exploited the situation to enlarge his own wealth and following while destroying that of the *myo wun*. Here, then, is an example not only of one official aggrandizing himself at the expense of another, but also of how such conflict fit into the factional struggle of the court, whereby the personal success of the *yei wun* strengthened his faction by weakening the opposition.

The triumph of the *yei wun* proved temporary, however, because the *myo wun* still had his rich appanage of Myei-de and the support of his powerful faction. He was soon permitted to return to Rangoon, where he discovered that his enemy had turned his house into a stable and granary. The *yei wun* was quickly put in his place by the *myo wun*'s superior resources (five thousand armed retainers versus the *yei wun*'s fifteen hundred), but was able to maintain his position through his daughter, his factional connections, and, it was widely thought, the fact that the ever-cautious Bo-daw-hpaya viewed him as a check on the *myo wun*. The *myo wun*'s superior political strength was manifested again in 1802, possibly in the wake of the abortive rebellion of the Taung-ngu prince, when his jurisdiction was extended to all of the realm south of Prome and east of the Irrawaddy River. The conflict between the two officials continued until 1809 when the political situation again changed. The crown prince had died the preceding year, leaving the future King Ba-gyi-daw as the heir apparent with but a shaky political base in the face of strong competition from two of his

The Officials 155

uncles. Jansey died that same year and was replaced by an Englishman named Rogers, who was a client of the more moderate of the uncles. The *yei wun*, while weakened by this turn of events, found a different ally and launched a new attack on his old enemy.

This new ally was U Shwei O, a man of considerable ability who had rapidly risen from his initial position as a secretary at the Hlut-taw to that of a secretary at the royal court about 1800, a time when court politics were in flux because Bo-daw-hpaya had deposed all of the *wungyis*. U Shwei O then became *wun* of the Daing Department, a post he continued to hold after his appointment as a *wun-dauk*. His real opportunity arrived when he was given broad powers to prosecute the war against Thailand in 1809, with Tavoy as his base. As behooved a shrewd official, however, he did not expend his time and strength against the enemy, but plundered the countryside to build up the large working capital necessary to further advance his career. That same year the *myo wun*'s jurisdiction over the south expanded, bringing him into sharp conflict with the *daing wun*. The latter was a prominent adherent of the anti–Ba-gyi-daw faction, while the *myo wun* had become the principal supporter of Bo-daw-hpaya at court. The conflict between the *myo wun* on one side and the *yei wun* and *daing wun* on the other was characterized by armed clashes and assassination plots until the latter two *wuns* succeeded in having the *myo wun* deposed in 1811 by charging him with lenience in prosecuting users of opium and spirits, a charge which struck a responsive chord in the puritanical king. The *daing wun*, in turn, fell to a charge of rebellion made the following year, but purchased the renewed favor of Bo-daw-hpaya with the vast treasure he had acquired as commander in the field, thereby regaining his position as *wun-gyi*. The *myo wun*, too, was restored that same year and remained in royal favor until his death in 1819. The subsequent fates of the *daing wun* and *yei wun* are not known.[48]

As the preceding story shows, the personal ambitions of officials and the factional nature of the politics of succession were mutually reinforcing. The dominant factors in the politics of appointive officeholding were possession or acquisition of wealth to buy influence or office and to support relatives and clients; armed retainers to literally enforce and defend official prerogatives and position; the vagaries of royal favor and wrath; and personal attacks emanating from complex webs of personal and political intrigue. Indeed parlous, the lives of officials demanded constant vigilance.[49] The corps of appointed functionaries was not a monolithic element in the political process, but riven with personal and factional rivalries, which, at the upper levels at least, tended to coalesce around the princely factions involved in the struggle for the royal succession.

Although the officials, both hereditary and appointed, were not homogeneous in their political interests, there were several factors which tended to unite them in a community of interest against the king in the contest for resources. The transitory nature of officeholding tended to force the individual functionary to concentrate not on his duties but on the acquisition of a financial and political base with which to maintain and advance himself. As such, financial considerations, including the uncertain nature of renumeration discussed above, almost drove officials to exploit any opportunity for financial gain. The most common and lucrative opportunities involved appropriating part of the crown due in revenue collections and services from the *athi taings* and crown service groups. Thus, the officials had a common need to deprive the ruler of part of his resources in order to ensure their own survival and betterment. The contest between ruler and officials over resources was one important aspect of politics and governance in the early Kon-baung period.

Corruption and Control

The moral climate of eighteenth-century Burma, like that of contemporary Europe, differed considerably from that of the modern western world. As a point of departure, some definition of *corruption* in the Burmese context is required. The *Oxford English Dictionary* defines *corruption* as the destruction or perversion of the integrity or fidelity of a person in the discharge of his duty or the inducement to act dishonestly or unfaithfully. James C. Scott has suggested that corruption is behavior that deviates from the formal duties of a public role for nonpublic (that is, personal, family, private clique or faction) pecuniary or status gains, or violates rules against certain types of nonpublic influence. This definition includes favors done for cash as well as for motives of loyalty or kinship.[50] Both definitions assume fairly specific rules and standards against which behavior can be measured and judged. In Burma, however, the lack of codified or even formal law and the general mutability of the edicts of rulers offered no specific standards. The upholding of justice and virtue were important themes in early Kon-baung customary law, which admonished officials to render wise and just decisions and not to oppress the people, but nowhere specified what constituted legal and illegal or moral and immoral behavior.[51] Customary law at best condemned official behavior that led to disruption of the social order. The duties of office, especially appointive office, were imprecise and flexible in nature.

To these factors must be added the prevalent custom of present-giving in connection with any contact with or between officials. This social custom, called *myet-hna pya*, or "something to show the face" in Burmese, was so well-established that many *sit-tans* record the presents required for different kinds of business with or service from local officials. The importance of present-giving for appointive officials has been discussed above.[52] Present-giving was an accepted and necessary aspect of officeholding, the line between presents and bribes being ambiguous. An official who accepted cash to reprieve a condemned criminal was corrupt, but one who sold his influence at court was within the bounds of accepted behavior.[53] The primary demander and receiver of presents was the monarch himself because he had the most to sell. The queens also made a business of selling their considerable influence.

The ultimate arbiter of official behavior was the king. From his point of view, the standard against which the actions of officials were judged was not a formal set of rules or even abstract ethics, but the *kadaw* oath of absolute fidelity and service. Officials were expected to exploit their positions for private gain; the sin was to carry this exploitation too far. Failure to uphold the *kadaw* oath, however, was considered anticrown activity and therefore to constitute unacceptable corruption. Such failures usually fell into one of three areas: treasonous activities, contravening the expressed will or orders of the ruler, and diverting the crown due in revenues and/or services to private ends.

A handful of officials did become involved in treasonous activities, but for the most part official corruption involved bribery or embezzlement. Bribery appears to have been widespread among both appointed and hereditary functionaries. The typical areas of bribery were related to the acquittal or reprieve of criminals, the settlement of disputes over local hereditary office, the adjudication of civil cases, and collusion in the corrupt acts of other officials.[54] Embezzlement was also apparently the rule rather than the exception among both kinds of officials. Of the many forms embezzlement took, the most common were the illegal appropriation and mortgage of state land by local officials, the underreporting of the tax receipts, and removing people from the official membership lists of crown service units, *athi taings*, and district registers of houses. In the last case, the dues and service of the people were appropriated to the private uses of officials. After the burning of Rangoon in January 1810, for example, local officials were directed to take a new census, but kept 1,000 of the 2,500 houses off the new registers, thus depriving the crown of 40 percent of its revenues and services. This example is probably the extreme, however, because the usual estimate of houses withheld was 10 percent.55

Records of the deposition of *wun-gyis* for the embezzlement of crown revenues show that such corruption reached the highest levels of government. The greatest embezzlement scandal of all broke in 1770, when it was discovered that the *wun-gyis* and *wun-dauks* had been in wholesale collusion with their subordinates and territorial officials to divert revenues through falsified records and to list *athi* villages as crown service villages to remove them from the tax rolls. The web of corruption and collusion was so tangled that an investigation proved impossible and left the king unable to "differentiate the guilty from the innocent."56

The essence of official corruption was that it deprived the crown of from 10 to 40 percent of its revenues and services, that it was inextricably linked to maladministration through overexploitation, and that the nexus of relationships supporting it tended to represent a political as well as an administrative threat to the crown. As discussed earlier, such overexploitation by officials drove a certain number of people into alternative statuses. In terms of the officials themselves, corruption fed on the need of lower officials to secure the protection of higher officials who, in turn, needed the assistance and support of lower functionaries and allies among their peers and superiors. Because political interest and corruption are natural allies, the lines of collusion in corruption tended to follow the lines of the political factions at court. The aggregate result was an often formidable ability on the part of officials to frustrate the royal will and policies.

Faced with this endemic corruption, the crown fought to protect itself and its resources with a variety of control devices. Two such devices were the fragmentation of administrative authority and the alternate communications systems described earlier. Another was control of the movements of officials, who were not permitted to travel to and from the capital without crown permission and were further required to report to the Hlut-taw every day while in the capital. Their wives, too, were required to remain in the capital and report to the women's palace each day, and exemption from these requirements was a mark of unusual royal favor. *Myo-zas* and *ywa-zas* were also not generally permitted to reside in their appanages.57

There were two further weapons employed by rulers in their struggle with the officials. One was the inquests or censuses undertaken during both the Restored Taung-ngu and early Kon-baung periods. The most immediate and drastic, however, was the harsh and arbitrary discipline imposed by rulers for deviance from the *kadaw* oath. Lapses of duty, corruption, and withholding or falsifying information were so endemic that status demotion, dismissal, banishment, or execution followed exposure. An edict of 1806, for example, records the punishment of three functionaries:

> Although they are officials of the crown, the Kyauk-padaung *myo-za*, Son *myo-za*, and *Lamaing wun* did not properly consider and report on affairs. The title of Min-hla Kyaw-thu held by the Kyauk-padaung *myo-za*, of Nei-myo Naw-rahta Kyaw-din held by the Son *myo-za*, and of Maha Thi-ha U-zana held by the *Lamaing wun* are revoked. Let those with previous titles serve with those titles and let those without previous titles serve with their personal names.[58]

In another instance, the general officers of the armies in the Chinese campaign of 1769 were banished for a month and their families publicly humiliated by Hsin-hpyu-shin, furious that the victorious Burmese generals had permitted the defeated Chinese to withdraw.[59] Local functionaries also felt the threat of crown discipline. Many of the 1802 *sit-tans* from Han-tha-wadi, for example, contain statements similar to the following by the headman of Kaw-li-ya Myo: "I submit the list of houses in full and in summary. If any have not been included in the list submitted by me, I will be punished by the king."[60]

Imprisonment and execution were common fates that befell even *wun-gyis*. Indeed, the severity of the discipline was sometimes counterproductive. During the Thailand campaign of 1785, for example, an officer who failed in his orders to organize adequate supplies was summarily executed. This caused other officers fearful of a similar fate to mislead the king concerning the adequacy of their own supply arrangements and thus undermined the logistic basis of the campaign.[61] The fact that rulers were reduced to the arbitrary infliction of extreme penalties is reflective of their general lack of systematic control over the official cadres.

An official of whatever rank could, therefore, expect summary and often severe punishment if detected in activity that could be construed as against the crown. Yet the deterrent effect of this threat can be questioned in light of the apparent prevalence of corruption and related activities among officials. Indeed, officials attacked each other freely with charges of treason, but it is perhaps telling that no overtly political cases have yet been found involving specific charges of corruption. The main reason is surely that treason charges were so much more effective in undoing a rival, but it is also possible that officials tacitly recognized their common interest in not spurring the crown into concerted action against bribery, embezzlement, and illegal land practices. The collusion among officials in protecting corrupt practices is perhaps best illustrated by the administrative inquests of the early Kon-baung period.

Such inquests were a longstanding feature of Burmese administration, possibly dating back to the fourteenth-century reign of Min-gyi-zwa-saw-ke.[62] The earliest extant records of inquests date from the early seventeenth-century reigns of Nyaung-yan and Anauk-hpet-lun, who used them as important tools in the organization of their expanding domain. The most extensive of the pre–Kon-baung inquests was that carried out by Tha-lun between 1635 and 1638 as part of his program to reorganize and centralize the administration of the realm. The specific dimensions of this inquest were to list the lands under cultivation and thus taxable; the people's names, ages, sex, birthdays, and children; the members and lands of the various crown service groups; the local officials and their office lands; and the boundaries of the jurisdictions.[63] It is very clear that such an inquest represented a major effort by the crown to gain control over revenues and services. But in so doing, the rulers struck directly at the vital interests of both the gentry and appointive officials. By establishing a central set of detailed records, the central authority attempted to reduce the capacity of all officials to embezzle and overtax and, particularly, to inhibit the shift of people from the crown sector to the private tenantry of the gentry and appointed officials.

The debility of later Taung-ngu administration and the licensed corruption engendered by the ministerial patronage networks meant that the gentry and officials had functioned virtually independently of crown control for decades prior to the debacle of 1752. Furthermore, the capture of Ava by southern forces not only ended the rule of the Taung-ngu kings, but destroyed the records of their administration. In his attempts to reassert control, therefore, Alaung-hpaya had to rely mainly on the oral evidence provided by local officials as to both their own legitimacy and their tax and service obligations. That matters remained in an unsatisfactory state can be seen from many of the edicts of Alaung-hpaya and Hsin-hpyu-shin regulating local affairs and the compilation of all extant Taung-ngu records into a slim work entitled the *Zam-bu-di-pa ok-hsaung kyan* [The crown of Jam-bu-di-pa], done in preparation for an inquest launched by Hsin-hpyu-shin in 1765.[64] It is difficult to assess how extensively this inquest was actually carried out because so few of its returns are extant. An edict of 9 February 1767 noted that the inquest was under way but that its returns had not yet been recorded on palm leaves for the Shwei-daik.[65] The combination of the lack of extant records, the embezzlement scandal of 1770, and the Thai and Chinese wars of the late 1760s strongly suggests that the inquest was virtually stillborn. The diversion of the king's attention to foreign and military affairs in those years appears to have allowed the demonstrably corrupt *wun-gyis* to turn the information-gathering process to their own ends, and the resultant scandal breaking in 1770 probably caused the project to be abandoned.

There the matter lay until 1783, when Bo-daw-hpaya launched the strongest possible attack on the problem of control. An edict of 2 December 1783 ordered a detailed inquiry into the population and boundaries of *myo* and village jurisdictions, crown service units, the hereditary lineages of local offices, revenue and service obligations, and glebe lands. Detailed statements of this information termed *sit-tans* were to be submitted by each *myo*, village, and crown service group. Two *wungyis* were placed in charge of the project with orders to work night and day. The king's recognition of the difficulty of the task is reflected in this revealing statement in his edict: "I will not allow this matter to be neglected and left unfinished like other matters."[66] Requiring almost three years to complete, the inquest struck directly at the power of the gentry and the peculating practices of all officials. Because his inquest was engendering substantial local opposition and remembering the fate of Hsin-hpyu-shin's inquest, Bo-daw-hpaya employed extreme measures to obtain accurate returns. Many officials were dismissed and some executed for submitting false information and spies and agents were sent to the districts to make inquiries and ascertain the correct information.[67]

In spite of these measures and the determination of the king, the inquest appears to have failed to obtain consistently accurate information. Court officials told Henry Burney half a century later that "when the lists were submitted to the king, he expressed his opinion that a third of the number of houses in each town must have been suppressed," a story confirmed by an edict of 19 April 1785 in which the king decreed:[68]

> There has been a crown inquiry to establish a correct list of hereditary posts. The headmen of the various *myos* and villages, the cavalry chiefs, the Shan Cavalry, the Southern and Northern Cavalry, the Myo-ba Cavalry, the chiefs of the four walls of the royal fort, the *wun* of the *daing* units, the *wuns* of the Western Court, the *lamaing wun*, the *wun* of the royal attendants and other *wuns*, and

> the heads of the crown service units submitted wildly incorrect information about their traditional duties in the *sit-tans* which were submitted in 1764, 1765, and 1783. The previous *sit-tans* are incorrect. Let only the correct information about traditional duties and customary taxes be submitted for the list which is presently being prepared.[69]

A second inquest in 1802 was presumably intended to correct the errors and misinformation of the 1783 survey.[70] Even so, the *sit-tans* of 1783 and 1802 were considered to be the authority for all cases of disputed inheritance of local office and boundary disputes. The latter involved jurisdictional conflicts between officials seeking to increase the size of their charges and hence their income and power.[71]

Apart from an ineffective census attempted by Ba-gyi-daw in the aftermath of the First Anglo-Burmese War, no more attempts of this type were made beyond the issuing of reams of ineffectual edicts by succeeding rulers down to Thi-baw. Indeed, the failure of the administrative reforms of Min-don in the mid-nineteenth century can be seen as one last high point in the centuries-old struggle between the crown and the officials and gentry over the size of their respective shares of the national product. In this struggle, corruption was the most important means by which the officials increased their share at the expense of the crown. Although they were at times able to reduce the share of the crown substantially, the officials acted from narrow self-interest rather than for group ends. Officials never came to constitute a group threat to the crown in the early Kon-baung period because the structure of the patronage and corruption network characterizing court politics discouraged the aggregation of their power. However questionable the effectiveness of the crown's controls may have been, that one fact left it in a dominant, if often frustrated, position.

Officials and Politics

Officeholding begat wealth and status and was the primary means of material accumulation and social mobility in early Kon-baung society. Even seemingly minor and unesteemed offices were important because they admitted their holders to the coveted status of *min*, and because their incumbents could use the money and influence accruing from such office to manipulate their way into positions of higher authority and prestige. Given the economic and social privileges stemming from incumbency, political power was translated into economic affluence. Rather than the sociopolitical structure being a reflection of economics, Burma in the early Kon-baung period represents a clear case where economics in general and land tenure in particular were a reflection of the sociopolitical structure.

The concentration of economic and social power in the hands of officials made them and their families one of the three elite status groups in society, a group I have labeled "gentry." Indeed, the local hereditary officials seem to be close to a perfect example of what Karl Wittfogel has termed a "bureaucratic gentry," a group whose economic and social position derives from officeholding.[72] The upper- and even some of the middle-level appointed officials might be aptly described as a "bureaucratic nobility." Incumbency in office made these men the recipients of part of the royal charisma and regalia and gave them high sumptuary privileges and trappings, appanages, and other economic perquisites. Many had multiple marriage relationships with the royal lineage and some had grandsons, nephews, and cousins in the royal pool of succession. There was, in fact, probably no clear line between the upper level of appointed functionaries and the extended royal lineage. Incumbency in crown office was in all cases the key to membership in both the bureaucratic gentry and the bureaucratic nobility.

As the basis of most social and economic reward in the society, possession of office had intrinsic value and was a primary object of popular aspiration. A central feature of early Kon-baung politics was the contest for office at all levels. The focus of local politics was the struggle to obtain or maintain office, a struggle in which hereditary claim was an important but by no means dominant factor. Among the appointed officials, the constant rivalries and attempts to exploit and expand relative position in the administrative hierarchy tended to be related to the factional lines of the struggle over the royal succession. The whole arena of the politics involving hereditary and appointive officeholding was characterized by the important roles played by wealth, marriage connections, and patronage and factional affiliations. While the officialdom was fragmented by its internecine struggles over individual position and status, the crucial role of wealth in maintaining and advancing their individual positions drove the officials as an inchoate entity to compete with the sovereign over respective shares of the national product through a wide variety of corrupt practices. The contest between ruler and officials over resources was second in importance only to that over the royal succession as an arena of political conflict.

The sovereign bound these officials to him through individual relationships of personal allegiance expressed in the *kadaw* oath and purchased their service through a system of specific material rewards and incentives available only through service to the crown. Underneath the veneer of the *kadaw* oath, the real political cement between rulers and officials was the reward of status, appanages, and sumptuary and economic perquisites conferred by virtue of the latter's active participation in the political hierarchy. In the absence of any real concept of dedication to the ideals of service to government or the commonweal, the reward system was the primary means by which officials were recruited into service. The flaw in the system was that political survival and advancement often required more than that produced by an individual's official reward. Despite their covert contest with the crown over resources, however, the officials were fundamentally dependent on the sovereign as the source of office and its attendant benefits.

Given the ruler's position as arbiter of office and reward, a second central feature of politics was the contest among individuals and factions for royal favor and relative influence over him. In a system which vested all political authority in the ruler, such influence was tantamount to power. Influence was also power in the sense that such influence, or access to those who had achieved it, was a salable commodity that could be translated into wealth, that most important ingredient of politics.[73] Thus, the contest for influence made the crown the highest focus of politics.

The officials were joined in the contest for influence by the other politically active group in Kon-baung society, the members of the extended royal lineage. The latter tended to exhibit some of the same group and political characteristics as the officials, but with one significant difference. The fact of their royal blood gave them a claim on the throne ranging from the immediate, as was the case of the princes of the blood, to the remote for royal relatives on the fringes of the lineage. To a greater or lesser extent, the members of the extended royal lineage could thus aspire to the ultimate office. In a system centered on officeholding, the ultimate office was the kingship, which lay at the core of political struggle. Given the centrality of this struggle to understanding the dynamics of the Kon-baung polity, the next two chapters examine the politics of the royal succession.

CHAPTER 6

THE ROYAL SUCCESSION

The main focus in the politics of the early Kon-baung period was the contest for the throne. Modern writers have tended to characterize this contest as both sanguine and chaotic, the dual result of the lack of any law or custom regulating the royal succession and the large numbers of sons produced by the rulers. "In the 'Indian' states of 'Burma' any one of a king's very numerous offspring might 'legitimately' succeed him and palace murders were the norm" is how the anthropologist E. R. Leach has described the Burmese succession.[1] Earlier the historian G. E. Harvey wrote, "Half the palace plots which were the bane of Burma proceeded from the lack of any clear law of succession."[2]

Although there was no formal, codified law in Burma, there was, in fact, an identifiable rationale and order underlying Kon-baung succession patterns. This included customary genealogical priorities for selecting the heir, institutionalized means of preparing and protecting him, and formal procedures for the smooth passage of power at his accession. The customary rules of the royal succession succeeded quite well in achieving those goals so important in Burmese political thought: preserving the continuity and bloodlines of the lineage and eliminating unfit candidates. In so doing, however, the rulers were left faced with a difficult political dilemma which none proved able to resolve satisfactorily. The discussion that follows considers the structure, recruitment, and status definition of the royal family; how the royal pool of succession was delimited; and how kings and custom attempted to provide a smooth passage of power despite the ever-present dilemma of the royal succession.

Chapter 6

The Royal Women and the Succession

The queens, princesses, concubines, and female relatives of the king comprised the royal women. The center of residence and administration for these women was the Western Court, which contained the apartments of the queens, princesses, and other women of the royal establishment, with the exception of those of the chief and north queens. The administration of the Western Court was usually, but not always, directed by four *anauk wuns*, each with the assistance of a secretary. The specific duties of the *anauk wuns* concerned the security, direction, and maintenance of the court and its dozen or so service units, and confining queens and princesses under punishment in the gaol of the court.[3]

The court itself was kept under strict discipline and control. Queens, princesses, and their maids were permitted to go out only with specific permission, while only males on duty at the court or under seven years of age were permitted entrance. On occasions when monks, outside servants or courtiers had business with queens in their apartments, an *anauk wun* and his secretary first ascertained the nature of the business and then monitored the discussion. Of the various bureaucratic posts, the duties of the *anauk wuns* were among the most difficult and delicate. Hence it is not surprising that the qualities listed in contemporary sources as requisite for these positions were great circumspection, great and habitual fear and respect for the power of the ruler, and the "blessing of being content with his own wife."[4]

Queenship was not hereditary nor was it automatically attained from forming a conjugal relationship with the king. Royal marriage paralleled the polygamous pattern of the commoners in that the first woman married to the king became the head and legal wife. The other queens were comparable to the lesser but still legal wives of the commoners and the concubines just that. When the king underwent his first *abhiseka*, or royal consecration, his current head wife received the highest of the six classes of titles for queens and underwent the *mahei abhiseka*, or consecration of a queen.

Tradition held that the chief queen should receive the *abhiseka* because the son of a king and queen so consecrated was called *ya-za pok-ta* (Pali, *raja putta*), or a king's son of the royal lineage. Because the chief queen was the head wife, her eldest son was the *aw-ra-tha* and entitled to his father's office and estate. This distinction is reflected in palace terminology, as the son of the chief queen was always termed *shwei-go-daw-gyi hpaya*, or (roughly) "the great golden person of the lord," while the sons of other queens were termed only *ko-daw-myat hpaya*, or "the noble person of the lord." A similar terminological distinction was made between the daughter of the chief queen and those of other queens.[5]

As the main consort of the king, tradition defined a special role and qualities for the chief queen. Her role was to produce the heir, to be the mother of the people (as the king was the father), and to be the head of the status hierarchy for females.[6] Due to her special position, the chief queen was given extensive appanages and several crown service units were devoted solely to her protection and service.

Ever since James G. Scott wrote "the kings of Burma according to traditional law had eight queens . . . [these] eight queens every constitutional king was bound to have," succeeding writers have tended to accept this statement as the norm.[7] However, the number of queens was one of the few matters not governed by tradition. A king was only "bound to have" a chief queen and the number of supplemental queens varied in all three Burmese dynasties.[8] In order of precedence the queens were the chief queen, or queen of the south palace; the queen of the north palace; the queen of the middle palace; and, lastly, the queen of the west palace. These were known as *nan-ya* queens, or queens who had a palace. As such, they were the principal or senior queens and the legal wives of the ruler.

During the reign of Bo-daw-hpaya, two important innovations were made in the organization of the royal women whereby the number of queens increased significantly. In addition to three principal queens, two second-rank queens—the queens of the south apartment and of the north apartment with the golden lining—were installed. A second innovation was the creation of a third rank of queens titled after the locality of their appanages, as were princesses, princes, and high officials. Bo-daw-hpaya installed a total of twelve such queens, sometimes referred to as "*myo-za* queens" in early Kon-baung documents. Because of their identification with parts of the palace, the second-rank queens had higher status than the *myo-za*, or third-rank queens. The latter were essentially concubines and were, perhaps, given the designation of queen (*mi-baya*) to raise their status and thus draw their families closer to the throne.[9] Table 4 illustrates the evolution and expansion of the Kon-baung royal women.

The sociological origins of the royal women reveal definite patterns. The first two kings, Alaung-hpaya and Naung-daw-gyi, were firmly rooted in the polygamous marriage pattern common to the upper Burma gentry. The pattern began to shift slightly with Hsin-hpyu-shin, who took two daughters of the last king of the Taung-ngu dynasty and a daughter of a *saw-bwa* as concubines, but drew mostly on women

Table 4. The Royal Women, 1752–1885

King	Chief Queen	North Queen	Middle Queen	West Queen	Queen of the North Apartment	Queen of the South Apartment	Queen of the North Apartment with the Golden Lining	Queen of the South Apartment with the Golden Lining	Myo-za Queens	Concubines
Alaung-hpaya	*	*								5
Naung-daw-gyi	**	**	*							3
Hsin-hpyu-shin	*	*	**							9
Sin-gu	*	**	*	*						7
Bo-daw-hpaya	*	**	*				*		12	35
Ba-gyi-daw	*	**	**	*						
Tha-ra-wadi	*	*	*	*	*	*	*	*	4	4
Pagan	*	*	*	*						
Min-don	*	*	*	**	**	*	**	**	37	2
Thi-baw	**									

Notes: Two asterisks indicate that the first incumbent died and was replaced, although such replacement was not mandatory. When Bo-daw-hpaya's chief queen died in 1806, for example, she was not replaced, and there was no chief queen from 1806 to 1819. When the north queen died that same year, she was replaced by the promotion of the queen of the north apartment with the golden lining, whose former position was then left vacant. On her death in 1813, this queen was also not replaced. The table is therefore a static composite and does not reveal that a given king did not necessarily have all the queens listed at the same time. For Thi-baw, the two asterisks mean that there were two chief queens concurrently. Maung Maung is omitted because his rule in 1782 lasted only seven days.

Sources: KBZ 1 and 2, passim; MMM, 191–251 passim; BL OR. 3470, "A Historical Memorandum of Royal Relations of Burmah Hunters Family," passim.

related to Mok-hso-bo area officials and some court functionaries for the remainder of his consorts. The same was true of Sin-gu and Bo-daw-hpaya, whose thirty-five known concubines also included a few daughters of commoners, *thu-gyis*, and *myo-thu-gyis*.[10]

Two generalizations can be made about the origins of the royal women, the first of which is that all the early Kon-baung monarchs maintained important marriage connections with the Mok-hso-bo District. These connections are well illustrated in the relationship between the royal lineage and one particular gentry family. The *shwei-ga htaung-hmu*, or chief of a military unit of one thousand "golden shields," Min Thi-ri Yan-daza of Si-bok-tara was father-in-law of the founder of the new dynasty. As grandfather of the chief queens of both Hsin-hpyu-shin and Bo-daw-hpaya, this important figure of the later Taung-ngu and early Kon-baung periods became the grandfather or great-grandfather of all the succeeding early Kon-baung kings. The connection cannot be traced beyond Bo-daw-hpaya. In addition to the foregoing, Min Thi-ri Yan-daza and three of his sons-in-law—the Ava *bo-hmu*, Mok-hso-bo *myo wun*, and Si-tha *min-gyi*—provided a number of women to the royal lineage. A picture emerges from the royal genealogies of extensive intermarriage among the gentry and officials and between this group and the royal lineage.[11] The web of Shwei-bo connections emanating from Min Thi-ri Yan-daza was an important factor in the politics of royal succession through at least 1782.

A second generalization is that the royal women were in the main recruited from the ranks of officialdom. By the reign of Hsin-hpyu-shin, the emphasis on daughters of officials and gentry from Mok-hso-bo and neighboring districts was diminishing relative to the number of daughters provided by court officals. The queens and concubines of Sin-gu, Bo-daw-hpaya, his son the crown prince, and his grandson the future Ba-gyi-daw reveal a distinct preference for the daughters of court functionaries. Sister marriage was reintroduced during the reign of Bo-daw-hpaya, but since half-sisters contributed only three principal queens during the entire early Kon-baung period, this source of queens is of minor sociological significance.

The queens and princesses were a body of women with affinal, consanguine, or fictive consanguine relationships with the sovereign. The term queen, or *mi-baya*, denoted not only a consort of the king, but was also used for others among the royal women. The head wife of the crown prince was known as the *ein-shei mi-baya*, or queen of the eastern house while, as another example, upon her marriage the youngest daughter of Bo-daw-hpaya and his chief queen was given Prome as an appanage and was known thereafter as the Prome *mi-*

baya. The term *min-thami*, or princess, was used not only for daughters and sisters of the king but also for other women whom he wished to honor by conferring by title a fictive consanguinity with him.[12]

This body of royal women constituted a status group in Burmese society and, as such, had its own internal grading. The royal women were graded into three ranks, and those in at least the first two were ordered as to the specific status of the individuals within them. An important aspect of status grading was clothing and ornaments, those of the royal women being divided into seven classes. The first five applied to queens and princesses and the last two to concubines and others. Conferred on each individual at the whim of the king, a given status brought specified clothing and ornaments. Corresponding to the seven classes of clothing and ornaments were the six classes of personal honorific titles, the seventh and lowest class of ornamentation and clothing presumably being for untitled women.[13]

The status hierarchy of the Western Court was composed of 112 places, 56 of the left and 56 of the right. In Burman tradition, the left had a higher status than the right, but the reverse was true at the Western Court. As the court of the chief queen, who sat on the right of the king and played the major role in the ceremony, the right took precedence over the left. The other significant division in the court was between women of the "inner side," who resided at the court, and the women of the "outer side," who lived elsewhere. The largest portion of the women of the outer side were the wives of officials, who were under the charge of officials of the Western Court called *kadaw* secretaries. These officials were responsible for organizing the wives at palace ceremonies and festivals by carrying out orders as to which women were permitted to attend, what clothes and ornaments they were entitled to, and recommending who was deserving of what honors.[14]

The full formal expression of the female hierarchy of status took place annually during the last three days of the month of Thadin-gyut (roughly September-October) at the end of the Buddhist Lent. At this time, the king and chief queen ascended the Lotus Throne in the Western Court to receive the homage of the female hierarchy. A formal ceremony was held in which the king formally inquired of the women present about certain distaff matters in the realm and received the prescribed answers, after which he was presented with gifts. In this ceremony, the king sat in the middle of the hall with the chief queen on his right.

Though smaller in scale, the hierarchy of the Western Court was similar to that of the main court. As Michael Symes aptly observed in 1795: "in this assembly, as much state and ceremony are observed as at the court of his Majesty. The rank, which each lady bears in right of her husband, is expressed by her dress and ornaments; female priority being not less scrupulously maintained, than precedency among men."[15] The female status hierarchy is another example of the extent to which the Burmese formalized the expression of social rank and the social distance between ranks, in this instance extending the control inherent in the hierarchies to the distaff side of society.

The functions of the Western Court also had some politically oriented aspects. Paralleling the duties of princes and officials for attending the ruler were similar duties for queens and princesses. The principal queens had no fixed turns, but were assumed to be in attendance on the king at his pleasure, while the remainder of the queens and concubines had a regular assignment for attendance day or night. Princesses had no fixed turns, but were expected to show themselves several times a day and render any needed service, and the ladies in waiting had a regular rota for duty. Wives of officials were expected to make an appearance at the court almost every day, another manifestation of the physical control to which officials were subjected. Another function of the Western Court was to take in and educate the daughters of courtiers and officials in the apartments of the queens and princesses. Marriages were subsequently arranged for these women with the heirs of Shan *saw-bwas* and other important personages. The court was also an important avenue for purchasing influence since, as the Italian missionary Vincentius Sangermano remarked, large sums for procurement of office had to be paid "not only to the Emperor, but also to his queens."[16] The buying of influence through the royal women was apparently fairly common, because there are numerous examples of their intervention in patronage and political matters, some of which will be mentioned later.

In sum, the royal women were organized into a distinct hierarchy of status which depended on affinal, consanguine, and fictive consanguine relationships with the king and which, more importantly, determined the status and political positions of the royal children. The polygamous structure of the royal family was as significant for the royal succession as was the gentry family structure for succession to local office, but with political ramifications that affected the entire polity.

The Royal Men

The royal men comprised the king, crown prince, and the *min-nyi min-tha*. Literally translated, this last term means the "younger brothers and sons of the king." In fact, however, it was used more broadly to refer to the upper level of the male status hierarchy as expressed both in terms of personal honorific titles and of place. There were three ranks of *min-nyi min-tha* titles, each with four classes, making a total of twelve classes. In terms of place, the crown prince, as the second most important personage in the realm, was followed by the nine great *min-tha* (princes) of the left and nine of the right, the nine middle *min-tha* of the left and nine of the right, and finally the nine great cavalry captains (*myin-hmu*) *min-tha* of the left and nine of the right for a total of fifty-four places. Below the *min-nyi min-tha* were the other four hundred or so places of the hierarchy occupied by various officials and *saw-bwas*. As with the female hierarchy, status was denoted by clothes, ornaments, and trappings of rank. The elite and semiroyal status of the *min-nyi min-tha* is further demonstrated in the fact that the daughters of its members were designated *hteik-tin* ("placed on top"?), as were the grand and great-granddaughters of the king and all but one of the daughters of the crown prince.[17]

Although the *min-nyi min-tha* was collectively the central group at court and in politics, it is difficult to determine its exact membership. Most, but not all, of the sons and brothers of the ruler were members. A son or brother advanced by grades up the ladder of status to the *min-nyi min-tha* level, but conferment of this or any status rank was not automatic and depended on the favor of the king. There were some cases of sons who remained untitled at maturity, the result of disfavor incurred by either their mothers or by themselves or as a result of physical or mental impairment. All nine of the sons of Alaung-hpaya, including the two by concubines, were holders of *min-nyi min-tha* titles, the three mature sons having first-rank titles and the remainder second- and third-rank titles. The reigns of Naung-daw-gyi and Sin-gu produced no sons old enough to be titled. Three sons of Hsin-hpyu-shin, all still in their teens, had lower-class, third-rank titles.

The numerous sons and grandsons of Bo-daw-hpaya provide a better picture of how the system may have worked. Of his sixty-two sons, one was the crown prince, one did not receive a *min-nyi min-tha* title, and twenty-two died in infancy. Of the remainder, nine had first-rank titles, six had second-rank titles, and twenty-two had third-rank titles. Most elder sons by principal queens had first-rank titles and, as might be expected, sons by concubines were mostly of the third rank. Notable exceptions were the eldest son of the middle queen who held a bottom-class, third-rank title, presumably because his "mind was not clear," while the son of the second north queen held a similar title, in marked contrast to the first-rank title of his younger brother by the same mother.[18] Another interesting exception was the Nat-mauk prince, son of a concubine, who held a first-class title at a young age. His grandfather, however, was the head officer of the chief queen, which may help to explain the unusual favor shown to him.

The eldest son of Bo-daw-hpaya was installed as crown prince in 1784 and sired his first son, the future Ba-gyi-daw, that same year. At his death in 1808 at the age of forty-six, he had produced thirty-two sons, sixteen of whom survived infancy. Ba-gyi-daw was given a title above the highest rank of the *min-nyi min-tha* system, but his two brothers by the same mother received first-class, first-rank titles, higher than any awarded to Bo-daw-hpaya's own sons by principal queens. The crown prince had four more sons by his second queen, the first queen having died in 1793, and all were awarded second-rank titles. The remainder of his sons were born of concubines and were given second- and third-rank titles of varying classes, as would be expected.[19]

With an occasional exception, therefore, it appears that the ranks of the *min-nyi min-tha* were in the main filled with the sons, grandsons, if any, and brothers of the king. Together these blood relatives constituted the great and middle *min-tha*. There were, however, other persons within the designation *min-tha*, persons with no blood ties to the king, but whom he honored by conferring fictive consanguinity. This last group of *min-nyi min-tha* falls into several rough categories. The most discernible were the eighteen cavalry captain *min-tha* chosen from among the various cavalry regiments, the cavalry being the elite of the Burmese army. There were also occasional individuals whom the king wished to distinguish by awarding second- or third-rank titles, though never first-rank, apparently reserved for blood relatives. This custom can also be found in the late Taung-ngu period, when an occasional *wun-gyi* received a second-rank title.[20] Thus, royal birth alone did not guarantee admission to the royal status group nor did nonroyal birth absolutely forbid it.

Broadly speaking, the *min-nyi min-tha* had only two specific functions. In time of war, they were supposed to be assigned field commands, while at all other times they attended the king. The nonroyal members of this group invariably had other specific offices or posts and even some of the royal members received administrative duties or such posts as *bayin*, or viceroy. The *min-nyi min-tha* were required to attend the daily public audiences of the king and were subject to all the physical controls placed on officials.[21]

In sum, the royal men were a relatively small group which comprised the top of the elite hierarchy by virtue of their genuine or fictive kinship with the king and, by virtue of that same relationship, were preeminent in the management of the country. Those with a blood relationship to the king can be fairly well known through the royal genealogies, but it is difficult to form a picture of the nonroyal *min-nyi min-tha* beyond the fact that they were high officials whose service and trustworthiness in the eyes of the king merited bestowal of this distinction.

The Royal Pool of Succession

As there was no codified or formally enacted and ongoing law governing other aspects of Burmese society, so too there was none governing the royal succession. Still, the descent of the crown was subject to clearly defined custom sanctified by tradition and Buddhist historiography. As discussed in chapter 3, lineage was one of the two major sources of political legitimacy for Burmese kings. The two ideal characteristics of the royal lineage were that it was unbroken back to its founder figure (whether Maha Thamada or Pyu-saw-hti) and pure in its bloodlines, as idealized in the Sakyan lineage. Therefore, the individual Burmese ruler theoretically represented the current end of an unbroken and undiluted chain of blood relationships stretching back to the original and legitimate source of governmental authority as given in Theravada Buddhist thought.[22]

Qualified by the special lineage needs of the crown, the royal succession was governed by much the same customary principles of inheritance as was succession to local gentry office. Blood relatives were preferred over affinals, and lineals (sons) over collaterals (brothers). The special position of the *aw-ra-tha* son was emphasized in formal court edicts and proclamations, which referred to him as *tha-gyi yadana*, literally the "precious eldest son." The preference for lineal descent through the eldest son is clearly expressed in many of the stock formulae of early Kon-baung (and Restored Taung-ngu) documents, one of the most common being "stemming from the ancient and noble race of kings descended son to grandson to great-grandson." The edict announcing the coming investiture of Bo-daw-hpaya's eldest son as crown prince in 1783 is an excellent statement of the ideal of the royal succession:

> In accordance with the tradition that the precious eldest son receives the eastern house in order that he may strive equally for the efflorescence of the religion and welfare of

the king, his sons and grandsons in succession and of all the people, noble kings of yore in succession from Maha Thamada have at the noble and auspicious time installed their precious eldest sons in the eastern house with all the establishment and treasure suitable to the station of the Lord of the Eastern House.[23]

As noted earlier, in order to be installed as crown prince, the eldest son had to be deemed competent in much the same way as did the inheritor of a local office. For the crown princeship competence required, first, that the prospective heir be the product of the legal marriage of the king and one of his principal queens and thus both a *yin-gya-thu*, or blood relative, and legitimate son in terms of customary law. Competence also required an "attractive appearance," which can be taken to rule out a diseased, maimed, or physically or mentally infirm prince.[24] Finally, the determination of competence in these respects lay with the king in consultation with his courtiers. The prerogative of selecting the crown prince belonged to the sovereign, whose choice from the pool of succession was constrained only by his awareness of the need for some consensus among his courtiers. Selection of a candidate without reasonable support at court simply was not in accord with the political realities of the age.

With the succession defined to include only sons by principal queens, the number of eligible candidates tended to be small and was limited by several other factors. The number of children produced by a king depended both on the length of his life and the length of his reign. The rate of child mortality was high from natural (and sometimes political) causes, at times reducing the number of royal children by over 50 percent. These figures are given in table 5. In some cases, the number of royal children was comparatively small, and in all cases, save that of Alaung-hpaya, significantly reduced by the high mortality rates. As shown in table 6, the number of potential heirs produced by any king of the early Kon-baung period never exceeded seven.

Concubinage was another important factor restricting the growth of the royal pool of succession. If a king came to the throne as a mature adult, he had usually already married the women who became his principal queens at an early age, or if he succeeded at a younger age, he had done so early in his reign. As these women passed prime childbearing age and perhaps became sexually less attractive to the king, he began to take younger women as concubines or, as was the case from the reign of Bo-daw-hpaya on, as both minor queens and concubines

Table 5. The Royal Children

King	Lifespan (years)	Period of Reign (years)	Sons Total	Sons Died	Daughters Total	Daughters Died	Total	Total Children Died	Total Children % Mortality
Alaung-hpaya	45.75	8.00	10	1	6	0	16	1	6.3
Naung-daw-gyi	29.25	3.50	5	3	2	1	7	4	57.1
Hsin-hpyu-shin	40.00	12.00	18	6	23	9	41	15	36.6
Sin-gu†	25.75	5.66	5	1	6	3	11	4	36.4
Bo-daw-hpaya	75.00	38.00	62	22	58	25	120	47	39.2
Crown Prince	46.80	—	32	16	26	16	58	32	55.2

†All of Sin-gu's living children were executed along with their father after the coup of 1782 by Bo-daw-hpaya.

Sources: MMM, 191–225 passim; KBZ 1 and 2 passim.

Table 6. Sons by Principal Queens

King	Chief Queen	North Queen	Middle Queen	West Queen	Total	Total Surviving Infancy
Alaung-hpaya	6	1	—	—	7	7
Naung-daw-gyi	1	1	0	—	2	2
Hsin-hpyu-shin	4	0	1st: 0; 2d: 5	—	9	1
Sin-gu	0	1st: 0; 2d: 0	1	0	1	0
Bo-daw-hpaya	0	1st: 2; 2d: 2	2	—	6	5
Crown Prince	1st: 4; 2d: 5	—	—	—	9	7

Sources: MMM, 191–225 passim; KBZ 1 and 2 passim.

and to focus his procreative energies on them. With this shift in attention, kings continued to produce children, but not potential heirs.

For both the gentry and the royal family, the multiple potential heirs stemming from multiple legal wives were the means essayed to ensure the continuity of the lineage. But the concern of the royal family went beyond lineage continuity to include the purity of its bloodline. In emulation of the Sakyan example, it was common for Taung-ngu kings to take, if possible, one of their half-sisters as chief queen in order to produce an heir with royal blood from both parents. There were, however, no princesses of the blood from the preceding dynasty available to Alaung-hpaya and his successors who, with the exception of Sin-gu, also had legitimate sons from their gentry marriages to whom they wished the crown to pass. Thus, the issue of purity of bloodline through sister marriage did not arise until the reign of Bo-daw-hpaya. At his investiture as crown prince in 1783, Bo-daw-hpaya's eldest son, born of the north queen, was married to a daughter of the chief queen, who had born three daughters but no sons. Observing that both of these queens had received the *mahei abhiseka*, the *Kon-baung-zet* states that the crown prince and his half-sister "were married with the intent that the Sakyan lineage of Okkamukha not be broken."25

Cousin marriage was almost as important as sister marriage, because brothers of the king by principal queens produced daughters with blood pedigrees as suitable as those of the daughters of the monarch himself. Not only were crown princes married to one half-sister, but also to either several half-sisters or to the daughters of uncles of the royal blood. From the reign of Bo-daw-hpaya on, it also became customary for the other princes of the blood and minor princes to practice sister and cousin marriage.

Thus, the royal lineage began to shift from a completely open marriage system drawing all its women from the outside to a partially closed system, a clear trend from complete exogamy to partial endogamy. While multiple queens were intended to ensure the adequacy of the pool of succession and hence lineal descent, the introduction of more than one principal queen of the blood was intended to preserve the bloodline. The political effect of sister and cousin marriage on the royal succession was that princes with royal blood from both parents had a theoretically better claim to the throne than did the other members of the pool of succession. The introduction of this distinction was a major point of political conflict during the later part of the reign of Bo-daw-hpaya.

As with gentry lineages, the royal succession, with its pool of potential heirs and competency requirements, left considerable scope for conflict and challenge. There were instances in which the chief queen produced no sons, forcing the king to turn to another principal queen. In other cases, the son or sons of the ruler were deemed incompetent because they were yet children and, in still others, the ruler failed to appoint his heir. Even when appointed, a crown prince could expect challenges from his brothers and his uncles of the blood, who tended to be more mature and experienced. The uncles, in fact, were often more qualified and attractive candidates for the throne than their nephews.

Because the often large group of sons by minor queens and concubines was defined out of the succession, it was not considered a factor and was therefore well treated. Alaung-hpaya's two sons by concubines, for example, lived honored but politically inactive lives under Bo-daw-hpaya as the *myo-zas* of Myin-gun and Mya-wadi, respectively. Maung Naga, a son of Hsin-hpyu-shin by a concubine, was honored with gifts and trappings alongside three of Bo-daw-hpaya's sons in 1785, appointed cavalry captain of Let-ywei-nge, and then made *myo-za* of Patana-go.[26]

These minor sons only became politically significant in abnormal circumstances. During the Kon-baung period such circumstances arose in 1752, 1878, and 1885. In 1752 and 1885, foreign invasion and the occupation of upper Burma left the country without a government, because the victors physically removed the king. In each case this was accompanied by strong local resistance. In 1752 all of the princes save two were carried off with the king and later killed by the southerners. Neither of the remaining princes was able to exert effective leadership and so control of the resistance passed to men not of the royal line. In the second instance, there were seven alleged royal princes in the field against the British from 1885 to 1887, but only one—the Myin-zaing prince—would have been part of the pool of succession in more normal circumstances. As it was, virtually the entire pool of succession and corpus of minor princes had been liquidated by Thi-baw in the so-called massacres of the kinsmen in 1879 and 1883. In the third instance, the customary succession had failed in 1878 because there were no sons by principal queens and Min-don had not formally designated his successor. As a result, the minor princes were projected into the running for the throne. Any claim to royal blood apparently became significant when the pool of succession had been eliminated, but until such time the minor children of the king were very much on the political fringe.

The Crown Prince

The institution of the crown princeship was apparently well established, at least in Burmese tradition, as early as the Pagan period. The *Glass Palace Chronicle* makes various references to the appointments of crown princes in the Pagan period and the *Law-ka byu-ha kyan* [Treatise on customary terms] of the late 1750s, a detailed record of royal traditions and customs, states that since the founding of Ava by Thado Min-bya in 1364, there was a total of twenty-nine kings, all of whom appointed their sons to the post.[27] In the early Kon-baung period there were three appointed crown princes. Alaung-hpaya installed his eldest son, who became Naung-daw-gyi, and Bo-daw-hpaya installed first his eldest son and, on the latter's death, his grandson, who became Ba-gyi-daw.

The crown prince was termed *ein-shei min*, or "lord of the eastern house," and also *maha u-payaza*, or "great under-king." These appellations are indicative of the crown prince's position in relation to the king. As the most exalted being in the realm, the king on his throne faced east, that being where the sun rose and hence the most important direction. As the second most exalted being, the crown prince was installed in the eastern house. The term *maha u-payaza* is also literally descriptive of the position of the crown prince as deputy ruler.

Once selected by the king, a prince was not formally installed as heir apparent until he came of age, which in Burma usually occurred about the age of sixteen. At this time he was also married to his future chief queen. As the time for investiture approached, the eastern house was constructed. It was similar in form to the palace of the king, as it was considered to be an "embryo" palace for an "embryo" king.[28] Like all Burmese houses, both the royal palace and the eastern house had a post or pillar (*kun*) for the Maha Gi-ri *nat*, the guardian spirit of houses and realm alike. The eastern house itself was composed of eastern, middle, and western apartments with subsidiary quarters for the *atwin wuns* of the crown prince. The house was surrounded by a wall with twelve gates, outside of which was the main court (*yon*) on the left, a smaller court on the right, and a western court by the western gate. Inside the wall was an armory, treasury, stables, and quarters for attendants while outside were more quarters for attendants and barracks for the regiments of the prince's guard.[29]

The investiture itself was held on an auspicious day determined by the court astrologers. The record of the installation of the eldest son of Bo-daw-hpaya on 13 July 1783 provides a detailed description of that occasion.[30] Held at the Bye-daik, the ceremony was witnessed by the full court, with the place holders headed by the four *wun-gyis* in their assigned spots. Gathered around the galleries and edges of the audience hall was a multitude of people who were to be appointed to the service of the crown prince. Accompanied by his retinue, the heir apparent arrived on his palanquin and entered the hall, where he was seated on a fine reed mat before which were placed four umbrellas of state. Walking along a path of mats surrounded by his attendants, the king entered from the royal apartments and seated himself on his dais as the auspicious moment drew near. In front of the Bye-daik were dancers and people reciting verses appropriate to the occasion. The ceremony began as a herald read aloud the investiture order:

> For the benefit and welfare of the people and of themselves and for the efflorescence of the religion, the noble and great kings of old who were replete with glory, strength, and power, always gave their precious eldest sons the eastern house. I am of the line and flesh of kings stemming from Okkamukha and rule my patrimony in accord with the kingly laws. I vow to strive for the expansion of the religion and for my welfare and the welfare, happiness, and prosperity of all the people.
>
> My son is one who is worthy to assist me in this noble endeavor. In accord with the duty of the law [that is, *dhamma*], the duty of kings, and proper conduct, I invest my precious eldest son with the insignia, trappings, jewels, elephants, horses, retinue, attendants, and service groups proper to the Lord of the Eastern House in order that he carry on the royal line in succeeding generations, be the refuge of all the people, and strive diligently for their welfare and the welfare of the religion.[31]

The king's endowment of lands, goods, and servants to the crown prince was then read aloud and formally transferred. The crown prince on that occasion received a substantial establishment, including quantities of piece goods, gold, silver, and numerous servants and household attendants. More importantly, he was granted a number of cavalry, artillery, and musketeer units as well as a personal elite guard unit for his protection. The armory of the eastern house was also well stocked with cannons, muskets, powder and shot, and edged weapons. With his own walled compound, arsenal, and army, the crown prince was militarily the second most powerful figure in the realm, as was intended.[32]

Similarly, the extensive towns, districts, and service units assigned to the crown prince were intended to give him a private demesne second only to that of the monarch. Lastly, he was given an administrative establishment which mirrored in microcosm that of the ruler. Two *anauk wuns* ran his household with a full complement of supporting personnel. His treasure, material goods, insignia and trappings, lands, revenues, service units, and security were administered by two *atwin wuns* of the eastern house. Comparable to *wun-gyis*, two *wuns* of the eastern house were charged with looking after his affairs in the governmental sphere, most importantly his relations with the Hlut-taw, in which capacity they made daily written reports to him on the business conducted. Supporting them was a full roster of heralds, secretaries, couriers, and other personnel. The total establishment of the crown prince, excluding military and other service groups, was around five hundred functionaries, including two doctors, two astrologers, and six reciters of *parittas* and *mantras*.[33]

At an astrologically determined time later that day, the bride of the crown prince arrived with her retinue and the marriage ceremony took place.[34] This ceremony completed the formation of the crown prince's establishment as a microcosm of that of his father. The bride was invested as the *ein-shei mi-baya*, or queen of the eastern house. Her role was to become the chief queen and produce the next heir to the crown. On a separate day, the crown prince's new status was acknowledged by the court in a formal *kadaw* ceremony where the princes and courtiers, according to rank and status, presented him with gifts and homage.

The point of the investiture was to establish the heir in a position that was politically and materially unassailable by any save his father and to transfer to him some of the charisma surrounding the throne—hence the embryo palace, embryo queen, embryo establishment, and public approbation of his father. Once formally installed, the process of preparing the crown prince for the kingship was continued by giving him a definite role to play in public affairs. In the early Kon-baung period, only two of the three crown princes installed held that post as mature adults. Both Naung-daw-gyi and Maha U-payaza, eldest son of Bo-daw-hpaya, at times assumed complete responsibility for the kingdom.

The crown prince was generally expected to participate in the daily audiences held by the king and to lead military expeditions. Naung-daw-gyi was one of his father's more active and able field commanders and Maha U-payaza led both the successful 1784 expedition against Arakan and subdued the major Tavoy rebellion of 1792. There is no record of military command for Ba-gyi-daw as crown prince. The crown prince's other major governmental role was to act as superintendent of the Hlut-taw. For this purpose two officials of the prince were designated *nagans*, whose duties were to sit in the Hlut-taw each day beside the *nagans* of the king and make copies of letters received and sent and to report on business transacted by the *wun-gyis* and the deaths of any officials, courtiers, or *saw-bwas*. When a *myo-za, saw-bwa*, or other important official died, one of the crown prince's officers was appointed to accompany the officers sent from the Hlut-taw to the domain or jurisdiction of the deceased and to render one-half of the assistance given by the crown. The crown prince also had a minor role to play in some of the ceremonies and festivals of the Buddhist calendrical cycle as well as receiving *kadaw* in the same fashion as the king.[35] The essential difference between the *kadaw* of the king and that of the crown prince was that allegiance was sworn only to the king. In terms of material power, institutional charisma, and role in government, however, it was intended that the crown prince truly be the "under-king."

The Passage of Power

On the demise of a ruler, the passage of power was immediate and was supposed to follow customary procedures. These procedures were observed at the accessions of Sin-gu in 1776, Ba-gyi-daw in 1819, and probably Naung-daw-gyi in 1763. Because it was the role of the *atwin wuns* to oversee the well-being and health of the king, they were in constant attendance in rota when he was indisposed and were the first to know of his death. When this event occurred, they immediately dispatched a herald to the eastern house to report the death in writing to the crown prince. A laquered *parabaik* conveyed this standard message: "Your father was ill and although he was treated with medicine and prayers, he is today discontented with the world of people and now dwells in the realm of the spirits. Pray rule over the palace and kingdom."[36] When this message had been formally read aloud and transferred, the crown prince ordered the herald to return to the palace to announce the coming of the new king. His military and civil establishment then formed a procession led by the military units in prescribed order, followed by the civil establishment headed by the *wuns*, the prince himself in his palanquin with his personal attendants and umbrellas of rank, and finally a corps of his infantry bringing up the rear. Arriving at the fort, the crown prince went first to the Hlut-taw and then to the Bye-daik, each of which was taken over by the appropriate parts of his establishment. He then entered the palace itself where he was met by the former king's *atwin wuns*. At that point, a proclamation proclaiming his occupancy of the throne was read out: "My father the king was wearied of the world of people and now that he dwells in the realm of the spirits, I rule my heritage in accord with the law."[37]

As soon as the prince had formally proclaimed his occupancy of the throne, some elements of his establishment began to take over important parts of the palace, replacing personnel of the former king, while others merged with existing units in the palace and fort. The most important moves were taken by the military units, which moved to replace the personnel at major security points such as the main gates, and by the *anauk wuns* who moved their men into control of the Western Court. While this process was going on, the death of the old king and the accession of his heir was announced to the capital by members of cavalry units who were dispatched to the main roads and crossroads within and without the city to read this proclamation: "My father the king was wearied of the world of people and now that he dwells in the realm of the spirits, I rule my inheritance in accord with the law. Let the people be not afraid and conduct their daily business as usual."[38]

As the fort and capital area were being secured by the personnel of the crown prince, the formal transition of power continued within the palace. In a customary act of continuity, all of the princes and courtiers renounced their titles, trappings of rank, and appanages, which were then reinstated by the new king. On the day following the funeral, the process of receiving the fealty of the court and country began. With the new king on the throne, the princes and courtiers in order of rank performed the *kadaw* ceremony under the watchful eyes of the personal troops of the sovereign.

Three days after taking possession of the palace and fort, the new ruler was supposed to perform that act of Burmese kings known as *maha u-gin-bwin*, or appearing on the throne in full and formal audience. He was then considered to be king *de jure* as well as *de facto* and entitled to be addressed with the standard appellation for kings: "the lord whose glory is exceedingly noble and great, the lord of life, the king of righteousness." Up until that point in his occupancy of the palace he had only been termed "the lord whose glory is very great," whereas from his installation as crown prince he was termed "the lord of the eastern house who has great glory."[39] Similarly, prior to the *u-gin-bwin* (literally, the opening of the doors behind the throne through which the king appeared), he could only give verbal orders, which were not written down, whereas normally all pronouncements of the ruler were recorded on the spot. The process of becoming king was still incomplete, however, as ceremonies were held at two successive seven-day intervals in which the incumbent took formal possession of first the Hlut-taw and then the Bye-daik. A proclamation was then issued to inform the people of the municipal area that in seven days the sovereign would in great procession take possession of the city and fort along a prescribed route, hence the streets and houses must be cleaned and prepared. On completion of this act, the heir was well established as ruler in terms of customary procedures and could set about the more pragmatic aspects of organizing his administration.

With the court and capital dealt with in such fashion, it remained for the provinces to be informed. Letters prepared in the Hlut-taw under the direction of the *wun-gyis* were sent to the provincial officials, *myo-zas*, and *saw-bwas* to inform them of the death of the king and the accession of the heir. Officials were directed to send their gifts and oaths of allegiance in the customary way and also to inform the people in their jurisdictions, so that they would not be afraid and continue their business as usual. In the case of appointed officials such admonition was important, for the accession of a new king meant not only the lapse of the titles, trappings, and appanages of the royal men and courtiers, but those of the *myo wuns* and other appointed officials as well. Most importantly, this involved the officials of such large districts as Hantha-wadi, Tavoy, Taung-ngu, Prome, and Martaban, whose loss of position might be permanent for, in contrast to officials at court, there was no customary act of continuity for appointed officials and royal favor alone dictated reappointment.

The Dilemma of the Royal Succession

Through the customary rules governing the royal pool of succession, the institution and role of the crown prince, and the customary procedures for the transfer of authority, the Burmese political system did attempt to make careful institutional preparation for the orderly passage of power. The number of legitimate claimants was limited by the genealogical priorities of the customary succession, which was, however, by no means inflexible. If not for selecting the ablest candidate, there was at least provision for eliminating the obviously unfit. Once selected, the heir apparent was endowed with a preponderant and institutionalized position, which left him with a significant advantage over the remainder of the pool of succession. As lord of the eastern house, he had an important formal role in government and partook of some of the royal charisma as well. When it came time for him to assume the throne, he already had the nucleus of his administration, a corps of officials who had served him as crown prince and whose futures, and thus loyalties, were bound to him. At his accession, his personal army protected him and secured the palace and capital. Had he been old enough to serve what amounts to an apprenticeship in kingship while his father still lived, the prince assumed the throne already conversant with the business of government and the subtleties of politics and with allegiances already formed with the important officials.

The genealogical priorities of the customary succession were intended to limit the competition for the throne and ensure a supply of qualified heirs. Too much precision in defining genealogical qualifications might force the accession of a fundadamentally unsuitable candidate; hence beyond having a blood relationship with the king through a principal queen and basic personal competence, no qualification was absolute. While usually ensuring a minimally qualified and competent heir, this lack of absoluteness made the royal succession the central and constant focal point of political conflict in the polity through the basic eligibility of all the sons and uncles of the blood. The primary actors in the struggle were the ruler and his candidate, if any, the factions pressing the claims of other princes, and the senior officials who, if possible, attempted to seize control of the succession in order to place the weakest and most malleable candidate on the throne.[40] The result was a struggle in which the winner was not necessarily the most able candidate, but the one put forth by the strongest faction.

The dilemma of the royal succession was not restricted to these debilitating factional struggles, but extended to the surviving members of the pool of succession. The struggle tended not to end with the victory of one candidate because the defeated usually remained a continuing source of tension and challenge. Two solutions to this dilemma appeared in the Restored Taung-ngu period. The first of these was attempted on two occasions, when rulers made their eldest son and heir designate promise that the remaining sons of the blood would rule in succession by order of seniority.[41] Such promises were not a viable solution, however, because in both cases the eldest son wished to pass the crown to his own son and ignored the promise. A second solution was tried on two other occasions, when kings tried to eliminate the threat posed by their brothers to the kings' eldest sons by making the former viceroys. This solution, too, was unsatisfactory because on both occasions the brothers used their positions as viceroys to contest the succession militarily on the death of the king.[42] Thus, one solution was to attempt to decree collateral rather than lineal succession. The other was to try to buy off other eligibles by making them literally mini-kings with governance over a small part of the realm in the hope that the maxi-king would ultimately be able to control them. The same dilemma characterized the politics of the royal succession in the early Kon-baung period. The royal succession and the solutions essayed by Alaunghpaya and his sons are the subject of the following chapter.

CHAPTER 7

THE PASSAGE OF POWER, 1752-1819

In early January 1760, Alaung-hpaya launched a major invasion of the Thai state of Ayuthia, the historic enemy of Burma. Advised against even by the court astrologers, the campaign was ill-fated from its inception and expired in a miasma of fever and flux before the walls of Ayuthia some four months later. With more than half of his force suffering from fever, Alaung-hpaya began an ignominious retreat on 17 April. After a march of twenty-four days, he too succumbed to the fever at dawn on 11 May at the little village of Kin, a two-day march from Martaban. Attended by his second son Maung Ywa and various officers, the king on his deathbed gave two last orders. The first was to continue the war against Ayuthia and the second directed that his sons should occupy the throne in succession, eldest to youngest.[1] The first of the deathbed orders was executed when Maung Ywa, then King Hsin-hpyu-shin of Ava, put an end to the Ayuthia kings of Thailand with the sack of the Thai capital in 1767. But the second order was to become Alaung-hpaya's unfortunate legacy to the line of kings he founded, confounding the royal succession for the next twenty-five years. The Italian missionary Vincentius Sangermano, a contemporary observer, wrote that it was "a most fatal proposition, as it was the cause of the many troubles and civil wars that shortly arose."[2] The first half of this story of the passage of power concerns the effects of this "most fatal proposition," and the second looks at the efforts of Alaung-hpaya's fourth son, Bo-daw-hpaya, to prevent such a situation from arising again.

Alaung-hpaya and His Pool of Succession

Born U Aung Zei-ya in August 1714 in what is the modern Shwei-bo District of upper Burma, Alaung-hpaya was truly a man of destiny.

The specific position and rank of his father are not known, but judging from the account of the family's long official and gentry lineage recorded in the *Kon-baung-zet* and the advantageous marriages Alaung-hpaya's father was able to make for his son, he must have been a person of some local and political consequence. Alaung-hpaya himself was a local official who had received the personal honorific title of Bala Nan-da Kyaw from Maha Dama Ya-za Di-pati, the last Taung-ngu ruler.[3] As a titled person and one of the local authorities, in local opinion he was a man of no little stature. Known for his resourcefulness and strength, it was natural for local leadership to devolve on him in the unsettled years preceding the fall of the Taung-ngu dynasty.

There were various cases of local resistance to the southern occupation of upper Burma in 1752, but that led by Alaung-hpaya was the most visibly successful.[4] Eliminating or coopting his competition, he apparently began to harbor aspirations toward the vacant crown at an early stage. For this reason he fell out with the Shwei-daung prince, eldest son of the last Taung-ngu king, who had escaped capture and entered his camp. Following their split, the prince had fled first to the Shan Hills and later to Ayuthia, where he was only marginally successful in enlisting Thai support for his cause. Scarcely a month after the fall of Ava in March 1752, Alaung-hpaya bestowed titles and honors on his followers and acceded to their request that he himself assume the royal title of Alaung-min-taya-gyi, or "Embryo Buddha, King of Righteousness," in accord with a hermit's prophecy about the coming of a new king. A palace and fort were built in June of the following year at Mok-hso-bo, which became the royal capital of Yadana Thein-hka. At that time, he held coronation ceremonies for himself and his head wife and appointed his eldest son as crown prince.[5] Alaung-hpaya went on to clear upper Burma and establish his authority there as ruler, then reconquered central and lower Burma in a series of well-conducted campaigns which ended in 1757 and left him the unchallenged king of Burma.

One of Alaung-hpaya's main strengths in his pursuit of the crown was the large number of relatives on whose support he could draw. As Walter Alves, a 1755 visitor to Mok-hso-bo, noted in his journal: "He has also abundant Relations and Dependants, which he generally employs in Posts of trust or consequence."[6] Alaung-hpaya's family was well intermarried with the gentry of neighboring towns, providing him with a broad range of blood and marriage ties. Many, if not most, of the key posts in his reign were held by such relatives. His head wife was Me Yun San, a daughter of Min Thi-ri Yan-daza, a highly respected and powerful local figure in the neighboring town of Si-bok-tara. This marriage probably took place around 1730. A year older than her husband, Me Yun San was a strong woman who bore Alaung-hpaya six sons and three daughters. All of the sons survived the perils of infancy and childhood, the two eldest reaching manhood in time to assist their father in his rise to power.

Alaung-hpaya's pool of succession consisted of these six sons by his head wife and one son by a lesser wife. Although the date of the marriage is not recorded, it is known that Alaung-hpaya took a second wife, Shin Pyei, a daughter of the Si-tha *min-gyi*, Si-tha being another town in the district. A granddaughter of Min Thi-ri Yan-daza, Shin Pyei bore a son named Maung Hla in 1753 who was later known as the Si-tha prince after his appanage. As was the practice with the early Kon-baung kings, on Alaung-hpaya's assumption of the crown, Me Yun San, as head wife, became chief queen while Shin Pyei, as second wife, became the north queen. Of three other sons by concubines, one died in infancy and the others appear to have played no role in politics and would, in any case, have had no formal claim to the throne. At Alaung-hpaya's death in 1760 there were thus seven potential heirs to the crown. The first six were all grandsons of Min Thi-ri Yan-daza and the seventh a great-grandson.

At the time of the southern occupation in 1752, the first son, Maung Hlauk, was eighteen years of age, and the second son, Maung Ywa, was sixteen. By the standards of the time, both were already men and became lieutenants to their father. They took an active part in the early discussions on resistance to the southerners and it was, in fact, Maung Hlauk who proposed the plan that was finally accepted. During the ensuing skirmishes around Mok-hso-bo, both fought beside their father, after which they shared command of a successful expedition against an enemy fort at Myaung-wun. Maung Hlauk, as the *aw-ra-tha* son, was subsequently installed as crown prince. Probably due to the bad feeling between himself and the Shwei-daung prince, heir apparent of the fallen dynasty, Alaung-hpaya gave his own heir apparent Shwei-daung Myo as an appanage. From this time on, Maung Hlauk appears to have begun to perform the administrative role of crown prince. He is seen less frequently as a field commander, instead being left in charge of the capital as his father continued the conquest of the country.

Now holding *min-nyi min-tha* status with the title of Thado Min-zaw, the second son came to the forefront as a field commander, being exceptionally distinguished for his capture and subsequent defense of Ava in 1753-1754. As a reward, his title was raised to Thi-ri Dama Ya-za and he was given Myei-du and Salin *myos* as appanages. He was thereafter known as the Myei-du prince, after his major appanage.

The two brothers appear again as a team during the 1754 campaign in central Burma, where they distinguished themselves in the bloody assault on the southern fort at Hsan-daw-shin. Each was rewarded with a golden sword and a golden umbrella, marks of royalty. During the final campaigns in Han-tha-wadi, the brothers further distinguished themselves, sometimes acting alone, sometimes in tandem. Having early proved themselves as soldiers, the two sons became trusted commanders of their father and contributed importantly to his establishment as ruler.

Alaung-hpaya's two eldest sons inherited the good qualities of their father—strength, driving ambition, bravery, and flair for leadership—but also shared his volatile temper, religious austerity, and arrogance. To these the crown prince added a certain vindictiveness, a trait for which he was subsequently to pay dearly. Neither son had the charisma of the father, that intangible quality that made the common people venerate him and whisper that surely their king was a *bodhisatta*.[7] Driven by their ambitions, the relationship between the two brothers was probably one of respect tinged with rivalry, but perhaps not without genuine affection. They had to function in a highly competitive context, as their father had gathered about him a body of able men from the area, a number of whom quickly emerged as civil officials and military commanders of drive and ambition. Some of these men continued to play important and even dominant roles in military and political affairs for almost half a century. With such talent available, the early councils of state and war were the stage of many conflicts and the origin of some lasting resentments.

When Alaung-hpaya marched on Ayuthia early in 1760, the crown prince was left in charge of court and country and the Myei-du prince commanded the advance guard. The arrival at court on June 6 of the news of Alaung-hpaya's death found the crown prince securely in control of the capital and upper Burma, while his most probable rival was struggling back in defeat from Thailand. The crown prince ascended the throne the following day at the age of twenty-six to become the second king of the Kon-baung dynasty.[8] Known as Naung-daw-gyi in Burmese history, his reign was short and turbulent—even before he knew he was king, challenges were in the making.

Challenges to Naung-daw-gyi

The first challenge came from his younger brother the Myei-du prince, but the details are somewhat obscure. The only contemporary account, that of Walter Alves who visited Mok-hso-bo in 1760, states that the Myei-du prince announced that his father had designated him as heir on his deathbed and tried to claim command of the army then retreating from Thailand. The main body of officers resisted this claim and suppressed news of the king's death for as long as possible. Taking what followers he had, the prince then established himself at Taung-ngu. Finding little support, however, he quickly opened negotiations with his brother through their mother and was forgiven for his aberration.[9]

A later indigenous source, the *Kon-baung-zet*, relates a more detailed and somewhat different story. Due to the adverse circumstances in which the invasion army found itself before Ayuthia, this account claims that the Myei-du prince and a leading general titled Min-gaung Naw-rahta both counselled retreat, counsel which was readily accepted by the ailing Alaung-hpaya. Min-gaung Naw-rahta was appointed to command the rear guard of six thousand foot and five hundred horse and ordered to remain before Ayuthia as the main force departed. After a day's march, the king reinforced the rear guard with thirty-two hundred men under another proven general, Min-hla Naw-rahta, the future *wun-gyi* U Hnaung. The still outnumbered Min-gaung Naw-rahta beat off a major attack and drove the Thai back within their walls, sending Min-hla Naw-rahta to rejoin the king. After menacing the cowed Thai for four or five more days, Min-gaung Naw-rahta then began his own retreat.

The *Kon-baung-zet* continues that only the Myei-du prince and the attending courtiers knew of the death of the king on 11 May. The body was preserved as well as possible and carried in a closed palanquin as though the king was simply ill. As the main force crossed the Sittang River on its way to Pegu, it was overtaken by the detachment of Min-hla Naw-rahta. Gathering provisions along the way, Min-gaung Naw-rahta moved slowly and made no effort to catch up, finally coming to a complete halt near the Sittang River. Apprised of this information, the Myei-du prince ordered Min-gaung Naw-rahta to resume the march and join him at Pegu. Unaware that the king was dead, the latter refused to do so without a formal order from Alaung-hpaya and announced his intention to return via Taung-ngu. Arriving at Rangoon, the body of the king was placed on a boat for transport to the capital. As the news had become generally known about Rangoon, the Myei-du prince realized that it was now futile to try to keep the secret and sent two messengers to the capital.

Soon after the news arrived and the crown prince assumed the throne, he apparently received word from Min-gaung Naw-rahta, one of the first and most trusted followers of his father, that the Myei-du prince and some of the officers had formed a group based on a blood oath of allegiance at the Mya-thein-dan Pagoda in Martaban, and that the prince had further directed the *myo-thu-gyi* of Sittang not to send supplies to the rear guard. From this word, the new king began to surmise that his brother was up to no good. His suspicions were reinforced by reports of remarks made by his brother's second wife, although the *Kon-baung-zet* does not reveal the nature of these remarks. When the Myei-du prince arrived at Ywa-thit-kyi with the body, he was ordered to the capital posthaste, and the *wun-gyi* Nei-myo Shwei-daung was summarily executed for his complicity in the failed plot.[10] The Myei-du prince defended himself by saying that he had become suspicious of Min-gaung Naw-rahta because the latter lagged behind, refused to obey orders, and elected to return via Taung-ngu. Although no action was taken against the prince, the *Kon-baung-zet* records that the king did not believe his brother and continued to doubt him.[11]

Although differing in detail, the two accounts do agree that the Myei-du prince made but an ineffectual challenge to his brother. He did not, however, go to Taung-ngu, traditionally a base for rebellions because of its remote geographic position and proximity to Thailand. Walter Alves's account probably confused the Myei-du prince with Min-gaung Naw-rahta, who did briefly pass through Taung-ngu. Remote from the reality of court and power, the seeming opportunity of the moment at Kin Village may have unleashed the strong ambition of the second son. But with his brother installed as crown prince as the publicly announced choice of the father for the crown and firmly in command of court and country, there was no way that the Myei-du prince could have gained the throne without a bloody and protracted struggle, even had the retreating army fully supported him. His plan apparently had been to use this army to support his claim to the throne and his first problem was the lack of their anticipated support. His second problem was, of course, the independence of Min-gaung Naw-rahta. This problem later turned to his advantage, however, because he was able to make Min-gaung Naw-rahta the scapegoat of the affair, a scapegoat who Naung-daw-gyi for reasons of his own readily accepted. Being but twenty-four years old at the time, it seems certain that the Myei-du prince was the recipient of some bad counsel from his own retainers, who surely misled him as to the amount of his support. Be that as it may, Naung-daw-gyi was not a popular choice to succeed his father, and there are indications that his younger brother did have powerful supporters.

The reason for the speedy adjudication of the differences between the brothers was the very real threat to both posed by the disaffected General Min-gaung Naw-rahta, whose fate was sealed by two factors. First, the new king nursed a strong animosity toward him that apparently stemmed from past conflicts. Indeed, he had already summarily executed two other officers toward whom he bore similar grudges. Second, to help save himself from the consequences of his rash actions, the Myei-du prince with support from his mother had charged Min-gaung Naw-rahta with rebellious intentions, a charge which gained credence as the latter hung back with his army for fear of meeting the same fate as the two other officers. He was finally pushed into open rebellion by news of the charges against him at court. The *Kon-baung-zet* places these words in his mouth as he explained his plight to his old comrade-in-arms Min-hla Naw-rahta, sent by the king to persuade him to return to the capital:

> I have been accused so that the crime of the Myei-du prince may remain unnoticed. Since they are elder and younger brother, the elder will surely believe the words of the younger. As our lord and benefactor, Alaung-hpaya, who could have saved me, now is no more, I and all my family are surely ruined. A man cannot entertain any fear in attempting to fight for his survival. Since such a thing happens but once in a lifetime as ordained by one's *kamma*, I will not go with you, come what may.[12]

Popular with his troops and able to play on their resentment of the king's perfidious execution of the two other generals, Min-gaung Naw-rahta brushed aside the initial opposition offered by Thado Thein-ga-thu, *myo wun* of Taung-ngu and younger brother of Alaung-hpaya, and seized Ava. There he fortified himself with twelve thousand seasoned and loyal troops and called on the country to join him in the overthrow of the king. Lacking cannon capable of breeching the walls, as popular disaffection with him mounted Naung-daw-gyi was forced to rely on direct and costly assaults. Starvation finally accomplished what his soldiers had failed to gain and, after a siege lasting over nine months, Min-gaung Naw-rahta and his remaining men were forced to cut their way out. The rebel general remained at large for several more months before finally falling victim to a musket shot from one of his pursuers in a remote forest.[13]

Presented as a tragiheroic victim of circumstances not of his own making by the *Kon-baung-zet*, the length and strength of Min-gaung

Naw-rahta's resistance illustrates the weakness and unpopularity of Naung-daw-gyi. The former was also able to tap a substantial and ill-concealed reservoir of support for the restoration of the previous dynasty in the person of the Shwei-daung prince, then in Thailand. The crown worn by Naung-daw-gyi was by no means secure and he could ill-afford to alienate his younger brother's supporters in the face of their common enemy.

Lasting more than a year, Min-gaung Naw-rahta's rebellion forced Naung-daw-gyi to postpone his coronation, performance of the *maha u-gin-bwin*, and the formal assumption of regnal titles for himself and his chief queen until 9 February 1761. Less than three months later, news of a third serious challenge to his throne reached the capital. The rebellion mounted by his uncle Thado Thein-ga-thu was not to end until a year and a day after the coronation.

Alaung-hpaya had an elder brother who receives but a single mention in the *Kon-baung-zet* and a younger brother named Maung Nyun. Apparently close to Alaung-hpaya, the younger brother served him from the beginning as a commander and governor in posts of increasing importance. After the completion of his Manipur campaign in 1759, Alaung-hpaya appointed his younger brother, now titled Thado Thein-ga-thu, *myo wun* of the Taung-ngu region and sent him to live there with his family.[14] This appointment was in keeping with Alaung-hpaya's practice of placing close relatives in key positions. Even before his posting to Taung-ngu, there were signs that Thado Thein-ga-thu had pretensions, as shown in an edict of 1757 reprimanding him and his family for putting on the airs of royalty and oppressing the people of their district.[15]

Virtually independent administratively and made more so by the geographic difficulty of communication with the capital, in 1761 Thado Thein-ga-thu and six of his lieutenants apparently believed the moment opportune to challenge his nephew. Never a popular sovereign, Naung-daw-gyi had alienated many military and civil officers with his petty vindictiveness, and Min-gaung Naw-rahta's long rebellion had left the country in confusion and Naung-daw-gyi himself in a politically shaky position. Walter Alves noted that the king was unable to impose his will on his officials and "in the present Posture of his Affairs, will not quarrel with them for a Trifle."[16] Raising the standard of revolt on 18 April, Thado Thein-ga-thu and his lieutenants probably planned to harness the resources of the Taung-ngu area and Sittang Valley and, following the example of Tabin-shwei-hti over two centuries earlier, strike at the unsettled Irrawaddy Valley.

Whatever his defects of character may have been, Naung-daw-gyi was a man of action and immediately dispatched the trusted Min-hla Naw-rahta with an advance force to harry the rebels while he gathered the much larger main force. This latter army did not depart until near the end of the monsoon in September, perhaps because of the rains but perhaps also due to the king's difficulties in mustering active support. The arrival of the main force under Naung-daw-gyi saw the defeat of the rebels in the field and the commencement of a formal siege. Cut off from supplies and reinforcements from its hinterland, the city finally fell to a bloody assault on 10 February 1762. Thado Thein-ga-thu was found with his family sitting on the floor of his house and brought before his nephew. Despite the fact that his uncle had violated his oath of allegiance, Naung-daw-gyi did not execute him, but forced him to live as a monk. The entire family was kept under house arrest in Mok-hso-bo, where Thado Thein-ga-thu appears to have remained until well into the reign of Bo-daw-hpaya. Even more puzzling was the fate of the surviving lieutenants, who only had their possessions confiscated and were forced into royal service, appearing in subsequent years in positions of middle-level military command on various occasions.[17]

Just two months after the end of this second rebellion, the victorious king formally took possession of the rebuilt capital of Sagaing, which was renamed Zei-ya-pu-ra, or the "City of Victory." He also maintained his boyhood home of Mok-hso-bo as a second capital, dividing his time between the two. Emerging from the affair of Thado Thein-ga-thu somewhat strengthened politically, the remainder of Naung-daw-gyi's reign was relatively peaceful, except for some disturbances among the Shans, an occurrence common to the reign of any Burmese king.

Details of the queens of Naung-daw-gyi are sketchy. The chief queen was Shin Hpyo U, a daughter of Maha Thi-ri Thin-hkaya who had served as a *wun-gyi* under the last king of Ava. She bore a son named Maung Maung on 12 September 1763 but no other children. A daughter of the Min-ywa *bo*, the north queen had only one child, a son named Maung Nu who died in infancy. The middle queen, Min Shwei Gya, was a minor daughter of the last king of Ava. She bore two daughters, only one of whom survived infancy. Of Naung-daw-gyi's three sons by concubines, only one reached maturity. Named Maung Chit O, his mother was Thi-da Dei-wi, a daughter of the Northern Cavalry *wun*. Beyond the fact that he died in prison during the reign of Bo-daw-hpaya, nothing more is known.

Naung-daw-gyi's reign continued for only a year and nine months after his victory at Taung-ngu. Several strands of evidence suggest that he succumbed to a fourth challenge, this time of a covert nature.

In addition to his general unpopularity and precarious political position, he also may have been neither overly able nor intelligent. Although Alaung-hpaya had left his son in charge of the realm, he had enough misgivings about Naung-daw-gyi to dispatch a number of letters from the field with detailed instructions and admonitions. In a letter of 4 January 1760, for example, he directed the chief queen to keep Naung-daw-gyi near her, superintend him in the execution of the king's instructions, and not to let him flag in his duties. These things were necessary, the king regretfully concluded, because Naung-daw-gyi was young and needed to be exhorted and cautioned.[18]

These misgivings perhaps shed further light on the motivation behind what appears on the surface to have been the rash attempt on the throne by Naung-daw-gyi's younger brother in 1760. The Myei-du prince may well have believed that he was more than a match for his less able brother. After the failure of his first plot there is no doubt that his ambition and intrigue continued. This was apparently such common knowledge that even Walter Alves recorded in October 1760: "I also heard of a Conspiracy, to place the present king's younger Brother on the Throne, which it was said was ripe for Execution, the first opportunity."[19] Naung-daw-gyi himself was surely aware of his brother's continuing machinations, as evidenced by the fact that he made a point of including the Myei-du prince in the main expedition against Taung-ngu in a rather minor capacity, presumably to keep him under surveillance.[20]

Yet the reign of Naung-daw-gyi came to an early end with his sudden death on 28 November 1763 at the age of twenty-nine. There is no evidence to suggest ill health and some to indicate physical vigor.[21] Given Alaung-hpaya's concern for his crown prince, the continuing intrigues of the Myei-du prince, and Naung-daw-gyi's sudden and unexpected early death there is at least some possibility that he was poisoned by his brother. This possibility is further strengthened by the fact that Naung-daw-gyi's only lineal heir was his son Maung Maung, then scarcely three-months-old.[22] In the eyes of the customary succession, his infancy made him an incompetent heir, hence the *atwin wuns* sent the customary formal message announcing the death of the king to the only acceptable heir. In this instance, the new king was also supported by his father's deathbed order that the sons succeed in turn. As the second son of Alaung-hpaya, the Myei-du prince began the process of assuming the kingship at dawn the following morning. One of his first acts was to give the order that his brother receive the funeral of a *cakkavatti*, or universal monarch, two days later in the northeast corner of the Hlut-taw.

The Passage of Power, 1752–1819   199

The deathbed order on succession is puzzling, however, because although the European sources refer to it freely, only one brief mention occurs in a Burmese source. Two explanations of the order are offered in the European sources. An Italian missionary letter of 1778 states that because only the youngest son of the chief queen, the Pin-dale prince, was born after Alaung-hpaya officially became king, the latter desired the succession to pass through the other sons to this son, who was then to begin a lineal succession according to Burmese tradition.[23] Writing six years later, the Italian missionary Gaetano Mantegazza observed that Alaung-hpaya loved his six sons by the chief queen so much that he wanted them all to enjoy the crown in succession.[24]

Despite these and other European sources, the absence of mention of the order in indigenous sources would make its veracity questionable were it not for one reference in the *Kon-baung-zet*. In giving his reasons for seizing the throne in 1782, the Badon prince is recorded as saying: "The original statement of our father was that his sons should succeed in order like the fingers on a hand."[25] Furthermore, the virtual absence of reference to the order in Burmese sources becomes more understandable in light of two points. First is the fact that a Buddhist cannot make a will concerning the disposition of his estate, which is why, in fact, the rules of inheritance were treated at such length in the customary law of the eighteenth century. Also closely regulated by customary law, the descent of office was a similar case and was not completely within the control of the bequeathor. Second, given the general mutability of the edicts of kings, no formal edict or informal wish concerning the succession would be binding on successors. As such, collateral succession as a solution to the dilemma of the royal succession proved a vain hope for rulers.

Hsin-hpyu-shin and Sin-gu

The succession of 1763 took place with no apparent conflict, the Myei-du prince having no rivals for the crown among the sons of Naung-daw-gyi or his younger brothers. Although Maung Maung was a babe in arms with no following, he did represent a potential danger for the future because he had all the blood qualifications for the throne. He was therefore given into the charge of an aunt and placed in a monastery with the intent that he remain there for the rest of his days. Known to history as Hsin-hpyu-shin, the Myei-du prince assumed the throne in a strong position in terms of his legitimacy as ruler. Only twenty-seven years old at his accession, he received the *abhiseka* over five months later on 17 May 1764, at the same time taking his regnal title and performing the *maha u-gin-bwin*. This occasion was also marked by honoring his four remaining brothers with new titles, trappings, and many gifts.

The new king's chief queen was Me Hla, a daughter of the *myo wun* of Mok-hso-bo and a granddaughter of Min Thi-ri Yan-daza. She bore four sons, but only the Sin-gu prince, born 10 May 1756, survived infancy. A daughter of King Tanin-ganwei (1714–1733), the north queen produced no children. The first middle queen was a daughter of the Si-tha *min-gyi* and a granddaughter of Min Thi-ri Yan-daza and also produced no children. When she died, her successor, a daughter of the Shwei-daik *wun*, conceived five sons and five daughters. Hsin-hpyu-shin also took as a concubine a minor daughter of the last king of Ava. She died before he reached the throne, but bore him a son named Maung Paung Chaung, who was later known as the Salin prince after his appanage.

Thus, the pool of succession in the reign of Hsin-hpyu-shin was small. Because the sons of the second middle queen were all infants, only Sin-gu, as the *aw-ra-tha* son of the chief queen, was eligible. Given the fact that the mother of the Salin prince had been a princess of the preceding dynasty, he was also an acceptable candidate, but he was about five years younger than his half-brother. It must also be remembered that Sin-gu had five uncles of the blood and that at least four of these could use the deathbed order of his grandfather as one pretext for claiming the crown. The position of the fifth brother, the Si-tha prince, is vague. He does not appear in the lists of honors and titles with his half-brothers and, as the son of a lesser queen, was probably considered to be of lower status and therefore not included in the deathbed order.

Hsin-hpyu-shin went on to become perhaps the most powerful ruler in Burmese history and yet his reign is paradoxical. He extended the empire to limits not seen since the sixteenth-century reign of Bayin-naung, but was unable to control his officials or carry out his inquest. He was faced with considerable internal political opposition and, in that respect, fared little better than his predecessor.

One of the key points of political conflict during his reign was his early and visible intention to make Sin-gu heir rather than his next youngest brother. Taking his father's order on the succession as binding, however, Alaung-hpaya's third son was highly offended at the obvious intentions of the king. Thirty-years-old at the time of Hsin-hpya-shin's accession, Maung Po was known as the Amyin prince after his largest appanage of Amyin Myo. Too young to hold field commands, as had his elder brothers during the campaigns of the 1750s, he had, however, been given some modest responsibilities by his father. In 1755, for instance, he had been left in charge of the capital, though this commission may have been a charge in name only. On the eve of Alaung-hpaya's campaign in Tenasserim and Ayuthia in 1759, he had also been placed in charge of the royal retinue sent from Rangoon to the capital.

As a result of the Salin prince's growing resentment, an abortive plot was laid for the assassination of Hsin-hpyu-shin who, on discovering the plot, imprisoned his brother and began the search for accomplices. The search revealed, however, the large number of officials who were actual accessories or disapproved of his choice of Sin-gu. Hardly knowing who to trust amid the growing political turmoil, Hsin-hpyu-shin turned to the Frenchmen Milard and San Prive, the first the commander of the palace guard and the other the *wun* in charge of foreigners. Reduced to sleeping in the same room with Milard for fear of his life, the king was forced to pardon his brother and abandon prosecution of his brother's accomplices in a turn of events foreshadowing his later inability to punish his blatantly corrupt and disobedient *wun-gyis* and other high officials. After some time the crisis passed and the king was finally able to name his son crown prince only after he had required important officials and his brothers to send their sons to court to be educated and, in effect, maintained them as hostages. Moreover, the internal position of the king apparently remained under challenge. The French envoy Feraud, visiting Ava in 1770, reported that Hsin-hpyu-shin was surrounded by enemies only awaiting the right moment to strike, and that he had made overtures through Milard concerning possible military assistance from the French East India Company in the form of soldiers.[26] Bereft of any adherents in the wake of his abortive coup, the Amyin prince remained a helpless spectator as the events surrounding the succession of his nephew began to unfold.

The king fell ill in the spring of 1776, whereupon the high courtiers, well aware of the frustrated aspirations of the Amyin prince, made arrangements among themselves to ensure the accession of the crown prince, who was then twenty-years-old. Aside from the fact that he was the formal choice of his father, the Sin-gu prince was an easygoing lad who gave every evidence of malleability in the hands of the ministers. When Hsin-hpyu-shin finally expired on 10 June 1776, the *atwin wuns* informed Sin-gu, who occupied the palace that same day. The new king was to have a stormy reign, his first troubles coming from an unexpected quarter only three weeks after the death of his father. This threat centered on his younger half-brother the Salin prince, a favorite of their father and then in his sixteenth year. Along with the *atwin wun* Maha Thin-hka Si-thu and two other officials, this prince concocted a plot against his brother that led to the execution of all four on 1 July.[27]

Made understandably insecure by this incident, Sin-gu took steps to strengthen his position. His father had renewed operations in 1774–1775 against a resurgent Thailand, sending the generals Maha Thi-ha Thu-ra, Min-ye Zei-ya-gyaw, and Nei-myo Thi-ha Patei into the field. For reasons of their own, these three veterans were all firm supporters of Sin-gu. For instance, Maha Thi-ha Thu-ra was Sin-gu's father-in-law, his daughter Ma Min Aung being the north queen of the young ruler.[28] Sin-gu also had marriage ties with Min-ye Zei-ya-gyaw and Nei-myo Thi-ha Patei, the former a brother-in-law and the latter the grandfather of the chief queen and an old follower of Alaung-hpaya. To shore up his position, Sin-gu recalled Maha Thi-ha Thu-ra from the field and appointed him *athi wun-gyi*. Along with the redoubtable old general Min-hla Naw-rahta (U Hnaung), Nei-myo Thi-ha Patei was appointed *wun-gyi*. The fourth *wun-gyi* appointed was Zei-ya-thu, the *myo wun* of Tavoy and a loyal servant of Hsin-hpyu-shin. Thus, Sin-gu shrewdly protected himself with powerful relatives by marriage and loyal followers of his father. As a further precaution, the king had his four uncles confined to their respective houses, allowing each only twenty-five retainers and servants.[29]

Having weathered his brother's plot and having enlisted powerful support for himself, Sin-gu began his reign competently enough. He also ended the foreign adventures of his father and, as the *Kon-baung-zet* comments, the country was peaceful and prosperous with taxes, war, banditry, and diplomacy at a minimum.[30] On 23 December 1776, he received the *abhisekha* and performed the *maha u-gin-bwin*. Appearances were deceiving, however, and conflict simmered just beneath the surface of this tranquility. In May 1777, the royal anger fell on Maha Thi-ha Thu-ra, who was stripped of office and sent into exile with his family at Sagaing. His daughter was also deposed as north queen and sent to her father. Sin-gu again became angry with her and recalled her to be drowned.[31] The later British envoy Michael Symes relates that he was told the daughter was "a young woman endowed with virtue, beauty, and accomplishments" of whom the king was very fond, but that due to his irrascible, intemperate, and jealous nature the relationship was a stormy one, with irrational accusations of infidelity from the king.[32] Whether the father fell from favor because of the daughter or vice versa cannot be guessed from the sources, but it is also possible that each had separate problems with Sin-gu.

A second plot against the throne was uncovered only four months later. Still nursing his aggrieved ambition, the Amyin prince had succeeded in finding a modest following led by the Nat-su *bo* Thein-hka Pyan-chi and another person with the low-rank title of Le-ya Du-da. Those involved, including the Amyin prince, were executed on 1 October 1777. Gaetano Mantegazza's 1784 account goes so far as to claim that Maha Thi-ha Thu-ra, stripped of all in exile, refused to join the plot and even informed Sin-gu of the danger.[33] If this was in fact the case, it still did not restore the exiled general to favor.

In the aftermath of the plot of the Amyin prince, a paranoid Sin-gu found it prudent to send his three remaining uncles into exile in 1778. The Badon prince was sent to Sagaing, the Pahkan prince to Pin-ya, and the Pin-dale prince to Ywa-thit-kyi. The exile was particularly difficult for the Badon prince, who was then thirty-four. The fourth son of Alaung-hpaya, he had been a favorite of his father, who reportedly once said of him: "The Badon Prince Thado Min-hla Shwei-daung, my son who is replete with glory, wisdom, and the signs, will like me probably become the future lord of all the umbrella-bearing kings of the great countries."[34] Although only sixteen at the death of his father, the prince had shown himself to be responsible in the conduct of the minor assignments he had received. During the reigns of his two older brothers, he had led a circumspect life and received high rank and trappings. It must have come as a shock to first be confined to his house and then to be stripped of his appanages of Badon and Mya-wadi *myos* for the insecurity of poverty-stricken exile at Sagaing. Oral tradition relates that the prince with his family and a few loyal servants eked out a meager living by gardening, weaving, and making small articles for sale in the local bazaar.[35] The following year the sixteen-year-old Maung Maung was removed from his monastery and sent to Hpaung-ga Village in Sagaing District. The position of the Si-tha prince remains vague, as he is not mentioned along with his brothers.

In terms of the pool of succession, Sin-gu's situation was similar to that of his uncle Naung-daw-gyi. Neither reigned long enough to produce the sons to challenge the strong corps left by Alaung-hpaya. A daughter of the granary *atwin wun* and a granddaughter of the *wun-gyi* Nei-myo Thi-ha Patei, Sin-gu's chief queen bore one daughter. The north queen, daughter of Maha Thi-ha Thu-ra, was apparently executed before she conceived. The middle queen was a daughter of the palace attendant Nga Kyaing and bore one daughter who died in infancy. On the execution of the first north queen, she was elevated to the north palace and her two younger sisters were placed in the middle and western palaces, respectively. The second middle queen bore a son and a daughter while her younger sister remained barren.

Apparently thinking the situation well under control, Sin-gu began to devote himself to the worship and repair of pagodas on the one hand and to the enjoyment of life on the other. The former occupation began to require increasing periods away from the palace and the latter gradually turned into long orgies of drinking, gaming, cock-fighting, hunting, and fishing trips with his personal retainers and courtiers. "Of the courtiers, guards, and attendants, those that were not drunk were few" records the *Kon-baung-zet*, while an epic poem composed in 1783 versified: "unseemly as it was, sins stormed their way into the royal palace, the wrong path was pursued, virtues were thrown to the winds, and misdeeds prevailed."[36] On various occasions, the inebriated king returned to the palace at odd hours or went to the water palace rather than the main palace. Stories of his unseemly behavior circulated among the people, who surely muttered that not only were these acts contrary to the five basic precepts of Buddhist morality, but that they had even been punishable by death in the reigns of his grandfather, uncle, and father. Such conduct was contrary to the laws governing kingship and caused unease among the people, who wondered how long the *kamma* of the king could withstand this torrent of demerit. These sentiments were joined by considerable alienation among the officials and gentry at the dismissal of the popular Maha Thi-ha Thu-ra, the summary execution of his daughter, and the harsh exile of the uncles.

The Coups and Attempted Coups of 1782

By early 1782, the king's failure to exercise royal power and the general alienation of people and officials engendered by his erratic behavior provided a fertile ground for intrigue. There were three potential sources of such intrigue against Sin-gu. First was the disgraced Wun-gyi Maha Thi-ha Thu-ra, a respected and popular figure with important marriage connections. Second were the exiled uncles, who could also call on powerful support through marriage ties. Third was the young Maung Maung exiled in Hpaung-ga Village a little over ten miles from Ava. As the reins of government grew increasingly slack and the king failed to use his power effectively, a complicated drama involving all three sources began to unfold.

The initiator of events was Maung Maung. As the *aw-ra-tha* son of Naung-daw-gyi, he possessed excellent credentials for the crown. Then a few months past his eighteenth birthday, the lad had spent virtually his entire life inside a monastery. At best he was inexperienced and naive compared to his peers, who had grown up in the midst of the sophistication and intrigue of the court. At worst he may have been a dullard. Whatever the case, he found or was found by supporters led by Ga-mani (a low-level title) and Nga Kya Gyi, who were probably local officials of the village of Hpaung-ga. Who first proposed the plot is not known, but if it was indeed someone else, Maung Maung would seem to have fallen in with alacrity. Learning that Sin-gu had been away from the palace for several days to worship at a pagoda upriver, on the evening of 5 February 1782 Maung Maung and about forty men from Hpaung-ga set out for the capital. Joined by more people *en route*, they arrived at the Man-aung Gate of the palace at midnight. Impersonating the king, Maung Maung demanded admission and was admitted by guards long accustomed to the erratic comings and goings of their lord. Once within the fort, the other gates were quickly seized and the various officials of the palace and government summoned in the name of the king. Most came immediately in the belief that the king was drunk and therefore more dangerous than usual. They found instead Maung Maung, whose followers extracted oaths of allegiance at sword point. The armory was opened and the fort secured as many people from the city came to swell the ranks of the adventurers.

Maung Maung's next move was to mobilize the former servants of his father and those who were known to be disaffected with Sin-gu. Some exiled officials were recalled, including Maha Thi-ha Thu-ra, who took command of military operations. Strong positions were established to the north of the city and to the east across the river, while a large force of boats was dispatched upriver in search of Sin-gu. At the same time, Maung Maung invited his three uncles to return to Ava from exile and live in their own houses again. In accord with the order of Alaunghpaya, the young adventurer then offered the crown to each in turn, but all refused and drank the water of allegiance to him. Because the credentials of the uncles were as suitable as those of Maung Maung, the offer was obviously a test to see where dangerous ambition might lurk. Sensing the danger, however, the uncles avoided the trap and gave Maung Maung no grounds to act against them. Maung Maung was proclaimed king and issued a proclamation declaring Sin-gu to be an outlaw.

On the night of the coup, one of the courtiers had escaped from the fort before it was fully secured to warn the king, who was camped at the NgaPat Monastery thirty miles away. Unaware of the authorship of the coup, Sin-gu accepted the advice of his attendants to cross to the east side of the Irrawaddy River to his old appanage of Sin-gu Myo and there to raise a strong force to attack the capital. The move began on 6 February, but when definite word of Maung Maung arrived later that day, the plans were changed. Because it had been an auspicious place for his grandfather, Sin-gu was advised to establish himself at Kyauk-myaung, build a temporary fort and palace, and dispatch officers and men to rally the countryside for a move against Ava. The first objective was to seize Mok-hso-bo, the seat of early Kon-baung power, and then take Sagaing as a base for an attack on Ava.[37] With the three thousand men of his retinue already at his command, Sin-gu could have marched immediately against Ava, where he had supporters who would either suffer at the hands of a new king or lose their positions if the coup was successful. On the bad advice of his attendants, however, Sin-gu committed the cardinal error of dividing his already inadequate force and moving away from rather than advancing on the enemy. During the march to Kyauk-myaung, his force rapidly melted away while most of the parties sent to raise the countryside were either captured by or fled from rebel units sent out from Ava. His campaign strategy a disaster, Sin-gu decided to abandon the fight and flee to China via Bhamo, and there to seek the aid of the Chinese emperor. With the remains of his followers, he set out upriver on the eleventh, accompanied by his mother, sister, and queens. His men now deserted to the point that none were left to draw the boats, bringing the flight to an end at San-pe-nago. His remaining officials pointed out to the king that it was unsuitable for a ruler to flee his own country in such a manner. His *kamma* and *hpon* (kingly glory) were low and would only rise again if he faced his enemies at Ava. With his *wun-gyis* and *atwin wuns* dragging his boat, the gullible king was led downriver to meet his fate, sold out by his own advisers.

While Sin-gu floundered in the field, the capital remained in a confused and tumultuous state. Initially welcomed by the majority of the people, in the space of days Maung Maung came to be heartily detested. It was quickly obvious to all that he was little more than an ignorant lout who knew nothing of manners, let alone politics and government. Well aware that Sin-gu was still very much a factor in the situation, the officials and courtiers were disconcerted to see Maung Maung devote himself to his two new queens and three concubines while his peasant followers plundered the city and maltreated the people. In the later words of one of Ava's inhabitants, "The people were greatly oppressed and they hated Maung Maung."[38] It was all too apparent that a bad master had been exchanged for one who was worse.

The three uncles of Maung Maung now made their debuts on stage. To this point they had been wary but passive spectators to events but, deeply suspicious of their nephew, they now felt forced to take action for their own protection. In a statement summing up their view, the Badon prince told his servants and retainers:

> The original order of our father was that his sons should succeed in order like the fingers on a hand and rule for the welfare of the religion, the people, and the monks. When Naung-daw-min-taya-gyi died, Hsin-hpyu-shin became king in accord with the order and looked after religious and secular affairs. When Hsin-hpyu-shin died, the original order was not upheld. Prince Sin-gu became king and cast aside the officials who had governed the kingdom in earlier reigns. He put ignorant rustics in important posts and let them govern. Listening to the words of stupid officials, he seized our lands and people and exiled us under guard. Now our nephew has taken the throne and restored us, appearing to care for us, but the signs of betrayal are there. I do not wish to become king and increase the law of *akusala* [demerit], but it does not seem that we can otherwise live peacefully.[39]

The uncles felt no loyalty to Sin-gu because of his mistreatment of them and considered Maung Maung to be their definite enemy. The references to the order on succession and Sin-gu's misrule were intended to help legitimize action against the king. Thus, the motives were a mixture of a deep grievance against Sin-gu, a real fear of Maung Maung, and a genuine desire on the part of the Badon prince to be king. It was easy for the prince to rally support because the officials and people shared his view that Maung Maung was unfit to rule. Sin-gu, too, was now to pay a heavy price for having alienated so many important officials and their families.

In beginning his move, the Badon prince called on the formidable family connections of his head wife for support. The lineage of Min Thi-ri Yan-daza was large and controlled many important offices at both the court and provincial levels. Maha Thi-ha Thu-ra, too, was married into this powerful lineage. Sin-gu's drowning of the north queen and his exile of Maha Thi-ha Thu-ra and the uncles clearly made this large and powerful family more than willing to take the field against him on behalf of its own. With four thousand men from the Mok-hso-bo area, the Badon prince occupied Sagaing and on the eleventh struck at

Maung Maung in Ava, the same day that Sin-gu began his return downriver to the capital.

When the attack began early in the morning, one of the *myo wuns* of the city immediately defected to the cause of the Badon prince. Maung Maung was captured and drowned that same day in the manner customary for royalty. Begun on 5 February, his reign had ended seven days later, which is why the Badon prince derisorily dubbed him the "seven-day king." Sin-gu's party was captured several days later by the force under the *wun-gyi* U Hnaung, then titled Maha Si-thu. On the fourteenth, Sin-gu and his family were, in the words of the *Kon-baung-zet*, "dealt with according to custom." Custom would normally mean drowning, but the European accounts all state that the queens, concubines, and children of Sin-gu were burned alive.[40]

When the palace fell at noon on the eleventh, the Badon prince was proclaimed king and immediately reappointed the former *wun-gyis* of Hsin-hpyu-shin: Maha Thi-ha Thu-ra, Maha Si-thu, and Nei-myo Thi-ri Naw-rahta. The fourth *wun-gyi* named was Nei-myo Zei-ya Ga-mani, the *myo wun* of Ava who had defected earlier that day during the attack. Liberal rewards of offices and presents went to the retainers who had shared the prince's exile, to the followers who had supported the coup, and to the palace officials who had aided the attack.

Hardly had the dust of his own coup settled when the new king, known to history as Bo-daw-hpaya, found his throne under attack. There had been a clear indication of its incubation, so the plot could not have been unexpected. At the time when the Badon prince and his two brothers had decided to take the field against Sin-gu and Maung Maung, the courtier Min-hla Si-thu was sent to find the Si-tha prince in order to bring him to the council of war. Failing to find the prince at his own house, Min-hla Si-thu had discovered him at the residence of Maha Thi-ha Thu-ra deep in consultation with the general and his formidable wife Me Talaing. Without making his presence known, Min-hla Si-thu slipped away to report what he had seen to the Badon prince, who sent him back to keep watch on the house.[41] Perhaps giving his half-brother and the old general the benefit of the doubt, or enough rope to hang themselves, Bo-daw-hpaya took no action, but accepted the support of each during his coup, after which he restored Maha Thi-ha Thu-ra to his rank and position. Yet only twelve days later on 23 February, the *Kon-baung-zet* records that the Si-tha prince and Maha Thi-ha Thu-ra "devised an unsuitable plan" and were "dealt with according to custom."[42]

Although his motives cannot be known for certain, it might be surmised that Maha Thi-ha Thu-ra's experiences with Sin-gu had so embittered the long-time servant of the Kon-baung rulers that he determined to test the strength of his *kamma* in a bid for the crown. Gaetano Mantegazza and Vincentius Sangermano both state that he wanted the crown for himself and only used the Si-tha prince as a means to this end.[43] Well aware of his lower status and remote prospects of ever ascending the throne, the Si-tha prince was undoubtedly a willing conspirator. With the country in a generally unsettled state from the slack rule of Sin-gu and the effects of two coups in rapid succession, the two conspirators may have hoped to strike while the situation was still fluid. Bo-daw-hpaya reportedly found the attempted coup so unnerving that he adopted the practice of changing the room in which he slept every night.[44]

He was even more unnerved when, nine months later on the night of 4–5 October, he awakened to the sound of cannon fire and the clash of hand-to-hand combat. Hastily gathering some palace attendants, he organized a resistance in the Inner Palace while his eldest son, who had been on duty that night in the Hlut-taw, rallied other forces and carried the fight to the intruders. By dawn the attack had been broken and the remnants of its force were being hunted down in the city. When captured later that day, the leaders were revealed to have been Ga-mani and Nga Kya Gyi of Hpaung-ga Village, who had escaped the collapse of Maung Maung's moment of power and found a new candidate to promote for the throne. Commonly known as Nga Hpon, this new aspirant was a Shan necromancer, tattooer, and astrologer named Nga Shun from the Maing-gaing area who had for several years been attracting a following in the Pok-pa region by representing himself as a son of the last Taung-ngu king. Like Maung Maung, he had been a willing recruit for the proposed scheme, a scheme for which all three paid with their heads. On their part, Ga-mani and Nga Kya Gyi had been inspired to this second plot by the ease with which Maung Maung had seized the palace. Their participation in both plots is also indicative of the extent to which the lure of the crown affected even the commoners and, in the case of Nga Hpon, inflamed the popular imagination.[45]

Bo-daw-hpaya Establishes His Heir

Coming to power at the age of thirty-seven, Bo-daw-hpaya was already a mature man who had married his head wife in 1760 when he was sixteen and she seventeen. Named Me Lun Me, her father was the Ava *bo-hmu* and her mother belonged to the lineage of Min Thi-ri Yan-daza. Bearing no sons for her husband, Me Lun Me did present him with three daughters in 1761, 1763, and 1764. The king's second wife was Me Lun Thu whose father was the *kyei-gaing* (that is, *myei-daing*) of Thabut-taw, a jurisdiction in Shwei-bo District. This union was more fruitful for the succession, giving him sons in 1762 and 1765. Bo-daw-hpaya also had a concubine, a daughter of the secretary of a cavalry unit, whom he had taken around 1760. Her first son died in infancy in 1761, but a second was born in 1778. When Bo-daw-hpaya ascended the throne in 1782, his head wife became the chief queen, his second wife the north queen, and his concubine the middle queen. At that time his unions with these women had produced sons aged twenty, seventeen, and five. He also had a son born to him in 1767 by a second concubine, the daughter of an *athi* villager, who had died before he came to power. This son, aged fifteen at the time of the king's accession, was a favorite of his father, but not technically part of the pool because his mother had not been a queen before she died. At the time of Bo-daw-hpaya's accession, therefore, his pool of succession consisted of two sons already eligible by virtue of having reached manhood, and one who was still a child. The three eldest sons had fought with their father in the coup and subsequently received many gifts and honors from him. Also in the pool of succession at that time were the king's two remaining brothers, the Pahkan prince, aged thirty-three, and the Pin-dale prince, then twenty-eight.

With two sons and two brothers of the blood available, the new ruler was faced with the need to select a crown prince. Always a strong traditionalist, he chose to appoint his *aw-ra-tha* son. This son, whose given name is not recorded but who was then known as the Shwei-daung prince after his appanage, was installed as crown prince on 13 July 1783, and on the same day married to his half-sister, the Taung-dwin-gyi princess. This princess was the middle daughter of the chief queen, hence the crown prince and his princess were considered *ya-za pok-ta*, or true royalty, because each had royal blood from both mother and father and all three parents had received the *abhiseka*. On 23 July of the following year, the crown princess bore a son in whose birth the king rejoiced, saying that the child would continue his line unbroken. This grandson, the future Ba-gyi-daw, was given Sagaing as an appanage, and taken out of the hands of his parents to live in his grandfather's palace.[46] In this Bo-daw-hpaya was firmly adhering to the customary lineal succession of "father to son to grandson" and, as had his own father, was beginning an attempt to manipulate the succession beyond his immediate heir apparent.

Although Bo-daw-hpaya had installed his *aw-ra-tha* son as crown prince to end uncertainty over the succession, one last scene in the drama initiated by Alaung-hpaya's deathbed order had yet to be enacted. On becoming king, Bo-daw-hpaya had restored his younger brothers, the Pahkan and Pin-dale princes, to their ranks and appanages. Of the seven sons of Alaung-hpaya, the fire of ambition would seem to have burned lowest in the Pahkan prince, but the Pin-dale prince was an impetuous youth who had earnestly desired the crown princeship. Perhaps realizing his brother's intentions concerning the succession, the Pin-dale prince gathered a few fellow conspirators. The plot was discovered, however, and all the conspirators executed except the prince himself. Made the responsibility of a senior official, both the prince and his innocent brother were confined to their houses and permitted out only when their presence was required for state occasions. Gaetano Mantegazza, who was in Burma at that time, reports a popular suspicion that the scenario had been arranged by the king's ministers to compromise the only prince of the blood with the spirit to challenge the appointment of the eldest son as heir apparent.[47]

The question of official complicity aside, it is clear that the Pin-dale prince continued to harbor his ambitions, and with fateful results. The *Kon-baung-zet* records that he "devised an unsuitable plan" and was drowned on 19 June 1785.[48] He had apparently decided on one last desperate gamble for the crown, a gamble which he lost and which also compromised his blameless and politically innocuous brother. Thereafter the Pahkan prince lived an obscure and miserable life under house arrest until 11 December 1802, when he died of what one court official termed "the sickness of the heart," but received the honor of the funeral of a prince of the blood.[49]

The execution of the Pin-dale prince ended the drama initiated in 1760 by Alaung-hpaya's deathbed order on succession. Three of his seven sons had mounted the throne, three had been executed, and one had been condemned to lifelong confinement. There had always been potential conflict among the princes of the blood for the throne, but it tended to be restricted by the customary emphasis on primogeniture. Alaung-hpaya's order had loosened this inhibiting factor and caused twenty-five years of conflict between lineal and collateral succession. By 1785, lineal succession had won with the removal of the last two sons of Alaung-hpaya and the installation of his grandson as crown prince. Coming to the crown with two mature and two nearly mature sons of his own, however, Bo-daw-hpaya's efforts to ensure the lineal succession against the collateral frustrations of his younger sons constitute the second part of the story of the passage of power.

Governance and Princely Politics, 1783–1808

With the succession issue seemingly settled and no apparent threats to his crown remaining, Bo-daw-hpaya allowed a new pattern of governance to evolve. He largely withdrew from the day-to-day management of affairs and physically absented himself from the capital for long periods. His mature sons, particularly the first and second, came to have large amounts of authority and strong personal bases of power. This enabled them to eclipse and ultimately displace the senior officials, a pattern that ended only with the premature death of the crown prince in 1808. Although the king and crown prince were firmly in control throughout, the question of succession remained very much in the foreground.

By the late 1780s, Bo-daw-hpaya began increasingly to devote himself to religious affairs. In 1790, he conceived a plan to build the largest pagoda in the world, presumably as an exercise in state merit-making, and hence left the capital on 21 November for Min-ywa to inaugurate his project. Renaming Min-ywa as Min-gun, on this occasion the king did not return to the capital for nearly four months. Apparently obsessed by the project, he went to Min-gun again early in 1792 for three months. From January 1793 to June 1795, Bo-daw-hpaya was again continuously in residence in Min-gun. He moved virtually the entire court to Min-gun at the end of 1800, so that he could supervise the pagoda construction personally. After that he returned to the capital only for several brief visits until 1812, when he again took up permanent residence there.

Although ultimate power lay with the king, the actual reins of government were largely in the hands of his two eldest sons, the crown prince and the Prome prince. The crown prince bore the major burden of government during this period and was given charge of the capital and the affairs of the realm during his father's long absences from the court. In fact, the crown prince was held in such high esteem by his father that the latter often talked of abdicating in his favor. This news had even reached India and formed part of the instructions given to the envoy Michael Symes in 1802.[50] Both of the same mother, the two princes were competent individuals with stable personalities, an important factor as their father became increasingly difficult with the passing years. The Prome prince was, in fact, almost a second crown prince himself. In a union paralleling that of the crown prince, he was married to the youngest daughter of the chief queen in 1785. When a daughter was born in 1788, she was taken to live in the main palace, as had been the son of the crown prince.

Thus, the crown prince was left with a large measure of power and independence, but Bo-daw-hpaya drew his other sons into governing roles as well. In January 1791, the Prome prince was made *bayin*, or viceroy, of Prome and given complete governance of that region. The third son—the one not in the pool of succession—was made *bayin* of Taung-ngu with similar powers, and became known as the Taung-ngu prince. The fourth son was made *myo-za* of Bassein. Since ascending the throne Bo-daw-hpaya had sired two more sons and they, too, were assigned appanages. The sixth and youngest son was given the large and important district of Pagan as his appanage. The fifth son does not seem to have enjoyed the esteem accorded to his brothers, receiving only Mek-hkaya Myo for his support. With the exception of the Taung-ngu prince, there were five princes of the blood.

The date is not certain, but around 1800 the king deposed his four *wun-gyis* and did not formally appoint replacements. The administration of the fort and city was conducted by the Prome prince and one of the *wuns* of the crown prince, while the crown prince himself conducted the affairs of state and carried the most influence with his father. The chief executive officer of the crown prince was apparently the second-ranking *wun-dauk*. In May 1803, the king conferred "extraordinary" powers on the crown prince, giving him complete management of all government business. Although the crown prince enjoyed this formal position of power and on occasion even countermanded orders of the king, there was never any question as to where ultimate power lay. A notable demonstration of this occurred when the king, displeased with the administration of the crown prince, punished him by confinement to his house for six days.[51]

Thus, the upper level of the official establishment was displaced by the sons of the king and the governance of the country fell largely into their hands. With the moderating influence of the ruler increasingly absent during this period, the three most important princes after the crown prince were the Prome, Taung-ngu, and Sagaing princes who developed large and well-armed factions to become powers in their own right. The growth of the princely factions was made possible by their strong territorial bases, the eclipse of the *wun-gyis* and other top officials in government, and the preoccupation of the king with the Min-gun Pagoda and religious affairs. The retainers of the princes often looted merchants and fought with the retainers of other princes in an aggressive expression of rivalries. At one point the followers of the Sagaing prince almost created a serious diplomatic incident by looting a Chinese trading caravan near Amara-pu-ra.[52] As a measure of their growing strength, in 1795 Michael Symes was told that the Taung-ngu prince had around ten thousand armed and unruly followers.[53] The main princely rivalry was between the Prome and Taung-ngu princes, the second and third sons of the king. Immersed in his own concerns, the king allowed this state of affairs to flourish, passing out only occasional reprimands to the princes for particularly flagrant actions. The focal point of politics had become the rivalries among the princes of the blood, whose material power and governmental roles made them the dominant powers in the land.

Despite the fact that Bo-daw-hpaya had settled the succession early in his reign by installing his *aw-ra-tha* son as crown prince and demonstrated his wish that his grandson succeed in turn, as his other sons became mature men the succession issue came increasingly to dominate the political scene. The Prome prince was apparently a competent and reasonable person who accepted the primacy of his elder brother, but considered himself second in line for the throne should his brother be removed from the scene. It was generally accepted that this prince would contest the succession of his nephew even against the expressed wish of his father. The Taung-ngu prince also made little secret of his desire to succeed, despite his lack of a royal mother. To this end, a rumor was bruited about that his mother had been a princess of the Taung-ngu period, when, in fact, she was Shin Min Si, the daughter of Maung Pu of Shun-zet Village north of Mok-hso-bo. The Mek-hkaya and Pagan princes were too young to be factors at this time, and the Bassein prince was not mentally competent.[54] Thus, the two challengers to Bo-daw-hpaya's succession plans were the Prome and Taung-ngu princes.

Bo-daw-hpaya never kept secret his desire for the succession to pass to his grandson, who was of a purer royalty than his own sons and thereby closer to the Sakyan ideal. In an unprecedented move, he bestowed a title on the grandson at the age of one, saying publicly, "My grandson will surely be like me the lord of all the umbrella-bearing kings of the great continent. He shall have the title which my father Alaung-min-taya-gyi gave to me."[55] The child was taken from the eastern house to live in the main palace and treated literally as a son of the king. In 1793, when he underwent the ear piercing and hair-dressing ceremonies at the age of nine, he also received an extensive endowment that included the towns of Mok-hso-bo, Ava, Myei-du, NgaSin-gu, Myin-zaing, Pyin-zi, Kyauk-hsauk, and Taung-dwin-gyi. With the addition of Sagaing, which he had received at birth, this gave him control of a total of over twenty-five thousand houses. He was also given an establishment of fifty-eight officials and secretaries, and thirteen companies of musketeers totalling 3,620 men as well as an eighteen-strand *salwe*, or sash of rank.56 By contrast, his uncle the Prome prince had only the approximately ten thousand houses of Prome and the Taung-ngu prince the twenty-five hundred houses of Taung-ngu. The grandson was also made head of a miniature court composed of the sons of courtiers, who were designated *wun-gyi*, *wun-dauk*, and other court officers. In terms of rank at court, he took precedence over all except his father and grandfather. The partiality with which he was treated so struck Michael Symes in 1802 that he wrote "the Prince of Chagain [Sagaing] . . . is treated with homage little inferior to what is paid to the king himself, while courtiers and those who seek favors are taught to believe that the accomplishment of their views can best be attained through his influence."57 No mistake could be made by either of his uncles as to the intended succession after their elder brother the crown prince. This must have been especially galling to the Prome prince who, in terms of credentials for the crown, was a carbon copy of his eldest brother.

Yet the Prome prince, "a very corpulent young man . . . pleasant and easy in his manners," accepted the situation and sensibly bided his time.58 Not so his younger half-brother. The Taung-ngu prince was a great favorite of his father, who tolerated the remarkable power amassed by the prince. Described as able, courageous, and lacking in scruples, he had used these qualities and his prosperous but remote base in Taung-ngu to gather a large and well-armed following. Rumors had reached even India that the prince would probably contest by force the succession of his half-brother the crown prince. "The military character of the Prince Tongho Tickien, and the resources which he is enabled to command, may be supposed to render his opposition extremely hazardous to the stability of his brother's power" was the comment included in the instructions to Symes for his mission to Burma in 1802.59

At least two factors had been at work to create this situation. First was the strong and ill-concealed ambition of the Taung-ngu prince for the throne, and an equally strong defensive reaction from the crown prince. Second was a reportedly irreconcilable enmity that had existed between the two from the days of their youth. Given the threat that he represented and the dislike borne him by his half-brother, the Taung-ngu prince was surely fated for a short life once the crown prince ascended the throne. And given the ability and temperament of the Taung-ngu prince, the natural solution to his predicament was to challenge his father and brother for the throne.

In the end, even Bo-daw-hpaya could not ignore the danger presented by his third son. Hearing rumors that the prince was fortifying himself in Taung-ngu, considered to be the strongest fort in the realm and the scene of earlier serious rebellions, at the end of 1798 the king led an expedition of fifty thousand men to that city to discover that, indeed, the fort had been repaired and the prince had gathered many followers. Word had leaked out too soon for the prince to consider resistance, however, hence he submitted peacefully. The fort was dismantled and his closest retainers executed. The prince himself was returned to the capital and placed under house arrest. He was still under house arrest when Symes paid him a courtesy visit in 1802, but appears to have been rehabilitated by 1806, because his name again appears in its proper place in the lists of presents offered to the king on state occasions and references occur to his role in governmental affairs.[60] He also retained Taung-ngu as his appanage, although the king reduced its territory.

The Future Ba-gyi-daw as Crown Prince, 1808–1819

The crown prince died on 9 April 1808, two months short of his forty-sixth birthday.[61] The king's careful preparation of his grandson now came to its natural conclusion. On 27 April 1808, the Sagaing prince was installed as crown prince in his father's stead and received the traditional endowment of treasure, arms, and civil and military establishments.[62] Then twenty-four years old, his accession set in motion significant shifts in the pattern of politics and government.

The deceased crown prince had been the center of the moderate clique at court, a group that had tried with greater or lesser success to dilute or neutralize the more extreme actions of the king and to remain on civil terms with the East India Company. The new crown prince took over his father's role as leader of this clique. Described by the British envoy John Canning as "a young man of moderate talents, pleasing and affable manners, and a mild peaceable disposition," he was under pressure from two quarters: the first his grandfather and the second his two uncles.[63]

The interests of grandfather and grandson coincided, hence there was a natural alliance between them. Yet Bo-daw-hpaya was apparently so erratic at this time that the crown prince had his hands full. A number of court officials told Canning in 1810 that the king appeared to be deranged and sometimes sat in a deep melancholy, barely speaking for days. At other times he fell into ferocious rages, physically attacking courtiers and issuing incredible orders, which officials tried not to carry out until one of the princes had talked to him and the king was again reasonable. Although Bo-daw-hpaya had given the crown prince authority equal to his own, it was well known that all orders issued by the crown prince were submitted to the king before execution.[64]

Yet beneath this facade of madness can be detected an acute awareness of the political situation on the part of the king. All accounts describe his grandson as an easygoing person of moderate ability who would have difficulty coping with his able and aggressive uncles. His grandfather surely shared the same doubts, for he kept a close eye on the crown prince and a tight hand on the reins of government. More importantly, the king now tried to neutralize the power of his sons by forbidding them to visit their appanages, the main source of their strength, and allowing them only a handful of retainers each at the capital. As a further measure, he appointed the four princes of the blood to be the *wun-gyis*, so that each had to attend the Hlut-taw daily. The princes were also required to wait on the king early each morning and to make in his presence an obeissance to the crown prince. In order that they not use their positions as *wun-gyis* to amass partisans, he periodically deposed one or another of them for a fortnight or a month and cancelled all the appointments they had made. The king also employed an army of spies to report on every action of the princes and high officials.[65] Thus, a major change resulting from the death of the first crown prince was the king's resumption of a more direct role in government and the curbing of the power of the princes.

With the king no longer relying on his sons to play serious roles in governmental affairs, a second change was the reemergence of officials in positions of real power. Several such figures can be discerned, but each was prevented from obtaining too much power by periodic deposition and reappointment in the same manner as the princes. The most important of these officials were Min-hla Naw-rahta, *myo wun* of Hantha-wadi, and the Daing *wun-gyi*, whose careers have been discussed in chapter 5. In this way, it appears that the king was able to retain control of the princes and officials and prevent any combination from tipping the balance of power too far away from the crown prince.

Dependent as it was on the king, the position of the crown prince was precarious. His support from other quarters was lukewarm because he was young, inexperienced, and thought to be of weak character. In fact, many preferred one of his older, more experienced, and stronger uncles for the throne. His right to the throne was also subject to question in terms of the customs of succession, as John Canning reported:

218   Chapter 7

> Tho' the general opinion seems to favor the Prince of Chagain [Sagaing], there are not wanting well informed Natives who entertain doubts on the subject. Had the late Engy Teckien [crown prince] been in possession of the throne for but one day, no doubt, they say, could exist for the right of his son to succeed but he having died while only heir apparent, the Prince of Prome, the next brother in succession, has in their opinion at least a dubious claim. Whoever the rightful heir, that at the decease of the present Sovereign the crown will be disputed appears extremely probable.[66]

Despite their curbing by the king, the Prome and Taung-ngu princes still possessed considerable power and support and remained formidable opponents. Then aged forty-four, the Prome prince was described as "possessed of good abilities and generally liked because of an open and frank disposition," and the Taung-ngu prince at forty-two was pictured as "a resolute unprincipled ruffian."[67] The other two sons of the blood, the Mek-hkaya and Pagan princes, were not really involved in the struggle, given the former's youth and the academic and religious penchant of the latter.[68] There was particular tension between the crown prince and the Taung-ngu prince, which was expressed in armed clashes between their retainers. The crown prince held his own in this militant rivalry, partly due to the vigorous support of his younger brother the Thayet prince (the future King Tha-ra-wadi), who was in great favor with the king and more aggressive in disposition than the crown prince to whom he was strongly attached.

Apprehending the weakness of his position, in 1810 the crown prince used the *myo wun* of Han-tha-wadi as intermediary to discuss with Canning the circumstances under which the East India Company would support him militarily against his uncles. Canning decribed his initial conversation with the *myo wun* on the subject thus:

> After mentioning in general terms the factions and turbulent spirit of the Burmah Princes, he took occasion to introduce the subject of the Succession to the Crown at the death of the present King. He observed that the present Heir apparent from his youth and mild disposition, was but ill-calculated to struggle against the opposition he is likely to meet from his uncles and particularly the Prince of Tongho [Taung-ngu], and asked me whether, in case of

need, the British Government would be disposed to afford him assistance.69

The assistance discussed was five thousand East India Company troops, which, combined with the forces of the crown prince, would constitute a larger army than it was thought the Taung-ngu prince could muster. Canning thought that the company might be inclined to respond positively because the crown prince's father had been well-disposed toward the British and the crown prince gave evidence of the same orientation. The negotiations ended with Canning instructing the crown prince how to communicate with the company most expeditiously in case of need, and the crown prince promising to do his best to moderate the views of the king on the Arakan boundary issue and the Burmese claim to Chittagong and Dacca.

Apart from this one episode, however, the question of British intervention in the succession struggle never arose again. On his mission to Burma in 1811-1812, Canning discovered a surprising change. In the interim, the crown prince had established himself as the dominant power and was apparently conducting the real business of government virtually independently. He seldom informed the king of sensitive matters, thereby keeping his grandfather remote from the affairs of state and politics. In one instance, for example, one of Canning's spies briefly gained possession of a letter from the *myo wun* of Han-tha-wadi to the crown prince, which contained this revealing passage: "Your royal highness, who now governs the empire, ought seriously to reflect, and not allow anything to reach the golden ears of his Majesty but what you may think proper."70 Canning himself wrote of the crown prince in his diary: "He alone dares oppose the will of his grandfather" and "the crown prince who may in fact now be considered the real sovereign of the country.... This indeed seems to be the general opinion of the best informed natives and others whom I have consulted on the subject."71

In less than two years, the crown prince seems to have gained the upper hand over his uncles and to have assumed *de facto* as well as *de jure* control of the government. His success, however, took place against a background of extreme social and political turbulence, which tended to militarize the succession struggle as well. The country had been in visible and accelerating decline since the late 1780s, and in virtual anarchy and insurrection since 1805. The main factors causing the decline have already been identified in chapter 2 as overtaxation and maladministration, overexploitation of the demographic base for external adventures and internal construction projects, and recurring natural calamities such as droughts. In growing numbers people sought protection and livelihood in alternative statuses under bandit chiefs and other figures of power. The largest beneficiaries of this movement were members of the royal family with appanages. In an effort to control this, as early as 1795 the king prohibited queens, princes, princesses, and others from accepting service and offering refuge to any person not on the official list accompanying the grant of the appanage.[72] Despite this edict and augmented by a steady influx of clients, as law and order progressively broke down after 1800 and as the food situation became more desperate, the princes and their private armies assumed increasing importance. By nature rapacious, the princes became the biggest bandits in the country, fighting among themselves and plundering as they wished, even in the capital.

The outbreak of serious peasant rebellions from around 1805, the renewed war with Thailand in 1809, and the rebellion of Chin Pyan in Arakan in 1811 contributed greatly to the internal disorder and militarization of life. The English missionary Felix Carey wrote to his father in 1811: "This country is entirely split to pieces, and things are beginning to wear a terrible aspect. . . . The Burmans themselves are forming large parties under the various princes."[73] In the same vein Canning reported: "The whole time and attention of the Government is said to be taken up by numerous insurrections in various parts of the Country."[74]

The difficult years between 1805 and 1812 seriously weakened the formal administrative systems and structures necessary for the crown to mobilize labor and material resources. Many of these resources became "floating" or unattached to any point of authority, be it legitimate or illegitimate. The remainder tended to coalesce around existing loci of power such as the princes. This process appears to have enabled the Taung-ngu prince, in particular, to recoup his power to the point where his military threat impelled the crown prince to seek assistance from the East India Company. But the deep and widespread suspicion in Burmese court circles of British complicity with Chin Pyan probably removed the possibility of the company as a military ally from the minds of the crown prince and his supporters.[75] Lacking further details of this period, it appears that, in any case, Bo-daw-hpaya's efforts to curb his sons and those of the crown prince to build a network of allies within the corps of officials met with sufficient success to contain the threat.

Although resident in the capital since 1812, the king continued to travel frequently about the country to worship at pagodas, to dedicate religious buildings, and generally to oversee affairs. While on a visit to Mok-hso-bo in March 1819, he fell ill and returned to the capital. The illness proved mortal, however, and on 5 June Bo-daw-hpaya died at the age of seventy-five with his grandson at his bedside.[76] After consultation with learned monks, the crown prince arranged a huge funeral, that of a universal monarch, which took place in the northeast corner of the Hlut-taw two days later. On the same day, he ascended the throne at the age of thirty-five to become known to history as Ba-gyi-daw.

As the first *wun-gyi*, the *myo wun* of Han-tha-wadi, Min-hla Nawrahta, a key supporter of both the crown prince and his father before him, emerged as the dominant figure in government. In the words of the American missionary Ann Judson, he "is next in rank to the king, and has the management of all the affairs of the kingdom."[77] Three of Ba-gyi-daw's former chief officials were appointed to the other *wun-gyi* positions. All four *wun-dauks* and all four *atwin-wuns* were also drawn from his previous establishment, as were those who filled many of the lesser posts. It was not until the following November, however, that Ba-gyi-daw performed for the first time the *maha u-gin-bwin* and took his regnal title. At that time he took the daughter of his uncle the Pagan prince, who had died in 1814, as his north queen, the daughter of his uncle the Bassein prince as middle queen, and a daughter of Bo-daw-hpaya as a titled concubine.[78] Thus, cousin and half-sister marriage was extended well beyond the chief queen.

From John Canning's last mission in 1811–1812 to the death of Bo-daw-hpaya in 1819, there are only hints in the meager American and British missionary sources that the politics of succession continued to be tense. One hint is found in the diary for 1817 of Ann Judson, who wrote: "The heir-apparent is, I understand, a mild prince. His accession to the throne, on the king's demise, will undoubtedly be tracked with blood."[79] Evidence of continued rivalry is stated more strongly in the journal of her husband, the missionary Adoniram Judson. On 21 June 1819, he records that Rangoon was "in the utmost anxiety and alarm," with many rumors of rebellion and the illness or death of the king, and further that the *myo wun* had been urgently summoned to court with all his troops.[80] In an aside, Judson noted that the crown prince had two powerful uncles who would probably contest his accession and that there existed a genuine prospect of civil war. On the following day, Judson wrote that a dispatch boat had arrived with a royal order announcing the death of Bo-daw-hpaya and the accession of the crown prince. The business had been settled so expeditiously, he concluded, that the provinces had felt scarcely a shock.[81]

The long-expected challenge of Ba-gyi-daw's uncles did not materialize. It can only be surmised that Ba-gyi-daw and his allies were able to effect the passage of power in such a way that the uncles had no chance to muster their forces. In the case of the Taung-ngu prince, according to the *Kon-baung-zet* the new king believed that he had no grounds for leniency because the latter had habitually oppressed the people and had plotted against both father and grandfather. The prince and most of his family were drowned on 10 June. Ba-gyi-daw's queen as crown prince had been a daughter of the Prome prince, for whom he also had genuine affection. Because of his good character and clean political record, the Prome prince was only confined with the intent that he be released when the passage of power was complete and the throne secure. But, on 16 June, the unfortunate prince was murdered in prison by retainers of the chief queen Me Nu and her powerful brother the Salin prince.[82] American missionary sources report that thousands of the clients and supporters of the two princes were also executed as the new king made a clean sweep of his enemies.[83]

With the deaths of the Prome and Taung-ngu princes, the story of the politics of the royal succession in the early Kon-baung period drew to a close. Ba-gyi-daw reigned for the next eighteen years, but the succession in the later Kon-baung period remained confused and turbulent. As the first Kon-baung ruler, Alaung-hpaya had attempted to manipulate the succession with his deathbed order in 1760, which at least partly released the inhibitory mechanism of customary succession on the aspirations of the various princes of the blood. Perhaps the major effect of the order was to create an atmosphere of suspicion among his sons. No subsequent king could be certain that his brothers would not make an attempt on the crown. Indeed, each time a king designated the succession for his *aw-ra-tha* son, he provoked Alaung-hpaya's other sons into attempts on the throne. Alaung-hpaya's attempt to decree collateral succession was a failure that led directly to the deaths of three of his sons and the long imprisonment of another.

The story of the Kon-baung succession after 1785 involves Bo-daw-hpaya's effort to reestablish customary lineal succession and channel his remaining sons of the blood into subordinate roles in government as *bayins* and large *myo-zas*. Ironically, he too allowed a collateral struggle to develop by giving too much independent power to other members of his pool of succession. In particular, had he early on curbed the power of the Taung-ngu and Prome princes, the princely rivalries might have been contained within manageable limits. Alaung-hpaya and Bo-daw-hpaya tried to solve the dilemma of the royal succession in different ways and, like their Taung-ngu predecessors, each failed to determine the succession beyond the end of his own reign.

CONCLUSION

Although early Kon-baung society was multi-ethnic, social and political cleavages did not generally follow ethnic lines. The major cleavage lay between the upland-dwelling, animist practitioners of shifting cultivation and the far more numerous rice-cultivating Burmans, Mons, and Shans of the lowlands. Although linguistically diverse, the lowland peoples shared a common culture and world view derived from Theravada Buddhism. That fact enabled them to live for the most part within the same political system and subscribe to common leaders regardless of ethnic origin. The Shans and Mons were further drawn into the dominant Burman system through a certain amount of translocation for organization into crown service units and what was apparently a fairly steady process of cultural assimilation. Notions of ethnic identity were flexible and ethnicity *per se* was not usually a major factor in the internal politics of the society.[1]

The dominant Burman society drew its world view and social ideology from Theravada Buddhism, which provided a comprehensive and acceptable rationale for individual differences and social inequalities as well as some transcendental provision for individual improvement. The social order itself was thought to be modelled on the hierarchical world view of Theravada Buddhism, which sees existence as a merit-graded pyramid of beings from demons to deities. The population was divided into rank-ordered status groups, each with its own internal subdivisions, which were precisely defined and regulated by customary law and sumptuary rules backed by the coercive power of the state. Individual station and social distance were both visible and real. As each individual had a designated place in the social order, so too each had a place in the framework of the state. The generality of people were required to provide service and taxes to the state along a gradient running from *athi* (more taxes and less service) to the elite crown service groups (complete service and no taxes). While the differential between the statuses of *athi* and crown service was distinct and meaningful in contemporary Burmese eyes, its practical effects were far less clear-cut. The emphasis placed on social control and organization stemmed from the need to control and mobilize what was a relatively sparse population, a fact that mandated maximum control over what were limited resources.

The precise sociopolitical definition and high degree of social and spatial control were deemed necessary for cosmic, social, and hence dynastic stability. Even so, the system made explicit provision for individual social mobility and, in spite of its best efforts, was faced with considerable geographic mobility by its populace as well. A related and constant problem was the fact that the people, sometimes in sizable numbers, opted out of their designated places in the state for alternative statuses as debt slaves, private clients of powerful patrons, or membership in the floating population in general and bandit groups in particular. Thus, the high degree of control and organization which the state attempted to impose on the population provoked inevitable reaction, the strength of which varied with the ability of the state to enforce its demands.

The state tended to dominate the economic as well as the social order. Burmese society was characterized by a small-scale economy that was predominantly agricultural and by the absence of real economic cleavages and conflict, at least in class terms. The state monopolies over surplus labor and goods, the channeling of much of the remainder of the surplus into economically nonproductive pursuits, the lack of market opportunities, and the inhibition of conspicuous consumption by the sumptuary rules kept the level of material accumulation low. This prevented the formation of economically based classes or large concentrations of private economic power to compete with the state.

Early Kon-baung Burma was clearly not a nation state in the modern western sense of the term. Although it possessed a centralized bureaucratic framework, its administrative cadres were not true bureaucrats. There was to an undetermined extent some ideal of unity and imperial destiny, but loyalties were directed to a hierarchy of personal leaders, not to a political abstraction. That one person would hold supreme power at the top of this hierarchy was never called into question because the well-being and prosperity of the realm were deemed to be dependent on his strength. Only a king had enough power to control the anarchy thought to be intrinsic to human affairs. Such strength could only stem from and such power could only be entrusted to a man of superior morality and virtue, personal qualities which enabled him to bring harmony to both the cosmos and mundane society. If a ruler failed in that combination of right conduct and virtue termed *raja dhamma*, he remained king until his *kamma* was depleted because even a bad king was preferable to no king. The emphasis in kingship was on the personal qualities of the incumbent, an emphasis further reflected in the role of the ruler as a military leader. Indeed, military victories were a well-trodden path to the crown, as the careers of Tabin-shwei-hti, Bayin-naung, Nyaung-yan, Tha-lun, and Alaung-hpaya demonstrated.

Whether by Manu or the Buddha, the *dhamma*, or natural law governing the universe, had been revealed to humankind, hence the king had no power to enact law *per se*. His judgments were final, but they constituted orders rather than permanent laws and, with the exception of those relating to religious donations, expired with his demise. Rather than promulgating their own laws, rulers were supposed to uphold the revealed law, maintain order, protect the realm from internal and external dangers, adjudicate disputes between subjects, punish those contravening custom, and ensure that the collective merit-making functions of the state on behalf of its subjects were discharged.

Because most of the subgroups and subordinate institutions in Burmese society were to some extent self-regulating, beyond some sporadic irrigation projects the monarchy did not attempt to provide the positive services and administrative activism characteristic of modern governments. Perhaps the main function of the crown was to provide a point of political orientation and a sense of ordered interrelationships for the subgroups and subordinate institutions of the society. When the monarchy weakened, the relationships between the parts of the social system began to deteriorate, a deterioration which characterized the Restored Taung-ngu dynasty after the reign of Tha-lun and which commenced midway through the reign of Bo-daw-hpaya in the Konbaung period. When the monarchy was destroyed, as it was in 1752 and again in 1885, political organization devolved to its lowest constituent units, the jurisdictions of the local hereditary officials, particularly the *myo-thu-gyis*. These functionaries provided an important element of stability and continuity in a society that was characterized by chronic political instability above their level and demographic flux, induced both by nature and the policies of the central authority.

Although endowed with absolute political authority, the monarch had to rule through subordinates and bartered part of his authority and resources for their services. Entry into officialdom was determined only partly by hereditary claim at the local level, and was achieved through wealth, marriage connections, and patronage and factional affiliations at all levels, especially for the higher appointive offices. Official position automatically brought important status and material rewards and was the main means of social and economic advancement. Because the primary objectives of state action—order, salvation, maintenance and sometimes expansion of the imperial system—were static and unquestioned, the politics of policy formation and problem solving tended to be more peripheral than the politics of personal advancement. The status and affluence of official position were sought as ends in themselves rather than as the means to achieving societally defined goals. Despite the structured hierarchy of fixed statuses and offices, the sociopolitical order was characterized by constant and at times very rapid individual mobility. One of the most common avenues of such mobility was for the holders of minor offices to use the influence and money accruing from these posts to manipulate their way into positions of higher authority. For nonroyal members of early Kon-baung society, officeholding at whatever level was the most important channel for garnering wealth and exerting influence.

The determining relationship between officeholding and socioeconomic position made the former the main focus of popular aspiration and the central feature of politics among the nonroyalty. Officeholding at all levels was characterized by instability. Incumbents were subject both to attacks from subordinates and those covetous of their positions and to the whim of the ruler, who could depose them with a single command. Position and advancement were further contingent on the ability to muster political support through allegiances and associations with court factions and the capacity to attract and support retainers and clients. The role of wealth was central in these endeavors, and made its accretion the foremost concern of the ambitious functionary. Because they received no salaries from the state, officals depended on appropriation from their jurisdictions and clienteles. The higher- and some favored middle-level officials received appanages from the crown, while local hereditary officers often enjoyed the benefit of office land. Even so, the appointed officials, in particular, tended to suffer constant pressures from the financial demands of their positions. The rather casual system of official recompense made maladministration, bribery, embezzlement, and other corrupt practices the rule rather than the exception.

Besides the officials, there were two other elite groups in the society, the extended royal lineage and the monkhood. To some extent the former overlapped with the officials because some of its members were themselves middle- and lower-level functionaries. There was extensive intermarriage between the royalty and the bureaucratic gentry and nobility. The second and third generations of the royalty appear to have been absorbed by the official elite in a process of downward mobility in status. The main support of members of the extended royal lineage stemmed from appanages and the influence they had to sell at court. With the exception of the princes of the blood, in the normal course of events members of the royalty were excluded from the royal succession and owed their position to their relationship with the reigning monarch. But they, too, were subject to the vagaries of royal favor and the eddies of court politics, and hence often joined with officials in the congeries of factions that competed for influence with the ruler and supported the various candidates in the royal succession. In the constant maneuvering for influence over the ruler, the common interests of the officials and the royalty were never enough to overcome their internal rivalries. As a result, political coalitions cut across both groups to include a heterogenous array of functionaries and royalty, all seeking to advance their own personal interests and relative positions. The officials and royalty were therefore interrelated through overlapping positions, marriage ties, and some of the same political needs, with the royalty generally occupying a somewhat more stable position by virtue of their blood ties to the throne.

In contrast to the continuously high level of political activity by the officials and royalty, the monkhood in early Kon-baung Burma was notable for its political passivity. The *sangha* was inherently divided into small units and individuals spread across the land in village and forest monasteries, with large concentrations of monks only in the capital and Rangoon.[2] The *sangha* had two basic characteristics, the first its general amorphousness and lack of organizational ties. Such unity as there was stemmed from common values, which, in given situations, tended to produce uniform but not concerted responses. The second was the monastic order's fundamental dependence on the secular power for protection and assistance in the maintenance of its socioeconomically privileged position. In return, the essential functions of the professional monks—those who had passed the state examination—were the rescension of the sacred texts, the political socialization of the youth through schooling, spiritual and moral advice to the rulers, and affirmation of the basic values of the society in general and of the legitimacy of the political order in particular.

This reciprocal relationship between the state and the *sangha* was one of the two basic political exchanges in the polity. Because of its lack of organizational autonomy and its correspondingly close identification with state organs and institutions, the monkhood could not be an active participant in the central political struggle of the polity. Indeed, the dependence of the *sangha* on the state closely tied the fate of the former to that of the latter, as the troubled history of the monkhood in the colonial and independence periods illustrates.[3] The reduction of the *sangha* to this condition of passivity and dependence is part of the linear trend toward political centralization that characterized the series of dynastic regimes in Burma and represents the monarchy's one notable success in curbing the potential threat of an elite group.

In contrast, the officials and royalty were deeply involved in the two main arenas of political struggle within the polity: the basic distribution of wealth and privilege and the possession of the crown. In the case of the *sangha*, although a substantial portion of the national surplus was expended in the religious sphere by the state and individuals, it was not directly involved in the process of determining the size of the expenditure, nor did it have any real control over the result. This left the main conflict over the relative distribution of national resources between the crown and the politically active elites, the officials to a greater extent and the royalty less so.

In the second basic political exchange, the crown bartered part of its authority and monopoly over material and labor resources in return for the service and loyalty of its officials. The constant issue in this relationship was how much officials were able to appropriate to their use resources exceeding those offered by the crown. Here was the only arena in which the officials had a common interest sufficient to cause them to collude to protect illegal appropriations from crown attack. Rulers, in turn, tried a variety of devices aimed at restricting this illegal income, most notably the inquests. The royalty was probably a minor factor in this conflict, given its small size and peripheral involvement with the formal structure of administration. Over the long term, the victors in this contest for control of resources were the officials.

Since the ruler was imbued with absolute political authority, he was *ipso facto* the arbiter of position and reward in the social order. Thus the contest for possession of the throne was clearly associated with that for resources, since the character of the king and his political debts were important factors in the maneuvers for influence and reward at court. Although commoners sometimes mounted armed challenges for the throne, one notable feature of politics was the near complete exclusion of all but the princes of the blood from the contest for the crown. The lineage qualifications for the kingship had broad social acceptance. As such, in most cases the genealogical priorities of the customary succession succeeded in limiting the number of eligible candidates and in eliminating those who were unacceptably incompetent, but remained loose enough in their definition of eligibility to engender competition. Hence, despite its emphasis on the *aw-ra-tha* son, the customary succession was characterized by hostilities between contending segments of the royal lineage, segments which were the ultimate organizing foci for the various factions and coalitions of court politics. The existence of more than one eligible candidate for the throne created a dilemma for rulers because the succession made no provision for removing the unsuccessful candidates as political factors. The two unsuccessful solutions to this dilemma were, first, lineal succession with important roles in government to the other eligibles, and, second, collateral succession in which the eligible sons succeeded in order of seniority.

Yet the ambiguity of the royal succession and the related competition may have been, on the one hand, an important means of renewing the political cement that held the polity together; on the other, it was a primary factor in the gradual weakening of the monarchy. The first three kings of the Kon-baung dynasty were preeminently military figures whose legitimacy stemmed from right of conquest. All three played important political and military roles in the founding of the dynasty and Naung-daw-gyi had also to defend his kingdom against strong internal military challenges as well. The military origins of the dynasty resulted in the development of a strong network of personal allegiances to Alaung-hpaya among his followers. A perfect example of this phenomenon is the *thwei-thauk* of sixty-eight of his closest followers formed by Alaung-hpaya in 1749, a formalization of the allegiances which bound them to his personal service and cause. The value of the *thwei-thauks* as a means to cement royal power is reflected in the fact that others were formed in 1752 and 1753.[4] Many of these men became leading officials in his government and those of succeeding kings. These bonds of personal loyalty were based on shared struggle and goals and were further reinforced with the award of offices, social rank, and intermarriage with the royal line. The state in its early phase was held together by the political cement of these personal allegiances to the original ruler. The strength of this bond can be seen in the continuity of high officials from the reign of Alaung-hpaya on and the sustained bias in recruitment toward the Shwei-bo area, where Alaung-hpaya's quest for power had its origins.

As participants in the struggle for power, the first king and his elder sons understood the nature of the personal ties on which their rule was established. But the transfer of power from the dynastic founder to his eldest son through inheritance tended to weaken the bonds of loyalty of these early officials to the crown. This weakness became more pronounced as later recruits to the administrative apparatus obtained their positions and advancement through family and patronage connections and the use of wealth rather than as a reward for service. Over time the nature of the relationship between crown and officials tended to change from loyalty based on service and common struggle to a more cynical and self-serving relationship characterized by the politics of personal advancement. The notable characteristic of this later relationship was the uncertain loyalty of the officials and the employment of selective acts of brutality by the king to sustain it.

While the loyalty of the generality of early Kon-baung officialdom was sustained for three or four decades after Alaung-hpaya's death, it is very clear that Naung-daw-gyi, Hsin-hpyu-shin, and Sin-gu were never able to draw on loyalties of the same nature and strength as had the first Kon-baung king. Thus, one function of the succession struggles that characterized the passage of power was to allow the successful candidate to assume the throne with a new network of personal allegiances originating in his own struggle for power. The creation of such a new network of loyalties can be seen in the military seizure of the throne by Bo-daw-hpaya in 1782. The elements of military struggle and shared goals, later reinforced by office and marriage ties, created a corps of supporters that was ultimately sufficiently strong to sustain the accession of Ba-gyi-daw over strong opposition.

It must also be remembered, however, that there were more abstract ideas of proper and improper behavior for kings. Cold-blooded murder was considered conduct unbecoming a monarch; nor were rivals for the crown to be eliminated until they had offered a visible threat or provocation. Naung-daw-gyi certainly eroded the loyalties of officials by his arbitrary execution of two of his army officers and his shabby treatment of Min-gaung Naw-rahta. Hsin-hpyu-shin's possible murder of his older brother would explain some of the continuing hostility toward him by many officials. Similarly, Sin-gu's unwarranted execution of his north queen, high-handed treatment of his uncles, and other unseemly behavior was completely counter to contemporary standards for royal conduct. Indeed, one of Bo-daw-hpaya's main assets in mounting his successful coup in 1782 was that he was seen as a decent person, in contrast to his three predecessors. The changing nature of the loyalties of officials in the early Kon-baung period was no doubt influenced by such abstractions.

Important as the weakening and transformation of loyalties were in the erosion of the royal position, the circumstances surrounding the raising of the princes must also be considered. The founder king and his elder sons were not raised in a palace, but learned about the realities of politics and social conditions in the course of their own upbringing and struggle for power. The first two Kon-baung rulers to be raised completely within the confines of the court were Sin-gu and Ba-gyi-daw. Alaung-hpaya's fourth son Bo-daw-hpaya and his three eldest sons all had a certain amount of experience in and exposure to the real world, culminating in the seizure of power in 1782. After 1782, however, princes were cloistered in the palace and had little opportunity to gain practical experience in the real world. Deprived of realistic contact with affairs and conditions, princes so reared tended to become erratic rulers, a problem compounded by the sycophancy inherent in the officialdom and the well-founded fear on the part of the functionaries of impulsive royal reaction to displeasing news and events. The institution of the crown princeship was intended to remedy this deficiency at least for the heir apparent but, as the careers of Sin-gu and Ba-gyi-daw suggest, does not appear to have been effective with young princes raised in the palace. Two important political features of the early Kon-baung state were thus the initial strength and cohesion it drew from the network of personal allegiances centered on the charismatic military figure of Alaung-hpaya, and the combination of the subsequent weakening of these bonds with less effective leadership and control by kings raised in the palace. With these features in mind, a review of the rise and decline of the Kon-baung state and some comparisons with the preceding Restored Taung-ngu period are in order.

There appear to have been two constant features of the early Kon-baung monarchy. The crown always lost a given amount of its resources through the corruption that was endemic to the system due to the nature of officeholding and the *myo-za* system. The policies of the crown itself, most notably during the reign of Bo-daw-hpaya, contributed to the loss of resources, as did recurring natural calamities. A second constant feature was the crown's concern to protect itself by preventing any point or individual in the administrative apparatus from acquiring too much power—thus the dichotomies, fragmentation, overlapping of jurisdictions, creation of administrative conflicts, alternate communications channels, and arbitrary personnel practices used to manage the bureaucratic apparatus. Such devices cannot but have impaired the efficiency of government and encouraged the chronic corruption, but they did allow even weak kings to survive, albeit at a heavy price. Under the best of circumstances, the crown was therefore subject to an attrition of its resource base and a relatively low level of administrative efficiency.

As the dynasty progressed through the reigns of Naung-daw-gyi, Hsin-hpyu-shin, and Sin-gu, the weakening and gradual transformation of the network of allegiances and the first experience of less competent leadership under Sin-gu caused a gradual decline in the ability of the monarchy to cope with governing the realm. As this decay set in, the corruption endemic to the system increased, becoming rampant as early as midpoint in Hsin-hpyu-shin's reign, as evidenced by the great embezzlement scandal of 1770. While Bo-daw-hpaya ascended the throne with a new network of personal allegiances and generally strong popular support, the decline accelerated during his reign for three main reasons. First, the failure of his administrative reforms, as exemplified by the inquests of 1783 and 1802, suggests that the crown was already past the point of being able to deal effectively with the entrenched interests of the bureaucratic gentry. Second, the large-scale overexploitation of the entire country for the military campaigns of the 1780s and the public works of the 1790s caused demographic loss to the crown, which I estimate at 17 percent. The lack of data makes it impossible to provide even rough estimates for demographic loss during the famine, social disorders, and renewed warfare of the years from roughly 1800 to 1812, but the descriptions of conditions in the contemporary European sources indicate that it must have been considerable. Third, Bo-daw-hpaya's tenacity in ensuring the ultimate victory of the least competent of all the candidates for the throne during a long and bitter succession struggle between 1808 and 1819 was the final touch in pushing the dynasty irretrievably downhill. There were, of course, other factors, such as the expansion of the royalty and the corresponding enlargement of the resources allocated to its support through the *myo-za* system and the fading military capability of the dynasty. It may also have been that the collective memories of the disorders and collapse of the Taung-ngu period and the ensuing desire for strong rulers faded over time, as new generations with no direct experience of that societal trauma came of age.

The long reign of Bo-daw-hpaya was the transition from the initial period of vigor to the long phase of decline. Bo-daw-hpaya himself attempted to rule with the imperial and administrative style characteristic of Alaung-hpaya, Naung-daw-gyi, and Hsin-hpyu-shin, but fundamental transformation in political cohesiveness and loss of resources were already too far advanced. As the fourth son of Alaung-hpaya, Bo-daw-hpaya had reached manhood in the mid-1760s, almost a decade after the struggle for power was over. His youth had not been spent entirely within the palace, but he was given no opportunity to gain the practical experience of his older brothers and had not participated in the empire building of his father. In terms of background and experience, he is closer to the princes raised in the palace than to the worldly warrior figures he sought to emulate. While seeking to be a monarch cut from the same mold as his father and two brothers, Bo-daw-hpaya is instead characterized by his military and administrative failures on the one hand, and his masterful orchestration of court politics to ensure the ascendancy of himself and his two chosen successors on the other.

Raised in his grandfather's palace, Ba-gyi-daw was quickly captured by one court faction after his accession in 1819. His deposition in 1837 by Tha-ra-wadi was a reaction against the extreme dominance of this faction. Succeeding rulers were also dominated by their high officials, including Min-don, who owed his throne to the support of the families of several powerful officials to whom he was related by marriage. The death of this ruler in 1878 saw the first complete failure of the customary succession because none of his four major queens had borne a son. An intense power struggle ensued as the various factions of the court promoted the claims of a number of minor princes. In the end, a strong faction led by the third-ranking *wun-gyi*, known as the Kin *wun min-gyi*, and the middle queen succeeded in placing the nineteen-year-old Thi-baw prince on the throne in the firm expectation that he would prove to be a malleable monarch. The intensity of the struggle is reflected in the fact that four of the unsuccessful candidates fled the country to continue the fight from abroad. Most of the remaining minor princes and their families, a total of perhaps fifty persons, were eliminated in the so-called massacre of the kinsmen in January 1879. Government fell into the hands of the faction centered on the Thi-baw prince and remained so until the war that broke out with Britain in November 1885 brought the end of the monarchy the following month.[5]

Victor Lieberman has argued that the starting point of dynastic decline in the Restored Taung-ngu period was the inherent tendency of the monarchy to exploit the nuclear zone around the capital more heavily than less accessible areas.[6] The result was both a geographic movement of people from this zone and a political movement from state to private service with princes and other important *myo-zas*. This attrition from the crown sector not only strengthened the latter, but also forced the throne to exploit the nuclear zone ever more heavily. As the crown was weakened through this process, the princely contenders for the throne augmented their resources through alliances with important ministers who controlled the administrative and military functions of the state. Over time these officials became king-makers able to reduce the monarchs to figureheads. The dominance of officials over the crown also gradually displaced the formal administrative apparatus with informal networks of clients. These, in turn, allowed corruption and maladministration to run unchecked, leaving the state increasingly unable to cope with its internal and external enemies. The officials over the long term succeeded in gaining control over both the allocation of resources and over the royal succession.

The Kon-baung dynastic pattern has a number of features in common with that of the Restored Taung-ngu period: their common origins as conquest dynasties, the military attributes of their first three kings, the immediate appearance of the dilemma of the royal succession accompanied by attempts to decree collateral succession by the founding kings, the overexploitation of resources, the abrupt change in dynastic fortunes linked to the first accession of a king raised in the palace, and the gradual dominance of the high officials. Whether the Kon-baung dynasty would have repeated the pattern of extreme ministerial dominance that characterized the later Restored Taung-ngu period cannot be known, given British political pressure and military intrusions during the later Kon-baung period.

The ways in which the British influenced later Kon-baung dynastic politics and administration await another study, but one aspect is obvious. Its highly centralized nature and the existence of conflict between alternative candidates for the throne made the Kon-baung state vulnerable to outsiders as the contenders sought allies. Naung-daw-gyi sought arms from the English East India Company while Hsin-hpyu-shin and Ba-gyi-daw considered the possibility of the intervention of French and English soldiers, respectively. Starting with Michael Symes's second mission in 1802, there was a keen British awareness of the opportunities offered by the politics of the royal succession. One reason the early Kon-baung monarchs were generally reluctant to have European factories established at Rangoon was the fear that these outsiders with their superior military capability would become the decisive factor in internal politics.

It is not, however, completely appropriate to compare the respective dynastic developments of the Restored Taung-ngu and Kon-baung periods because the history of the dynastic period exhibits linear as well as cyclical characteristics. The early rulers of the Restored Taung-ngu dynasty learned from the sad history of the First Taung-ngu period and transformed Burma from an administratively decentralized polity composed of a dominant center with relatively weak institutional ties with a series of subordinate centers of varying size into a centralized bureaucratic polity. In this new state, power was organized hierarchically and exercised by a sovereign with absolute and immediate control over the fate of an appointive elite consisting of higher functionaries and a quasi-hereditary bureaucratic gentry. This transformation took half a century to complete and brought with it new structures of power relationships and styles of politics. By contrast, Alaung-hpaya appears rather quickly to have been able to create a copy of the later Taung-ngu state, in which he had been a minor functionary. It would further appear that the early Kon-baung kings learned from the ministerial dominance of the later Taung-ngu period. They enlarged the royal lineage and assigned it a more important role in the governance of the realm in the vain hope of providing a counterbalance to the power of the officials. Thus, the various cycles of the dynastic period in Burma do have causes and processes in common, but the relative importance of these varied in accord with the specific circumstances of any given period and the advance of the linear features of Burmese history.

APPENDIX 1

POPULATION TRENDS, 1783–1802

Although the size of the population of the early Kon-baung state was subject to various estimates done by British visitors, the Burmese themselves left significant records of their population. Inquests that included census material were an important feature of Burmese administration from at least the fourteenth century.[1] Four inquests were held between 1765 and 1826, whose administrative function and political significance are discussed in chapter 5. No statistical material is known to survive from the inquest of 1765 and the surviving statistics from 1826, except for those of the immediate capital area, can largely be discarded as straightforward repetition of earlier figures. However, two extant sets of district-by-district figures for 1783 and one set for 1802 provide the basis for some estimates. The "45 hku myo-zu shwei-daik sa-yin win-daw-gu naing-ngan-daw atwin myo-kyei-ywa-mya" (hereafter termed "Population Summary of 1783") gives figures for the crown service and *athi* populations for 123 *myos*, ten *taiks*, or special revenue jurisdictions, and six departmental jurisdictions.[2] A second set of figures for 1783, in the main identical with the first, for 145 *myos*, twelve *taiks*, and six departmental jurisdictions was compiled by Henry Burney, British Resident at Ava from 1830 to 1837, from Burmese lists clandestinely shown to him by court officials.[3] The "Sit-tan sa-yin" (hereafter termed the "Population Summary of 1802")

---

[1] Yi Yi, "Kon-baung hkit sit-tan-mya" [*Sit-tans* of the Kon-baung period], JBRS 49, no. 1 (1966): 71.
[2] HRD 2984, 44–50.
[3] "Census of the Population of the Kingdom of Ava as Taken in the Burman Year 1145 A.D. 1783, and as Revised in 1188 A.D. 1826," Royal Commonwealth Society, Henry Burney Papers, B.I.

provides crown service and *athi* figures for 141 *myos*.[4] These three lists appear in annotated translation in *Sit-tans*, chapter 11, and are summarized in table 7.

Table 7
Comparison of Early Kon-baung Population Summaries

Population Summary of 1783		Burney's Census		Population Summary of 1802	
Unit	Population	Unit	Population	Unit	Population
123 *myos*	210,724	145 *myos*	228,623	141 *myos*	178,806
10 *taiks*	42,101	12 *taiks*	43,508	—	—
6 depts.	29,526	6 depts.	23,926	—	—
Totals	**282,351**		**296,057**		**178,806**

In terms of comparability, the population summaries of 1783 and 1802 and Burney's census of 1783 all cover only Burma proper and do not include Arakan, the littoral to the east of Martaban, or the northern and southern Shan states. The western, Burmanized Shan principalities were under closer Burmese administrative control, hence the apparent reason for their inclusion, while the other Shan states were not required to participate in the inquests.[5] Thus, the three lists are comparable in geographic coverage. There is an important structural difference, however, in that the two 1783 lists include sections on *taik* and departmental jurisdictions while the 1802 document does not. A modest divergence also occurs in the coverage of small, marginally

---

[4] BL OR. 3449-B.
[5] For a list of thirty-two northern and southern Shan principalities that did not participate in the 1783 inquest, see HRD 2984, 50.

important *myos*. The 1802 list has 125 *myos* in common with the combined 1783 lists, while the Burney document has identical figures with its Burmese twin and contains a number of *myos* not in the latter. The "Population Summary of 1783" and Burney's "Census" are almost completely coincident in terms of the *myos* and the figures given for individual *myos*. This replication, coupled to the fact that the number of *myos* in the latter is roughly equal to the "Population Summary of 1802," means that the best rough comparison can be made between the 1802 document and Burney's list.

A question remains as to whether individual comparison of the 125 *myos* included in both the 1783 and 1802 figures is valid. Of the 125 *myos*, 79 have completely identical figures, 11 show increases, 29 show decreases, and 6 have internal increases and decreases that offset their respective changes, thereby yielding the same totals for 1783 and 1802. The total for the 11 *myos* showing increases is 5,328, while the total for the 29 showing decreases is 46,511. As such, the increases and decreases are greatly disproportionate. In addition, 31,166, or 68 percent, of the decreases are divided among 8 major *myos* in north and northwest Burma, while the remainder is concentrated among the major *myos* of central Burma. Neighboring *myos* show no changes or slight decreases. Given these facts and the high degree of replication between the 1783 and 1802 figures for individual *myos*, it is clear that changes in the boundaries of *myos* can explain neither the disproportion in decreases over increases nor the geographic concentration of the shift. Comparison of the boundaries of specific *myos* as recorded in the *sit-tans* of 1783 and 1802 also produces little evidence of jurisdictional change between 1783 and 1802. Because the territories of individual *myos* appear to have been stable, it can be concluded that the 1783 and 1802 data are comparable on a *myo* by *myo* basis.

Despite the fact that the Burmese inquests carefully gathered information about the age, sex, birthday, service affiliation if any, and place of residence of individuals, the authorities only compiled lists of houses because the house was the traditional unit of taxation and service. The figures given in the three lists presented here therefore represent houses and were not intended to provide demographic information *per se*, but an overview of the tax/service units of each district. For demographic purposes, the authorities generally reckoned each house to contain between five and seven individuals.[6] It was also commonly

---

[6] See J. Crawfurd, *Journal of an Embassy from the Governor General of India to the Court of Ava in the Year 1826*, 2d ed., 2 vols. (London, 1834), 2: 8; and H. Burney,

acknowledged that local officials standardly underreported their figures by around 10 percent.[7]

There are no figures for Arakan, the northern and southern Shan states, or the littoral east of Martaban other than those provided by Burney. Based on comparisons with later British censuses, his total of 4,286 houses for Yei, Tavoy, and Mergui is probably realistic, but his totals of 232,301 houses for Arakan and 152,800 for the Shan states can justly be suspected of being too generous. It seems improbable that the Shan states could contain over a million people or that the population of Arakan was almost as large as that of Burma itself. Beyond guesswork, there does not seem to be any reasonable way to estimate the population of these two areas.

For these reasons, I have opted to include only the figures from the 1793 and 1802 population summaries in the regional data given in table 8. In addition to providing totals for Burma's seven main regions, table 8 provides separate figures for the primary centers of population concentration, which show the relative decline or increase locally. In most cases, I have listed only centers having one thousand or more houses and combined the figures for smaller *myos* under the category "other *myos*."

In addition to Burney's census, other British visitors made various estimates of the population of Burma proper by extrapolating both from their own observations and from conversations with Burmese officials.[8] In 1795 Michael Symes guessed a figure of 14.4 million for all the Kon-baung dominions, while two years later Hiram Cox halved that figure. John Canning was told in 1810 that the registered houses did not exceed 400,000 and, on that basis, estimated the population at between 2 and 2.4 million. John Crawfurd, writing in 1829, suggested 2 to 2.1 million for Burma proper and 4 million overall. Utilizing the figures from his census for 1783 and calculating at 7 persons per house, Henry Burney produced a figure of almost 2.3 million for Burma proper and 4.2 million for the empire.

Multiplication by 7 persons per house and correction of 10 percent for underreporting gives a figure of roughly 2.2 million for the popula-

---

"On the Population of the Burman Empire," *Journal of the Royal Statistical Society* 4 (1842): 335–47; reprinted in JBRS 31, no. 1 (1941): 26.
[7] See Crawfurd, *Journal of an Embassy*, 2: 8; and Burney, "Population of the Burman Empire," 26. MMOS (3: 48–49) gives an edict of 1785 which also complains of the erroneous nature of the returns.
[8] Burney, "Population of the Burman Empire," passim, critically reviews the various estimates and offers his own calculations.

tion summary of 1783 and 1.8 million for that of 1802. The Burmese figure for 1783 is therefore quite in harmony with the estimates of Canning, Crawfurd, and Burney for Burma proper. Such estimates do not, however, account for that part of the population not living in registered houses: pagoda slaves, some retainers of officials and royalty, the large floating and debt-slave populations, and so on. Furthermore, the lists themselves may not be comprehensive in their coverage. The totals given in the population summaries of 1783 and 1802 are therefore probably on the low side, but it is impossible to estimate to what extent this was the case.

Table 8
Trends in Houses by Region, 1783–1802

Area	1783	1802	Change	Percent Change
Capital				
Ava	73	73	—	—
Amara-pu-ra	15,457	15,411	−46	(<1)
Sagaing	4,012	6,411	+2,399	+60
Pin-ya	533	533	—	—
Totals	**20,075**	**22,428**	**+2,353**	**+12**
North/Northwest				
Tabayin	14,662	8,197	−6,465	−44
Alon	17,418	5,590	−11,828	−68
Myei-du	7,998	6,190	−1,808	−23
Amyin	4,683	883	−3,800	−81
Kan-ni	8,196	5,710	−2,486	−30
Mok-hso-bo	1,753	1,753	—	—
NgaSin-gu	1,156	1,023	−133	−12
Htan-dabin	1,077	1,077	—	—
Pyin-zala 5 *myos*	3,922	4,130	+208	+5
Other *myos*	8,193	8,198	+5	(<1)
Totals	**69,058**	**42,751**	**−26,307**	**−38**

Area	1783	1802	Change	Percent Change
Central				
Meik-hti-la	2,644	982	−1,662	−63
Yin-daw	1,012	1,012	—	—
Yame-thin	5,917	5,917	—	—
Nyaung-yan	1,698	712	−986	−58
Kyauk-hse†	—	—	—	—
Pin-dale	6,505	3,766	−2,739	−42
Pyin-zi	3,292	518	−2,774	−84
Kyauk-hsauk	1,698	404	−1,294	−76
Pin	1,313	1,613	+300	+23
Kyauk-padaung	924	510	−414	−45
Talok	4,311	3,565	−746	−17
Pagan	3,980	3,623	−357	−9
Salin	7,586	7,127	−459	−6
Pahkan-gyi	2,818	4,100	+1,282	+45
Taung-dwin-gyi	5,008	5,008	—	—
Magwei	1,005	993	−12	—
Myin-gun	1,020	892	−128	−13
Other *myos*	6,906	6,896	−10	(<1)
Totals	**57,637**	**47,638**	**−9,999**	**−17**
Prome				
Sagu	2,270	1,764	−506	−22
Malun	1,191	1,191	—	—
Myei-de	1,602	1,602	—	—
Ka-ma	1,130	1,130	—	—
Shwei-daung	1,811	1,811	—	—

†The figures for the nine *myos* in the Kyauk-hse wunship are too patchy to be included. The "Population Summary of 1783" gives figures for only Mek-hkaya and Pyin-mana *myos*, while Burney's census has figures only for Myit-tha Myo. Figures for seven *myos* appear in the "Population Summary of 1802." Kyauk-hse was densely settled by crown service groups, but the overall total for the seven *myos* in 1802 was only 2,262 houses. In 1783 Mek-hkaya alone had 3,021 but by 1802 had declined by 92 percent to 230. This suggests that Kyauk-hse suffered the same serious population decline as did the other major population centers.

Area	1783	1802	Change	Percent Change
Prome	9,091	9,091	—	—
Padaung	3,507	2,670	−837	−24
Kanaung	2,062	2,062	—	—
Le-gaing	1,690	1,690	—	—
Other *myos*	5,835	5,775	−60	−1
Totals	**30,189**	**28,786**	**−1,403**	**−5**
Irrawaddy Delta				
Henzada	2,515	2,515	—	—
Tha-ra-wadi	5,388	5,388	—	—
Bassein	1,676	1,676	—	—
Dala	1,566	1,566	—	—
Han-tha-wadi	5,852	5,852	—	—
Other *myos*	3,122	3,210	+88	+3
Totals	**20,119**	**20,207**	**+88**	**(<1)**
Taung-ngu				
Taung-ngu	1,698	2,529	+831	+49
Other *myos*	634	634	—	—
Totals	**2,332**	**3,163**	**+831**	**+36**
Martaban				
Martaban	4,411	4,411	—	—
Other *myos*	296	296	—	—
Totals	**4,707**	**4,707**	—	—

APPENDIX 2

TRENDS IN CROWN SERVICE HOUSES BY REGION, 1783–1802

Area	1783 Houses		1802 Houses		Percent Service Houses	
	Service	Total	Service	Total	1783	1802
Capital						
Ava	51	73	51	73	70	70
Amara-pu-ra	11,472	15,457	10,964	15,411	74	71
Sagaing	3,179	4,012	5,139	6,411	79	80
Pin-ya	284	533	284	533	53	53
Totals	**14,986**	**20,075**	**16,438**	**22,428**	**75**	**73**
North/Northwest						
Tabayin	8,107	14,662	4,295	8,917	55	48
Alon	9,684	17,418	3,524	5,590	56	63
Myei-du	4,799	7,998	3,985	6,190	60	64
Amyin	1,407	4,683	567	883	30	64
Kan-ni	1,677	8,196	899	5,710	20	16
Mok-hso-bo	1,103	1,753	1,103	1,753	63	63
NgaSin-gu	871	1,156	776	1,023	75	76
Htan-dabin	973	1,077	793	1,077	90	74
Pyin-zala 5 *myos*	1,040	3,922	1,246	4,130	27	30
Other *myos*	3,174	7,930	2,786	7,935	39	34
Totals	**32,835**	**68,795**	**19,974**	**43,208**	**48**	**46**

	1783 Houses		1802 Houses		Percent Service Houses	
Area	Service	Total	Service	Total	1783	1802
Central						
Meik-hti-la	682	2,644	182	982	26	19
Yin-daw	421	1,012	491	1,012	42	49
Yame-thin	2,567	5,917	2,567	5,917	43	43
Nyaung-yan	542	1,698	120	712	32	17
Kyauk-hse†	—	—	—	—	—	—
Pin-dale	1,161	6,505	720	3,766	18	19
Pyin-zi	734	3,292	231	518	22	45
Kyauk-hsauk	542	1,698	213	404	32	53
Pin	64	1,313	64	1,613	5	4
Kyauk-padaung	148	924	19	510	16	4
Talok	2,291	4,311	1,889	3,565	53	53
Pagan	1,225	3,980	1,142	3,623	31	32
Salin	2,406	7,586	2,328	7,127	32	33
Pahkan-gyi	1,001	2,818	954	4,100	36	23
Taung-dwin-gyi	446	5,008	446	5,008	9	9
Magwei	167	1,005	155	993	17	16
Myin-gun	224	1,020	210	892	22	24
Other *myos*	1,124	6,906	1,161	6,896	16	17
Totals	**15,745**	**57,637**	**12,892**	**47,638**	**27**	**27**
Prome						
Sagu	493	2,270	395	1,764	22	22
Malun	289	1,191	289	1,191	24	24
Myei-de	169	1,602	169	1,602	11	11
Ka-ma	108	1,130	130	1,130	10	11
Shwei-daung	111	1,811	111	1,811	6	6

†Again, the figures for Kyauk-hse are too scanty to be included. See the note to table 8, appendix 1.

	1783 Houses		1802 Houses		Percent Service Houses	
Area	Service	Total	Service	Total	1783	1802
Prome	1,852	9,091	2,042	9,091	20	22
Padaung	950	3,507	95	2,670	27	4
Kanaung	271	2,062	271	2,062	13	13
Le-gaing	384	1,690	384	1,690	23	23
Other *myos*	1,965	5,835	2,037	5,775	34	35
Totals	**6,592**	**30,189**	**5,923**	**28,786**	**22**	**21**
Irrawaddy Delta						
Henzada	546	2,515	546	2,515	22	22
Tha-ra-wadi	691	5,388	691	5,388	13	13
Bassein	264	1,676	264	1,676	16	16
Dala	32	1,566	32	1,566	2	2
Han-tha-wadi	2,517	5,852	2,517	5,852	43	43
Other *myos*	567	3,122	555	3,210	18	17
Totals	**4,617**	**20,119**	**4,605**	**20,207**	**23**	**23**
Taung-ngu						
Taung-ngu	1,118	1,698	1,795	2,529	66	71
Other *myos*	92	634	482	634	15	76
Totals	**1,210**	**2,332**	**2,277**	**3,163**	**52**	**72**
Martaban						
Martaban	1,162	4,411	1,289	4,411	26	29
Other *myos*	7	296	7	296	2	2
Totals	**1,169**	**4,707**	**1,296**	**4,707**	**25**	**28**

APPENDIX 3

NOTE ON SOURCES

In contrast to earlier periods, a substantial range of contemporary sources in Burmese, English, French, and Italian is available for the study of the early Kon-baung dynasty. The Burmese-language materials themselves fall into four general categories. First, a large number of the edicts of the early Kon-baung rulers are extant, a portion of which have been examined in printed form.[1] These edicts provide information on a wide variety of administrative and political matters. Second, another important body of records are the *sit-tans*, or land rolls, which primarily comprise the statements of local and provincial officials submitted during the crown's administrative, census, and cadastral surveys of 1765, 1783, and 1802, together with three related compilations of population statistics. Of the five hundred or so *sit-tans* thought to be extant, at least 80 percent have been collected and studied. My extensive use of the *sit-tans* in this study reflects the fact that during much of the time my thesis was in train, I was also engaged in a project to translate and publish a collection of these documents. This work was done under the auspices of the Burma Research Project of New York University.[2] Through the good offices of my collaborators, the late Professor Frank N. Trager of New York University and the late Dr. Yi Yi of the Historical Research Department, Ministry of Culture, Rangoon, copies of a large number of *sit-tans* from Burma were

---

[1] Khin Khin Sein's, *Alaung-min-taya-gyi amein-daw-mya* [Edicts of Alaung-hpaya] (Rangoon, 1964) (abbreviated AA) is a collection of ninety-nine edicts of Alaung-hpaya. Yi Yi, "Additional Burmese Historical Sources, 1752-1776," *The Guardian* 15, no. 11 (1968): 33-35, and 15, no. 12 (1968): 21-23, renders some of these into English, along with edicts of Naung-daw-gyi and Hsin-hpyu-shin. Many more edicts are included in part or in full in MMOS.

[2] F. N. Trager and W. J. Koenig, *Burmese Sit-tans, 1764–1826: Records of Rural Life and Administration* (Tucson, Ariz., 1979) (abbreviated *Sit-tans*).

made available to me. The corpus of *sit-tans* is a mine of information on many aspects of local and provincial administration, revenue collection, the duties and nature of local officeholding, land tenure, and even some aspects of the state's religious role.

A third source of much material has been the many *damathats*, or compilations of customary law, from this period.³ The *damathats* are revealing contemporary treatises on the rules and conditions of social life and include numerous explicit statements on political thought, the nature and function of the state, the roles and duties of the king and of officials, and the nature and regulation of social relationships and administrative conduct. Finally, valuable information was obtained on the traditions and customary procedures of the court and royalty from treatises such as the *Law-ka byu-ha kyan* [Treatise on customary terms] of the late 1750s, the *Shwei-bon ni-dan* [A work on the Golden Palace] of 1782, and the court records and genealogical materials presented in U Ya Gyaw, *Myan-ma maha min-gala min-gan-daw* [Burmese royal ceremonies].⁴

These edicts, *sit-tans*, *damathats*, and court treatises and records constitute the main types of contemporary Burmese records available. The lithic inscriptions that are such an important source for the study of earlier periods of Burmese history are not yet available for the early Kon-baung dynasty. While there are hundreds and perhaps thousands of such inscriptions from this period, to date a mere handful have been collected and published, hence their exploitation as a source of early Kon-baung history awaits a future time.⁵ Apart from several biographies of Alaung-hpaya written in chronicle style, there were no royal or religious chronicles composed during the early Kon-baung period that focus on the period itself.⁶ The *First Glass Palace Chronicle*, composed by a committee between 1829 and 1832, covers the period from

---

3I relied most heavily on the *Manu-kye* of 1756 and the *Manu wunana* of 1770. For a useful perspective on the nature of the *damathats*, see M. B. Hooker, "The Indian-Derived Law Texts of Southeast Asia," *Journal of Asian Studies* 37, no. 2 (1978): 201–19, especially 201–6 and 215–19.
4Thi-ri U-zana, *Law-ka byu-ha kyan* [Treatise on customary terms] (Rangoon, 1958) (abbreviated LBK); Zei-ya Thin-hkaya, *Shwei-bon ni-dan* [A work on the Golden Palace] (Rangoon, 1960); and Ya Gyaw, *Myan-ma maha min-gala min-gan-daw* [Burmese royal ceremonies] (Mandalay, 1905) (abbreviated MMM).
5A few inscriptions of Alaung-hpaya and Hsin-hpyu-shin are included in Tun Nyein, *Inscriptions of Pagan, Pinya and Ava: Translation with Notes* (Rangoon, 1899). For an important inscription of Hsin-hpyu-shin, see Taw Sein Ko, "A Preliminary Study of the Po:U:Daung Inscription of S'inbyuhin, 1774 A.D.," *Indian Antiquary* 23, no. 1 (1893): 1–8.
6Hla Tin, ed., *Alaung-hpaya ayei-daw-bon hnazaung-dwe* [Two biographies of Alaung-hpaya] (Rangoon, 1961).

1752 to 1821, while the *Second Glass Palace Chronicle*, completed in 1869, carries the narrative to 1854. In 1908 a former court official, U Tin of Mandalay, published the *Kon-baung-zet* [History of the Kon-baung dynasty], which comprised the narrative of the Glass Palace chronicles from 1752 to 1854 and his own account of the subsequent reigns of Min-don and Thi-baw and the latter's exile.[7] As a narrative history compiled during the later Kon-baung period, the *Glass Palace Chronicle* provides a secondary rather than primary account. While giving fairly full descriptions of military, foreign, and religious affairs as well as the various coup attempts and rebellions between 1752 and about 1800, for the period from roughly 1800 to 1819 the chronicle confines itself largely to palace activities and related matters and sheds little light on the internal events and politics of this turbulent time. Other valuable secondary sources include two ecclesiastical chronicles from the later Kon-baung period as well as several treatises and compilations that provide information on the earlier period.[8]

Complementing the contemporary Burmese sources is a large but uneven array of European and American materials. Both the English and French East India companies became involved in the war of the 1750s, and the French were active in Burma in other ways between 1770 and 1784. In consequence, there are a modest number of eyewitness accounts by French and British participants. The British diplomatic missions to Burma between 1795 and 1812 produced a substantial body of reports and journals from the pens of Francis Buchanan, Hiram Cox, and especially Michael Symes and John Canning. Missionaries, too, were present throughout the period. The Italians Gaetano Mantegazza and Vincentius Sangermano lived in Burma from 1772 to 1784 and 1783 to 1806, respectively, and each wrote a long and comprehensive account.[9] The English Baptist missionary Felix Carey was in Burma from 1808 to 1816 and became an intimate of Bo-daw-hpaya and the future Ba-gyi-daw. Unfortunately, his letters and jour-

---

[7]*Hman-nan maha ya-zawin-daw-gyi* [Glass Palace chronicle], 3 vols. (Mandalay, 1921) (abbreviated *Hman-nan*); and Tin (of Mandalay), comp., *Kon-baung-zet maha ya-zawin-daw-gyi* [History of the Kon-baung dynasty], 3 vols. (Rangoon, 1967–1968) (abbreviated KBZ).

[8]Maha Dama Thin-gyan, *Tha-thana lin-ga-ya kyan* [Treatise to adorn the religion] (Rangoon, 1897); and Pannasami, *The History of the Buddha's Religion (Sasanavamsa)*, trans. by B. C. Law (London, 1952). On the derivative relationship of the latter to the former, see V. B. Lieberman, "A New Look at the *Sasanavamsa*," *Bulletin of the School of Oriental and African Studies* 39, no. 1 (1976): 137–49.

[9]R. Carmignani, *La Birmania, Relazione Inedita del 1784 del Missionario Barnabita G. M. Mantegazza* (Rome, 1950); and V. Sangermano, *A Description of the Burmese Empire*, trans. by W. Tandy, 5th ed. (London, 1966).

nals were lost when the Baptist Missionary Society Archives in London were bombed during World War II, leaving only the scattered letters preserved in printed form in publications of the society. Carey was joined on the Burmese scene by the American Baptist missionaries Ann and Adoniram Judson in 1813. Most of their letters and journals for the period 1813 to 1819 have also been lost. Some of their letters, along with a few of those by other American missionaries in Burma, can be found in American and English Baptist publications. In addition, in 1823 Ann Judson published a small but valuable volume of her letters to raise funds for the mission.[10] These European and American sources are important supplements to the Burmese materials because they provide descriptions of events, conditions, and personalities as well as report comments obtained from the Burmese, a type of commentary that tends to be absent from indigenous sources. The foreign sources must be used carefully, however, as they are often characterized by strong anti-Burmese bias and are frequently incorrect in terms of minor facts and dates.

10A. Judson, *An Account of the American Baptist Mission to the Burman Empire*, 2d ed. (London, 1827). To this edition are appended extracts from her husband's journal.

ABBREVIATIONS

AA	Khin Khin Sein, ed., *Alaung-min-taya-gyi amein-daw-mya* [Edicts of Alaung-hpaya]. Rangoon, 1964.
BL OR.	British Library Oriental Manuscript.
BPC	*Bengal Political Consultations.* India Office Records. London.
BSP	*Bengal Secret and Political Consultations.* India Office Records. London.
GUBSS	J. G. Scott, and J. P. Hardiman, comps. *Gazetteer of Upper Burma and the Shan States.* 5 vols. in 2 parts. Rangoon, 1900–1901.
Hman-nan	*Hman-nan maha ya-zawin-daw-gyi* [Glass Palace chronicle]. 3 vols. Mandalay, 1921.
HRD	Historical Research Department, Ministry of Culture. Rangoon.
JBRS	*Journal of the Burma Research Society.*
KBZ	Tin (of Mandalay), comp. *Kon-baung-zet maha ya-zawin-daw-gyi* [History of the Kon-baung dynasty]. 3 vols. Rangoon, 1967–1968.
LBK	Thi-ri U-zana. *Law-ka byu-ha kyan* [Treatise on customary terms]. Rangoon, 1958.
LN-AA	Let-we Naw-rahta. *Alaung-min-taya-gyi ayei-daw-bon* [Biography of Alaung-hpaya]. In Hla Tin, ed., *Alaung-hpaya ayei-daw-bon hnazaung-dwe* [Two biographies of Alaung-hpaya]. Rangoon, 1961.

Maha ya-zawin	Kala. *Maha ya-zawin-gyi* [Great chronicle]. 3 vols. Rangoon, 1929–1961.
Manu wunana	Wuna Dama Kyaw-din. *Manu wunana damathat kyan* [*Damathat* of 1771]. Rangoon, 1878.
Manu-kye	D. Richardson, ed. and trans. *The Damathat, or the Laws of Menoo, Translated from the Burmese.* Moulmein, 1847.
MMM	Ya Gyaw. *Myan-ma maha min-gala min-gan-daw* [Burmese royal ceremonies]. Mandalay, 1905.
MMOS	Tin (of Pagan). *Myan-ma min ok-chok-pon sa-dan* [The administration of Burmese kings]. 5 vols. Rangoon, 1931–1933.
SNT	Tin (of Mandalay). *Shwei-nan-thon waw-ha-ra abi-dan* [Terminology used in the Golden Palace]. Mimeo, n.d.
Sit-tans	F. N. Trager, and W. J. Koenig. *Burmese Sit-tans, 1764–1826: Records of Rural Life and Administration.* Tucson, Ariz., 1979.
ZOK	J. S. Furnivall, and Pe Maung Tin, eds. *Zam-bu-di-pa ok-hsaung kyan* [The crown of Jambudipa]. Rangoon, 1960.

NOTES

Preface

1. These works include A. P. Phayre, *History of Burma* (London, 1883; rpt., London, 1967); G. E. Harvey, *History of Burma from the Earliest Times to 10 March 1824* (London, 1925; rpt., London, 1967); Htin Aung, *A History of Burma* (New York, 1967); and Tin Ohn, "Modern Historical Writing in Burmese," in *Historians of South East Asia*, ed. D. G. E. Hall (London, 1961).
2. Of J. S. Furnivall's numerous writings on the society and administration of the dynastic period, the most important are *An Introduction to the Political Economy of Burma* (Rangoon, 1931); "Burman Rule in Hanthawaddy," JBRS 4, no. 3 (1914): 209–13; and (with Pe Maung Tin), *Zam-bu-di-pa ok-hsaung kyan* [The crown of Jambudipa] (Rangoon, 1960). Unfortunately, he died before completing his English version of this last work. He gave the administrative records he collected to U Wun of Rangoon. Most of these are included in F. N. Trager and W. J. Koenig, *Burmese Sit-tans, 1764–1826: Records of Rural Life and Administration* (Tucson, Ariz., 1979).
3. See MMOS 1–5.
4. Mya Sein, *The Administration of Burma* (Rangoon, 1938; rpt., Singapore, 1973).
5. Subsequently published as V. B. Lieberman, *Burmese Administrative Cycles: Anarchy and Conquest, c. 1580–1760* (Princeton, N.J., 1984).
6. On dynastic history and foreign relations in general, see the works of Phayre, Harvey, and Htin Aung cited in note 1 above. For surveys of Anglo-Burmese and Franco-Burmese relations, see D. G. E. Hall, *Europe and Burma* (London, 1945) and his *A History of South-East Asia*, 3d ed. (London, 1968); and P. Pres-

chez, *Les relations entre la France et la Birmanie au XVIII*ᵉ *et au XIX*ᵉ *siècles* (Paris, 1967). Burmese relations with China and Thailand are surveyed in Kyaw Thet, "Burma's Relations with her Eastern Neighbours in the Konbaung Period, 1752-1819" (Ph.D. thesis, University of London, 1950).

7. The role of the *sangha* and religious wealth in post-Pagan Burmese history has received attention recently. M. Aung Thwin argues that monastic economic power similar to that which sapped the late Pagan dynasty played a similar role in succeeding dynasties as late as the nineteenth century. See his "The Role of *Sasana* Reform in Burmese History: Economic Dimensions of a Religious Purification," *Journal of Asian Studies* 38, no. 4 (1979): 671-88. This argument is well rebutted by V. B. Lieberman in his "The Political Significance of Religious Wealth in Burmese History: Some Further Thoughts," *Journal of Asian Studies* 39, no. 4 (1980): 753-69.

8. Early Kon-baung Burma is an excellent example of what Michael Adas terms the "contest state structure of precolonial politics in Southeast Asia." See his "'Moral Economy' or 'Contest State'?: Elite Demands and the Origins of Peasant Protest in Southeast Asia," *Journal of Social History* 13, no. 4 (1980): 521-46.

Chapter 1

1. The preceding discussion relies on C. A. Fisher, *South-East Asia: A Social, Economic and Political Geography*, 2d ed. (London, 1966), chapter 14 passim.
2. The best general treatment of Pagan is G. H. Luce, *Old Burma— Early Pagan*, 3 vols. (Locust Valley, N.Y., 1969-1970), 1: 1-127 passim. M. Aung Thwin, "Kingship, the *Sangha*, and Society in Pagan," in *Explorations in Early Southeast Asian History: The Origins of Southeast Asian Statecraft*, ed. K. R. Hall and J. K. Whitmore, Michigan Papers on South and Southeast Asia, no. 11 (Ann Arbor, 1976), 205-56 passim, offers another interpretation of the period. Than Tun, "The Buddhist Church in Burma during the Pagan Period, 1044-1287" (Ph.D. thesis, University of London, 1955) is the most comprehensive treatment of Buddhism in this period, with chapter 3 dealing specifically with Pagan administration. For the most systematic treatment of Pagan kingship, see J. Stargardt, "Social and Religious Aspects of Royal Power in Medieval Burma, from Inscriptions from Kyanshattha's Reign,

1084–1112," *Journal of the Economic and Social History of the Orient* 13, no. 3 (1970): 289–308.
3. On this point, see P. J. Bennett, *Conference under the Tamarind Tree: Three Essays in Burmese History*, Yale University Southeast Asia Studies Monograph Series, no. 15 (New Haven, 1971), 14–15.
4. The foregoing and following discussions of the Early and Restored Taung-ngu periods are drawn from V. B. Lieberman, *Burmese Administrative Cycles: Anarchy and Conquest, c. 1580–1760* (Princeton, N.J., 1984). Chapter 1 details the rise and fall of the First Taung-ngu dynasty.
5. See ibid., chapter 2, for the administration of the Restored Taung-ngu dynasty.
6. On the collapse of Taung-ngu rule, see ibid., chapters 3 and 4; Yi Yi, *Myan-ma naing-ngan achei-anei 1714–52* [The state of Burma, 1714–1752] (Rangoon, 1973); and N. J. Brailey, "A Re-Investigation of the Gwe of Eighteenth Century Burma," *Journal of Southeast Asian Studies* 1, no. 2 (1970): 33–47.
7. For Alaung-hpaya's campaigns and administration, see Lieberman, *Burmese Administrative Cycles*, chapter 5.
8. R. Halliday, *The Talaings* (Rangoon, 1917), 18.
9. See AA, 149; and M. Symes, *An Account of an Embassy to the Kingdom of Ava, Sent by the Governor-General of India, in the Year 1795* (London, 1800; rpt., Westmead, England, 1969), 41–43. The rising occurred in December 1758 or January 1759.
10. AA, 117.
11. KBZ 1: 404. The ruler of Ayuthia, Boromoraja V, was in fact killed by a stray musket shot during the sack of the city. The story of the campaign is told in detail in KBZ 1: 346–410 passim.
12. Ibid., 1: 418–23. See also G. H. Luce, "Chinese Invasions of Burma in the Eighteenth Century," JBRS 15, no. 2 (1925): 119.
13. KBZ (1: 470–71) gives the text of the treaty; the three campaigns are described in KBZ 1: 424–79 passim.
14. See "Journal du voyage de M. Feraud au royaume d'Ava," in H. Cordier, "Mémoires sur le Pégou, tirés des Archives de la Marine et des Colonies," *Revue de l'Extrême-Orient* 2, no. 4 (1883): 531–32. Cited hereafter as *Feraud's Journal*.
15. This episode is analyzed in detail in Kyaw Thet, "Burma's Relations with her Eastern Neighbours in the Konbaung Period, 1752–1819" (Ph.D. thesis, University of London, 1950), 314–34.
16. KBZ 1: 487.
17. Ibid., 1: 490–91 and 493.

18. Ibid., 1: 494.
19. K. Wenk, *The Restoration of Thailand under Rama I, 1782-1809* (Tucson, Ariz., 1968), 55.
20. KBZ 1: 514.
21. D. K. Wyatt, "Siam and Laos, 1767-1827," *Journal of Southeast Asian History* 4, no. 2 (1963): 20.
22. KBZ 2: 22-39; Wenk, *The Restoration of Thailand*, 43-64.
23. KBZ 2: 49-54; Wenk, *The Restoration of Thailand*, 64-68.
24. Wenk, *The Restoration of Thailand*, 89-91.
25. KBZ 1: 292-300, 369-70, and 480.
26. Ibid., 2: 1-17.
27. Ibid., 2: 37.
28. Ibid., 2: 91-101.
29. The French officer Bruno, resident in Pegu in the late summer of 1751, reported that the southerners could only field about thirty thousand infantry, poorly armed with lances and swords, and had made a particular request for arms. See Cordier, *Revue*, 510-11.
30. Cordier, *Revue*, 539-51 passim.
31. Bussey to Castries, 4 August 1784, in E. Gaudart, *Catalogue des manuscrits des anciennes archives de l'Inde française*, 6 vols. (Paris and Pondichéry, 1926-1935), 1: 159-60.
32. C. R. Boxer, "Asian Potentates and European Artillery in the 16th-18th Centuries: A Footnote to Gibson-Hill," *Journal of the Malaysian Branch of the Royal Asiatic Society* 38, no. 2 (1966): 171.
33. So many cannon were captured during the Ayuthia campaign of 1764-1767 that 150 were sent back to Ava as unnecessary to the siege of the city. Numbers of guns were also taken from Arakan in 1784-1785. Various contemporary European observers also noted the presence of many rusty guns.
34. See Boxer, "Asian Potentates and European Artillery," passim.
35. S. C. Sarkar, "The Negrais Settlement and After," JBRS 22, no. 2 (1922): 63-64.
36. Cordier, *Revue*, 521.
37. Cossigny to Bussy, 7 July 1786; and enclosures in H. Cordier, "Mémoires sur le Pégou," *T'oung Pao*, series 2, 23 (1923): 117-18; "Report of Civil Commissioner Lescalier to the National Convention and Executive Council, Pondichéry, 15 October 1794," in Gaudart, *Catalogue des manuscrits*, 2: 446-47; and P. Preschez, *Les relations entre la France et la Birmanie au XVIIIe et au XIXe siècles* (Paris, 1967), 21-30.
38. Cordier, *Revue*, 548.

39. M. S. Khan, "Captain George Sorrel's Mission to the Court of Amarapura, 1793-1794: An Episode in Anglo-Burmese Relations," *Journal of the Asiatic Society of Pakistan* 2 (1957): 131-53 passim.
40. See Symes, *Account of an Embassy*, passim.
41. See H. Cox, *Journal of a Residence in the Burmhan Empire* (London, 1821); and Pechell to Adam, 12 November 1812, BSP, 25 November 1812, document 79. These figures were supplied to the company by the Arakanese rebel Chin Pyan and hence are suspect, but the levy undoubtedly was heavy.
42. D. G. E. Hall, ed., *Michael Symes: Journal of his Second Embassy to the Court of Ava in 1802* (London, 1955), passim. Francis Buchanan, however, had submitted a bold but unsolicited plan for military and political intervention in Burma to the company in 1796. See "Francis Buchanan's Account of Burma in 1796," India Office Records, *Home Miscellaneous Series*, vol. 388, ff. 599-613.
43. B. R. Pearn, "King-Bering," JBRS 23, no. 1 (1933): 55-85 passim.
44. Ibid., 85.
45. B. R. Pearn, "Felix Carey and the English Baptist Mission in Burma," JBRS 28 (1938): 67.
46. KBZ 2: 119 and 126-27.
47. Ibid., 2: 158-65, 181-82, and 189-94.
48. D. G. E. Hall, *A History of South-East Asia*, 3d ed. (London, 1968), 595-97.
49. The forces of Maha Ban-du-la carried off thousands of people from Assam and Cachar in the early 1820s, but there is no evidence that this resulted in systematic resettlement in upper Burma.
50. Hall, *Michael Symes*, 183-84; 1802 *sit-tans* of the *myos* of Ma-u, Htan-daw-gyi, Zaung-du, and Han-tha Zaing-ganein, in *Sit-tans*, 77, 78, 80-81, and 85.
51. KBZ 1: 493-94 and 499.
52. See Symes, *Account of an Embassy*, 229; H. Gouger, *Personal Narrative of Two Years' Imprisonment in Burmah* (London, 1860), 19-20; T. A. Trant, *Two Years in Ava: From May 1824 to May 1826* (London, 1827), 3, and 235; and H. Cordier, "Les Français en Birmanie au XVIIIe siècle: Notes et documents," *T'oung Pao* 2 (1891): 29-30.
53. KBZ (2: 22-25 and 37-39) gives the Burmese forces as approximately 147,000 in the campaign of 1785 and 55,000 in 1786.

Comment on the casualty rate is in Cox to Shore, 25 November 1797, BPC, 2 May 1798, document 4.
54. KBZ 2: 91–101.
55. Cox to Shore, 25 November 1797, BPC, 2 May 1798, document 4.
56. See GUBSS 1.2: 432 and 2.1: 276; W. F. Grahame, *Report on the Settlement Operations in the Shwebo District, Season 1900–1906* (Rangoon, 1907), 63; and W. A. Hertz, *Report on the Settlement Operations in the Magwe District, Season 1897–1903* (Rangoon, 1903), 6.
57. Canning to Tushington, 22 October 1809, BPC, 26 December 1809, document 57.
58. Canning to Edmonstone, 9 September 1812, BSP, 25 September 1812, document 11.
59. Ibid.
60. Letter of 14 November 1809, in *Periodical Accounts Relative to the Baptist Missionary Society* 4 (1810): 171.
61. Canning to Edmonstone, 26 November 1811, BPC, 26 December 1811, document 6.
62. F. Carey to W. Carey, 20 February 1812, in *Monthly Circular Letters Relative to the Mission in India* 4 (1812): 29.

Chapter 2

1. The concept of social class developed from the critical study of European society and is therefore distinctive to western history and culture. The inutility of its application to societies outside that history and culture is reviewed by G. Balandier, *Political Anthropology* (New York, 1970), 91–92.
2. The relationship between consorts and the foreigners to whom they were provided by lower-status Burmese for money did not constitute marriage, but the rental of chattel goods. The French officer Flouest reported that such transactions often involved a written contract, that the price was between one hundred and two hundred *kyats* in 1784, and that neither the woman nor any children could be removed from the country. See "Journal du voyage de Lt. Flouest," in H. Cordier, "Les Français en Birmanie au XVIIIe siècle: Notes et documents," *T'oung Pao* 2 (1891): 24–27. Cited hereafter as *Flouest's Journal*.

3. *Manu-kye damathat*, cited in Gaung, *Translation of a Digest of the Burmese Buddhist Law Concerning Inheritance and Marriages*, 2 vols. (Rangoon, 1903–1909), 2: 246.
4. The British envoy Michael Symes noted in 1795 that the law recognized only one wife, but "concubinage, however, is admitted to an unlimited extent." His Italian contemporary Vincentius Sangermano similarly observed "when they have the means of maintaining them, the Burmese, besides their lawful wife, have two or three concubines." See M. Symes, *An Account of an Embassy to the Kingdom of Ava, Sent by the Governor-General of India, in the Year 1795* (London, 1800; rpt., Westmead, England, 1969), 313; and V. Sangermano, *A Description of the Burmese Empire*, trans. by W. Tandy, 5th ed. (London, 1966), 164.
5. *Manu-kye*, 281.
6. There was a member of the central administration called the *amwei* (inheritance) *wun*, whose duty was to decide cases of disputed inheritance on the basis of the *damathats*. See MMOS 4: 76.
7. *Manu-kye*, 281.
8. Ibid., 267.
9. Ibid., 280.
10. Ibid., 281.
11. *Manu wunana damathat*, cited in Gaung, *Translation of a Digest*, 1: 118.
12. *Manu-kye*, 280.
13. The foregoing ideas are drawn from M. E. Spiro, *Buddhism and Society: A Great Tradition and its Burmese Vicissitudes* (London, 1971), chapters 2–5.
14. Ibid., 411–12.
15. See Sangermano, *Description of the Burmese Empire*, 116 and 122; and *Flouest's Journal*, 13.
16. On monastic education, see E. M. Mendelson, *Sangha and State in Burma: A Study of Monastic Sectarianism and Leadership* (Ithaca and London, 1975), 150–57 passim.
17. Ibid., chapter 1 passim, reviews the history and nature of sectarianism in the Burmese *sangha*. Although there have been many small sects (*gaing*) historically, the main cleavages within the *sangha* have been Mon versus Burman monks, town versus forest monks, meditating versus scholarly monks, a Burman versus Ceylonese ordination, and a long and bitter conflict in the eighteenth century between monks covering one shoulder with the robe and those covering both.

18. For example, in ethically motivated acts to prevent trangression of the fundamental Buddhist precept against the taking of life, monks occasionally prevented the execution of criminals. See Sangermano, *Description of the Burmese Empire*, 122; and *Flouest's Journal*, 13.
19. B. M. Barua, *Asoka and His Inscriptions* (Calcutta, 1968), chapter 7 passim, shows clearly that the early Indian *sangha* was also totally dependent on the state, and cites many approving references from Buddhist texts demonstrating that the monks felt this to be the natural state of affairs.
20. The attempt to identify possible monkish participation in political or governmental affairs is hampered by the fact that it is difficult to define what a monk was. In fact, the *sangha* was an open institution through which much of the male population passed for varying lengths of time. It is also important to differentiate between career monks, those who had spent ten years or more in the *sangha* and had passed the difficult state examination in the scriptures, and those who were merely spending time in a monastery for personal reasons. In either case, however, political or governmental involvement of whatever nature necessitated leaving the order. Michael Symes was quite to the point when he wrote in 1795: "In the various commotions of the empire, I never heard that the Rahaans had taken any active share, or publically interfered in politics, or engaged in war" (Symes, *Account of an Embassy*, 212).
21. Than Tun, "The Influence of Occultism in Burmese History with Special Reference to Bodawpaya's Reign, 1782–1819," *Bulletin of the Burma Historical Commission*, 1, no. 2 (1960): 117–45 passim, explores the nature of these histories of the future, particularly their influence on Bo-daw-hpaya. The most famous of the court astrologers during the reign of Bo-daw-hpaya was an official titled Ayu-daw-min-gala, whose skill in interpreting omens and prophecies gave him considerable influence over state affairs.
22. See Spiro, *Buddhism and Society*, 438–39.
23. General statements of the main levels of society and their grades are given in *Manu-kye*, 91, 125, and 149–50; *Manu wunana*, 376; and *Manu damathat*, cited in Gaung, *Translation of a Digest*, 2: 24–25. On the *thahteis* and their functions, see LBK, 372; *Manu-kye*, 149–50; and MMOS 4: 108. On the commoners, see *Manu-kye*, 150; and MMOS 2: 52.
24. *Manu-kye*, 149. The *damathats* are filled with similar examples. Body price is discussed in *Manu wunana*, 326 and 410.

25. For example, *Manu wunana* (306) says, "If a person is not suitably respectful and humble to a person of superior rank, abuses him verbally, let him pay 100 of silver. Why? Because that degraded person has broken his traditional duty."
26. MMOS (2: 51) gives the sumptuary rules for the wealthy.
27. Derivations and discussions of various titles can be found in Maha Zei-ya Thin-hkaya, *Waw-ha-ra li-nat-hta di-pani kyan* [Treatise on recondite words] (Mandalay, 1899). On the classes of titles, see MMOS (4: 154-55); and SNT, 35. BL OR. 3480/3 ("Statement of the Titles Usually Conferred on Burmese Officials and Men of Rank") is also useful as it relates functional offices with title classes and the associated trappings of rank.
28. SNT, 15-16 and 19; and LBK, 382-83. A detailed diagram of the places of the court can be found on the page facing MMOS 4: 130.
29. D. G. E. Hall, ed., *Michael Symes: Journal of his Second Embassy to the Court of Ava in 1802* (London, 1955), 163.
30. *Manu-kye*, 393.
31. On this point, see Sangermano, *Description of the Burmese Empire*, 158 and 161-62; Symes, *Account of an Embassy*, 123 and 243-44; B. R. Pearn, ed., "A Burma Diary of 1810," JBRS 27, no. 3 (1937): 292; and F. Carey to W. Carey, 28 January 1808, in *Monthly Circular Letters Relative to the Mission in India* 3 (1808): 37.
32. Symes, *Account of an Embassy*, 310.
33. Canning to Edmonstone, 9 September 1812, BSP, 25 September 1812, document 11.
34. On the fall from power of the *yei wun* of Rangoon, Canning reported "The materials of his dress and betel utensils, as likewise the height of his umbrella, are heavy charges against him." See Canning to Edmonstone, 9 August 1803, BSP, 5 July 1804, document 128.
35. *Manu-kye*, 126. The illustration is an adaptation of the Matanga jataka (see E. B. Cowell, ed., *The Jataka, or Stories of the Buddha's Former Births*, 6 vols. [London, 1957], 4: 235ff.), which is concerned with pride of caste and not positional change. *Manu wunana* (314) makes a similar statement on positional change without an illustration.
36. For example, Bo-daw-hpaya condemned the inhabitants of the village of Hpaung-ga, some of whom had supported the rebellion of Nga Hpon in 1782, to be perpetual slaves of the Aung-myei-law-ka Pagoda, which he had built on the site of the house in

which he had lived as an exile during the reign of Sin-gu. On slavery in general, see *Manu-kye*, 189–95.
37. *Flouest's Journal*, 394.
38. Sangermano, *Description of the Burmese Empire*, 156. See also *Flouest's Journal* (394), in which he further notes that many people preferred debt bondage to the rigors of continued taxation.
39. *Sit-tans*, 405 and 413.
40. Canning to Edmonstone, 19 January 1812, BPC, 21 February 1812, document 30.
41. For some examples and comments on the foregoing, see M. Laurie, *Report on the Settlement Operations in the Mandalay District, Season 1892–1893* (Rangoon, 1894), 28; R. S. Wilkie, *Burma Gazetteer—Yamethin District*, vol. A (Rangoon, 1934), 35; and A. Judson, *An Account of the American Baptist Mission to the Burman Empire*, 2d ed. (London, 1827), 70. On the reciprocal relationship between bandits and officials, see H. S. Spearman, *British Burma Gazetteer*, 2 vols. (Rangoon, 1879–1880), 2: 376; and Laurie, *Report on Settlement Operations*, 28.
42. A striking example of the extensiveness of this mobility is found in the 1803 *sit-tan* of Hkwei-gyo Village in Salei Myo, in which the headman reported that thirty-nine of the sixty *athi* houses in his jurisdiction had moved elsewhere since 1783 and only two houses had moved in (see *Sit-tans*, 329–30). For the mobility of the members of a crown service unit, see the *sit-tan* of Let-ma Wun Daing in *Sit-tans*, 384ff.
43. The 1765 land roll of Pagan is published in English in *Sit-tans*, 191ff.
44. G. H. Luce, *Old Burma—Early Pagan*, 3 vols. (Locust Valley, N.Y., 1969–1970), 1: 4.
45. For the 1784 and 1802 *sit-tans* of Taywin-daing and the 1783 *sit-tan* of Ywa-tha, see *Sit-tans*, 278ff.
46. Dr. F. Buchanan's "Journal of Progress and Observations during the Continuance of the Deputation from Bengal to Ava in 1795," India Office Records, MSS.Eur.C.12, f. 43. Cited hereafter as *Buchanan's Journal*.
47. See M. Adas, *The Burma Delta: Economic Development and Social Change on an Asian Rice Frontier, 1852–1941* (Madison, Wis., 1974), chapter 1 passim, for a discussion of the agricultural environment of the delta in precolonial Burmese society.
48. For the extant parts of the Han-tha-wadi land rolls of 1784 and 1802 and the Martaban land roll of 1784, see *Sit-tans*, 62–131 passim.

49. The 1783 and 1802 *sit-tans* of Bassein given in *Sit-tans* (131ff.) are uninformative about agriculture, but see H. P. Hewlitt and J. Clague, *Burma Gazetteer—Bassein District*, vol. A (Rangoon, 1916), 32–35.
50. For a survey of Burmese industries c. 1800, see Tun Wai, *Economic Development of Burma from 1800 till 1940* (Rangoon, 1961), 11–20 passim.
51. For example, see the description of road systems in *Buchanan's Journal*, ff. 7, 29, and 247.
52. KBZ (1: 419–21) refers to caravans of individual Chinese traders numbering four hundred oxen and one thousand pack horses in 1765.
53. Tun Wai, *Economic Development of Burma*, 22.
54. For examples, see the description of the *kins* in Taung-ngu and the maritime *kins* around Rangoon in *Sit-tans*, 73–75, 143, and 179; also MMOS 4: 1–3.
55. The largest of these companies was a group of eight Burmans who, in the early nineteenth century, made an annual payment of two thousand *viss* of silver to the crown for the privilege of being the sole merchants of timber, sticklac, arsenic, and related products at Rangoon, Bassein, and the towns of the interior where they maintained agents. See Canning to Edmonstone, 19 January 1812, BPC, 21 February 1812, document 30.
56. The two most extensive discussions of Burmese specie are given in Cox to Mornington, 15 September 1798, BPC, 10 October 1799, document 5; and H. Burney, "Observations on the Currency of Ava," BSP, 15 April 1831, document 13. See also the remarks in "Journal du voyage de M. Feraud au royaume d'Ava," in H. Cordier, "Mémoires sur le Pégou, tirés des Archives de la Marine et des Colonies," *Revue de l'Extrême-Orient* 2, no. 4 (1883): 565–66. Coins or bits did circulate to some extent in Martaban prior to the reign of Hsin-hpyu-shin and in the coastal areas of Arakan due to the coasting trade. Bo-daw-hpaya attempted to introduce copper and silver coins minted with equipment brought by Hiram Cox in 1797, but the face value of the coins was fixed so unrealistically above their actual metallic value that people refused to use them. The effort was finally abandoned in 1812. See MMOS 3: 139 and 4: 91–92.
57. MMOS (3: 51) and the Taung-ngu land roll of 1784, in *Sit-tans* (146) both give the market price of paddy as one *kyat* of silver per five bushels.

58. Most of these factors are discussed in Adas, *Burma Delta*, 22–28 passim.
59. On the concept of levelling mechanisms, see M. Nash, *Primitive and Peasant Economic Systems* (San Francisco, 1966), 35–36.
60. J. Crawfurd, *Journal of an Embassy from the Governor General of India to the Court of Ava in the Year 1826* (1829 ed., 470), cited in Tun Wai, *Economic Development of Burma*, 27.
61. See V. B. Lieberman, "Ethnic Politics in Eighteenth-Century Burma," *Modern Asian Studies* 12, no. 3 (1978): 455–82, especially 456–62, for a discussion of contemporary ethnicity.
62. For a general discussion of the Mons, see R. Halliday, *The Talaings* (Rangoon, 1917), passim.
63. On the military use of the Mons by Thailand, see K. Wenk, *The Restoration of Thailand Under Rama I, 1782–1809* (Tucson, Ariz., 1968), 43. Hall, *Michael Symes* (211) also notes the military contribution of the Mons to Thailand.
64. On the maladministration leading to the rising of 1758–1759, see AA, 149 and 172; on the rising itself, see Symes, *Account of an Embassy*, 41–43; and Hpo Kya, *Pathein ya-zawin* [History of Bassein] (Rangoon, 1933), 81–82. For the rising of 1774, see KBZ (1: 493–94); and *Flouest's Journal*, 31. The rising of 1783 is described in *Flouest's Journal*, 32–39; Espinassy to Bussy, 15 October 1783, in H. Cordier, "Mémoires sur le Pégou," *T'oung Pao*, series 2, 23 (1923): 111–16; and Sangermano, *Description of the Burmese Empire*, 69–70.
65. On the Mon migrations, see R. Halliday, "Immigration of the Mons into Siam," *Journal of the Siam Society* 10, no. 3 (1913): 1–13 passim.
66. *Buchanan's Journal*, f. 250. Cox to Shore, 25 November 1797, BPC, 2 May 1798, document 4, contains a similar observation.
67. F. Carey to W. Carey, 10 March 1813, in *Periodical Accounts Relative to the Baptist Missionary Society* 5 (1813): 257.
68. B. A. N. Parrott, *Report on the Settlement Operations in the Hanthawaddy and Pegu Districts, Season 1882–1883* (Rangoon, 1884), 3.
69. For a general discussion of Shan society, see E. R. Leach, *Political Systems of Highland Burma: A Study of Kachin Social Structure*, London School of Economics Monographs on Social Anthropology, no. 44 (London, 1954), 213–16 passim.
70. MMOS 4: 116 and 120.
71. See LN-AA, 65 and 90; and KBZ 2: 22–25.
72. MMOS 4: 318.

73. See F. K. Lehman, *The Structure of Ch'in Society*, Illinois Studies in Anthropology, no. 3 (Urbana, Ill., 1963), 27–28; and Leach, *Political Systems*, 124, 208, and 242.
74. See MMOS 4: 122; and the *sit-tans* of Kaw-li-ya, Htan-daw-gyi, Kyaung-bya, Hpaung-lin, Hmaw-bi, and Maw-lon in Han-tha-wadi and the 1784 Martaban *sit-tan*, in *Sit-tans*, 70–71, 75, 76, 79, 80, 85, and 102. See also Pyin-nya, *Kayin ya-zawin* [History of the Karens] (Rangoon, 1929), passim.
75. *Buchanan's Journal*, f. 23. On this movement see also Hewlitt and Clague, *Burma Gazetteer*, 23.
76. For the Karen roles in the campaigns of 1774, 1785, and 1786, see KBZ 1: 504 and 2: 30 and 38.
77. An eyewitness to the rising of 1783, the French officer Flouest noted the extent of this concern on the part of the Burmans. See *Flouest's Journal*, 30.

Chapter 3

1. *Manu-kye*, 7. The foregoing discussion is a composite account based on *Manu-kye*, 5–8; *Manu wunana*, 4–6; *Hman-nan*, 1: 29–34; and *Maha ya-zawin*, 1: 5–14. Early Buddhist thought does not contain any concept of the supreme morality or bodhisattahood of Maha Thamada. On this point see T. W. R. Davids, trans., *Dialogues of the Buddha*, 3 vols. (London, 1899–1921), 3: 88.
2. *Manu-kye*, 8. Identical passages occur in *Maha ya-zawin*, 1: 14; and *Hman-nan*, 1: 34.
3. The *Loka niti*, a standard ethical text studied in eighteenth-century Burma, repeatedly emphasizes the necessity of monarchy, saying, for example, "Dreary is a sonless home, dreary a kingdom without a king" and "In whatever place these five—a man of wealth, a man of learning, a king, a river, a doctor—are not to be found, there a man should not live for even a day." See J. Gray, *Ancient Proverbs and Maxims from Burmese Sources or, The Niti Literature of Burma* (London, 1886), 26. On classical Buddhist political theory, see B. G. Gokhale, "Early Buddhist Kingship," *Journal of Asian Studies* 26, no. 1 (1966): 15–22 passim.
4. LN-AA, 18. This may have been a common chronicle cliché, however, as *Maha ya-zawin* (3: 113–14) says that the people

beseeched Nyaung-yan to save them from anarchy, just as the first people had beseeched Maha Thamada.
5. KBZ 1: 20–21.
6. *Manu-kye*, 148.
7. Maung Tin, ed. and trans., "Rajadhiraja Vilasini or The Manifestation of the King of Kings, a Pali Historical Work," JBRS 4, no. 1 (1914): 18. This is a paraphrase of a passage concerning *dhamma* and *cakkavattis* in the *Anguttara nikaya*. See F. L. Woodward and E. M. Hare, trans., *The Book of the Gradual Sayings (Anguttara Nikaya), or More Numbered Suttas*, 5 vols. (London, 1932–1936), 3: 115.
8. J. Stargardt, "Social and Religious Aspects of Royal Power in Medieval Burma, from Inscriptions from Kyanshattha's Reign, 1084–1112," *Journal of the Economic and Social History of the Orient* 13, no. 3 (1970): 305.
9. *Manu-kye*, 154.
10. *Maha ya-zawin*, 1: 44; *Hman-nan*, 1: 88.
11. See *Maha ya-zawin*, 1: 45; *Hman-nan*, 1: 89; and Maung Tin, "Manifestation," 16. The texts of the Pali canon give the rate of tax as one-sixth. See the discussion of the fiscal system in chapter 4.
12. Ibid.
13. LBK, 5–6.
14. AA, 9–10.
15. *Manu-kye*, 7.
16. Ibid., 51.
17. Ibid., 117 and 129.
18. M. Symes, *An Account of an Embassy to the Kingdom of Ava, Sent by the Governor-General of India, in the Year 1795* (London, 1800; rpt., Westmead, England, 1969), 306–7.
19. MMM, 27.
20. Davids, *Dialogues*, 3: 134.
21. Ibid., 3: 137–38.
22. C. Drekmeier, *Kingship and Community in Early India* (Stanford, 1962), 162–63 and 203.
23. Davids, *Dialogues*, 3: 62.
24. Ibid., 3: 63–64 and 139–65. The seven treasures are given as the wheel, the flying white elephant, the flying horse, the radiant gem, the perfect woman, the perfect treasurer, and the perfect adviser (ibid., 2: 204–8).
25. Ibid., 3: 73–74. The advent of the Buddha Metteyya and his relation to Sankha is the subject of a brief Pali work entitled

Anagatavamsa [History of the future], which was and continues to be well known in Burma. A printed Burmese text is *Anagatawin kyan* (Mandalay, 1927).
26. Compare LBK (17) with Woodward and Hare, *Gradual Sayings*, 3: 117.
27. Compare LBK (88 and 119) with Davids, *Dialogues*, 2: 208.
28. *Hman-nan*, 1: 87–88. In essence the duties enjoin the *cakkavatti* to treat beneficently the various elements of society and the beasts and birds, to consult with wise men, and to distribute wealth.
29. Davids, *Dialogues*, 2: 3.
30. In orthodox Buddhism the *arahat* was a monk so unattached to the world that he achieved *nibbana* on his death. In popular Burmese belief, the *arahat* postpones his extinction and uses his miraculous powers to remain in the world to help people until the coming of Metteyya. See J. P. Ferguson, "The Arahat Ideal in Modern Burmese Buddhism," unpublished paper presented at the Association for Asian Studies Annual Meeting, New York, March 1977 (cited by permission of the author). On popular messianism and cults, see E. M. Mendelson, "A Messianic Buddhist Association in Upper Burma," *Bulletin of the School of Oriental and African Studies* 24, no. 3 (1961): 560–80 passim.
31. Than Tun, "Religion in Burma, A.D. 1000–1300," JBRS 42, no. 2 (1959): 53.
32. G. H. Luce, *Old Burma—Early Pagan*, 3 vols. (Locust Valley, N.Y., 1969–1970), 1: 87–88.
33. Ibid., 1: 61. As befitted a future buddha, Kyan-zit-tha also had a personal set of *jatakas* relating his previous lives in India.
34. On this point, see V. B. Lieberman, *Burmese Administrative Cycles: Anarchy and Conquest, c. 1580–1760* (Princeton, N.J., 1984), 229ff. The popular name Alaung-hpaya is the Burmese word for *bodhisatta*, while his regnal title of Buddhankura Maha Dama Ya-za meant "Embryo Buddha, King of Righteousness."
35. See Pannasami, *The History of the Buddha's Religion (Sasanavamsa)*, trans. by B. C. Law (London, 1952), 127–28; and Yazein-da, *Tha-thana bahu thu-ta paka-thani* [Explanation of religious topics] (Rangoon, 1928), 100.
36. See, for example, KBZ 1: 245 and 298.
37. Taw Sein Ko, "A Preliminary Study of the Po:U:Daung Inscription of S'inbyuhin, 1774 A.D.," *Indian Antiquary* 23, no. 1 (1893): 2; and Tun Nyein, *Inscriptions of Pagan, Pinya and Ava: Translation with Notes* (Rangoon, 1899), 21–22 and 169.

38. H. Cox, *Journal of a Residence in the Burmhan Empire* (London, 1821), 229–30.
39. Letter from Luigi de Grondona, Vicar Apostolic of Ava, to John Canning, extracted in Canning to Adam, 6 October 1813, BPC, 20 October 1813, document 25. V. Sangermano, *A Description of the Burmese Empire*, trans. by W. Tandy, 5th ed. (London, 1966), 75, also gives an account of the episode, which, since he left Burma in 1806, is undoubtedly derived from letters from other Italian missionaries still in Burma. In a letter dated 5 August 1816 the American missionary Adoniram Judson wrote "just at this time, the monarch of the country has taken a violent hate to the priests of his own religion, and is endeavouring, with all his power, to extirpate the whole order" (see *American Baptist Magazine and Missionary Intelligencer*, new series, 1 [1817–1818]: 99). Subsequent letters of missionaries printed in this publication report that the conflict ended only with the accession of Ba-gyi-daw in 1819. A modern Burmese writer, U Ya-zein-da, says only that Bo-daw-hpaya "apostatized" and made changes in the religion, but encountered so much opposition from the monks and people that he had to order a return to the *status quo ante* (see Ya-zein-da, *Tha-thana bahu*, 114). The indigenous religious and royal chronicles do not mention the episode.
40. A similar incident occurred in Thailand when the ruler Phya Tak (1767–1782) claimed arahatship over the opposition of the Thai *sangha*. Elements in common with Bo-daw-hpaya's claims were a strong belief in his personal *kamma* and in his destiny to restore the realm and religion, which combined to produce something of a "Buddhist superman complex." Phya Tak also severely punished the *sangha* for rebuffing his aspirations. See R. Lingat, "La double crise de l'eglise Bouddique au Siam (1767–1851)," *Cahiers d'Histoire Mondiale* 4, no. 2 (1958): 409–10.
41. LBK, 119.
42. Maung Tin, "Manifestation," 21.
43. Symes, *Account of an Embassy*, 448.
44. LBK, 371–72.
45. KBZ 1: 558 and 2: 228. The "four important precepts" are the first four of the five moral precepts.
46. Ibid., 1: 70–71. See also the Hnget-pyit-taung inscription of 1758 in Tun Nyein, *Inscriptions*, 56.
47. LBK, 381.
48. Maung Tin, "Manifestation," 21. On the general use of capital punishment by all the early Kon-baung rulers in cases of viola-

tion of the precepts, even by members of the royal family, see Sangermano, *Description of the Burmese Empire*, 74 and 116; Symes, *Account of an Embassy*, 51; *Periodical Accounts Relative to the Baptist Missionary Society* 3 (1806): 435; Canning to Edmonstone, 19 January 1812, BPC, 21 February 1812, document 30; and "Journal du voyage de Lt. Flouest," in H. Cordier, "Les Français en Birmanie au XVIIIe siècle: Notes et documents," *T'oung Pao* 2 (1891): 13.

49. The most sacred structure in Buddhism, the true pagoda is a reliquary believed to have the same uncanny power as buddhas, monks, and kings. Pagoda worship is an ancient Buddhist custom prescribed by the scriptures. For ruler or subject, there was and continues to be no title of greater prestige than that of donor of a pagoda. See M. E. Spiro, *Buddhism and Society: A Great Tradition and its Burmese Vicissitudes* (London, 1971), 204.
50. KBZ 1: 349; 2: 211–14.
51. LBK, 380–81, 383, and 394.
52. See ibid., 382 and 394–95.
53. On the use of crown revenues for state merit-making in Prome and Taung-ngu, see *Sit-tans*, 136 and 147.
54. See, for example, the 1805 *sit-tan* of the Magyi-yon palace guards, in *Sit-tans*, 391.
55. On Asoka, see H. G. Van Zeyst, "Asoka," in *Encyclopedia of Buddhism*, ed. G. P. Malalasekara (Colombo, 1961).
56. S. Dutt, *Buddhist Monks and Monasteries of India* (London, 1962), 80.
57. On the development of the Asoka legend and traditions of *sangha* reform in Theravada Buddhism, see H. Bechert, "Theravada Buddhist Sangha: Some Observations on Historical and Political Factors in its Development," *Journal of Asian Studies* 29, no. 4 (1970): 761–78, especially 763–64.
58. KBZ 1: 556. For Hsin-hpyu-shin's association of himself with the legendary Asokan tradition of pagoda building, see Taw Sein Ko, "Po:U:Daung Inscription," 2. On the Asokan influence in Burmese coronation traditions, see MMM, 1; Maung Tin, "Manifestation," 18; and Ya-zein-da, *Tha-thana-bahu*, 88. Luce, *Old Burma—Early Pagan* (1: 109, 235, 238, and 246) notes the varied Asokan influences in the early Pagan period.
59. LBK, 64–65.
60. See, for example, KBZ 1: 535.
61. For example, apparently to neutralize the deaths of his rivals Maung Maung and Sin-gu, in 1782 Bo-daw-hpaya offered robes

with his own hands to five thousand monks he had invited to the palace (KBZ 1: 545). During the contest for the throne in early 1782, he is reported to have told his followers: "I do not want to become king and cause the law of demerit to increase" (KBZ 1: 527).

62. *Hman-nan*, 1: 247–48. This translation is from Pe Maung Tin and G. H. Luce, trans., *The Glass Palace Chronicle of the Kings of Burma* (London, 1923), 60. See *Hman-nan* (1: 299) for a similar explanation of the death of Anaw-rahta.
63. See, for example, KBZ 1: 24; and AA, 9–10.
64. KBZ 1: 524.
65. Woodward and Hare, *Gradual Sayings*, 3: 116.
66. See *Maha ya-zawin*, 1: 43; and *Hman-nan*, 1: 87.
67. The most developed statement of this origin story is in *Maha ya-zawin*, 1: 143ff. G. H. Luce, "Old Kyaukse and the Coming of the Burmans" (JBRS 42, no. 1 [1959]: 90) derives the origin story of Pyu-saw-hti from a Buddhist legend brought from Nanchao by the migrating Burmans. Not yet Buddhist, the Burmans ignored the Buddhist parts of the legend and remembered only the heroic aspects.
68. LN-AA, 8.
69. For examples of these edicts from 1755, see AA, 12 and 16.
70. Pe Maung Tin, *Myan-ma sa-bei thamaing* [History of Burmese literature] (Rangoon, 1955), 197–98.
71. *Hman-nan*, 1: 191.
72. Yi Yi, "Kon-baung hkit sit-tan-mya" [*Sit-tans* of the Kon-baung period] (JBRS 49, no. 1 [1966]: 76), citing a manuscript biography of Alaung-hpaya. *Kyei-gaing* was a position subordinate to headman, but in some cases functioned as headman. The same source states that Alaung-hpaya held the personal honorific title of Bala Nan-da-gyaw, so he must have been a man of some local consequence. KBZ (1: 24) says that Alaung-hpaya was the *asi-yin* of Mok-hso-bo, another local office that could function as headman.
73. See Lieberman, *Burmese Administrative Cycles* (239–40) on Alaung-hpaya's early quest for legitimacy.
74. All sources agree on these facts. See, for example, LN-AA, 12–13; and KBZ 1: 15–16.
75. Than Tun, "History of Burma, A.D. 1000–1300," *Bulletin of the Burma Historical Commission* 1, no. 1 (1960): 51–52.
76. I am indebted to Professor Hla Pe for this point.

77. B. C. Law, "A Short Account of the Wandering Teachers at the Time of the Buddha," *Journal and Proceedings of the Asiatic Society of Bengal*, new series, 14, no. 7 (1918): 399–406 passim. On Kautalya and the Arthashastra school, see Drekmeier, *Kingship and Community*, chapters 11 and 12 passim.
78. M. H. Bode, *The Pali Literature of Burma* (London, 1909), 107.
79. L. Sternbach, "The Pali Lokaniti and the Burmese Niti Kyan and Their Sources," *Bulletin of the School of Oriental and African Studies* 26, no. 2 (1963): 329–45 passim.
80. Gray, *Ancient Proverbs*, 19.
81. Ibid., 132.
82. Wuna Dama Kyaw-din, *Manu tha-ra shwei-myin damathat* [*Damathat* of 1772] (Rangoon, 1879), 18–19. Compare this passage with Gray, *Ancient Proverbs*, 79–80 and 133. See also *Manu wunana* (374–75) on kingcraft and punishment.
83. Gray, *Ancient Proverbs*, 137. Gokhale, "Early Buddhist Kingship" (17 and 21) notes that the early Buddhist theory of kingship contained most of these Arthashastran elements, as it could not avoid the realistic necessity of force in government.
84. Taw Sein Ko, "Po:U:Daung Inscription," 4.
85. The thirteen kinds of *abhiseka* are given in SNT, 232.
86. These ceremonies are described in Yi Yi, "Life at the Burmese Court under the Konbaung Kings," JBRS 44, no. 1 (1961): 85–129 passim; and in MMM, 1–188 passim.
87. On Brahmans, see MMOS 4: 111; LBK, 105–6; SNT, 97; and Symes, *Account of an Embassy*, 100. Than Tun, "The Influence of Occultism in Burmese History with Special Reference to Bodawpaya's Reign, 1782–1819," *Bulletin of the Burma Historical Commission* 1, no. 2 (1960): 117–45 passim, also has interesting material on this subject.
88. Cox to Shore, 25 November 1797, BPC, 2 March 1798, document 4.
89. *Manu-kye*, 29.
90. Ibid., 43, 179, and 228.
91. Ibid., 91. For a similar statement, see Gray, *Ancient Proverbs*, 126.
92. For examples from the Burmese *Raja niti*, see Gray, *Ancient Proverbs*, 120, 124–25, 126, 128–29, and 140–41.
93. "Journal du voyage de M. Feraud au royaume d'Ava," in H. Cordier, "Mémoires sur le Pégou, tirés des Archives de la Marine et des Colonies," *Revue de l'Extrême-Orient* 2, no. 4 (1883): 543.
94. Gokhale, "Early Buddhist Kingship," 22.

Chapter 4

1. V. B. Lieberman, *Burmese Administrative Cycles: Anarchy and Conquest, c. 1580–1760* (Princeton, N.J., 1984), chapter 5 passim, discusses Alaung-hpaya's administrative reconstitution.
2. S. P. Blake, "The Patrimonial-Bureaucratic Empire of the Mughals," *Journal of Asian Studies* 39, no. 1 (1979): 77–94, especially 79–80.
3. The Hlut-taw is discussed extensively in MMOS 3: 162–207 passim.
4. After 1798, for example, the adult princes of the blood directed the Hlut-taw, and orders were issued in the names of the crown, Sagaing, Prome, Pagan, and Pahkan princes. For examples, see Yi Yi, "Kon-baung hkit-u myo-ne ok-chok-pon" [Early Kon-baung provincial administration], *Pyei-daung-zu myan-ma naing-ngan sa-bei hnin lu-hmu-yei gya-ne* 1, no. 2 (1968): 381–82.
5. ZOK, 66.
6. There seems to have been no real differentiation made between domestic and foreign affairs until 1827, when one *wun-gyi* was made responsible for relations with the East India Company. See MMOS 3: 205.
7. Ibid., 4: 312–13. A 1783 *sit-tan* for one of these groups is extracted in MMOS 4: 317. There were similar groups in Taung-ngu and Martaban, but they were under the territorial authorities who collected and submitted the silver revenue.
8. HRD 6361, 47. See the 1765 and 1784 *sit-tans* of one of these thirteen villages, the Four Villages of Maw-hkwin (*Sit-tans*, 370–75). The 1784 document traces the increase of the jurisdiction's gold tax from the original $4^{1/8}$ *kyats* at the establishment of the tract by Bayin-naung in the sixteenth century to $36^{1/4}$ *kyats* in 1784.
9. *Sit-tans*, 405. See also the comments in W. F. Grahame, *Report on the Settlement Operations in the Shwebo District, Season 1900–1906* (Rangoon, 1907), 120.
10. MMOS 4: 79. See *Sit-tans* (384–86) for the 1805 *sit-tan* of a *daing* unit assigned to capital garrison duty. One of the elite *thwei-thauks* of the exterior, formed by Hsin-hpyu-shin in 1764, was composed of sixty-five chiefs of *daing* units (KBZ 1: 362–63).
11. *Sit-tans*, 405–6.
12. MMOS 4: 112.
13. HRD 2984, 49; "Census of the Population of the Kingdom of Ava as Taken in the Burman Year 1145 A.D. 1783, and as Revised

in 1188 A.D. 1826," Royal Commonwealth Society, Henry Burney Papers, B.I., contains similar lists of *taiks* and their house totals. The latter also gives the number of villages per *taik*. See *Sit-tans* (400ff.) for an analysis of these documents. The major *taiks* should not be confused with the local jurisdictions called *taik* existing in lower Burma during the later Kon-baung period.

14. See MMOS 4: 305; and SNT, 40–41 and 47.
15. These figures are taken from "Census of the Population of the Kingdom of Ava" (see note 13).
16. This phrase is one of a number of minor omissions in the printed text of the Han-tha-wadi 1802 *sit-tan* included in J. S. Furnivall, "Some Historical Documents" (JBRS 6, no. 3 [1916]: 213–23; 8, no. 1 [1918]: 40–52; and 9, no. 1 [1919]: 33–52), and is taken from the manuscript version (MSS 469–470) in the National Library, Rangoon. Dr. Yi Yi collated these materials with the printed text and kindly allowed me to use them. See *Sit-tans* (71ff.) for a revised translation. Information on the garrisons of Martaban, Taung-ngu, and Prome is in U Pyin-nya, *Mok-tama ya-zawin-baung-gyok hnin Mok-tama sit-tan sa-haung kyan* [Complete history of Martaban with the old Martaban land roll] (Thahton, 1927), 33–34; and *Sit-tans*, 136–39 and 142–43.
17. MMOS 4: 111.
18. SNT (101) lists eleven *myos* under the Myei-lat Wun: Mainggaing, Maing-byin, Maing-naung, Maing-don, Tahpet Lamaing, Kan-ta-rawadi, Zaga, Non-gan-win-gan, Kyaing-gan, Maing-maw, and Lwe-bon.
19. MMOS 4: 111. There are a number of references in the *sit-tans* to villages and *myos* in the jurisdictions of the Myo-lat and Ywa-lat *wuns*. A list of fifteen newly established villages in the charge of the latter *wun* is given in *Sit-tans*, 406. Identifiable names were located in Shwei-bo, Kyauk-hse, Tha-ra-wadi, and Martaban districts.
20. MMOS 4: 111.
21. "*Sit-tan* of the Nine Districts (Kyauk-hse) for 1784," in Ba Thein, *Ko hkayaing thamaing* [History of the nine districts (Kyauk-hse)] (Mandalay, 1910), 43.
22. Yi Yi, "Early Kon-baung Provincial Administration" (363–64) provides a discussion of the complexity of the Kyauk-hse wunship and the irrigation system. The 1784 *sit-tan* of Pyaung-bya Weir gives an interesting picture of the duties of a local unit of the crown weir department, its relations to the *athi* and crown

service cultivators in its irrigation jurisdiction, and its relations with the Kyauk-hse Wun and crown weir department (*Sit-tans*, 394–97).
23. For information on these aspects of the super *myos*, see the sources cited in note 16 above. The *sit-tans* of Prome and Taung-ngu contain details concerning military matters and the use of crown revenues for state merit-making activities. Other useful information is provided in the appointment order of the *wun* of Martaban in MMOS 4: 164–65.
24. MMOS 4: 111 and 166–69.
25. For example, every *myo* in the realm was required to send a labor contingent to work on the Meik-hti-la lake and irrigation project in 1795 and, that same year, construction of a local water channel resulted in the drafting of one person per house in the capital area (KBZ 2: 90 and 95ff.). Similarly, the *myo wun* of Han-tha-wadi levied one person per house in the Rangoon area for the construction of a pond two miles from the city (Hough to Carey, 8 November 1816, in *Periodical Accounts Relative to the Baptist Missionary Society* 6 [1817]: 278). A special levy of $33^{1/3}$ *kyats* of silver on every house in the kingdom was made in 1798, and the *myo wun* of Han-tha-wadi made a levy of 20 *kyats* per house in Rangoon to pay for the cost of the 1809 British mission to Burma (with a further levy to defray the cost of sending a newly caught white elephant to the capital). See J. Crawfurd, *Journal of an Embassy from the Governor General of India to the Court of Ava in the Year 1826*, 2d ed., 2 vols. (London, 1834), 2: 173; and Canning to Edmonstone, 8 May 1810, BPC, 29 May 1810, document 1.
26. Edict of 20 April 1788, in MMOS 3: 49–50.
27. For the mechanics of the formation of *thwei-thauks*, see LBK, 296–98. The *thwei-thauks* discussed here are not to be confused with the Burmese military units of the same name comprising fifty men and six officers, for which see MMOS 4: 157.
28. Edict of 11 September 1764, in KBZ 1: 356.
29. For the membership rosters of twenty-nine *thwei-thauks* formed by Hsin-hpyu-shin in 1764, see KBZ 1: 356–68. For the formation of *thwei-thauks* by Bo-daw-hpaya in 1782, 1784, and 1786, see KBZ 1: 538 and 559–60; and 2: 39. The first Kon-baung *thwei-thauk* was, in fact, formed by Alaung-hpaya in 1749 to bind sixty-eight of his most trusted followers and relatives to his service (see KBZ 1: 27–33).

30. The Let-thon-daw, for example, were the immediate bodyguard of the king chosen from the sons of trusted courtiers. The Inner Hpanat-taw were twenty-one men selected at the age of twelve from the families of high courtiers, officials, royal relatives, and *saw-bwas* to attend the king night and day (SNT, 24 and 27).
31. *Manu-kye*, 54.
32. "Population Summary of 1783," in *Sit-tans*, 405–6.
33. *Manu-kye*, 256 and 257. According to customary law, assault or abusive language against these people was viewed with the same gravity as similar offenses against the lower ranks of royalty.
34. For example, Bo-daw-hpaya selected able-bodied Burmans from eighteen villages in his former appanage of Alon (Badon) Myo to form six units of interior palace guards, each assigned to the specific chamber of the palace from which the unit took its name (SNT, 179–80).
35. For a description of three such units along with their duties, see *Sit-tans*, 394ff. The servicemen at the capital performed a wide variety of nonmilitary functions related to the court's observance of the Buddhist calendrical cycle, and also carried messages and orders to various parts of the realm, enforced certain royal orders, and read aloud proclamations to capital-area residents. For some examples, see LBK, 105–7 and 393–95.
36. See the *sit-tans* cited in H. F. Searle, *Burma Gazetteer—Mandalay District*, vol. A (Rangoon, 1928), 58 and 59; and J. A. Stewart, *Burma Gazetteer—Kyaukse District*, vol. A (Rangoon, 1925), 120.
37. The 1802 figures available for seven of the nine *myos* give an overall crown service sector of 79 percent while the 1783 figures for Mek-hkaya, Myit-tha, and Pyin-mana *myos* are 90, 98, and 75 percent. The overall population of the seven *myos* in 1802 was 2,262 houses, but Mek-hkaya and Myit-tha alone had 3,021 and 2,122, respectively, in 1783. Extrapolating from the three figures available for 1783, there may have been roughly 20,000 houses in the nine *myos* of Kyauk-hse in 1783, compared to the 2,262 houses in the seven *myos* in 1802, and the 69,000 houses in the north/northwest area in 1783.
38. *Sit-tans*, 104.
39. Than Tun, *Ne-hle ya-zawin* [Field notes on local history], 3 vols. (Rangoon, 1968–1969), 1: 177.
40. Some Manipuris devised a simplistic and abortive plot to burn the capital in 1774. See KBZ 1: 495; and V. Sangermano, *Description of the Burmese Empire*, trans. by W. Tandy, 5th ed. (London, 1966), 63.

41. G. H. Luce, "Old Kyaukse and the Coming of the Burmans," JBRS 42, no. 1 (1959): 97.
42. KBZ 1: 556.
43. See MMOS 4: 5–6 and 212.
44. Ibid., 4: 4; and 5: 33–34.
45. Ibid., 2: 52. For the funerary privileges of *athi*, see the 1784 *sit-tan* of Mya-daung Myo, in *Sit-tans*, 379.
46. MMOS 4: 5. References to the organization of *athi* and *kyeik-su taings* occur in the *sit-tans* of Taung-zin, Ywa-tha, and Taywindaing *myos*, in *Sit-tans*, 277, 280, and 290.
47. Ba Thein, *Ko hkayaing thamaing*, 19, 21, 28, 31, 38, and 55.
48. Cited in Yi Yi, "Additional Burmese Historical Sources, 1752–1776," *The Guardian* 15, no. 12 (1968): 21. A Hsin-hpyu-shin edict, also cited in Yi Yi (22), further states that servicemen as well as others must share in the community's burden of governmental monetary levies.
49. The 1783 *sit-tan* of the Salin-gathu Cavalry Charge in Kyaukhsauk states: "When crown service is not required, ten houses constitute one unit (*taing*), and each unit has to pay 25 *kyats* of copper per month" (see *Sit-tans*, 298).
50. For some examples of exemptions, see the *sit-tans* cited in Searle, *Burma Gazeteer*, 61–62. For the land taxes paid by crown service units, see the 1802 *sit-tan* of Myit-tha Myo and the 1803 *sit-tan* of Let-ma Wun Daing, in *Sit-tans*, 355 and 385.
51. MMOS 4: 265–71; and KBZ 1: 369. In 1770 the French visitor Feraud reported that about six thousand troops accompanied the ruler when he left the fort. See "Journal du voyage de M. Feraud au royaume d'Ava," in H. Cordier, "Mémoires sur le Pégou, tirés des Archives de la Marine et des Colonies," *Revue de l'Extrême-Orient* 2, no. 4 (1883): 543.
52. MMOS 3: 208.
53. Pagan land roll of 1784, in *Sit-tans*, 264.
54. On conscription, see H. Cordier, "Les Français en Birmanie au XVIIIe siècle: Notes et documents," *T'oung Pao* 2 (1891): 30; and India Office Records, MSS.Eur.C.12, Dr. F. Buchanan's "Journal of Progress and Observations during the Continuance of the Deputation from Bengal to Ava in 1795," f. 54. See also Cox to Shore, 27 November 1797, BPC, 2 March 1798, document 4; and MMOS 4: 262–63.
55. MMOS (4: 258–60) and KBZ (1: 57) describe the organization of conscripts in the field. Two participant accounts of Burmese campaigns against Thailand in 1785 and 1809 are "Memo-

randum on the Kingdom of Ava," Royal Commonwealth Society, Henry Burney Papers B.II., ff. 1–40; and "Journal of a Route from Rangoon to Murtumana, in the Year 1809 by Bro. Felix Carey," *Monthly Circular Letters Relative to the Mission in India* 3 (1810): 43–49. Comments on artillery and muskets are given in "Francis Buchanan's Account of Burma in 1796," India Office Records, *Home Miscellaneous Series*, vol. 388, f. 599; and M. Symes, *An Account of an Embassy to the Kingdom of Ava, Sent by the Governor-General of India, in the Year 1795* (London, 1800; rpt., Westmead, England, 1969), 168–69. On the significance of firearms, see Lieberman, *Burmese Administrative Cycles*, 126–27.
56. Lieberman, *Burmese Administrative Cycles*, chapter 3 passim.
57. B. G. Gokhale, "Early Buddhist Kingship," *Journal of Asian Studies* 26, no. 1 (1966): 16.
58. See, for example, *Manu-kye*, 61; *Hman-nan*, 1: 89; and MMOS 3: 51.
59. For the classical Indian background of both bases of taxation, see A. L. Basham, *The Wonder that was India* (London, 1971), 109–10.
60. *Manu-kye*, 176.
61. For example, in the case of fixed assessment for agricultural land the traditional Burmese practice was to use elastic measures of area that took into account variation in quality and productivity (as opposed to varying the tax rate). The most common spatial measures were the *pe* and the amount of land worked by a yoke of buffalo in a season. Each measure of poorer land was larger than the same amount of better land and also varied with respect to the type of cultivation: wet rice, dry rice, alluvial rice, dry millet, etc. Much useful information on these and related points can be found in *Sit-tans*, 43; O. S. Parsons, *Report on the Settlement Operations in the Minbu District, Season 1893–1897* (Rangoon, 1900), 57 and 73; and W. A. Hertz, *Report on the Settlement Operations in the Magwe District, Season 1897–1903* (Rangoon, 1903), 53.
62. ZOK, passim. One *sit-tan* of 1601 cited in ZOK (42) specifically used the terms "fixed" and "variable" assessment.
63. For the taxation of agriculture, see *Sit-tans* in general and also MMOS 3: 51–52 and 4: 307–8. For the betel tax, see especially the 1784 land roll of Taung-ngu, in *Sit-tans*, 139ff.
64. The port dues, miscellaneous charges, and presents for Han-thawadi and Bassein are given in *Sit-tans*, 73–75 and 133. "Tavoy and Mergui Accounts, 1819–1821," Royal Commonwealth Soci-

ety, Henry Burney Papers, D.XXIV, provides fragmentary port accounts for Mergui showing the levy of the 10 percent port duty, other charges, and presents. Contemporary accounts of the conduct of port officials and customs practices at Rangoon are those of the French officer Flouest in 1782 (H. Cordier, "Les Français en Birmanie," 189–91); and the American missionary Colman in 1818 (*American Baptist Magazine and Missionary Intelligencer*, new series, 2 [1819–1820]: 213). For the China trade and its taxation, see MMOS (5: 4); and Crawfurd, *Journal of an Embassy*, 2: 183 and 192–94.

65. See R. Carmignani, *La Birmania, Relazione Inedita del 1784 del Missionario Barnabita G. M. Mantegazza* (Rome, 1950), 103–4; Cox to Shore, 27 November 1797, BPC, 2 March 1798, document 4; and MMOS 2: 157.

66. The *sit-tans* contain much information about toll stations, landing stages, fisheries, ferries, and brokerage, but see particularly the 1765 *sit-tan* of Pagan Town and the 1784 *sit-tan* of Mya-daung Myo (*Sit-tans*, 194ff. and 377–78). On the Baw-dwin silver mines, see Crawfurd, *Journal of an Embassy* (2: 204); and Cox to Shore, 25 November 1797, BPC, 2 March 1798, document 4. On the ruby mines, see E. C. S. George, *Burma Gazetteer—Ruby Mines District*, vol. A (Rangoon, 1915), 109. Yo Pe, *Yei-nangyaung myo thin-hkei-pa sa-dan* [Abridged history of Yei-nangyaung] (Rangoon, 1913), passim, especially 20–22, gives information on the oil-well concession. Canning to Edmonstone, 9 September 1812, BSP, 25 September 1812, document 11, observes that in order to raise revenue Bo-daw-hpaya sold monopoly licenses over many areas of trade to individuals and syndicates.

67. On local levies, see Canning to Edmonstone, 8 May 1810, BPC, 29 May 1810, document 1; and Sangermano, *Description of the Burmese Empire*, 92. "Tavoy and Mergui Accounts, 1819–1821," contains the accounting of several local levies in Mergui in 1819 (see note 64). On the national levy of 1798, see "Observations on the Currency of Ava by H. Burney, Resident at Ava, 9 March 1831," BSP, 15 April 1831, document 13; and Crawfurd, *Journal of an Embassy*, 2: 173. Crawfurd's statement (174) that the capital districts were always exempted from levies is definitely not true for the period before 1819 (see Yi Yi, "Provincial Administration," 383).

68. See H. Cox, *Journal of a Residence in the Burmhan Empire* (London, 1821), 341–43; and Sangermano, *Description of the Burmese Empire*, 92.
69. The Prome *sit-tans* of 1784 and 1802 are the best example of the religious nature of local crown expenditures, but see also the Taung-ngu land roll of 1784, all in *Sit-tans*, 136 and 147.
70. M. Aung Thwin, "Kingship, the *Sangha*, and Society in Pagan," in *Explorations in Early Southeast Asian History: The Origins of Southeast Asian Statecraft*, ed. K. R. Hall and J. K. Whitmore, Michigan Papers on South and Southeast Asia, no. 11 (Ann Arbor, 1976), 212.
71. J. W. Hall, "Feudalism in Japan—A Reassessment," *Comparative Studies in Society and History* 5, no. 1 (1963): 15–51 passim, especially 21–22, reviews the issue of feudalism as a category of social organization. Hall defines the two fundamental characteristics of feudalism as the personal and military nature of the lord/vassal relationship and arms bearing as a class-defining profession of the vassals/aristocracy.
72. The *sit-tans* of Htanaung-daing and Pyo-gan in Talok, Zi-gan in Pyin-zi, and Salin-gathu in Kyauk-hsauk indicate that these villages might be classified as fiefs in that they were held as appanages by the hereditary chiefs of cavalry units (see *Sit-tans*, 297–99, 314–15, 319, and 344–48).
73. *Sit-tans*, 181. The principle is further demonstrated in a case in which the crown ruled that because the throne is entitled to one-tenth of treasure trove and a *myo-za* receives the crown's share, a man who found treasure in the domain of a *myo-za* had to pay one-tenth to the *myo-za* (edict of 11 August 1812, in MMOS 3: 62).
74. *Sit-tans*, 75 and 143–44. See also MMOS (4: 105) on the appanages of the chief and other queens.
75. On the alienation of the Rangoon export duties, see Canning to Edmonstone, 19 January 1812, BPC, 21 February 1812, document 30. On the Irrawaddy *kins*, see Cox to Mornington, 15 September 1798, BPC, 1 October 1799, document 5.
76. MMOS (3: 209) denies that servicemen allotted land within an appanage paid revenues to the *myo-za*, but the *sit-tans* indicate otherwise. See, for example, the 1802 *sit-tan* of Let-ma Wun Daing in *Sit-tans* (384) and the 1792 Kyauk-hse *sit-tan* in Ba Thein, *Ko hkayaing thamaing*, 58. The Pagan land roll of 1765, in *Sit-tans* (191ff.) has many references to glebe lands as appanages in which the *myo-za* received all revenues except the basic

land tax of one-tenth, an arrangement also noted as common in Crawfurd, *Journal of an Embassy*, 2: 165.

77. The 1784 *sit-tan* of Mya-daung Myo in *Sit-tans* (375–79) has the best information on the relationship of *myo-za* and appanage, but see also Carmignani, *La Birmania*, 104; and Yi Yi, "Provincial Administration," 382–83.
78. Lieberman, *Burmese Administrative Cycles*, 78–80.
79. Sangermano, *Description of the Burmese Empire*, 83.
80. Lieberman, *Burmese Administrative Cycles*, chapter 3 passim.
81. Sangermano, *Description of the Burmese Empire*, 93.
82. For example, with the exception of eighteen villages in the jurisdiction of the Silver Tax Department, by virtue of dedications occurring between the eleventh and fifteenth centuries, the entire district of Pagan was glebe land. See the Pagan land roll of 1765, in *Sit-tans*, 191ff.
83. The Han-tha-wadi 1802 *sit-tan* states that the Shwei-dagon glebe lands were cultivated by *hkwa*, or true hereditary glebe serfs (see *Sit-tans*, 75).
84. S. Westlake, *Report on the Settlement Operations in the Kyaukse District, Season 1890–1891 and Part of Season 1891–1892* (Rangoon, 1892), 26–27. This report also cites an 1802 *sit-tan* from Kyauk-hse as an interesting example of the alienation of glebe land over the centuries. The head pagoda serf of the Shwei-tha-lyaung Pagoda in Kyauk-hse stated that the pagoda had been built by Asoka and repaired by Anaw-rahta. Only 94 *pe* remained of the original land endowment of 1,236 *pe*.
85. See Than Tun, "History of Burma, A.D. 1000–1300," *Bulletin of the Burma Historical Commission* 1, no. 1 (1960): 39–57.
86. See Ya-zein-da, *Tha-thana bahu thu-ta paka-thani* [Explanation of religious topics] (Rangoon, 1928), 169–70 and 173; Than Tun, "Administration under King Thalun (1629–1648)," JBRS 51, no. 2 (1968): 173–88; and Lieberman, *Burmese Administrative Cycles*, 111. A 1637 edict states, "Let all matters connected with glebe land be submitted to the Maha Dan Wun" (ZOK, 66).
87. See MMOS 4: 74–75; SNT, 49 and 94–96; and Parsons, *Report on the Settlement Operations*, 52.
88. See MMOS 3: 55–56; and KBZ 2: 88.
89. The robe wrapping dispute can be followed in Burmese in Maha Dama Thin-gyan, *Tha-thana lin-ga-ya kyan* [Treatise to adorn the religion] (Rangoon, 1897), 186ff.; and, in English, in Pannasami, *The History of the Buddha's Religion (Sasanavamsa)*, trans. by B. C. Law (London, 1952), 123ff. On the monastic disputes of

the late seventeenth and early eighteenth centuries, see Lieberman, *Burmese Administrative Cycles*, 178–80.
90. See LBK, 170–71, 283–84, 300–2, and 368–76; Ya-zein-da, *Tha-thana*, 175; MMOS 3: 135; and Lieberman, *Burmese Administrative Cycles*, 110.
91. See Ya-zein-da, *Tha-thana*, 171–73 and 178–79; MMOS 3: 128 and 4: 111; and Lieberman, *Burmese Administrative Cycles*, 110.
92. On the Bye-daik, see MMOS 1: 14–27 and 89; and SNT, 50. On the Shwei-daik, see MMOS 4: 72–73 and 89–90; and SNT, 61–62 and 131. The pivotal position of the *atwin-wuns* is noted in Cox to Shore, 27 November 1797, BPC, 2 March 1798, document 4.
93. Edict of 2 June 1762, cited in Yi Yi, "Additional Burmese Historical Sources," 21. On the *nagans*, see MMOS 3: 187; 4: 7–11 and 165–66.
94. In 1802 the British envoy Michael Symes noted both the widespread use of spies and monitoring at the court, and his own use of palace functionaries for intelligence purposes. See D. G. E. Hall, ed., *Michael Symes: Journal of his Second Embassy to the Court of Ava in 1802* (London, 1955), 155, 171, 182, 203, and 208. See also Sangermano, *Description of the Burmese Empire*, 94.
95. On the interesting career of U Paw U, see Tin Swe, "Pandit U Paw Oo," *The Guardian* 13, no. 5 (1966): 22–24. The texts of *Nan-zin pok-hsa* and *Amei-daw ahpyei* have been published, but were not available to me.
96. *Sit-tans*, 354.
97. For example, Yi Yi, "Early Kon-baung Provincial Administration" (383) cites an 1805 edict concerning a dispute over tax collection involving the Granary and Yame-thin *wuns*.

Chapter 5

1. See, for example, *Hman-nan*, 1: 35.
2. *Manu wunana*, 239.
3. See *Hman-nan*, 1: 85 and 87; and J. Gray, *Ancient Proverbs and Maxims from Burmese Sources or, The Niti Literature of Burma* (London, 1886), 120–22.
4. See V. Sangermano, *A Description of the Burmese Empire*, trans. by W. Tandy, 5th ed. (London, 1966), 156; and Htin Aung, ed. and trans., *Epistles Written on the Eve of the Anglo-Burmese War* (The Hague, 1968), 29.

5. Hla Pe, "Officials' Titles in Burmese" (School of Oriental and African Studies, November 1967, mimeo), comments on popular attitudes toward officials.
6. Sangermano, *Description of the Burmese Empire*, 152. When an American missionary asked a reprieved man why he had become a bandit, "he replied that it was because he had not been made a governor, or raised above the grade of the common people." See Hough to Carey, 20 February 1817, in *American Baptist Magazine and Missionary Intelligencer*, new series, 1 (1817–1818): 371.
7. The 1784 *sit-tan* for Mya-daung Myo, in *Sit-tans*, 379. As evidenced by other *sit-tans*, the silver bowl of five *kyats* was the standard *kadaw* offering for *myo-thu-gyis*, while village headmen usually submitted a roll of cotton cloth twenty-five cubits in length. Information on the court formalities related to *kadaw* are given in LBK, 23–34, 46–48, 168–70, 309, and 315. See also MMOS 3: 52 and 4: 114–15.
8. For an enumeration of local offices, see MMOS 2: 172–73 and 197. The 1637 *sit-tan* of Myaung-mya lists virtually all of the local offices found in Kon-baung times (ZOK, 59). In some cases the *asi-yin* also served as headman. KBZ 1: 18, for example, gives Alaung-hpaya as the *asi-yin* of Mok-hso-bo.
9. These figures are from early Kon-baung census materials translated in *Sit-tans*, 400ff.
10. On the privileges of local officials, see MMOS 2: 183–85; and *Manu-kye*, 253. Many *sit-tans* contain detailed records of the privileges of the *myo-thu-gyi*. See, for example, the *sit-tans* for Wun-tho in 1802, Salin-gathu and Talok in 1783, and Pagan in 1765, in *Sit-tans*, 202–23, 262, 298–99, 341, and 369–70.
11. *Sit-tans*, 335.
12. Ibid., 340.
13. Ibid., 325.
14. Ibid., 343.
15. See MMOS 4: 29–34; *Manu-kye*, 226–27; J. S. Furnivall, *Report on the First Regular Settlement Operations in the Myingyan District, Season 1909–1913* (Rangoon, 1915), 63; and W. A. Hertz, *Report on the Settlement Operations in the Magwe District, Season 1897–1903* (Rangoon, 1903), 69–73.
16. *Sit-tans*, 324. Other *sit-tans* contain similar statements. See also MMOS 2: 185.
17. On the famine and its effect on land tenure, see Hertz, *Report on the Settlement Operations*, 72–73; R. A. Gibson, *Report on the*

Settlement Operations in the Meiktila District, Season 1896–1898 (Rangoon, 1900), 52; and GUBSS 2.2: 274.
18. On the private status of office lands, see MMOS 2: 159. On the size of estates, see Furnivall, *Report on the First Regular Settlement Operations*, 64–67; and Gibson, *Report on the Settlement Operations*, 51–52; as well as O. S. Parsons, *Report on the Settlement Operations in the Minbu District, Season 1893–1897* (Rangoon, 1900), 45 and 70. On the size of individual land allotments for members of crown service units, see the *sit-tan* cited in H. F. Searle, *Burma Gazetteer—Mandalay District*, vol. A (Rangoon, 1928), 58.
19. For example, the 1784 *sit-tan* of Sin-gu Myo records one hereditary *myo-thu-gyi* and ten hereditary *myei-daings*, while Pagan had four *myo-thu-gyis* and over one hundred subordinate hereditary officials. See *Sit-tans*, 191ff. and 271.
20. MMOS 3: 17.
21. Extracted in U Gaung, *Translation of a Digest of the Burmese Buddhist Law Concerning Inheritance and Marriages*, 2 vols. (Rangoon, 1903–1909), 1: 119. That same volume (168) gives a similar statement extracted from the *Dama vinnicchaya* of 1752. See also *Manu-kye*, 281.
22. Hlut-taw record of 1806, extracted in Yi Yi, "Kon-baung hkit-u myo-ne ok-chok-pon" [Early Kon-baung provincial administration] *Pyei-daung-zu myan-ma naing-ngan sa-bei hnin lu-hmu-yei gya-ne* 1, no. 2 (1968): 347.
23. Examples of all these instances can be found in the *sit-tans*.
24. H. Burney, "On the Population of the Burman Empire," *Journal of the Royal Statistical Society* 4 (1842); reprinted in JBRS 31, no. 1 (1941): 24.
25. Mya Sein, *The Administration of Burma* (Rangoon, 1938; rpt., Singapore, 1973), 59, notes the case of a *myo-thu-gyi* of Pagan who obtained office by bribing the Shwei-daik officers to falsify the records, but was deposed when the true claimant appealed to the Hlut-taw and the corruption was discovered. AA (240) refers to the case of a man who bribed a Hlut-taw official with 350 *kyats* of silver for a document recognizing him as *myo-thu-gyi* of Thamyin-don Myo during the reign of Alaung-hpaya. GUBSS (2.2: 117) also comments on the insecurities of local office.
26. MMOS 2: 183.
27. Ibid.
28. Ibid.
29. Ibid., 2: 179.

30. See Hla Pe, "Officials' Titles."
31. See Sangermano, *Description of the Burman Empire*, 82; and Canning to Edmonstone, 9 September 1812, BSP, 25 September 1812, document 11.
32. On retinues and insignia of rank, see MMOS 3: 183–85 and 4: 111. LBK (224–38) is a catalogue of some of the trappings of top officials. On the sumptuary rules for officials' houses, see Sangermano, *Description of the Burman Empire*, 160–62.
33. For example, the 1784 *sit-tan* of Kyaung-bya Yaw-min-dat in Han-tha-wadi states, "When the main tax is ten baskets, there is one *kyat* for the *wun*, two *mats* for the writers, one *kyat* for transport, and two *mats* for the chief of the crown storehouse" (*Sittans*, 70). Similar statements occur in other *sit-tans*. See also MMOS 3: 54.
34. In 1819, for example, the *myo wun* of Mergui was called to the capital and levied a total of 10,772 *kyats* from the people of his jurisdiction, not all of which went to finance the trip. See "Tavoy and Mergui Accounts, 1819–1821," Royal Commonwealth Society, Henry Burney Papers, D.XXIV.
35. "Journal du voyage de M. Feraud au royaume d'Ava," in H. Cordier, "Mémoires sur le Pégou, tirés des Archives de la Marine et des Colonies," *Revue de l'Extrême-Orient* 2, no. 4 (1883): 523 (cited hereafter as *Feraud's Journal*). See also the resigned comments of the East India Company agent Walter Alves in 1760 on the relationship of presents to business in A. Dalrymple, *Oriental Repertory*, 2 vols. (London, 1808), 1: 373 and 380–81.
36. "Tavoy and Mergui Accounts" (see note 34).
37. Canning to Edmonstone, 26 November 1811, BPC, 26 December 1811, document 6. See similar statements in *Feraud's Journal*, 523; Sangermano, *Description of the Burmese Empire*, 94; and H. Cox, *Journal of a Residence in the Burmhan Empire* (London, 1821), 170.
38. On "official banditry," see H. S. Spearman, *British Burma Gazetteer*, 2 vols. (Rangoon, 1879–1880), 2: 376; and B. R. Pearn, "Felix Carey and the English Baptist Mission in Burma," JBRS 28 (1938): 60. For comments on the commercial activities of officials, see Canning to Edmonstone, 26 November 1811, BPC, 26 December 1811, document 6; and same to same, 29 February 1812, BPC, 26 March 1812, document 1.
39. W. F. Grahame, *Report on the Settlement Operations in the Shwebo District, Season 1900–1906* (Rangoon, 1907), 9, notes the

40. case of inhabitants of a village who mortgaged most of their land to the second-ranking officer of the Shwei-daik, an indication that here, at least, was one official who had acquired working capital.
40. A list is provided in KBZ 1: 28–32. Further details about the *wun-gyis* in particular can be found in Min-gyaw Ya-za, "Wun-gyi hmu-gyi-mya akyaung" [Concerning ministers and officials], JBRS 45, no. 2 (1962): 146ff.
41. Min-gyaw Ya-za, "Ministers and Officials" (150–51) gives several examples of the careers of officials' sons who advanced from betel box bearers to *wun-gyis*.
42. Htin Aung, *Epistles*, 35.
43. See Min-gyaw Ya-za, "Ministers and Officials," 152–53; Cox, *Journal of a Residence*, 405; and R. R. Langham-Carter, "Four Notables of the Lower Chindwin," JBRS 30, no. 1 (1940): 336–37.
44. See Min-gyaw Ya-za, "Ministers and Officials," 150; Thein, *Pazat ya-zawin (By-ways of Burmese History Being the Unrecorded History of Burma During the Reign of King Bodawpaya)* (Rangoon, 1926), 23–27; and F. Carey to W. Carey, 28 January 1808, in *Monthly Circular Letters Relative to the Mission in India* 3 (1808): 36. Kyaw Ywei was a common figure in the accounts of the various East India Company visitors to Burma between 1795 and 1812 as the *maywoon*, or viceroy, of Rangoon. Another long-time personal retainer of Bo-daw-hpaya was Paw U, who also weathered the exile and became one of the most trusted counsellors of the king.
45. On the formal procedures for appointing officials, see MMOS 3: 197–200.
46. MMOS (2: 193) claims that certain middle- and lower-level appointed officials came to have quasi-hereditary claims to their offices because these had remained in their families for generations, but I can identify no such instances in the early Kon-baung period.
47. Min-gyaw Ya-za, "Ministers and Officials" (145–52) records a number of cases from the reigns of Hsin-hpyu-shin to Bo-daw-hpaya in which *wun-gyis* and other ranking officials were stripped of office or executed. For example, the Wun-gyi Maha Thi-ha Thu-ra (U Tha Gyi) was deposed and restored by Hsin-hpyu-shin twice, deposed by Sin-gu, and restored and later executed by Bo-daw-hpaya. Despite their close personal relationships with Bo-daw-hpaya, Kyaw Hkaung, Kyaw Ywei, and Paw U, all were deposed and, in Paw U's case, banished on at least one occasion.

48. This running conflict is described in D. G. E. Hall, ed., *Michael Symes: Journal of his Second Embassy to the Court of Ava in 1802* (London, 1955), 173, 187, and 200; and in the letters of John Canning, 1809–1812. For the latter, see particularly BPC consultations of 26 December 1809, document 57; 9 January 1810, document 72; 29 May 1810, document 1; 26 December 1811, document 6; 21 February 1812, document 30; and 29 October 1813, document 25. On the *daing wun*;, see Min-gyaw Ya-za, "Ministers and Officials" (151); and Canning to Edmonstone, 9 September 1812, BSP, 25 September 1812, document 11. For the background of Jansey, see Hall, *Michael Symes*, lxxii-lxxiii.
49. See, for example, A. Judson, *An Account of the American Baptist Mission to the Burman Empire*, 2d ed. (London, 1827), 26–27, on the *myo wun* of Dala, who was murdered by an underling covetous of his office; and Tin Swe, "Pandit U Paw Oo," *The Guardian* 13, no. 5 (1966): 24, on how one of Bo-daw-hpaya's favorites cleverly countered a charge of treason. Cox, *Journal of a Residence*, discusses the politics of the treason charges against the Wun-gyi Kyaw Hkaung in 1797, and Kyaw Hkaung's own intrigues after the position of the Pahkan Wun-gyi (U Hnaung) (343–50 and 335, respectively). See also S. C. Sarkar, "The Negrais Settlement and After," JBRS 22, no. 2 (1922): 64–65, on the politics of the Bassein wunship in 1760–1761 and their relation to court factions; Yi Yi, "Provincial Administration" (381) on the deposition and restoration of the Bassein *wun* in 1806; and Canning to Edmonstone, 19 January 1812, BPC, 21 February 1812, document 30, on the conflict between the *myo wuns* of Han-tha-wadi and Danu-byu. Finally, Htin Aung, *Epistles* (27–38) contains four letters discussing *inter alia* such dangers as intrigue and the enemies that are inherent in service as an official.
50. J. C. Scott, "An Essay on the Political Functions of Corruption," *Asian Studies* 5, no. 1 (1967): 501–2.
51. See, for example, *Manu-kye*, 51, 116, 148, 150, 171, and 187; and *Manu wunana*, 239 and 311.
52. Cox, *Journal of a Residence* (170) records the statement of the *yei wun* of Rangoon that "it was customary amongst the Burmhans never to go empty-handed to court, and that he himself had nothing of his own to offer, having been stripped during his nine months residence here."
53. The moral milieu of officialdom is suggested by the advice of a headman to his son in the service of a high official: "You must be

blind to certain actions of your lord as if you had lost the sense of sight, and you must be deaf to certain words of your lord as if you had lost the sense of hearing" (see Htin Aung, *Epistles*, 29).

54. See, for example, Cox, *Journal of a Residence* 322; Mya Sein, *Administration of Burma*, 59; Sangermano, *Description of the Burmese Empire*, 94; Min-gyaw Ya-za, "Ministers and Officials," 152; Hall, *Michael Symes*, 51–52; and B. R. Pearn, ed., "A Burma Diary of 1810," JBRS 27, no. 3 (1937): 292.

55. On embezzlement, see Yi Yi, "Provincial Administration," 383; Mya Sein, *Administration of Burma*, 67; Min-gyaw Ya-za, "Ministers and Officials," 151; Canning to Edmonstone, 18 November 1811, BPC, 26 December 1811, document 6; J. Crawfurd, *Journal of an Embassy from the Governor General of India to the Court of Ava in the Year 1826*, 2d ed., 2 vols. (London, 1834), 2: 8; and "Account of the Trade, etc. of Rangoon," Royal Commonwealth Society, Henry Burney Papers, B.XXVII.

56. On the scandal of 1770, see the edict of 28 January 1770 cited in Yi Yi, "Additional Burmese Historical Sources, 1752–1776," *The Guardian* 15, no. 12 (1968): 22–23.

57. See Yi Yi, "Provincial Administration," 381–82; GUBSS 1.2: 92 and 97; and Judson, *Account of the American Baptist Mission*, 54.

58. Edict of 14 June 1806, extracted in Yi Yi, "Provincial Administration," 381. As noted in chapter 2, loss of title was a serious degradation for an official.

59. KBZ 1: 479–81.

60. *Sit-tans*, 77.

61. KBZ 2: 26.

62. Yi Yi, "Kon-baung hkit sit-tan-mya" [*Sit-tans* of the Kon-baung period], JBRS 49, no. 1 (1966): 71. ZOK (41) is a 1580 edict that specifically refers to registers of tax-paying *athi*, *ala*, *kat-pa*, adult males, male children, and district registers of crown service groups. References to audits of glebe lands suggest that the information-gathering and record-keeping functions in Burmese administration were already evolving in the Pagan period.

63. ZOK, passim, contains all known records of the Restored Taung-ngu inquests. V. B. Lieberman, *Burmese Administrative Cycles: Anarchy and Conquest, c. 1580–1760* (Princeton, N.J., 1984), chapter 2 passim, discusses the administrative development of the Restored Taung-ngu period and places the inquests in perspective.

64. Some of these edicts are summarized in English in Yi Yi, "Additional Burmese Historical Sources," passim. In Burmese, see AA, passim.
65. Cited in Yi Yi, "Additional Burmese Historical Sources," 22–23.
66. The text of the edict is in To Hla, "Kon-baung hkit-u ok-chok-yei sit-tan" [A *sit-tan* from early Kon-baung administration (Talok)], *Pyinya law-ka sa-zaung* 7, no. 3 (1976): 35.
67. Burney, "Population of the Burman Empire," 24.
68. Ibid.
69. MMOS 3: 48–49.
70. Most of the extant materials relating to the inquests of 1765, 1783, and 1802 are published in F. N. Trager and W. J. Koenig, *Burmese Sit-tans, 1764–1826: Records of Rural Life and Administration* (Tucson, Ariz., 1979). Cited in the notes as *Sit-tans*.
71. The *sit-tans* record numerous disputes between *myos* over the control of villages, the forcible seizure of villages, and the mortgage of villages to other jurisdictions. The 1802 *sit-tan* of Wuntho illustrates the latter two points: "Mya-daung *Myo* in the year 1158 [1796] seized and now has charge of the villages of Magyibin, Kyauk-o, Leik-in, Htan-daw, Let-hpet-aik and Kya-in. Mogaung *Myo* has seized and has charge of Man-gat Village. Mohnyin *Myo* has seized and has charge of.... I do not have charge of [the eleven villages listed] as they have been mortgaged to the chief of the Maw-naing Gold Tract in the jurisdiction of the *wun* of the crown granaries" (*Sit-tans*, 368–69).
72. K. Wittfogel, *Oriental Despotism: A Comparative Study of Total Power* (New Haven and London, 1963), 312–16 passim.
73. See, for example, the description by Walter Alves of the structure of influence at court and its use to achieve his mission in 1760 in Dalrymple, *Oriental Repertory*, 1: 380.

Chapter 6

1. See E. R. Leach, "The Frontiers of 'Burma,'" *Comparative Studies in Society and History* 3, no. 1 (1960): 57.
2. G. E. Harvey, *History of Burma from the Earliest Times to 10 March 1824* (London, 1925; rpt., London, 1967), 264. R. C. Temple, "The Order of Succession in Alompra Burma," *Indian Antiquary* 21 (1892): 288, also argues that every brother and every son saw himself as a possible heir, which precipitated a general struggle on the death of a king.

3. On the Western Court and the *anauk wuns*, see MMOS 1: 181-82 and 4: 39-52 passim; also, SNT, 50 and 55-56. The *sit-tan* of a unit of *yuns* assigned to the *anauk wuns* gives some description of their duties in the Western Court (*Sit-tans*, 386-92). On other crown service groups of the Western Court, see SNT, 129 and 134.
4. SNT, 50.
5. There were eleven separate *abhiseka* ceremonies for the king, one for the elevation to queenship, and one for elevation to the crown princeship. On the *mahei abhiseka* and its significance for the heir apparent, see SNT, 4 and 210.
6. MMOS 1: 167-68.
7. GUBSS 1.2: 89.
8. The kings of both Taung-ngu dynasties generally had from one to three queens, as did the majority of the Pagan rulers. A few sovereigns of Pagan such as Kyan-zit-tha and Alaung Si-thu had four queens.
9. The data on the royal women are drawn from MMM, 191-251 passim.
10. Ibid., passim.
11. This particular relationship can be followed in the genealogical material in MMM, 191-251 passim. On Min-Thi-ri Yan-daza and the hereditary *myo-thu-gyi* lineage of Si-bok-tara, see the 1765 *sit-tan* of Si-bok-tara extracted in Yi Yi, "Kon-baung hkit sit-tan-mya" [*Sit-tans* of the Kon-baung period], JBRS 49, no. 1 (1966): 79. On the Si-tha Min-gyi's relationship to and early support of Alaung-hpaya, see KBZ 1: 32.
12. Little information is available about the fictively consanguine *min-thami*, but such examples as there are suggest that these were in the main relatives of the royal family. The mother of Alaung-hpaya, for example, had a *dei-wi* title and the mother of Bo-daw-hpaya's chief queen was similarly honored. The younger sister of the chief queen is recorded as having the funeral of a queen, another indication of *min-thami* status.
13. For the details of clothes and ornaments, see MMOS 4: 217-18. On the title classes for the royal women, see SNT, 35. Within each title class, status was further elaborated by the composition of words in the title, some having more importance than others, and, more importantly, by the number of syllables. The syllable length of titles for the royal women also increased noticeably under Bo-daw-hpaya, as opposed to his predecessors. Daughters tended to move up one status level over their mothers, presum-

ably because they had a consanguine rather than affinal relation to the king. See MMM, 191–225 passim.
14. The most extensive discussion of the status hierarchy of the Western Court is in MMOS 2: 200ff. The *kadaw* secretaries are briefly described in MMOS 4: 47. For a shorter discussion, see SNT, 16ff.
15. M. Symes, *An Account of an Embassy to the Kingdom of Ava, Sent by the Governor-General of India, in the Year 1795* (London, 1800; rpt., Westmead, England, 1969), 423.
16. V. Sangermano, *A Description of the Burmese Empire*, trans. by W. Tandy, 5th ed. (London, 1966), 94.
17. On the *min-nyi min-tha*, see MMOS 4: 106; SNT, 8–9, 15–16, 35, and 212; and LBK, 71, 127, and 343–45. On the appointment of eleven *myin-hmu min-tha* by Ba-gyi-daw at his coronation in 1819, see KBZ 2: 235.
18. MMM, 206.
19. The information on the titles of princes is derived from MMM, 191–225 passim.
20. Such material as there is can be found in LBK, 185ff.; and in Min-gyaw Ya-za, "Wun-gyi hmu-gyi-mya akyaung" [Concerning ministers and officials], JBRS 45, no. 2 (1962): 140–46.
21. See SNT, 9; and GUBSS 1.2: 91–93 and 476.
22. The importance of the unbroken and pure lineage in Burmese political thought is reflected in many Kon-baung documents. One contemporary comment is contained in *Hman-nan*, 1: 239, which relates the story of Pok-pa Saw-yahan, an early king of Pagan (613–640), who was not related to the royal lineage. After the Maha Gi-ri spirit withdrew its support of the realm, he was forced to make the son of his predecessor the heir apparent. The story associates national welfare with the restoration of the lineage because this spirit was the guardian of the kingdom.
23. Edict of 16 June 1783, National Library (Rangoon), 96/1948/170.
24. MMOS 1: 171 and 2: 227–28 and 236; also SNT, 6.
25. KBZ 1: 554.
26. Ibid., 1: 538 and 563.
27. LBK, 8. This statement is, of course, not meant to be taken literally, but only as the expression of a general ideal.
28. Zei-ya Thin-hkaya, *Shwei-bon ni-dan* [A work on the Golden Palace] (Rangoon, 1960), 63. For other details on the Eastern House, see LBK, 11–12.
29. LBK, 8.

30. A summary of the record is in MMM, 29–45 passim. Consistent in most details is the general description of the investiture of a crown prince found in LBK, 12ff. The edict of 16 June 1783 cited in note 23 directed that the ceremony be held on 10 July, but it was apparently postponed three days.
31. MMM, 35–36.
32. When the British envoy Michael Symes paid a courtesy visit to the crown prince in 1802, his soldier's eye noted "about 300 tolerable-looking troops, much better equipped than those of his Majesty" in evidence at the Eastern House. See D. G. E. Hall, ed., *Michael Symes: Journal of His Second Embassy to the Court of Ava in 1802* (London, 1955), 192.
33. On the endowment and establishment of the crown prince in 1783, see MMM, 36; and KBZ 1: 554–55.
34. The marriage ceremony of 1783 is described in MMM, 46ff.; and KBZ 1: 554.
35. MMOS 3: 169; SNT, 7; LBK, 26–27, 30–50, 61, and 384.
36. LBK, 64–65. The reference to "prayers" meant the recitation of appropriate sections of the Buddhist scriptures as a form of religious healing, in contrast to conventional medical treatment.
37. Ibid., 67.
38. Ibid., 68–69.
39. A basic difference between the titles of the king and that of the crown prince is hidden by translation. The term translated as "lord" for the crown prince is *ashin*, while the word *hpaya* is used for the king. *Hpaya* is legitimately translated as "lord" in this context, but it should be noted that it is used only in reference to objects or beings considered to have uncanny power. It is usually applied only to buddhas, pagodas, monks, and kings.
40. On at least three occasions in Restored Taung-ngu and Konbaung history, officials succeeded in dictating the succession: Min-ye Kyaw-din in 1673, Sin-gu in 1776, and Thi-baw in 1878. On the selection and accession of the first, see V. B. Lieberman, *Burmese Administrative Cycles: Anarchy and Conquest, c. 1580–1760* (Princeton, N.J., 1984), 146–48. On the last, see P. J. Bennett, *Conference Under the Tamarind Tree: Three Essays in Burmese History*, Yale University Southeast Asia Studies Monograph Series, no. 15 (New Haven, 1971), 57–99 passim. The accession of Sin-gu is described in chapter 7.
41. On the attempts of Nyaung-yan and Min-ye Kyaw-din to decree collateral rather than lineal succession, see Lieberman, *Burmese Administrative Cycles*, 57, 149–53, and 183.

42. On the brothers appointed viceroys by Pin-dale in 1648 and by Sanei in 1698, see ibid., 143–44 and 183–84.

Chapter 7

1. On the reasons for and course of this campaign, see V. B. Lieberman, *Burmese Administrative Cycles: Anarchy and Conquest, c. 1580–1760* (Princeton, N.J., 1984); and KBZ 1: 302–19. Thai accounts used by W. A. R. Wood, *A History of Siam from the Earliest Times to the Year A.D. 1781* (Bangkok, 1859), 241–42, are the source of the story that Alaung-hpaya was mortally wounded by a bursting cannon as he directed its loading. Walter Alves, an agent of the East India Company who was in Burma at the time of the death, wrote that "common report" said Alaung-hpaya died of the same fever and flux that reduced his army by half (see A. Dalrymple, *Oriental Repertory*, 2 vols. [London, 1808], 1: 261). This version of the death is supported by references in KBZ to the ill-health of the king, and a letter of 1778 from the Italian missionary Carpani who had arrived in Burma in 1765 (KBZ 1: 314 and 315). This letter states that Alaung-hpaya died of the bloody flux (extracted in R. Carmignani, *La Birmania, Relazione Inedita del 1784 del Missionario Barnabita G. M. Mantegazza* [Rome, 1950], 109).

   The exact date of the death is also uncertain. LN-AA, 152, the most contemporary source, gives 13 April, which is much too early because the reason for the retreat given in both it and KBZ was the approach of the monsoon. If Alaung-hpaya marched twenty-four days before dying, the retreat would have begun in mid-March, but the monsoon would not have arrived before late May, at the earliest. Two later secondary sources (MMM, 191; and "A Historical Memorandum of Royal Relations of Burmah Hunters Family," BL OR. 3470, f. 1) both give 2 May as the date of the death, but I have used 11 May, as given in KBZ 1: 319 and 322. KBZ is both closer in time to the actual event and the "official" history of the dynasty.
2. V. Sangermano, *A Description of the Burmese Empire*, trans. by W. Tandy, 5th ed. (London, 1966), 62.
3. On the family background, see KBZ 1: 15–16. KBZ (1: 18) specifically refers to Alaung-hpaya as the *asi-yin* of Mok-hso-bo, a term usually meaning an appointive administrative officer, but which could also mean a headman. A manuscript biography of

Alaung-hpaya cited in Yi Yi, "Kon-baung hkit sit-tan-mya" [*Sittans* of the Kon-baung period], JBRS 49, no. 1 (1966): 76, states that he was a *kyei-gaing*, a position equivalent in function to that of *myei-daing*. M. Symes, *An Account of an Embassy to the Kingdom of Ava, Sent by the Governor-General of India, in the Year 1795* (London, 1800; rpt., Westmead, England, 1969), 6, is the most probable source of the fiction that Alaung-hpaya was a huntsman (*mok-hso*) and that the name Mok-hso-bo Myo translates literally as "town of the hunter chief." A more realistic derivation for Mok-hso-bo is suggested by a story in KBZ, which relates that a prophecy of a true king appearing at Mok-hso-bo prompted King Narapati Si-thu of Pagan to build the Shwei-daza Pagoda on the site and to charge a hunter named Nga Po to build a town to look after the pagoda. Over time Mok-hso Nga Po Myo (the town of the hunter Nga Po) became contracted to Mok-hso-bo (KBZ 1: 67). The origin of the name Kon-baung stems from the Kon-baung channel built by King Alaung Si-thu of Pagan, east of Mok-hso-bo, giving the whole area its name. The name Shwei-bo derives from wordplay in court poetry on the term *shwei-pyei-daw* ("golden royal capital") and was only brought into general usage by Tha-ra-wadi in 1837.
4. On the other gentry leaders in the field against the southern forces, see Lieberman, *Burmese Administrative Cycles*, 232–33.
5. See KBZ 1: 34–35 and 65–69; and BL OR. 3464, 144.
6. Dalrymple, *Oriental Repertory*, 1: 169 and 152.
7. See Pannasami, *The History of the Buddha's Religion (Sasanavamsa)*, trans. by B. C. Law (London, 1952), 127–28; and Ya-zein-da, *Tha-thana bahu thu-ta paka-thani* [Explanation of religious topics] (Rangoon, 1928), 100.
8. KBZ 1: 320.
9. Dalrymple, *Oriental Repertory*, 1: 362–63.
10. Nei-myo Shwei-daung was U Pwin, one of a handful of Alaung-hpaya's earliest followers from the 1740s who subsequently received one of the first four *wun-gyi* appointments. See Min-gyaw Ya-za, "Wun-gyi hmu-gyi-mya akyaung" [Concerning ministers and officials], JBRS 45, no. 2 (1962): 146.
11. KBZ 1: 316–21.
12. Ibid., 1: 327. I am indebted to Professor Hla Pe for his assistance with this translation.
13. The story of Min-gaung Naw-rahta is told in KBZ 1: 325–36. Walter Alves provides an eyewitness account of the siege of Ava and popular disaffection (see Dalrymple, *Oriental Repertory*, 1:

362–64, 371–73, and 381–82). Symes, *Account of an Embassy* (55–63) has a later hearsay account with many incorrect names and facts.
14. KBZ 1: 301.
15. AA, 270.
16. Dalrymple, *Oriental Repertory*, 1: 381. Symes, *Account of an Embassy* (61–62) also notes that at this time subordinate officers were not well regulated and quite "voracious," having little dread of the king.
17. On Thado Thein-ga-thu's rebellion, see KBZ 1: 337–46; and, on his earlier career, see LN-AA, 23, 35, 44, 55, 61, 111, and 141. The European sources all rely on hearsay accounts from decades after the event and are often confused about the facts and names. Examples of this include Carmignani, *La Birmania*, 107; Sangermano, *Description of the Burmese Empire*, 62; and Symes, *Account of an Embassy*, 64.
18. AA, 142.
19. Dalrymple, *Oriental Repertory*, 1: 328.
20. KBZ 1: 338.
21. During the siege of Taung-ngu, for example, he personally led a charge astride his war elephant, annihilating a major enemy sally (ibid., 1: 341).
22. I am indebted to Dr. Yi Yi for suggesting this interpretation. A further piece of circumstantial evidence is the treatment of Hsin-hpyu-shin in KBZ, which differs from that of other rulers. The prose is cold and matter-of-fact, with none of the encomiums usually lavished on rulers. Even Sin-gu, for all his failings, receives warmer treatment and some laudatory remarks. It is as though the compilers of the chronicle projected their disapproval of Hsin-hpyu-shin in this manner.
23. Carpani to Cortenovis, 26 August 1778, extracted in Carmignani, *La Birmania*, 109.
24. Carmignani, *La Birmania*, 106–7. Sangermano, *Description of the Burmese Empire* (62) also states of Alaung-hpaya: "Before his death he declared his will to his nobles, that his seven sons should successively occupy the throne after his decease." Writing over twenty years after the other Italian missionaries, Sangermano missed the distinction they understood between the sons of the chief queen and the son of the north queen.
25. KBZ 1: 526. It is interesting that this source refers to Alaung-hpaya's order as a *ya-za-than*, or statement of a king, as opposed to the more forceful *amein-daw*, or formal edict.

26. "Journal du voyage de M. Feraud au royaume d'Ava," in H. Cordier, "Mémoires sur le Pégou, tirés des Archives de la Marine et des Colonies," *Revue de l'Extrême-Orient* 2, no. 4 (1883): 533–34. The most informative source on the internal politics of the reign of Hsin-hpyu-shin is Carpani to Cortenovis, 26 August 1778, extracted in Carmignani, *La Birmania*, 109–10.
27. KBZ 1: 508, 512. Of the European sources, Carmignani, *La Birmania* (109–11) provides the best account, but see also Sangermano, *Description of the Burmese Empire*, 63–64; and Symes, *Account of an Embassy*, 87–90.
28. Named U Tha Gyi, this general had been one of the original sixty-eight followers of Alaung-hpaya in 1752. An able field commander, he had served with distinction in the various campaigns of the 1750s, had been appointed *myo wun* of Taungngu following the rebellion of Thado Thein-ga-thu, and had achieved the distinction of *wun-gyi* in 1764. His wife was Me Talaing, a sister of Hsin-hpyu-shin's chief queen and a granddaughter of Min Thi-ri Yan-daza. Me Talaing had not approved of her daughter's match with the crown prince, perhaps because she doubted his chances for a safe passage to the crown. On U Tha Gyi and Me Talaing, see Min-gyaw Ya-za, "Ministers and Officials," 147; and KBZ 1: 30.
29. KBZ 1: 514.
30. Ibid., 1: 531.
31. Ibid., 1: 515.
32. Symes, *Account of an Embassy*, 51. A late Kon-baung source, Min-gyaw Ya-za, "Ministers and Officials" (147) relates that Singu suspected the north queen of plotting with the uncles.
33. KBZ 1: 516; and Carmignani, *La Birmania*, 112.
34. LN-AA, 134.
35. Thein, *Pazat ya-zawin (By-ways of Burmese History Being the Unrecorded History of Burma During the Reign of King Bodawpaya)* (Rangoon, 1926), 23–26.
36. See KBZ 1: 519; and Let-we Thon-dara, *Tha-di-na pyo* (Rangoon, 1900), 53–54 (an epic poem composed in 1783). The latter source also makes specific references to drinking and revelry. I am indebted to Professor Hla Pe for the latter translation. Sangermano, *Description of the Burmese Empire* (64) also refers to Sin-gu's dissipation and intoxication.
37. Mok-hso-bo was believed to contain *aung-myei* or "victory earth," which endowed those who walked upon it with victory. Min-don robbed the land of this power by making it pagoda land.

38. Aung Thein, trans., "The Testimony of an Inhabitant of the City of Ava," *Journal of the Siam Society* 45, no. 2 (1957): 47.
39. KBZ 1: 526–27.
40. The most detailed account of the events of February 1782 is given in KBZ 1: 520–32. The shorter but near-contemporary Burmese account in Aung Thein, "Testimony" (47–48) accords well with the main points of KBZ, as does Mantegazza's contemporary account (Carmignani, *La Birmania*, 111–12) and Sangermano's near-contemporary narrative (Sangermano, *Description of the Burmese Empire*, 64–65). Symes (*Account of an Embassy*, 92–96) is based on hearsay from over a decade later and contradicts the consensus of the other sources on a number of points. Interestingly and unverifiably, a modern Burmese source relates that Me Talaing, redoubtable wife of Maha Thi-ha Thu-ra and mother of the drowned north queen, got her revenge because the four principal queens of Sin-gu were all turned over to her and perished in misery (MMM, 201–2). This embellishment of the story of Sin-gu probably belongs in the realm of popular tradition.
41. KBZ 1: 527.
42. Ibid., 1: 533.
43. See Carmignani, *La Birmania*, 113; and Sangermano, *Description of the Burmese Empire*, 65.
44. Ibid.
45. See KBZ 1: 540–44; Carmignani, *La Birmania*, 113–14; and Sangermano, *Description of the Burmese Empire*, 65–67. The latter incorrectly places the event in December.
46. See MMM, 219; and KBZ 1: 554 and 563.
47. KBZ makes no mention of such a plot, but see Carmignani, *La Birmania*, 114. Min-gyaw Ya-za, "Ministers and Officials" (149) supports the rumor reported by Mantegazza by noting that the chief accomplice of the Pin-dale prince was the *athi wun* who, contrary to other accounts, was not executed but only lost his position after the failure of the coup. He was soon restored to royal favor and, after holding several other important offices, became a *wun-gyi* in 1790.
48. See KBZ 2: 22.
49. See D. G. E. Hall, ed., *Michael Symes: Journal of His Second Embassy to the Court of Ava in 1802* (London, 1955), 206.
50. Hall, *Michael Symes*, 216.
51. See MMOS 3: 38–39; Hall, *Michael Symes*, 140, 149, 156–57, and 203; and Canning to Symes, 18 June 1803, BSP, 5 July 1804, document 127.

Chapter 7

52. See Tin Swe, "Pandit U Paw Oo," *The Guardian* 13, no. 5 (1966): 24.
53. See Symes, *Account of an Embassy*, 427.
54. Canning to Edmonstone (8 May 1810, BPC, 29 May 1810, document 1) observed that the Bassein prince had been sentenced to death by his father for the use of spirits, a capital offense under all the early Kon-baung rulers. Although pardoned at the last moment through the entreaties of his mother, frightened out of his wits as he was being led out to execution he lost his reason, "which he has never since recovered." See also MMM, 206.
55. KBZ 2: 40.
56. Ibid., 2: 85–86.
57. Hall, *Michael Symes*, 196.
58. Ibid., 214.
59. Ibid., 114–15.
60. KBZ (2: 126) records that the king with "the four components of war" set out for Taung-ngu to repair pagodas and ordination halls on 20 December 1798, and did not return to the capital until 8 December 1799. Although no mention of the nascent rebellion is made in this passage, it is specifically referenced in KBZ 2: 226. On the political rehabilitation of the prince, see KBZ (2: 155) and various edicts of 1806 cited in Yi Yi, "Kon-baung hkit-u myo-ne ok-chok-pon" [Early Kon-baung provincial administration], *Pyei-daung-zu myan-ma naing-ngan sa-bei hnin lu-hmu-yei gya-ne* 1, no. 2 (1968): 381–82.
61. KBZ 2: 167–68. The English missionary Felix Carey, also a doctor and frequent visitor to court, wrote of the death: "From all the accounts I heard, I believe he must have died of a cancer." F. Carey to W. Carey, 1 May 1809, in *Monthly Circular Letters Relative to the Mission in India* 2 (1809): 23.
62. KBZ 2: 173. On the endowment, see especially MMM, 220.
63. Canning to Edmonstone, 23 May 1812, BSP, 12 June 1812, document 24.
64. Canning to Edmonstone, 8 May 1810, BPC, 29 May 1810, document 1; same to same, 9 September 1812, BSP, 25 September 1812, document 10.
65. Canning to Edmonstone, 8 May 1810, BPC, 29 May 1810, document 1.
66. Ibid.
67. Ibid.
68. Ibid.
69. Ibid.

70. Ibid.
71. Canning to Edmonstone, 23 May 1812, BSP, 12 June 1812, documents 20 and 24.
72. Edict of 28 January 1795, in MMOS 5: 244.
73. See F. Carey to W. Carey, 6 July 1811, in *Periodical Accounts Relative to the Baptist Missionary Society* 4 (1811): 403.
74. See Canning to Edmonstone, 8 May 1810, BPC, 29 May 1810, document 1. This document also provides a running account of the largest and most serious of the peasant rebellions.
75. On this point, see Canning to Edmonstone, 25 October 1811, BPC, 22 November 1811, document 4.
76. KBZ 2: 208.
77. Letter of 4 August 1819, in *American Baptist Magazine and Missionary Intelligencer* 2 (1819): 383.
78. KBZ 2: 220-33.
79. A. Judson, *An Account of the American Baptist Mission to the Burman Empire*, 2d ed. (London, 1827), 90.
80. Ibid., 141-42.
81. Ibid.
82. Originally a lowborn concubine of the former crown prince, Me Nu had apparently also had some hand in the death in 1811 of the daughter of the Prome prince who had been the crown prince's first queen. There had been a long-standing enmity between the Prome prince and Me Nu since that time. KBZ (2: 226) only implies that the Taung-ngu prince was executed. Dates and immediate details of the deaths of the Taung-ngu and Prome princes are from "A Historical Memorandum of Royal Relations of Burmah Hunters Family," BL OR. 3470, ff. 11-12.
83. Colman to Lincoln, 14 June 1819, in *American Baptist Magazine and Missionary Intelligencer* 2 (1819): 289, gives a figure of three to four thousand. An unsigned article (295) entitled "Burmese Despotism" dated 1 September 1819 offers the hardly credible figure of ten to fifteen thousand.

Conclusion

1. For the complex relationship between ethnicity and politics, see V. B. Lieberman, "Ethnic Politics in Eighteenth-Century Burma," *Modern Asian Studies* 12, no. 3 (1978): 455-82.
2. The French officer Flouest estimated that there were six thousand monks in the Rangoon area in 1784, while the British envoy

John Canning reported more than ten thousand at Amara-pu-ra in 1812. See H. Cordier, "Les Français en Birmanie au XVIIIe siècle: Notes et documents," *T'oung Pao* 2 (1891): 12; and Canning to Adam, 6 October 1813, BPC, 20 October 1813, document 25.

3. The *sangha* in lower Burma quickly dissolved into corrupt practices and disorder, despite the best efforts of King Min-don to manage it from afar after the Second Anglo-Burmese War. In the aftermath of the Third Anglo-Burmese War, British authorities refused the request of *sangha* leaders to assume the historic role the monarchy played as protector and administrator of the monkhood. In result, monks became a more active element in politics. These developments are surveyed in J. F. Cady, *A History of Modern Burma* (Ithaca, N.Y., 1958), chapters 3–5 passim. But to read back into Kon-baung times the "political *pongyis*" of the colonial and postcolonial periods, as do Cady and other western scholars, is incorrect. Direct political involvement by monks was a phenomenon induced by the changes in Burmese society brought about by the imposition of British rule, and was not part of the dynastic Burmese political tradition.

4. The same principle can be seen at work in the blood oath sworn by the Myei-du prince (the future Hsin-hpyu-shin) and his followers in 1760 at the Mya-thein-dan Pagoda in Martaban during his challenge to the succession of his elder brother. The formation of *thwei-thauks* by individual kings, as described in chapter 2, was one way in which rulers tried to create and formalize such personal allegiance networks.

5. P. J. Bennett, *Conference under the Tamarind Tree: Three Essays in Burmese History*, Yale University Southeast Asia Studies Monograph Series, no. 15 (New Haven, 1971), 57–99 passim, provides an excellent essay on the politics of the royal succession during the reigns of Min-don and Thi-baw.

6. See V. B. Lieberman, *Burmese Administrative Cycles: Anarchy and Conquest, c. 1580–1760* (Princeton, N.J., 1984), chapters 3 and 4 passim.

GLOSSARY OF BURMESE AND PALI TERMS

abhiseka: the ritual consecration of a king

ala: the offspring of a union between an *athi* and a *kat-pa*

asi-yin: a subordinate officer of a village or *myo* primarily concerned with judicial matters, but sometimes serving as headman

athi: a person not enrolled in a crown service unit and maintaining permanent residence in a given locality, for which certain land and status rights were allowed

athi wun: the officer in charge of the crown department responsible for administering the *athi* sector of the population

atwin wun: a minister of the Bye-daik

aw-ra-tha: the eldest son of a head wife, possessing superior rights of inheritance to the father's estate and heritable office

bayin: a viceroy, usually of royal blood

bodhisatta: a being ultimately destined to become a buddha

Bye-daik: the crown department responsible for the administration of the inner palace and the personal affairs of the king

cakkavatti: a universal monarch in Theravada Buddhist thought

damathat: a compilation of customary law

dhamma: the transcendental natural and moral law of the universe

daing: an embossed leather shield one cubit square and hardened with a special putty; *daing* also denotes the infantry units that carried such shields

daing wun: the officer in charge of the crown department responsible for the administration of the *daing* units

Hlut-taw: the central administrative organ of the state headed by a council of ministers called *wun-gyis*

jatakas: stories of the Buddha's former lives

kadaw: the formal relationship of personal allegiance to the king

kamma: the course of personal destiny as determined by the results of volitional acts

Kathaung-myaung Taik: the central treasury for public monies in which were also deposited revenues from glebe lands designated for religious purposes

kat-pa: a person not enrolled in a crown service unit or one having left his unit, in each case taking up residence elsewhere and hence not entitled to the status and rights of *athi*

kyat: a measure of weight equal to .6 oz. or 16.3 g.

kyei-gaing: a subordinate local officer found in some localities whose function appears to have been equivalent to that of a *myei-daing*

myei-daing: a local hereditary official primarily concerned with recording and taking a commission on sales of immovable property, mainly land, but also in numerous cases performing the functions of headman

myo: a district, often quite sizable, comprising a main town and usually a market and a hinterland of smaller towns and villages; also used to denote a town only

myo-gaing: the local agent of a *myo-za*

myo-thu-gyi: the hereditary official in charge of a *myo*

myo wun: the crown-appointed governor of a larger *myo* or group of *myos*

myo-za: a person to whom the crown's share of the revenue of a *myo* was alienated

nagan: an officer whose function was to report to the king on the conduct of business in a larger *myo* or in one of such larger crown departments as the Hlut-taw

nat: a spirit

Glossary of Burmese and Pali Terms

parabaik: paper, cloth, or metal folded accordion-like and used for writing

parittas: extracts from the *Suttas*, one part of the Buddhist scriptures, used as prayers to ward off evil

pe: a spatial measure for crops, generally equal to about 1.75 acres but varying from locale to locale and from crop type to crop type

pitakas: the Buddhist scriptures, comprised of the *Vinaya, Suttas,* and *Abhidhamma*

sangha: the order of Buddhist monks

saw-bwa: a hereditary ruler of a Shan principality

Shwei-daik: the personal treasury of the king and also the repository for the *sit-tans* and population registers

sit-ke: usually the chief deputy of a *myo wun* with responsibility for judicial and criminal matters; also the deputy commander of a military expedition

sit-tan: a general term for record of an inquiry, but specifically used to denote a local return from a village or *myo* during one of the periodic crown inquests

taik: a revenue department comprising a number, often quite large, of villages that were not necessarily geographically proximate

taing: an *athi* service and tax unit

thu-gyi: the standard term for the headman of a village

thwei-thauk: an elite crown service unit, commonly used to refer to one of the guard units of the inner palace

wun: the most common term denoting an appointed official

wun-gyi: a minister of state at the Hlut-taw

Yun: the Burmese term for Shans and Laos from the Chiengmai area

ywa-za: a person to whom the crown's share of the revenue of a village was alienated

BIBLIOGRAPHY

Adas, M. *The Burma Delta: Economic Development and Social Change on an Asian Rice Frontier, 1852–1941*. Madison, Wis., 1974.

———. "From Avoidance to Confrontation: Peasant Protest in Precolonial and Colonial Southeast Asia." *Comparative Studies in Society and History* 23, no. 2 (1981): 217–47.

———. "'Moral Economy' or 'Contest State'?: Elite Demands and the Origins of Peasant Protest in Southeast Asia." *Journal of Social History* 13, no. 4 (1980): 521–46.

American Baptist Magazine and Missionary Intelligencer, new series. 1 and 2 (1817–1820). Boston.

Ana-gatawin kyan [History of the future]. Mandalay, 1927. A Burmese translation of the Pali work *Anagatavamsa*.

Anatriello, P. "La Chiesa Cattòlica in Birmania nella seconda meta des sec. XVIII in una relazione inedita della S. Congreg. de Prop. Fide." *Neue Zeitscrift für Missionswissenschaft* 23 (1967): 244–51.

Aung Thein, trans. "The Testimony of an Inhabitant of the City of Ava." *Journal of the Siam Society* 45, no. 2 (1957): 26–54.

Aung Thwin, M. "Kingship, the *Sangha*, and Society in Pagan." In K. R. Hall and J. K. Whitmore, eds., *Explorations in Early Southeast Asian History: The Origins of Southeast Asian Statecraft*. Michigan Papers on South and Southeast Asia, no. 11. Ann Arbor, 1976.

———. "The Role of *Sasana* Reform in Burmese History: Economic Dimensions of a Religious Purification." *Journal of Asian Studies* 38, no. 4 (1979): 671–88.

Ba Thein. *Ko hkayaing thamaing* [History of the nine districts (Kyaukhse)]. Mandalay, 1910.

Balandier, G. *Political Anthropology.* New York, 1970.

Banton, M., ed. *Political Systems and the Distribution of Power.* London, 1965.

Barua, B. M. *Asoka and His Inscriptions.* Calcutta, 1968.

Basham, A. L. *The Wonder that was India.* London, 1971.

Bechert, H. "Theravada Buddhist Sangha: Some Observations on Historical and Political Factors in its Development." *Journal of Asian Studies* 29, no. 4 (1970): 761–78.

Benda, H. J. "The Structure of Southeast Asian History." *Journal of Southeast Asian History* 3, no. 1 (1962): 103–38.

Bennett, P. J. *Conference under the Tamarind Tree: Three Essays in Burmese History.* Yale University Southeast Asia Studies Monograph Series, no. 15. New Haven, 1971.

Bigandet, P. A. *An Outline of the History of the Catholic Burmese Mission, from the year 1720 to 1887.* Rangoon, 1887.

Blake, S. P. "The Patrimonial-Bureaucratic Empire of the Mughals." *Journal of Asian Studies* 39, no. 1 (1979): 77–94.

Bode, M. H. *The Pali Literature of Burma.* London, 1909.

Boxer, C. R. "Asian Potentates and European Artillery in the 16th–18th Centuries: A Footnote to Gibson-Hill." *Journal of the Malaysian Branch of the Royal Asiatic Society* 38, no. 2 (1966): 156–72.

Brailey, N. J. "A Re-Investigation of the Gwe of Eighteenth Century Burma." *Journal of Southeast Asian Studies* 1, no. 2 (1970): 33–47.

British Library, London. Cited in the notes as BL OR., followed by the number of the corresponding manuscript:

OR. 3416. "Taung-ngu myo 1146 sit-tan" [Taung-ngu land roll of 1784]. Palm leaf manuscript.

OR. 3449-B. "Sit-tan sa-yin" [Population registers of 1802 and 1826]. Black rough copy *parabaik.*

OR. 3450-C. "Pyei myo 1145 hku, 1164 hku sit-tan" [1784 and 1802 *sit-tans* of Prome]. Black rough copy *parabaik*.

OR. 3469. Volume 3 of a Burmese translation of the Mon history by the Monk of Athwa. Bound paper manuscript.

OR. 3470. "A Historical Memorandum of Royal Relations of Burmah Hunters Family." Mandalay. 4 December 1866.

OR. 3480/3. "Statement of the Titles Usually Conferred on Burmese Officials and Men of Rank."

Buchanan's Journal. Listed under India Office Records, MSS.Eur.C.12.

Burling, R. *The Passage of Power: Studies in Political Succession*. New York, 1974.

Burney, H. "On the Population of the Burman Empire." *Journal of the Royal Statistical Society* 4 (1842): 335–47. Reprinted in JBRS 31, no. 1 (1941): 19–32.

Cady, J. F. *A History of Modern Burma*. Ithaca, N.Y., 1958.

Carmignani, R. *La Birmania, Relazione Inedita del 1784 del Missionario Barnabìta G. M. Mantegazza*. Rome, 1950.

Chan Mya. *Man-dalei hmat-tan-mya* [Records of life at court]. Rangoon, 1966.

Cordier, H. "Les Français en Birmanie au XVIIIe siècle: Notes et documents." *T'oung Pao* 1 (1890): 15–28, 189–217; 2 (1891): 1–48, 390–400.

———. "Mémoires sur le Pégou." *T'oung Pao*, series 2, 23 (1923): 99–152.

———. "Mémoires sur le Pégou, tirés des Archives de la Marine et des Colonies." *Revue de l'Extrême-Orient* 2, no. 4 (1883): 505–72. Abbreviated in the notes as Cordier, *Revue*.

Cowell, E. B., ed. *The Jataka, or Stories of the Buddha's Former Births*. 6 vols. London, 1957.

Cox, H. *Journal of a Residence in the Burmhan Empire*. London, 1821.

Crawfurd, J. *Journal of an Embassy from the Governor General of India to the Court of Ava in the Year 1826*. 2d ed. 2 vols. London, 1834.

Dalrymple, A. *Oriental Repertory*. 2 vols. London, 1808.

Davids, T. W. R., trans. *Dialogues of the Buddha.* 3 vols. London, 1899–1921.

Drekmeier, C. *Kingship and Community in Early India.* Stanford, 1962.

Dutt, S. *Buddhist Monks and Monasteries of India.* London, 1962.

Ei Kyaw. "Han-tha-wadi 32 myo sit-tan" [*Sit-tan* of the 32 *myos* of Han-tha-wadi]. *Tekatho pyinya padei-tha sa-zaung* 1, no. 4 (1966): 183–95.

———. "Mok-tama 32 myo sit-tan" [*Sit-tan* of the 32 *myos* of Martaban]. *Tekatho pyinya padei-tha sa-zaung* 5, no. 1 (1970): 241–54.

———. "Pathein 32 myo sit-tan" [*Sit-tan* of the 32 *myos* of Bassein]. *Tekatho pyinya padei-tha sa-zaung* 5, no. 2 (1970): 207–12.

Eisenstadt, S. "Political Struggle in Bureaucratic Societies." *World Politics* 9 (1956): 15–37.

Feraud's Journal. "Journal du voyage de M. Feraud au royaume d'Ava." In H. Cordier, "Mémoires sur le Pégou, tirés des Archives de la Marine et des Colonies." *Revue de l'Extrême-Orient* 2, no. 4 (1883): 505–72.

Ferguson, J. P. "The Arahat Ideal in Modern Burmese Buddhism." Unpublished paper presented at the Association for Asian Studies Annual Meeting. New York, March 1977.

Fisher, C. A. *South-East Asia: A Social, Economic and Political Geography.* 2d ed. London, 1966.

Flouest's Journal. "Journal du voyage de Lt. Flouest." In H. Cordier, "Les Français en Birmanie au XVIIIe siècle: Notes et documents." *T'oung Pao* 2 (1891): 1–48.

Forchhammer, E. *The Jardine Prize: An Essay on the Sources and Development of Burmese Law.* Rangoon, 1885.

Francklin, W. *Tracts Political, Geographical and Commercial on the Dominions of Ava.* London, 1811.

Furnivall, J. S. "Burman Rule in Hanthawaddy." *JBRS* 4, no. 3 (1914): 209–13.

———. *An Introduction to the Political Economy of Burma.* Rangoon, 1931.

———. *Report on the First Regular Settlement Operations in the Myingyan District, Season 1909–1913*. Rangoon, 1915.

———. "Some Historical Documents." JBRS 6, no. 3 (1916): 213–23; 8, no. 1 (1918): 40–52; 9, no. 1 (1919): 33–52.

———, and Pe Maung Tin, eds. *Zam-bu-di-pa ok-hsaung kyan* [The crown of Jambudipa]. Rangoon, 1960. Cited in the notes as ZOK.

Gaudart, E. *Catalogue des manuscrits des anciennes archives de l'Inde française*. 6 vols. Paris and Pondichéry, 1926–1935.

Gaung. *Translation of a Digest of the Burmese Buddhist Law Concerning Inheritance and Marriages*. 2 vols. Rangoon, 1903–1909.

George, E. C. S. *Burma Gazetteer—Ruby Mines District*. Vol. A. Rangoon, 1915.

Gibson, R. A. *Report on the Settlement Operations in the Meiktila District, Season 1896–1898*. Rangoon, 1900.

———. *Report on the Settlement Operations in the Yamethin District, Season 1898–1901*. Rangoon, 1902.

Gokhale, B. G. "Early Buddhist Kingship." *Journal of Asian Studies* 26, no. 1 (1966): 15–22.

Gouger, H. *Personal Narrative of Two Years' Imprisonment in Burmah*. London, 1860.

Grahame, W. F. *Report on the Settlement Operations in the Shwebo District, Season 1900–1906*. Rangoon, 1907.

Gray, J. *Ancient Proverbs and Maxims from Burmese Sources or, The Niti Literature of Burma*. London, 1886.

Hall, D. G. E. *Europe and Burma*. London, 1945.

———. *A History of South-East Asia*. 3d ed. London, 1968.

———, ed. *Michael Symes: Journal of his Second Embassy to the Court of Ava in 1802*. London, 1955.

———. "The Tragedy of Negrais." JBRS 21, no. 3 (1931): 1–133.

Hall, J. W. "Feudalism in Japan—A Reassessment." *Comparative Studies in Society and History* 5, no. 1 (1963): 15–51.

Halliday, R. "Immigration of the Mons into Siam." *Journal of the Siam Society* 10, no. 3 (1913): 1–13.

———. *The Talaings.* Rangoon, 1917.

Harvey, G. E. *History of Burma from the Earliest Times to 10 March 1824.* London, 1925. Reprint. London, 1967.

Hertz, W. A. *Report on the Settlement Operations in the Magwe District, Season 1897–1903.* Rangoon, 1903.

Hewlitt, H. P., and J. Clague. *Burma Gazetteer—Bassein District.* Vol. A. Rangoon, 1916.

Historical Research Department, Ministry of Culture, Rangoon. Cited in the notes as HRD:

Acc. No. 2984. Untitled bound volume of documents containing *inter alia*:

"45 hku myo-zu shwei-daik sa-yin win-daw-gu naing-ngan-daw atwin myo-kyei-ywa-mya" [The Shwei-daik list of the *myos* and villages of the country for the year 1783] (pages 44–50).

The 1784 and 1802 *sit-tans* of Mya-daung Myo (pages 53–59).

Acc. No. 6361. Bound volume of documents entitled "Wun-tho myo-ne sit-tan ya-zawin sa-thi-mya" [Wuntho District *sit-tan*, history, etc.].

Hla Myo, comp. *Pyei-daung-zu myan-ma naing-ngan thamaing-win sa-gyok-sa-dan-mya* [Historical documents of the Union of Burma]. Rangoon, 1968.

Hla Pe. "Officials' Titles in Burmese." Paper presented at the School of Oriental and African Studies, November 1967. Mimeo.

Hla Tin, ed. *Alaung-hpaya ayei-daw-bon hnazaung-dwe* [Two biographies of Alaung-hpaya]. Rangoon, 1961.

Hman-nan maha ya-zawin-daw-gyi [Glass Palace chronicle]. 3 vols. Mandalay, 1921. Cited in the notes as *Hman-nan*.

Hooker, M. B. "The Indian-Derived Law Texts of Southeast Asia." *Journal of Asian Studies* 37, no. 2 (1978): 201–19.

Hpo Kya. *Pathein ya-zawin* [History of Bassein]. Rangoon, 1933.

Htin Aung, ed. and trans. *Epistles Written on the Eve of the Anglo-Burmese War.* The Hague, 1968.

———. *A History of Burma.* New York, 1967.

Hunter, W. M. D. *A Concise Account of the Kingdom of Pegu.* Calcutta, 1785.

India Office Records, London:

Bengal Political Consultations. Cited in the notes as BPC.

Bengal Secret and Political Consultations. Cited in the notes as BSP.

Home Miscellaneous Series.

MSS.Eur.C.12. Dr. F. Buchanan's "Journal of Progress and Observations during the Continuance of the Deputation from Bengal to Ava in 1795."

Irwin, A. M. B. *The Burmese and Arakanese Calendars.* Rangoon, 1909.

Judson, A. *An Account of the American Baptist Mission to the Burman Empire.* 2d ed. London, 1827.

Kala. *Maha ya-zawin-gyi* [Great chronicle]. 3 vols. Rangoon, 1929–1961. Cited in the notes as *Maha ya-zawin.*

Khan, M. S. "Captain George Sorrel's Mission to the Court of Amarapura, 1793–1794: An Episode in Anglo-Burmese Relations." *Journal of the Asiatic Society of Pakistan* 2 (1957): 131–53.

Khin Khin Sein, ed. *Alaung-min-taya-gyi amein-daw-mya* [Edicts of Alaung-hpaya]. Rangoon, 1964. Cited in the notes as AA.

Khin Maung Kyi, and Tin Tin. *Administrative Patterns in Historical Burma.* Southeast Asian Perspectives, no. 1. Singapore, 1973.

Koenig, W. J. "The Early Kon-Baung Polity, 1752–1819: A Study of Politics, Administration and Social Organization." Ph.D. thesis, University of London, 1978.

Kyaw Thet. "Burma's Relations with her Eastern Neighbours in the Konbaung Period, 1752–1819." Ph.D. thesis, University of London, 1950.

Langham-Carter, R. R. "Four Notables of the Lower Chindwin." JBRS 30, no. 1 (1940): 336–42.

———. "Queen Me Nu and her Family at Palangon." JBRS 19, no. 2 (1929): 31–35.

Laurie, M. *Report on the Settlement Operations in the Mandalay District, Season 1892–1893.* Rangoon, 1894.

Law, B. C. "A Short Account of the Wandering Teachers at the Time of the Buddha." *Journal and Proceedings of the Asiatic Society of Bengal,* new series, 14, no. 7 (1918): 399–406.

Leach, E. R. "The Frontiers of 'Burma.'" *Comparative Studies in Society and History* 3, no. 1 (1960): 49–68.

———. *Political Systems of Highland Burma: A Study of Kachin Social Structure.* London School of Economics Monographs on Social Anthropology, no. 44. London, 1954.

Lehman, F. K. *The Structure of Ch'in Society.* Illinois Studies in Anthropology, no. 3. Urbana, Ill., 1963.

Let-we Naw-rahta. *Alaung-min-taya-gyi ayei-daw-bon* [Biography of Alaung-hpaya]. Cited in Hla Tin, ed., *Alaung-hpaya ayei-daw-bon hnazaung-dwe* [Two biographies of Alaung-hpaya]. Rangoon, 1961. Abbreviated in the notes as LN-AA.

Let-we Thon-dara. *Tha-di-na pyo.* Rangoon, 1900. An epic poem composed in 1783.

Lieberman, V. B. *Burmese Administrative Cycles: Anarchy and Conquest, c. 1580–1760.* Princeton, N.J., 1984.

———. "Ethnic Politics in Eighteenth-Century Burma." *Modern Asian Studies* 12, no. 3 (1978): 455–82.

———. "A New Look at the *Sasanavamsa.*" *Bulletin of the School of Oriental and African Studies* 39, no. 1 (1976): 137–49.

———. "The Political Significance of Religious Wealth in Burmese History: Some Further Thoughts." *Journal of Asian Studies* 39, no. 4 (1980): 753–69.

Lingat, R. "La double crise de l'eglise Bouddique au Siam (1767–1851)." *Cahiers d'Histoire Mondiale* 4, no. 2 (1958): 402–25.

———. "Evolution of the Conception of Law in Burma and Siam." *Journal of the Siam Society* 38, no. 1 (1950): 9–31.

Luce, G. H. "Chinese Invasions of Burma in the Eighteenth Century." JBRS 15, no. 2 (1925): 115–28.

———. *Old Burma—Early Pagan.* 3 vols. Locust Valley, N.Y., 1969–1970.

———. "Old Kyaukse and the Coming of the Burmans." JBRS 42, no. 1 (1959): 75–109.

Maha Dama Thin-gyan. *Tha-thana lin-ga-ya kyan* [Treatise to adorn the religion]. Rangoon, 1897.

Maha Zei-ya Thin-hkaya. *Waw-ha-ra li-nat-hta di-pani kyan* [Treatise on recondite words]. Mandalay, 1899.

Massachusetts Baptist Missionary Magazine. Volume 4 (1814–1816). Boston.

Maung Maung Tin, comp. *Myan-ma min let-htet-taw sa-dan-mya* [Documents from the reigns of Burmese kings]. Rangoon, 1967.

Maung Tin, ed. and trans. "Rajadhiraja Vilasini or The Manifestation of the King of Kings, a Pali Historical Work." JBRS 4, no. 1 (1914): 7–21.

Mendelson, E. M. "A Messianic Buddhist Association in Upper Burma." *Bulletin of the School of Oriental and African Studies* 24, no. 3 (1961): 560–80.

———. *Sangha and State in Burma: A Study of Monastic Sectarianism and Leadership.* Ithaca and London, 1975.

Min-gyaw Ya-za. "Wun-gyi hmu-gyi-mya akyaung" [Concerning ministers and officials]. JBRS 45, no. 2 (1962): 139–62.

Monthly Circular Letters Relative to the Mission in India. 1807–1815. Baptist Missionary Society, Serampore.

Mya Sein. *The Administration of Burma.* Rangoon, 1938. Reprint. Singapore, 1973.

Nash, M. *Primitive and Peasant Economic Systems.* San Francisco, 1966.

National Library, Rangoon:

(96)(1948)(170) Edict of 16 June 1783 (copy provided by Dr. Yi Yi).

Okell, J. W. A. *A Guide to the Romanization of Burmese.* London, 1971.

"Pagan myo 1127 sit-tan" [Pagan land roll of 1765]. JBRS 32, no. 1 (1948): 52–61; 33, nos. 1 (1950): 39–57, and 2 (1950): 230–59.

Pannasami. *The History of the Buddha's Religion (Sasanavamsa).* Translated by B. C. Law. London, 1952.

Parlett, L. M. *Report on the Settlement Operations in the Sagaing District, Season 1893-1900.* Rangoon, 1903.

Parrott, B. A. N. *Report on the Settlement Operations in the Hanthawaddy and Pegu Districts, Season 1882-1883.* Rangoon, 1884.

Parsons, O. S. *Report on the Settlement Operations in the Minbu District, Season 1893-1897.* Rangoon, 1900.

Pe Maung Tin. *Myan-ma sa-bei thamaing* [History of Burmese literature]. Rangoon, 1955.

———, and G. H. Luce, trans. *The Glass Palace Chronicle of the Kings of Burma.* London, 1923.

Pearn, B. R., ed. "A Burma Diary of 1810." JBRS 27, no. 3 (1937): 283-307.

———. "Felix Carey and the English Baptist Mission in Burma." JBRS 28 (1938): 1-91.

———. "King-Bering." JBRS 23, no. 1 (1933): 55-85.

———, ed. "The State of Burma in 1790." JBRS 29, no. 2 (1939): 250-56.

Periodical Accounts Relative to the Baptist Missionary Society. 1807-1817. London.

Phayre, A. P. *History of Burma.* London, 1883. Reprint. London, 1967.

Preschez, P. *Les relations entre la France et la Birmanie au XVIIIe et au XIXe siècles.* Paris, 1967.

Pyin-nya. *Kayin ya-zawin* [History of the Karens]. Rangoon, 1929.

———. *Mok-tama ya-zawin-baung-gyok hnin Mok-tama sit-tan sa-haung kyan* [Complete history of Martaban with the old Martaban land roll]. Thahton, 1927.

Richardson, D., ed. and trans. *The Damathat, or the Laws of Menoo, Translated from the Burmese.* Moulmein, 1847. Cited in the notes as *Manu-kye.*

Royal Commonwealth Society, London:

Henry Burney Papers:

B.I. "Census of the Population of the Kingdom of Ava as Taken in the Burman Year 1145 A.D. 1783, and as Revised in 1188 A.D. 1826."

B.II. "Memorandum on the Kingdom of Ava."

B.XXVII. "Account of the Trade, etc. of Rangoon."

D.XXIV. "Tavoy and Mergui Accounts, 1819–1821."

Sangermano, V. *A Description of the Burmese Empire*, trans. by W. Tandy. 5th ed. London, 1966.

Sarkar, S. C. "The Negrais Settlement and After." JBRS 22, no. 2 (1922): 47–67.

Sarkisyanz, E. *Buddhist Backgrounds of the Burmese Revolution*. The Hague, 1965.

Scott, J. C. "An Essay on the Political Functions of Corruption." *Asian Studies* 5, no. 1 (1967): 501–23.

———. "Patron-Client Politics and Political Change in Southeast Asia." *American Political Science Review* 66, no. 1 (1972): 91–113.

Scott, J. G., and J. P. Hardiman, comps. *Gazetteer of Upper Burma and the Shan States*. 5 vols. in 2 parts. Rangoon, 1900–1901. Cited in the notes as GUBSS.

Searle, H. F. *Burma Gazetteer—Mandalay District*. Vol. A. Rangoon, 1928.

Sonnerat. *Voyage aux Indes Orientales et à la Chine*. 2 vols. Paris, 1782.

Spearman, H. S. *British Burma Gazetteer*. 2 vols. Rangoon, 1879–1880.

Spiro, M. E. *Buddhism and Society: A Great Tradition and its Burmese Vicissitudes*. London, 1971.

Stargardt, J. "Social and Religious Aspects of Royal Power in Medieval Burma, from Inscriptions from Kyanshattha's Reign, 1084–1112." *Journal of the Economic and Social History of the Orient* 13, no. 3 (1970): 289–308.

Sternbach, L. "The Pali Lokaniti and the Burmese Niti Kyan and Their Sources." *Bulletin of the School of Oriental and African Studies* 26, no. 2 (1963): 329–45.

Stewart, J. A. *Burma Gazetteer—Kyaukse District.* Vol. A. Rangoon, 1925.

Stuart, J. M. B. *Old Burmese Irrigation Works, being a Short Description of the pre-British Irrigation Works of Upper Burma.* Rangoon, 1913.

Symes, M. *An Account of an Embassy to the Kingdom of Ava, Sent by the Governor-General of India, in the Year 1795.* London, 1800. Reprint. Westmead, England, 1969.

Taw Sein Ko. "A Preliminary Study of the Po:U:Daung Inscription of S'inbyuhin, 1774 A.D." *Indian Antiquary* 23, no. 1 (1893): 1–8.

"Taywin-daing myo sit-tan" [*Sit-tans* of Taywin-daing (1784 and 1802)]. JBRS 44, no. 1 (1961): 81–84.

Temple, R. C. "The Order of Succession in Alompra Burma." *Indian Antiquary* 21 (1892): 287–93.

Than Tun. "Administration under King Thalun (1629–1648)." JBRS 51, no. 2 (1968): 173–88.

———. "The Buddhist Church in Burma during the Pagan Period, 1044–1287." Ph.D. thesis, University of London, 1955.

———. "History of Burma, A.D. 1000–1300." *Bulletin of the Burma Historical Commission* 1, no. 1 (1960): 39–57.

———. "The Influence of Occultism in Burmese History with Special Reference to Bodawpaya's Reign, 1782–1819." *Bulletin of the Burma Historical Commission* 1, no. 2 (1960): 117–45.

———. *Ne-hle ya-zawin* [Field notes on local history]. 3 vols. Rangoon, 1968–1969.

———. "Religion in Burma, A.D. 1000–1300." JBRS 42, no. 2 (1959): 47–69.

Thapar, R. *Asoka and the Decline of the Mauryas.* London, 1961.

Thein (Hmaw-bi Hsaya). *Pazat ya-zawin (By-ways of Burmese History Being the Unrecorded History of Burma During the Reign of King Bodawpaya).* Rangoon, 1926.

Thi-ri U-zana. *Law-ka byu-ha kyan* [Treatise on customary terms]. Rangoon, 1958. Cited in the notes as LBK.

Tin (of Mandalay), comp. *Kon-baung-zet maha ya-zawin-daw-gyi* [History of the Kon-baung dynasty]. 3 vols. Rangoon, 1967–1968. Cited in the notes as KBZ.

———. *Shwei-nan-thon waw-ha-ra abi-dan* [Terminology used in the Golden Palace]. Mimeo., n.d. The printed version of this work appeared on the eve of the Japanese invasion of Burma in World War II and, with the exception of a handful of copies, was destroyed. A very limited mimeograph edition was issued in the late 1940s. Cited in the notes as SNT.

Tin (of Pagan). *Myan-ma min ok-chok-pon sa-dan* [The administration of Burmese kings]. 5 vols. Rangoon, 1931–1933. Cited in the notes as MMOS.

Tin Ohn. "Modern Historical Writing in Burmese." In D. G. E. Hall, ed., *Historians of South East Asia*. London, 1961.

Tin Swe. "Pandit U Paw Oo." *The Guardian* 13, no. 5 (1966): 22–24.

To Hla. "Kon-baung hkit-u ok-chok-yei sit-tan" [A *sit-tan* from early Kon-baung administration (Talok)]. *Pyinya law-ka sa-zaung* 7, no. 3 (1976): 32–36.

Trager, F. N., and W. J. Koenig. *Burmese Sit-tans, 1764–1826: Records of Rural Life and Administration*. Tucson, Ariz., 1979. Cited in the notes as *Sit-tans*.

Trant, T. A. *Two Years in Ava: From May 1824 to May 1826*. London, 1827.

Tun Nyein. *Inscriptions of Pagan, Pinya and Ava: Translation with Notes*. Rangoon, 1899.

Tun Wai. *Economic Development of Burma from 1800 till 1940*. Rangoon, 1961.

Van Zeyst, H. G. "Asoka." In G. P. Malalasekara, ed., *Encyclopedia of Buddhism*. Colombo, 1961.

Wales, H. G. Q. *Ancient Siamese Government and Administration*. London, 1934.

———. *Siamese State Ceremonies: Their History and Function*. London, 1931.

Wenk, K. *The Restoration of Thailand under Rama I, 1782–1809.* Tucson, Ariz., 1968.

Westlake, S. *Report on the Settlement Operations in the Kyaukse District, Season 1890–1891 and Part of Season 1891–1892.* Rangoon, 1892.

Wilkie, R. S. *Burma Gazetteer—Yamethin District.* Vol. A. Rangoon, 1934.

Williamson, A. *Burma Gazetteer—Shwebo District.* Vol. A. Rangoon, 1929.

Wittfogel, K. *Oriental Despotism: A Comparative Study of Total Power.* New Haven and London, 1963.

Wood, W. A. R. *A History of Siam from the Earliest Times to the Year A.D. 1781.* Bangkok, 1859.

Woodward. F. L., and E. M. Hare, trans. *The Book of the Gradual Sayings (Anguttara Nikaya), or More Numbered Suttas.* 5 vols. London, 1932–1936.

Wun Collection, Rangoon:

> Originally collected by J. S. Furnivall, this collection contains approximately 150 district and village *sit-tans* from Myin-gyan and adjacent districts in central Burma. Most of these are published in F. N. Trager and W. J. Koenig, *Burmese Sit-tans, 1764–1826: Records of Rural Life and Administration.* Tucson, Ariz., 1979.

Wuna Dama Kyaw-din. *Manu tha-ra shwei-myin damathat* [Damathat of 1772]. Rangoon, 1879.

———. *Manu wunana damathat kyan* [Damathat of 1771]. Rangoon, 1878. Cited in the notes as *Manu wunana.*

Wyatt, D. K. "Family Politics in Nineteenth Century Thailand." *Journal of Southeast Asian History* 9, no. 2 (1968): 208–28.

———. "Siam and Laos, 1767–1827." *Journal of Southeast Asian History* 4, no. 2 (1963): 13–32.

Ya Gyaw. *Myan-ma maha min-gala min-gan-daw* [Burmese royal ceremonies]. Mandalay, 1905. Cited in the notes as MMM.

Ya-zein-da (Hpaya-byu Hsaya-daw). *Tha-thana bahu thu-ta paka-thani* [Explanation of religious topics]. Rangoon, 1928.

Yi Yi. "Additional Burmese Historical Sources, 1752–1776." *The Guardian* 15, no. 11 (1968): 33–35; and 15, no. 12 (1968): 21–23.

———. "Burmese Historical Sources, 1752–1885." *Journal of Southeast Asian History* 6, no. 1 (1965): 48–66.

———. "Kon-baung hkit sit-tan-mya" [*Sit-tans* of the Kon-baung period]. JBRS 49, no. 1 (1966): 71–127.

———. "Kon-baung hkit-u myo-ne ok-chok-pon" [Early Kon-baung provincial administration]. *Pyei-daung-zu myan-ma naing-ngan sa-bei hnin lu-hmu-yei gya-ne* 1, no. 2 (1968): 343–95.

———. "Life at the Burmese Court under the Konbaung Kings." JBRS 44, no. 1 (1961): 85–129.

———. *Myan-ma naing-ngan achei-anei 1714–52* [The state of Burma, 1714–1752]. Rangoon, 1973.

———. *Thu-tei-thana abi-dan-mya hmat-su* [Dictionary of historical terms]. Rangoon, 1974.

Yo Pe. *Yei-nan-gyaung myo thin-hkei-ba sa-dan* [Abridged history of Yei-nan-gyaung]. Rangoon, 1913.

Zei-ya Thin-hkaya. *Shwei-bon ni-dan* [A work on the Golden Palace]. Rangoon, 1960.

INDEX

Amyin prince, succession position of, 200-1; attempted rebellion and execution of, 203
A-na, 75, 79, 85
Anagatavamsa, 76, 268-69, n. 25
Anauk-hpet-lun (r. 1606-1628), 7, 8, 9, 160
Animism. *See Nat* worship
Appanages, administration of, 110, 124, 140; in first Taung-ngu period, 5-6; and officials, 46, 123-24, 138, 139, 148-49, 158, 164, 184; in Pagan period, 3; and princes, 10, 11, 125, 182, 184, 191; in Restored Taung-ngu period, 8, 9, 10, 11; revenue of, 51; and royal family, 122, 123, 124, 125, 158, 167, 169-70, 214-15. *See also Myo-za*
Arakan, Bo-daw-hpaya annexes, 22-23, 31, 104, 122; and British, 23, 26; deportations from, 31, 113; maladministration of, 23, 26; military and labor levies on, 23, 26, 33; rebellions in, 23, 26-28, 35. *See also* Chin Pyan
Arthashastra, 89, 96
Artillery, 25
Asoka, 82-83. *See also* Kingship

Administration, of departments, 101-3, 131, 134-35; of territorial jurisdictions, 103-7, 134-35; local, 107
Agriculture, 34-35, 53-55, 57; and social disorders, 33-35; and irrigation, 54-55, 100-1; and surplus, 57-58; types of, 54-55. *See also* Famine; Banditry
Ahmu-dan. *See* Crown service groups
Alaung-hpaya (r. 1752-1760), 13, 30, 47, 62, 86, 115, 133, 149, 151, 167, 175, 178, 179, 180, 187, 195, 198, 201, 202; administration of, 13, 30, 32, 128, 143-44, 149-50, 160; death of, 16, 189, 192, 294, n. 1; imperial campaigns of, 14-16; legitimacy problem of, 86-89; lineage of, 86, 87-89, 190; messianic associations of, 74, 76-77, 95, 190, 191; relations with French and British, 24
Alaung Si-thu, 75
Alves, Walter, 190, 192, 193, 194, 196, 198
Amara-pu-ra, 27, 28, 34, 121, 151, 213; 1809 burning of, 35

323

Assam, 22, 28–29
Astrology, 41, 44
Athi, 59, 95, 110, 116, 134; administration of, 107–8, 113–15, 144; alienation of, 52; obligations, 103; in Pagan period, 4; in Restored Taung-ngu period, 8, 10, 11, 113; social and legal position of, 114; taxation of, 115; types of, 114
Athi taing, 10, 53, 108, 113–14, 115, 156, 157
Athi wun, 100, 103. See also Maha Thi-ha Thu-ra
Aung Zei-ya. See Alaung-hpaya
Ava, 7, 12, 20, 23, 69, 151, 180; Chinese threat to, 16–17, 18–19
Aw-ra-tha son, 40–41; in gentry succession, 144; in royal succession, 166, 174, 191, 204, 210, 211, 214, 229
Ayuthia, Alaung-hpaya's campaign against, 14–15, 189, 192; Hsin-hpyu-shin conquers, 16–17, 122; and Mons, 14–15
Badon prince. See Bo-daw-hpaya
Ba-gyi-daw (r. 1819–1837), 80, 162, 173; accession of, 28, 36, 221–22; birth of, 210; as crown prince, 152, 154–55, 180, 183, 214–15, 216–22, 231; as king, 233; and succession struggle, 217–20, 221–22, 234
Banditry, 33–36, 52–53, 56, 69, 220; and officials, 149; as social protest, 34–35. See also Floating population
Bassein, 104, 105, 120, 213
Bayin-naung (r. 1551–1581), 5, 6, 7, 14, 16, 200

Blake, Stephen, 99
Bo-daw-hpaya (r. 1782–1819; Badon prince), 28, 30, 31, 33, 36, 53, 79–80, 92, 104, 108, 125, 128, 129, 130, 133, 150, 152, 154, 161, 167, 169, 173, 175, 178, 179, 180, 197, 199, 209, 211, 216–17, 225, 231, 232; accession of, 20, 79, 208; coup of, 207–8; death of, 28, 30, 36, 221; domestic policies of, 20–21, 22–23, 33, 59, 62, 121; exile of, 203; military campaigns of, 17–18, 20–23, 27, 31–33, 34, 35, 62, 64, 104; relations with French and British, 23, 25, 26–27, 28, 29–30; and *sangha*, 44, 77–78, 94; succession plans of, 209–11, 214–17, 222
Bodhisatta, 66, 67, 68, 71–79; and *kamma*, 74–75; in Pagan period, 75, 76. See also Kingship
Brahmans, 91–92, 133
Bribery. See Corruption
Buchanan, Francis, 55, 61, 63, 251, 259, n. 42
Buddhism, Theravada, 37–38, 41, 223; doctrines of, 41–43; eschatology of, 65, 73, 76, 79, 94; in Pagan period, 42; Burmese salvation function in, 41–43; *sangha* in, 82
Buddhist monkhood. See *Sangha*
Burney, Henry, 110, 146, 161; census of, 237–39, 240, 241
Bye-daik, functions of, 115, 131–32; and Hlut-taw, 131–33, 134, 135, 136; and passage of power, 180–81, 183, 185; personnel of, 131–32

Cachar, 22
Cakkavatti, Asoka as, 82; role of, 71-74, 75-77, 78, 79; political emotiveness of, 74, 79
Canning, John, 27, 28, 35, 121, 149, 216, 217, 218-19, 220, 221, 240, 251
Carey, Felix, 28, 36, 61, 220, 251
Chao Phya Chakri (Rama I), 20, 21
Ch'ien Lung (Manchu emperor), 17, 18
Children, royal, number and mortality of, 175-78
Chin Pyan, 27-28, 29, 35-36, 220
China, and Shans, 62; trade with Burma of, 17, 18, 120; tributary relationship with Burma of, 18; wars with Burma of, 16-19, 111, 159, 161
Commerce. See Trade
Conscription. See Military system
Corruption, by officials, 10-11, 31, 156-62, 232, 233; officials' need for, 149; and political factions, 158; and scandal of 1770, 158, 232. See also Inquests; Gentry
Cox, Hiram, 26, 28, 33, 77, 120, 122, 240, 251, 265, n. 56
Crawfurd, John, 58, 240
Crown demesne, 102-3, 111
Crown prince (d. 1808). See Maha U-payaza
Crown princes, administrative and ceremonial establishment of, 180-83; consorts of, 178, 182; customary investiture of, 180-82, 183-85; institution of, 171, 172, 231; qualifications required for, 175, 186; power base of, 180, 181-82
Crown service groups, 53, 59, 95, 134-35, 156, 167; administration of, 101, 107-9, 157; ethnicity of, 111, 113, 240; land allotments of, 109-10; and military, 116-18; in Pagan period, 4; percent of population in, 110-13, 238; in Restored Taung-ngu period, 8, 10-11, 31; taxation of, 115; types of, 101, 106, 109
Currency, 57
Daing wun, 34-35, 102, 155, 217
Danda, 70. See also Political thought
Deathbed order on succession of Alaung-hpaya, 189, 198, 199, 200, 205, 207, 211, 222, 296, n. 24
Debt bondage, 51-52, 53
Dhamma, 44, 70, 71, 72, 82, 181; early Kon-baung interpretation of, 67-68; and sumptuary rules, 49. See also Kingship; Political thought
Dharma, 50, 68, 70
Dynastic cycles, xv, 231-35
East India Company, and Arakan problem with Burma, 23, 26-30; and Assam, 28, 29; and Burmese internal politics, 26, 218-19, 220, 234; and commerce with Burma, 23-24, 26, 29; diplomatic missions of, 26-27; and First Anglo-Burmese War, 29; and Manipur, 28, 29. See also French East India Company
Eastern Court, 46, 101

Factions, and officials, 52, 163; of princes, 213–15, 216, 217, 220; and royal succession, 186–87, 227, 233; and succession to local office, 146
Famine, 11, 118, 142; of 1805–1812, 33–36, 53, 59, 77, 143
Feraud (French envoy), 18, 24, 25, 26, 29, 95, 149, 201
Fief. *See* Appanages
First Anglo-Burmese War, 29, 30, 162
First Taung-ngu dynasty, administration of, 5–6; appanages in, 5–6; fall of, 6; rise of, 4–5; royal officials of, 5–6
Floating population, 34, 51, 52, 53, 219–20
Force, royal monopoly of, 95–96, 118
French East India Company, 23, 24–25, 26, 27, 29–30; possible military assistance to Hsin-hpyu-shin of, 201
Furnivall, John S., xvi
Gaurinath Singh, 28
Gentry, autonomy of, 32; in kingdom of Pegu, 12; marriage practices of, 39, 143; in Restored Taung-ngu period, 9, 10; socioeconomic position of, 143, 147
Glass Palace Chronicle, xvi, 73, 85, 87, 90, 180, 250–51
Glebe land, abuses of, 127–28, 143; administration of, 126–27, 130, 142, 143; and crown service units, 127. *See also* Land tenure
Gotama Buddha, 73, 74, 75, 78
Han-tha-wadi, 104, 106, 148, 185

Harvey, G. E., xvi, xviii, 165
Hlut-taw, 105, 117, 129, 144, 145, 147, 158; and Bye-daik, 131–33, 134, 135, 136; jurisdiction of, 100–1, 115–16, 131; and passage of power, 183, 185; personnel of, 100; in Restored Taung-ngu period, 9
Hpon, 75, 79, 85, 86, 88, 206
Hsin-hpyu-shin (r. 1763–1776), 19, 32, 108, 116, 124, 150, 160, 161, 167, 169, 172, 179, 202, 234; abortive contest of Naung-daw-gyi's accession, 192–95, 198; accession of, 16, 199–200; appoints crown prince, 200–1; and Arthashastra, 90–91, 96; and *bodhisatta* mission, 77; and *cakkavatti* attributes, 77; and Chinese wars, 17–19, 111, 159; conquers Ayuthia, 16–17; death of, 20, 30, 201; and French, 24, 25; queens of, 200
Inquests, 31, 131, 135, 158, 160–62, 237, 239
Irrigation, administration of, 105, 115; construction of, 100–1, 225; labor levies for, 33
Jansey (*shahbandar* of Rangoon), 154
Judson, Adoniram, 221, 252
Judson, Ann, 221, 252
Kamma, and collective merit-making, 42, 80–81; flux in, 42, 50, 85, 96, 138; and kingship, 72, 74, 75–76, 94, 206, 271–72, n. 61; and merit-sharing, 42, 80–81; neutralization in, 42; and officials, 138, 195, 209; and royal legitimacy, 84–86, 89, 225; and social

ideology, 45. *See also* Kingship; Political thought
Karens, in early Kon-baung polity, 62–64; infiltration by, 12–13; taxation of, 120
Kathaung-myaung Taik, 101, 102, 128
Kautalya, 89. *See also* Arthashastra
King who came to Han-tha-wadi. *See* Maha Dama Ya-za Di-pati
Kingship, appellations of, 73, 83; Arthashastran aspects of, 89–92; Asokan model of, 82–84, 128; authority of, 92–96, 132, 225; *bodhisatta* ideal in, 66, 67, 71–72, 74–77, 78–79, 96, 126; *cakkavatti* ideal in, 71–74, 78–79, 96; ceremonial aspects of, 73, 79, 91, 92; *dhamma* norm for, 67–70; kammatic basis of, 72, 84–86, 225, 271–72, n. 61; legitimacy in, 71, 84–89, 94, 174; lineage requirements of, 86–89, 174, 228; in Pagan, 3; personal qualities required for, 75; *raja dhamma* norm for, 69–70, 73, 85, 86, 138, 225; and stewardship of Buddhism, 49, 69, 80–81, 82–84, 126. *See also* Buddhism; Maha Thamada; Political thought; Sangha
Kyan-zit-tha, 76
Kyauk-hse, administration of, 103, 104–5, 120; crown service population of, 111, 113, 115; deportations to, 31; and inquests, 111
Kyaw Hkaung, 152
Kyaw Ywei (*myo wun* of Han-tha-wadi), conflicts with other officials of, 52, 154–55; followers of, 52; supports Ba-gyi-daw as crown prince, 218, 219, 221; as *wun-gyi*, 152, 217
Kyeik-su taing, 95. *See also* Athi; Athi taing
Land tenure, 141–43
Law-ka byu-ha kyan, 47, 180, 250
Leach, E. R., 165
Legitimacy, of king, 84–89, 174, 199, 229; of officials, 137–38. *See also* Kamma; Kingship; Political thought
Let-yon, 75, 79, 85, 88
Lieberman, Victor B., xvii, xix, 8, 10, 118, 125, 233
Lineage, royal, 235; and appanages, 125; and legitimacy, 86–89, 166, 174; and royal succession, 164, 166
Luce, G. H., 88
Maha Ban-du-la, 29, 259, n. 49
Maha Dama Ya-za Di-pati (r. 1733–1752; king of Ava), 12, 13, 69, 86, 88, 190
Maha Dan Department, 101, 128, 130. *See also* Glebe land; Sangha
Maha Thamada, 66, 69, 70, 71, 93, 137; and Burmese royal lineage, 86–87, 174; as *cakkavatti*, 73, 74, 78. *See also* Kingship; Political thought
Maha thayaw. *See* Famine
Maha Thi-ha Thu-ra, attempted coup and execution of, 208–9; background of, 297, n. 28; and Chinese wars, 17–18; and coups of 1782, 204, 205, 207; recalled from Thailand, 20, 202; as *wun-gyi*, 150, 202, 208

Maha U-payaza (crown prince, d. 1808), conquers Arakan, 22–23, 182; death of, 154, 212, 216; and Hlut-taw, 100; investiture of, 73, 172, 173, 174–75, 180–81, 210; moderate toward British, 27; political position of, 49; role in governance of, 182, 212–13

Maladministration, 118, 126, 153, 156, 233. See also Officials

Manipur, 22, 28, 113, 116

Mantegazza, Gaetano, 120, 199, 209, 211, 251

Manu, 66, 67

Manu-kye damathat, 39, 40, 41, 46, 49, 50, 66, 68, 70, 92, 93

Manu wunana damathat, 41

Marriage, and *athi*, 114; and concubines, 39, 166, 261, n. 4; with foreigners, 260, n. 2; and gentry, 39–41; and head wife, 39–41; and inheritance, 39–41; and officials, 143; and polygamy, 39, 149–50, 166

Marriage, royal, and officials, 150, 151, 163, 167, 169, 229; polygamous nature of, 87, 89, 166, 167, 178; of sisters and cousins, 87, 89, 169, 178, 210, 212, 221. See also Queens; Officials; Lineage

Martaban, 15, 19, 20, 32, 60, 111, 120, 148; administration of, 104, 105–6, 185

Maung Hlauk. See Naung-daw-gyi

Maung Maung (r. 1782), birth of, 197; coup of, 95, 204–6; execution of, 208; exile of, 203; as king, 6, 206–8; and royal succession, 198, 199

Maung Ywa. See Hsin-hpyu-shin

Merit-making and sharing, state, 79–85, 126, 212

Metteyya, Buddha, 73, 74, 75, 76, 95; and Alaung-hpaya, 74; and Bo-daw-hpaya, 78

Milard, Pierre de, 24, 25, 29, 201

Military system, description of, 115–18; and ethnicity, 116–17; conscription in, 33, 34–35, 117, 118

Min-don (r. 1853–1878), 147, 162, 179, 233

Min-gaung Naw-rahta, 193–96

Min-hla Naw-rahta. See U Hnaung

Min-nyi min-tha (royal men), 47, 171–74, 191

Min Thi-ri Yan-daza, lineage of, 207, 209; relationship with top royal lineage, 169, 190, 191

Min-ye Kyaw-din (r. 1673–1698), 10

Mok-hso-bo, 197, 294–95, n. 3

Money. See Currency

Monks, as officials, 151–52

Mons, and Alaung-hpaya, 13, 15; Burman fear of, 26, 60; in kingdom of Pegu, 12, 32; maladministration of, 14, 15, 19, 60; migration of, 14, 15, 21, 32, 60–61; and Thailand, 14–15, 21, 60

Munitions, foreign, 25, 26, 29

Myei-du prince. See Hsin-hpyu-shin

Myo-thu-gyi, functions of, 106–7, 139, 140, 169; and land control, 141–43; remuneration

Index

of, 140–41, 143. *See also* Officials, hereditary
Myo wun, of Arakan, 23; institutionalized, 8, 9; administrative role of, 103–7
Myo-za, 123–26, 127, 134, 158, 231. *See also* Appanages
Nan-da Bayin (r. 1581–1599), 6, 14
Nat worship, 41, 69, 80
Naung-daw-gyi (r. 1760–1763), accession of, 16, 192; as crown prince, 180, 182, 191, 198; death of, 16, 197–98, 230; queens of, 197; rebellions against, 16, 192–99; unpopularity of, 194, 196, 198
Negrais, 24, 25
Nei-myo Thi-ha Patei, 16–17, 19, 20
New Pagan Chronicle, 86
Nyaung-yan (r. 1597–1606), 7, 9, 67, 160
Officials, appointed, appointment of, 153, 185; behavior of, 153, 156; and factions, 151–52, 153–56; recruitment of, 151; remuneration of, 148–49, 156; skills required of, 148; socioeconomic situation of, 149, 151, 152–53
Officials, hereditary, appointment of, 106; duties of, 106–7; land control by, 142–43; and politics of officeholding, 143–47; remuneration of, 122, 140–41
Orasa. See Aw-ra-tha
Pagan dynasty, 2–4, 83, 86, 123
Patron-client relationship, 51, 52, 53
Pegu, 2, 5, 7, 12, 15, 24, 32, 60, 64

Phayre, Sir Arthur, xv
Pin-dale prince, 211
Political thought, concept of administration and control in, 132, 134–36; concept of royal authority in, 91–94, 96, 135–36; concept of sovereignty in, 71; *dhamma* in, 67–68, 71; first king ideal in, 65–67, 93, 137; officials in, 137–38; origin stories in, 86–89; reformation function in, 67, 71, 73, 74, 78–82, 96, 126, 137; regulation function in, 67, 70–71, 78–79, 93, 126, 137; royal succession in, 185–86; taxation in, 119. *See also* Kingship
Population, decline of, 58–59, 232; estimates of, 58–59; ethnicity in, 58–64, 111, 113; records of, 58–59, 237–43
Princes, marriage of, 178; and politics of succession, 126, 186–87, 200–3; rivalries of, 213–14, 218–20; role in governance of, 133–34, 192, 212–13, 216–17
Princesses, 169–70, 178
Prome, administration of, 104, 185; as appanage, 169. *See also* Prome, prince of
Prome, prince of, murder of, 222, 300, n. 82; role in governance of, 212–13; and succession struggle, 212–14, 215, 217–18, 221
Pyu-saw-hti, 86, 87, 174
Queen, chief, appanages and crown service units of, 167; role of, 166–67. *See also* Lineage, royal

Queens, evolution of, 167; political roles of, 171; origin and recruitment of, 167, 169, 170; and royal children, 175–79
Rangoon, 60, 121, 124, 154, 193; burning of, 35, 157; port of, 104, 120
Rebellion, 6, 9, 12, 15, 16, 21, 56, 182; of Mons, 15, 19, 21, 32, 60; and officials, 155; of peasants, 35–36, 89, 94–95, 209, 263–64, n. 36
Restored Taung-ngu dynasty, 7–12, 15, 47
Revenue, 122–23. *See also* Myo-za
Sagaing, 197
Sagaing, prince of. *See* Ba-gyi-daw
Salin prince, attempted coup of, 201–2; execution of, 202; parentage of, 200
San Prive, 201
Sanei (r. 1698–1714), 11
Sangermano, Vincentius, 51, 63, 121, 122, 125, 126, 138, 171, 189, 209, 251
Sangha, administration of, 101, 126, 128–30; as collective savior, 43, 81–82, 129; as elite group, xviii, 227–28; and politics, xviii, 262, n. 20; and problems of indiscipline and orthodoxy, 77–78, 82–84, 94, 126, 128, 261, n. 17; secular control of, 44, 83–84, 94, 129–30, 227–28, 262, n. 19, 301, n. 3; status hierarchy of, 129–30. *See also* Maha Dan Department
Sankha, 72, 73, 74, 75, 76, 78
Scott, James C., 156

Scott, James G., 167
Set-kya min, 75, 76
Shans, as Burman vassals, 14, 16, 17, 74; and Chinese wars, 17–18; in early Kon-baung polity, 61–62, 63; and Thai wars, 20, 21
Shore, Sir John, 26, 79
Shwei-daik, 102, 131, 146, 161
Si-tha prince, 191, 200, 208–9
Sin-gu (r. 1776–1782), 20, 21, 22, 30, 31, 32, 150, 169; accession of, 20, 200–1; birth of, 200; and *bodhisatta* mission, 77; as crown prince, 200–1, 231; dissipation of, 204, 205; domestic policy of, 20, 21, 30, 32; fall and execution of, 205–8; low *hpon* and *kamma* of, 86, 206
Singh, Gaurinath. *See* Gaurinath Singh
Sit-tans (land rolls), 50, 54, 55, 56, 109, 111, 117, 121, 124, 135, 139, 140, 145, 146, 147, 151, 157, 159, 249–50; and crown service groups, 109, 115; and glebe land, 126–27; and hereditary office lineages, 106–7, 144; and *myo-za*, 124, 125; and sumptuary privileges, 47
Slavery, pagoda, 51, 263–64, n. 36
Social disorders, 33–36, 53
Social ideology, hierarchical nature of, 45–46; kammatic basis of, 45; mobility in, 50–51, 138–39, 162–63; status grades in, 45–47. *See also* Sumptuary rules; *Kamma*
Social protest, 35, 51–53

Social structure, Burman, conjugal family in, 38, 53; endogamy in, 38; inheritance in, 39–41; marriage in, 38–40; polygamy in, 39

Sorrel, George, 26

Spirit worship. *See Nat* worship

Status hierarchy, court, 46–49, 109, 184; and court discipline, 49; and honorific titles, 47, 138, 148, 184; and place, 47–48. *See also* Women; Western Court

Succession, pool of, of Alaung-hpaya, 191; of Bo-daw-hpaya, 210, 214–16; of Hsin-hpyu-shin, 200; of local hereditary offices, 145; of royal lineage, 174–79

Succession, royal, customary aspects of, 174–75, 178–79, 185–87, 210, 228–29; and factions, 11, 186–87; and political conflict, xviii, 185–87, 229; politics of, 53, 144, 152, 155, 179, 185–87, 229, 233, 234. *See also* Children, royal; Crown princes; Lineage, royal; Marriage, royal

Sumptuary rules, 46–49; and *athi*, 114; and consumption, 57–58, 224; and officials, 49, 140, 163

Symes, Michael, 26, 27, 28, 49, 55, 70, 170–71, 202, 212, 213, 215, 216, 234, 240, 251, 261, n. 4, 262, n. 20

Tabin-shwei-hti (r. 1531–1550), 5, 196

Taik. See Crown demesne

Tak Sin, 19, 20, 21

Tanin-ganwei (r. 1714–1733), 11

Taung-ngu, 111, 117, 148; administration of, 104, 185; agriculture of, 55; service houses in, 52

Taung-ngu, prince of, attempted coup of, 215–16; execution of, 222; role in governance of, 212, 213; and succession struggle, 52, 213–16, 218–19, 222

Taxation, 119–23; basis of, 71, 119; officials' share of, 141, 143, 148–49; of trade and commerce, 120–21

Tha-lun (r. 1629–1648), administrative reforms of, 7, 9, 44, 128, 129; inquest of, 8, 9, 160

Tha-ra-wadi (r. 1837–1845), as Thayet prince, 218

Thado Thein-ga-thu, 195, 196–97

Thailand, Burmese wars with, 15–17, 19, 20–22, 27, 31, 33, 34, 35, 62, 64, 155, 159, 161. *See also* Mons

Than Tun, Dr., 88

Thi-baw (r. 1878–1885), 147, 162, 179, 233

Thu-gyi, duties of, 140, 169

Thwei-thauk, 46, 108–9, 116, 134, 150, 229

Trade, with China, 17, 18; control of, 56–58; domestic, 55, 56–57; maritime, 23–24, 26, 56

U Hnaung, 150, 193, 195, 202, 208

U Shwei O. *See Daing wun*

U Tha Gyi. *See* Maha Thi-ha Thu-ra

U Tin (of Pagan), xvi, 116, 120

Wealthy, and status hierarchy, 46; and court ceremonial, 71

Western Court, 39, 101, 109, 131, 152, 184; political functions of, 171; as residence of royal women, 166; status hierarchy of, 170–71

Wittfogel, Karl, 163

Women, as concessionaires, 41; as officeholders, 41, 50, 145–46; royal, 166–71; social and legal position of, 41; status hierarchy for, 47. *See also* Queens; Princesses; Western Court

Yi Yi, Dr., 121, 249, 296, n. 22